AF333455

CHANGING THE SCORE

Conceptualizing Music: Cognitive Structure, Theory, and Analysis·
Lawrence Zbikowski

Inventing the Business of Opera: The Impresario and His World in
Seventeenth-Century Venice
Beth L. Glixon and Jonathan Glixon

Lateness and Brahms: Music and Culture in the Twilight of Viennese
Liberalism
Margaret Notley

The Critical Nexus: Tone-System, Mode, and Notation in Early Medieval
Music
Charles M. Atkinson

Music, Criticism, and the Challenge of History: Shaping Modern Musical
Thought in Late Nineteenth-Century Vienna
Kevin C. Karnes

Jewish Music and Modernity
Philip V. Bohlman

Changing the Score: Arias, Prima Donnas, and the Authority of Performance
Hilary Poriss

CHANGING THE SCORE

Arias, Prima Donnas, and the
Authority of Performance

Hilary Poriss

OXFORD

UNIVERSITY PRESS

2009

OXFORD
UNIVERSITY PRESS

Oxford University Press, Inc., publishes works that further
Oxford University's objective of excellence
in research, scholarship, and education.

Oxford   New York
Auckland   Cape Town   Dar es Salaam   Hong Kong   Karachi
Kuala Lumpur   Madrid   Melbourne   Mexico City   Nairobi
New Delhi   Shanghai   Taipei   Toronto

With offices in
Argentina   Austria   Brazil   Chile   Czech Republic   France   Greece
Guatemala   Hungary   Italy   Japan   Poland   Portugal   Singapore
South Korea   Switzerland   Thailand   Turkey   Ukraine   Vietnam

Published by Oxford University Press, Inc.
198 Madison Avenue, New York, New York 10016

www.oup.com

Oxford is a registered trademark of Oxford University Press

Library of Congress Cataloging-in-Publication Data
Poriss, Hilary.
Changing the score : arias, prima donnas, and the authority
of performance / Hilary Poriss.
p. cm.—(AMS studies in music)
Includes bibliographical references and index.
ISBN 978-0-19-538671-4
1. Opera—Italy—19th century. 2. Operas—
Performances—Italy—History—
19th century. I. Title.
ML1733.4.P67 2008
782.10945'09034—dc22   2008046296

2   4   6   8   9   7   5   3   1

Printed in the United States of America
on acid-free paper

For my dad, Oscar Poriss
(1933–2008)

ACKNOWLEDGMENTS

This book has been written over many years and in many different places. It is a pleasure to be able to thank a number of people and institutions that were instrumental in helping me complete the project. My first gesture of gratitude must go to Philip Gossett, who has been a treasured mentor and friend over the years and whose example serves as the inspiration for this book. Francesco Izzo also deserves special mention for reading every chapter, for offering priceless input on translations, and for providing much-needed encouragement whenever and wherever I asked for it. I am deeply indebted to a group of musicologists and opera scholars who have taken an interest in my ideas, read drafts of individual chapters, and provided invaluable commentary: Jane Bernstein, Susan Boynton, Patricia Brauner, Joy Calico, Alessandra Campana, Rachel Cowgill, Will Crutchfield, Gabriele Dotto, Mark Everist, Andreas Giger, Ed Goehring, Helen Greenwald, Roberta Montemorra Marvin, Ryan Minor, John Platoff, Arthur Rishi, David Rosen, and William Weber. In addition, a number of friends from outside musicology graciously read and commented on portions of this book, offering perspectives from the fields of history and literature: Romina Crociani, Bradin Cormack, Jaclyn Maxwell, William Orchard, and Jay Rubenstein.

The research for this book was supported by the Gladys Krieble Delmas Foundation, the University of Cincinnati, and postdoctoral fellowships from the Columbia Society of Fellows and the Franke Institute for the Humanities at the University of Chicago. The writing was completed during a faculty leave, generously granted by Northeastern University for the 2006–2007 academic year, during which time I was able to accept the Millicent Mercer Johnson postdoctoral fellowship at the American Academy in Rome. Very special thanks go to my colleagues at Northeastern who supported me in this endeavor, especially Judith Tick, Ron Smith, Matthew McDonald, and chair of the music department, Anthony De Ritis. Additionally, I must express my gratitude to a number of friends and scholars at the American Academy who offered essential commentary and constant moral support: Tom Bissell, Hendrik Dey, Lisa Mignone, Jerry Passanante, Stephanie Pilat, Arman Schwartz, Kevin Uhalde, Hillary Zipper, and Sarah Zwerling. Martha Feldman visited me at the American Academy and provided a wealth of inspiration, as she has always done.

Support for the publication of this book was provided by the Dragan Plamenac Publication Endowment Fund of the American Musicological Society.

A number of archivists and librarians deserve special mention for the help they have extended to me over the course of this project. I am extremely grateful all of them, and especially to Luigi Ferrara (Fondazione Cini, Venice), Matteo Sartorio (Fondazione La Scala, Milan), Thomas Lisanti (New York Public Library, New York), and Revinder Chahal (Victoria and Albert Museum, London).

I thank the University of California Press for permission to publish material in chapter 3, which is a substantially revised and expanded version of my article "Making Their Way through the World: Italian One-Hit Wonders," published in *19th-Century Music* (2001): 197–224. © 2001. Reprinted with permission.

I am grateful to Mary Hunter, editor of the American Musicological Society Studies in Music, for having read several drafts of the manuscript and for encouraging me at every stage of the project. Two anonymous readers for AMS Studies in Music also provided crucial insight and suggestions, and I owe them both very special thanks. My gratitude also goes to Suzanne Ryan, editor at Oxford University Press, and Madelyn Sutton, editorial assistant, and Stephanie Attia, production editor, who have expertly ushered this project through to completion.

Finally, I owe an enormous debt of gratitude to my mother Julie and stepfather Don, and to my sister Sarah and brother-in-law Paul for their unflagging support. Sarah and Paul's dog Fredo—the greatest dog in the world—was always there to cheer me up when the writing was going slower than I wanted. I also wish thank my husband Chris, whose love and patience seem to know no bounds. Finally and sadly, my father Oscar Poriss passed away as this book was going into production. I miss him every day and wish he had been able to stick around for longer. I dedicate this book to him.

CONTENTS

CHANGING THE SCORE

INTRODUCTION

On a cold evening in January 1843, Anna De Lagrange (1824–1905)—one of the most beloved opera stars of the nineteenth century—made an unforgettable appearance at the Teatro Comunitativo in Piacenza, Italy. The opera was *Il bravo* by Saverio Mercadante, and De Lagrange sang the role of Teodora. When it came time to make her entrance, she stepped delicately onto the stage and then made a rather curious choice: instead of singing the cavatina that Mercadante composed for her character, she performed an aria that originated in a different opera (*Corrado d'Altamura*), and was written by a different composer (Federico Ricci).[1] Rather than cause confusion or concern, this alteration thrilled her spectators, who applauded loudly and called her back to the stage for three tumultuous curtain calls.

The explanation for this elated response is simple: by introducing an aria that did not belong to Mercadante's opera, De Lagrange was participating in a tradition that originated during the seventeenth century and persisted into the second half of the nineteenth century. Defined simply, "aria insertion" is the practice that allowed singers to introduce arias of their own choice into opera productions. These arias are also known as *arie di baule,* or "trunk arias," so named for the cumbersome luggage that singers stuffed with costumes, props, and most important for this context, musical scores of their favorite arias. Insertion arias might replace a portion of an opera (substitutions), or they might dislodge none of the original music (interpolations); they may have been authored by the composer of the opera, or they may have been written by someone else; they might have originated in an operatic context, or, more rarely, they might have been composed independently of the stage. Without exception, singers planned these insertions in advance, and everyone involved in the production (orchestra, other singers, and so on) was aware of when and where they would occur.

As widespread as this practice was throughout the nineteenth century, the assumption that aria insertion was essentially an eighteenth-century phenomenon, and that the nineteenth-century repertory was rarely subject to this type of alteration, has resulted in scholarly neglect of its later manifestations. Conventions of replacing one aria with another did not become obsolete at the turn of the century,

---

1. *Il pirata* anno 8, no. 55 (January 6, 1843): 222.

however; even after 1800, prima donnas and leading men still held on to what had long been one of their most prized possessions—the power to alter an operatic score to their liking. The present study is thus the first dedicated to examining how aria insertions shaped productions of the *bel canto* repertory throughout the nineteenth century, and how the practice changed and developed during that era. Exploring these pieces as manifestations of both individual and communal desires among performers and spectators, this book asks how aria insertions were woven into the authorial fabric of individual Italian operas, what principles guided the practice, and what the practice says about the relationship between singers, operatic works, and their authors. Most importantly, this study examines aria insertion as a creative endeavor through which the nineteenth century's most famous and powerful singers—especially the prima donnas—actively asserted their own authorial voices.

Although it is a commonplace in musicological scholarship to acknowledge that the creation and performance of an opera requires the collaborative efforts of composer, librettist, stage designer, and singers, it can still come as a surprise to find that such "collaborations" extended to the wholesale substitution of one aria for another. (Less common but equally plausible was the exchange of a duet or larger ensemble for another.) To learn, for instance, that a prima donna like Giuditta Pasta (1797–1865)—celebrated throughout Europe for her sensitive approach to the operas in which she appeared—insisted on concluding Rossini's *Tancredi* with a rousing rendition of "Il braccio mio conquisse" by Giuseppe Nicolini; to learn, furthermore, that this was one of many substitutions that she made throughout her twenty-five-year-long career, is to be confronted by a performance tradition that is rarely replicated in opera houses today.[2]

Since the 1950s, when ideas of authenticity began to exert influence over the performance of classical music, and when *bel canto* operas started to edge their way back into the repertory, the prevailing approach to operatic production has been to remain faithful to established conceptions of what constitutes a composer's work (whether or not those conceptions are fully accurate).[3] The late-twentieth and early-twenty-first centuries have witnessed a loosening of these restraints, most noticeably through iconoclastic visual approaches to staging.[4] Even so, altering an opera's aural landscape beyond certain cuts and transpositions can be a contentious endeavor, and transplanting an aria from one opera to another is taboo in all but the most restricted circumstances.[5] The result is a widespread unfamiliarity with many

2. For detailed information regarding Pasta's substitution, see the introduction of Gioachino Rossini, *Tancredi,* edited by Philip Gossett, in *Edizione critica delle opere di Gioachino Rossini,* series 1, vol. 10 (Pesaro: Fondazione Rossini, 1984), xxxiv–xxxv. For a piano-vocal score of this aria that includes ornaments that Rossini himself supplied for Pasta, see pp. 802–18 of that edition.

3. See Will Crutchfield, "What Is Tradition?" in *Fashions and Legacies of Nineteenth-Century Italian Opera,* ed. Roberta Montemorra Marvin and Hilary Poriss (Cambridge: Cambridge University Press, forthcoming); and Philip Gossett, *Divas and Scholars: Performing Italian Opera* (Chicago: University of Chicago Press, 2006).

4. For a discussion of the phenomenon of *Regieopern,* see Gundula Kreuzer, "Voices from Beyond: Verdi's *Don Carlos* and the Modern Stage," *Cambridge Opera Journal* 18 (2006): 151–79; and David J. Levin, *Unsettling Opera: Staging Mozart, Verdi, Wagner, and Zemlinsky* (Chicago: University of Chicago Press, 2007).

5. Roger Parker explores such issues in *Remaking the Song: Operatic Visions and Revisions from Handel*

aspects of nineteenth-century aria insertion, a practice that eschews strict notions of fidelity. A host of questions come to the fore: into which operas did singers typically introduce new numbers? In what way did inserted numbers conform, both dramatically and musically, to their new environments, and how important was it that they do so? What artistic, economic, and social factors motivated nineteenth-century singers to make these types of alterations? And how were aria insertions received by critics, spectators, and composers?

The present study engages with these questions at a pivotal stage in the history of aria insertion, the years between 1800 and 1850, decades during which the practice inched slowly toward extinction. Nineteenth-century performances of works by Mayr, Mercadante, Pacini, Paër, Rossini, Bellini, Donizetti, Verdi, and their many contemporaries were subject to frequent instances of aria insertion, just as eighteenth-century productions of *opera seria* and *opera buffa* had been. Unlike the earlier era, however, aria insertion began to encounter resistance during the first half of the nineteenth century, for it was during those decades that theaters, publishers, and composers began to wrest control from singers. Lydia Goehr marks the year 1800 as a decisive turning point, after which the "work-concept" dominated musical repertories, operatic and otherwise.[6] Although this shift toward a text-based aesthetic took root only slowly in the realm of Italian opera, newly blossoming concerns for authorial control and aesthetic purity nevertheless influenced the perception and production of these works. More and more throughout the first half of the nineteenth century, singers began to face a difficult choice: whether to perpetuate the practice of aria insertion or to forgo this privilege in favor of performing operas "as written." One of the primary goals of this book is to uncover how singers continued to employ substitute and interpolated arias in the face of this increasing strain.

There are many reasons why these performers continued to employ aria insertions, most of which will be explored in the following chapters. It is worthwhile, however, to address the most self-evident here: singers perpetuated the practice of aria insertion throughout the first half of the nineteenth century because they wanted to and because they could. Aria insertions offered a wealth of benefits that singers might have been unable to reap by remaining faithful to a score, especially if the opera in question was not written with their specific talents in mind. In a world where superior vocal performance was the most highly valued economic and artistic commodity that an opera house possessed, singers inserted arias to accommodate their individual vocal strengths and ranges and to augment their roles. The better they sang, after all, the more likely they were to attract large audiences to the box office. An excerpt from a review of an 1830 production of Rossini's *Il Turco in Italia* that took place at the Teatro Valle, Rome, illustrates the effectiveness of aria insertions in highlighting a performer's talents: "Even though the part of the *primo tenore,* taken by Signor Francesco Regoli is not among the major [roles] in this

---

to Berio (Berkeley and Los Angeles: University of California Press, 2006). For detailed discussions of cuts, transpositions, reorchestrations, and many other types of alterations that have been made to nineteenth-century Italian operas, see part II of Gossett, *Divas and Scholars,* 203–486.

6. Lydia Goehr, *The Imaginary Museum of Musical Works: An Essay in the Philosophy of Music* (Oxford: Clarendon Press, 1994).

drama, it was arranged as such nevertheless with the introduction into the first act of a cavatina by Maestro Morlacchi in which [Regoli's] bravura and uncommon agility stand out; we only wish that he would exert equal effort during the concerted pieces."[7]

It might be tempting for modern-day readers to chastise this singer for sacrificing the aesthetic "vision" of one composer in order to capture a few extra moments of applause through the aria of another. This temptation grows stronger, moreover, when one is reminded of the realities of the industry in which such alterations occurred. As the highest-paid employees, singers were granted generous license to determine which music they would and would not perform.[8] A modern response to such customs might be to write off aria insertions as the consequences of a decadent system, blatant manifestations of a capricious singer's will.[9] As this review of Regoli and many others suggest, however, most nineteenth-century critics and spectators operated under a different set of expectations, adopting a more generous attitude and evaluating these alterations on a case-by-case basis. In fact, aria insertions occurred so frequently and were so tightly wrapped up in the fiber of operatic performance that they were perceived not as curiosities, but rather as integral components of a production, subject to the same praise or criticism as were the authorial portions of a score. This book seeks to account for this ordinariness by evaluating these arias as did their contemporaries—on their own merits both as arias and as performances.

The mundane status of aria insertions can be attributed, in part, to the operatic marketplace, a system that affected both sellers (performers) and consumers (audiences). Throughout the first half of the nineteenth century and earlier, singers moved quickly from city to city and theater to theater, learning new roles at what today would be considered breakneck speeds. As will be explored further in chapter 1, a prima donna under pressure to sing well after only a few weeks of rehearsal might ease her burden considerably by introducing a familiar aria in place of, or in addition to, music that appeared in the opera she was scheduled to perform. Modes of spectatorship, moreover, also differed notably from today. Throughout the eighteenth and nineteenth centuries, audience members attended performances of the same opera on multiple occasions both within a single season and over multiple seasons. In some instances, repetition led to complacency (even boredom) on the part

7. "La parte di primo Tenore, affidata al signor Francesco Regoli, ancorchè in quel dramma non sia delle maggiori, nulladimeno è stata da lui ravvivata coll'introdurvi nel primo atto una Cavatina del Maestro Morlacchi, nella quale risalta la sua bravura, e non comune agilità, e vorremmo soltanto che un uguale impegno egli ponesse nei pezzi concertati." *Le notizie del giorno* (May 13, 1830).

8. For a comprehensive account of singer salaries, see John Rosselli, *Singers of Italian Opera: The History of a Profession* (Cambridge: Cambridge University Press, 1992), 114–46. According to Alessandro Roccatagliati, fixed expenditures of opera houses throughout Italy "could be planned accurately: the singers, orchestra, composer, and staging took up around 50, 12–15, 8, and 20–30 percent of the total budget respectively." See "The Italian Theater of Verdi's Day," in *The Cambridge Companion to Verdi,* ed. Scott Balthazar (Cambridge: Cambridge University Press, 2004), 17.

9. In "'La cantante delle passioni': Giuditta Pasta and the Idea of Operatic Performance," *Cambridge Opera Journal* 19 (2007): 107, Susan Rutherford adds, moreover, that views of aria insertion as a decadent practice, and of singers as "monstrous creatures," are not exclusively modern notions, originating long before the twentieth century.

of audiences, thus encouraging impresarios and performers to vary the internal structure of an opera by introducing one or more insertion arias. Such jolts of "freshness" injected during the middle of an opera's run were rare, however, and were typically limited to special occasions, such as benefit performances for a leading singer or an impresario—*potpourri* productions during which audiences expected to hear aria insertions in addition to full operas. The most common contexts for aria insertions, rather, and the ones on which this book focuses, were regularly scheduled opera productions that stretched from the beginning of a season to the end, the quotidian events of an opera house.

During such performances, the identities of new arias were frequently concealed; these musical numbers were not necessarily intended to protrude from their new environments, but rather to blend into the surrounding dramatic and musical fabric. Performers rarely aimed for an illusion of spontaneity when employing aria insertions. Indeed, it is important to note that audiences might have been completely unaware that a singer was performing an insertion aria. Although these pieces were planned in advance, they were not typically announced to spectators, and although their texts were frequently printed in librettos, they were not distinguished in any way from the rest of the poetry. If, therefore, both the opera and insertion aria were unfamiliar, there would be no way for the average operagoer to discern that an alteration had been made.

Audiences were by no means left entirely in the dark, however; there were many other ways to learn that a singer had performed an insertion aria, if they were interested. The most immediate sources were reviews of productions published in daily and weekly newspapers. As was the case with the excerpt concerning Regoli in *Il Turco in Italia,* cited above, critics often (though certainly not always) remarked on the presence of an insertion aria shortly following an opera's initial performance, some going so far as to list the title of the piece, the composer, and/or the opera in which it originated. Audience members who read these reviews could attend future performances fully aware of the alterations that had been made to an opera. How critics obtained this information is uncertain—as *cognoscenti,* they might have been able to identify the inserted aria on their own; it is also possible that the impresario, singer, or someone else involved with the production passed on to critics the relevant information. There are a variety of cases, moreover, in which insertion arias were familiar to spectators even without guidance from critics. These included popular numbers from famous operas, or arias that had taken on a life of their own as insertion arias, introduced by many singers into a variety of contexts. In general, whether an insertion aria was recognized by spectators, and whether a singer wanted audiences to recognize that she was performing an insertion aria, differed from situation to situation. These are issues that will arise frequently throughout the chapters that follow.

Because the focus of this volume falls primarily on Italian operas—works by Rossini, Bellini, Donizetti, and their contemporaries—the majority of the examples discussed come from productions that occurred on Italian stages. Aria insertion was an international phenomenon, however, and as such, this study is not limited to Italy alone. Examples from French, German, British, and American theaters arise frequently, providing an overview of the widespread effect of this practice throughout the operatic world. Broadly speaking, aria insertion did not differ radically from city to city or from country to country. Singers stood at the center of this practice, and as these artists traveled throughout Europe and the United States reprising many of their roles, they brought their own particular brand of aria insertion with them.

Throughout this book, moreover, my attention falls primarily on aria insertions made by women, the prima donnas who introduced these pieces on Italian stages and who exported their techniques to opera centers throughout Europe and elsewhere. This practice was by no means exclusive to women, and men are not ignored—chapters 1 and 3, in particular, take into account how, when, and why leading men participated in this practice as well. With only a few exceptions, however, aria insertions made by tenors, baritones, and basses were quickly forgotten, isolated events that made little impact on future performances or on other singers. Instead, moments that showcased aria insertions by the women of the operatic world have long exerted the greatest fascination over critics, historians, and operagoers.

This situation can be attributed to the widespread influence that women had over the operatic marketplace during the first half of the century. In her far-reaching survey of the cultural and social position of the figure of the prima donna, Susan Rutherford describes these decades as a watershed: "Women's greatest freedom on the operatic stage occurred between approximately 1800 and 1840. At this juncture the prima donnas enjoyed their most powerful moment in operatic history. They influenced compositional practices; they determined musical and dramatic interpretation; and they affected management decisions about the running of the opera house, the content of the season, the employment and use of other artists, and so forth."[10] The authority enjoyed by prima donnas during these years extended directly to the practice of aria insertions, and although some of their choices were undeniably the product of vocal reasons, many others must be interpreted as aesthetic tools wielded with a careful eye toward enhancing the dramatic and musical experience of an opera production. To recognize how these women approached aria insertion is to comprehend the practice as a whole. In focusing on prima donnas, this book aims to complement and contribute to the wealth of recent research concerning the creative involvement of women and the gender theory behind their careers, a field of inquiry that extends beyond the nineteenth-century operatic stage.[11]

10. *The Prima Donna and Opera, 1815–1930* (Cambridge: Cambridge University Press, 2006), 162.

11. Carolyn Abbate, "Opera; or, the Envoicing of Women," in *Musicology and Difference: Gender and Sexuality in Music Scholarship,* ed. Ruth Solie (Berkeley: University of California Press, 1993), 225–58; Suzanne Aspden, "'An Infinity of Factions': Opera in Eighteenth-Century Britain and the Undoing of Society," *Cambridge Opera Journal* 9 (1997): 1–19, and "The 'Rival Queens' and the Play of Identity in Handel's *Admeto,*" *Cambridge Opera Journal* 18 (2006): 301–31; Rachel Cowgill, "Re-gendering the Libertine, or, The Taming of the Rake," *Cambridge Opera Journal* 10 (1998): 45–66; Suzanne Cusick, "Gender and the Cultural Work of a Classical Music Performance," *Repercussions* 3 (1994): 77–110; Martha Feldman and Bonnie Gordon, eds., *The Courtesan's Arts: Cross-Cultural Perspectives* (Oxford: Oxford University Press, 2006); Bonnie Gordon, *Monteverdi's Unruly Women: The Power of Song in Early Modern Italy* (Cambridge: Cambridge University Press, 2004); Heather Hadlock, "Women Playing Men in Italian Opera, 1810–1835," in *Women's Voices across Musical Worlds,* ed. Jane Bernstein (Boston: Northeastern University Press, 2004), 285–307; Matthew Head, "Rethinking Authorship through Women Composers," *Women and Music* 6 (2002) 36–50; Mary Ann Smart, "The Lost Voice of Rosine Stoltz," *Cam-*

The evidence drawn on for this study is varied, including librettos, newspaper reviews, epistolary sources, anecdotal and biographical material, theatrical documents such as contracts, posters, and box-office receipts, printed and manuscript scores, and other assorted archival records. The most effective tools helping the modern scholar identify arias that were inserted into opera productions—and the prima donnas who made those changes—are librettos; according to nineteenth-century custom, these books were printed anew for each production and they frequently included the texts for aria insertions that were performed. Newspaper reviews are also vital, for in addition to offering clues regarding the identity of some aria insertions, they provide crucial insight into the reception of this music during the first half of the nineteenth century.

This study emerges, moreover, from a range of scholarship that has already made significant inroads into our knowledge of aria insertion by both prima donnas and leading men from the seventeenth and eighteenth centuries. Jennifer Williams Brown has presented the most systematic exploration of the practice as it affected operatic works during the seventeenth century. Through an exhaustive survey of extant librettos dating from 1672 to 1685, she compiled an elaborate database of thousands of aria texts, demonstrating that roughly half of all productions during those years featured one or more aria insertion.[12] Though no similarly comprehensive survey has been attempted for eighteenth-century productions, scholars working on the social history of *opera seria* and *opera buffa* have mapped out the procedures whereby these changes were made, and in many cases have explored the political and cultural implications—both contemporary and modern—of a handful of the century's aria substitutions.[13] What has emerged from this work is the sense that during the eighteenth century, aria insertion often dissolved into something of a free-for-all, singers interpolating arias whenever they pleased. Tracking both the connections and the distinctions between these earlier eras and nineteenth-century aria insertion represents a significant component of this book.

The most important scholarship concerning how and why this practice affected operas composed during the first half of the nineteenth century has been accomplished by the editors of the critical editions of works by Rossini, Donizetti, and

bridge Opera Journal 6 (1994): 31–50, and "Verdi Sings Erminia Frezzolini," *Women and Music: A Journal of Gender and Culture* 1 (1997): 33–45.

12. "'Con nuove arie aggiunte': Aria Borrowing in the Venetian Repertory, 1672–1685" (Ph.D. diss., Cornell University, 1992), and "On the Road with the 'Suitcase Aria': The Transmission of Borrowed Arias in Late Seventeenth-Century Italian Opera," *Journal of Musicological Research* 15 (1995): 3–23.

13. Daniel E. Freeman, "An 18th-Century Singer's Commission of 'Baggage' Arias," *Early Music* 20 (1992): 427–33; Robert Freeman, "Farinello and His Repertory," in *Studies in Renaissance and Baroque Music in Honor of Arthur Mendel*, ed. Robert Marshall (Kassel: Bärenreiter Verlag, 1974), 301–30; William C. Holmes, *Opera Observed: Views of a Florentine Impresario in the Early Eighteenth Century* (Chicago: University of Chicago Press, 1993), 44–45; Mary Hunter, *The Culture of Opera Buffa in Vienna: A Poetics of Entertainment* (Princeton, N.J.: Princeton University Press, 1999), and "'Se vuol ballare' Quoted: An Early Moment in the Reception History of *Figaro*," *Musical Times* 130 (1989): 464–67; Roger Parker, *Remaking the Song*, chapter 3, "Ersatz Ditties: Adriana Ferrarese's Susanna," pp. 42–66; and Reinhard Strohm, "Handel's Pasticci," in *Essays on Handel and Italian Opera* (Cambridge: Cambridge University Press, 1985), 164–211.

Bellini. For the past three decades, their research has resulted in scores that reflect the version, or versions, of these operas in which the composers directly participated. These volumes, whose introductions outline detailed performance histories of the operas, draw attention to select instances of aria insertions and often discuss the careers and specific vocal talents of the singers who performed the changes.[14]

Although the research I present in this book is heavily indebted to these editions, it differs in several respects. Most significantly, my focus does not lie with aria insertions that bear an authorial stamp—numbers that composers wrote with the explicit intention of introducing into revivals of their own works. Whether they undertook such revisions willingly (to mend weaknesses in their scores) or unwillingly (to comply with singers' demands or the pressures of censorship), these alterations are considered authentic and are thus well accounted for if a critical edition of the opera exists. Instead, my attention falls primarily on the inauthentic, aria insertions that were introduced without explicit intervention or permission from the opera's composer. These fall into two general categories. The first consists of numbers written by composers for insertion into operas that were not their own. Throughout the eighteenth and nineteenth centuries, rehearsals were frequently supervised by a house composer charged with rendering whatever alterations to a score were necessary to accommodate singers, including the composition of new arias. Almost every well-known opera composer prior to 1850 fulfilled these duties during the course of his career—examples include Mozart and Wagner, among many others— and the new arias occasionally garnered as much enthusiasm as portions of the original scores.[15] Although this first type of inauthentic aria insertion receives some attention in these pages, my primary emphasis falls on the second: arias that singers selected from preexisting works and which they dropped, often without change to music or poetry, into new operatic contexts. It is here where prima donnas grasped authorial control most firmly and where they exerted their own agency to influence the shape of an operatic work most powerfully.

Nineteenth-century composers, singers, impresarios, and critics engaged in a vibrant discourse about the persistent use of aria insertions in opera performances, de-

14. The intricacies of the critical edition projects, moreover, have been summarized by Philip Gossett in his study of Italian opera, *Divas and Scholars,* in which he explores the various transformations that occur as the *bel canto* repertory travels from score to stage. Gossett touches at length on a few instances of aria insertion, making note of their effects—both positive and negative—on the integrity of the operatic works in which they appeared. See *Divas and Scholars,* chapter 7, "Choosing a Version," pp. 203–40.

15. For a discussion of Mozart's aria insertions, see Gordana Lazarevich, "Mozart, Haydn, Cimarosa: Insertion Arias as Reflections of Operatic Customs," in *Internationaler Musikwissenschaftlicher Kongress zum Mozartjahr,* ed. Ingrid Fuchs (Baden-Wien: Schneider 1993), 725–50, and "Mozart's Insertion Aria 'Alma grande e nobil core,' K. 578: Criticism of Cimarosa or a Compliment to the Composer?" *Mozartjahrbuch* (1991): 262–67; and Roger Parker, *Remaking the Song,* 42–66. Also, see Rachel Cowgill, "'Wise Men from the East': Mozart's Operas and their Advocates in Early Nineteenth-Century London," in *Music and British Culture, 1785–1914,* ed. Christina Bashford and Leanne Langley (Oxford: Oxford University Press, 2000), 39–64, and "Mozart Productions and the Emergence of *Werktreue* at London's Italian Opera House, 1780–1830," in *Operatic Migrations,* ed. Roberta Montemorra Marvin and Downing A. Thomas (Aldershot, England: Ashgate, 2006), 147–48, for accounts of how some of Mozart's arias were employed as aria insertions on the early-nineteenth-century London stage.

bating their benefits and drawbacks, beauties and weaknesses. Chapter 1 taps into these conversations to explore the role that aria insertions played in day-to-day operatic life during the *Primo Ottocento*. This discourse illustrates that the first half of the nineteenth century witnessed the gradual formation of aesthetic boundaries that frequently (though not always) influenced the arias that performers chose for their insertions and limited the contexts into which they introduced this music.

Chapters 2, 3, and 4 explore the nature and extent of these aesthetic boundaries from varying perspectives. Chapter 2 focuses on one prima donna, Carolina Ungher (1803–1877), and one opera, Donizetti's *Marino Faliero*. This singer's relationship with Donizetti's opera is both unusual and illuminating—over the course of one year and three productions, she introduced three different arias into its first act. By examining each of these arias, this chapter addresses a series of logistical questions that apply broadly across all nineteenth-century aria insertions, as well as illustrating the painstaking efforts that many singers made in choosing these arias. Chapter 3 contextualizes nineteenth-century aria insertion by referring to its ancestry during the seventeenth and eighteenth centuries, noting the communal quality that surrounded the practice almost from its origins. This historical outline provides the background essential for introducing the concept of "favorite insertions," arias that were employed as substitutes or interpolations by a host of different singers in an assortment of operatic contexts during the nineteenth century. Chapter 4 begins with an overview of operatic moments that were typically affected by aria insertions, and then focuses on one scene in which change became standard during the nineteenth century: the "tomb scene" of Bellini's *I Capuleti e i Montecchi*. Maria Malibran (1808–1836), who played the trousers role of Romeo, famously eliminated Bellini's entire last scene and replaced it with the corresponding music from *Giulietta e Romeo* by Nicola Vaccai. This chapter investigates not only why Malibran made this change, but, more significantly, why dozens of prima donnas followed her lead.

The analyses and examples in chapters 1 through 4 illustrate that aria insertion during the nineteenth century often resulted from careful planning among its practitioners, who paid attention not only to their own vocal needs, but also to the dramatic and musical fabric of the opera into which insertion arias were sung. Chapter 5, on the other hand, serves as an important reminder that the boundaries developing around this practice were by no means unyielding and that singers still selected aria insertions that clashed notably with their new operatic surroundings. The lesson scene of Rossini's *Il barbiere di Siviglia* offers the most vibrant example in the entire *bel canto* repertory. This chapter investigates the almost two-hundred-year-long history of aria insertion in this scene, charting the vast range of arias that prima donnas introduced into Rossini's opera, and the freedom with which they did so. Chapter 6 returns to the discourse that surrounded aria insertion during the first half of the nineteenth century, focusing on one document: a short story published anonymously in 1849 titled "Memoir of a Song." The significance of this story stems from one if its strangest features: it is narrated by an insertion aria. Like the lesson scene of *Il barbiere di Siviglia,* it provides a glimpse of the "afterlife" of aria insertion, this time from a perspective that shifts past one individual opera toward broader aesthetic issues concerning the relationship between singer and song, image and actuality, opera and audience. This book concludes with an appendix containing the only modern edition of "Memoir of a Song."

The thread that ties together the examples of aria insertion discussed throughout this book is their ability to offer insightful commentary on the performance realities of Italian opera during the first half of the nineteenth century, on the audiences who applauded these changes, and on the prima donnas who made them. Although I rarely agitate explicitly for the practice of aria insertion to make its way back onto the modern stage, an implicit aim of this book is to suggest that today's singers seeking ways to reinvigorate operatic culture might look toward their nineteenth-century predecessors for ideas as to how they might do so. Perhaps some aria insertions can and should make their way back into today's opera houses, offering performers and spectators the opportunity to experience nineteenth-century operas in new, and quite unexpected, ways.

CHAPTER I

A DISCOURSE OF CHANGE

Donizetti's *melodramma comico, Le convenienze ed inconvenienze teatrali* (Naples, Teatro Nuovo, 1827), is an opera about an opera, a self-conscious gesture on the part of a composer who was ensconced in a theatrical world where prima donnas and leading men were firmly in charge. The setting is a provincial theater in which the singers of a small company have gathered to rehearse a new opera. Almost immediately, jealousy and petty bickering destroy any semblance of a professional atmosphere and in the ensuing confusion, Luigia (the *seconda donna*), the *musico,* and the tenor, all insist that special arias be added to their parts:

Mus.:	Dica un po' signor Maestro,	Tell me signor maestro
	vi sarà per me il rondò?	will there be a rondò for me?
Ten.:	Mie gran scene con trompete?	And for me, grand scenes with trumpets?
Luigia:	La Romance v'è, sì o no?	Is there a romance for me, yes or no?
Maestro:	Si dirigano al Poeta . . .	You need to ask the poet . . .
Poeta:	Al Maestro; io non lo so . . .	Ask the maestro; I don't know . . .
Maestro:	Ma il libretto . . .	But the libretto?
Poeta:	Lo spartito . . .	The score?
Maestro:	Or vi spiego . . .	Now I will explain to you . . .
Poeta:	Or vi dirò . . .	Now I will tell you . . .
Luigia,		
Mus. e Ten.:		
(*a tre*)	Basta, basta, ho ben capito;	Enough, enough, I've got it:
	il Poeta, ed il Maestro	the poet and the maestro
	han perduto per me l'estro,	have forgotten me because she
	perché lei già s'intrigò.	is already plotting against me.
	(*Indicando la prima donna*)	(*Pointing to the prima donna*)
	D'avvilirmi in questo modo	If to degrade me in this way
	se Madama ha nel pensier,	that woman has it in her head,
	qui fra poco a suo dispetto	to spite her
	chi son io farò veder.[1]	I'll soon show who I am.

1. Gaetano Donizetti, *Le convenienze ed inconvenienze teatrali,* ed. Roger Parker and Anders Wiklund, in *Edizione nazionale delle opera di Gaetano Donizetti* (Milan: Ricordi/Bergamo: Fondazione Donizetti, 2002), 57–63.

As art that imitates life, this scene embraces and pokes fun at the sorts of demands singers placed on composers and librettists to augment their roles, preferably with ample moments for solo display. In a rather satisfying turn, moreover, the life of this opera imitated the artifice exhibited within its plot when it was revived throughout Italy and elsewhere. As Roger Parker has observed in his introduction to the critical edition of *Le convenienze ed inconvenienze teatrali,* the textual history of this opera is enormously complicated, embodying almost as many versions as there were productions.[2]

This situation can be explained in part by the features it shares with most Neapolitan *farse:* the original contained dialect that had to be altered if it was to be understood outside of Naples, and as originally constructed, it was a slight work, requiring additions if it were to fill a whole night's entertainment. More significant, though, is that as an opera about an opera (a "metaopera"), this work encouraged singers to embrace openly the behavior of the fictional characters they were portraying.[3] Indeed, as it was revived, its real-life performers took even greater liberties with the libretto and score than did their fictional counterparts. A libretto for a revival in 1831 at the Teatro della Connobbiana, Milan, for instance, reveals that Fanny Corri-Paltoni in the role of the prima donna inserted variations on "Nel cor più non mi sento" from Paisiello's *La molinara.*[4] A second libretto, one that might reflect events at the opera's premiere, records an even more liberating mark: where text for an aria for the prima donna should be, nothing appears, indicating that she should insert an aria of her own choosing.[5] This improvisatory allowance permits a variety of interpretations. On the one hand, it might be read as a sign of resignation, a tossing up of hands at the inevitabilities of the opera house. Star singers—the line of thinking might run—will do as they please, so why bother suggesting an aria that will simply be discarded in the end? We might, however, glean a second, more affirmative interpretation, reading this particular directive (or, more precisely, nondirective) as a vague attempt on the part of the composer to assert an authorial voice over his work, permitting the singer to alter the score, but in a way that he himself controls. Indeed, this gesture might be read as an early hint of a new self-consciousness regarding the practice of aria insertion: an attempt not to rid operas of these pieces, but rather to articulate when, where, and why they might appear.[6]

2. Ibid., xi.

3. "Metaopera" is the umbrella term used by Francesca Savoia to describe this genre. See her collection of librettos from seven metaoperas in *La cantante e l'impresario e altri metamelodrammi* (Genoa: Edizioni Costa & Nolan, 1988).

4. See Parker, introduction to Donizetti, *Le convenienze ed inconvenienze teatrali,* xiii, where he explains that no printed libretto for this production exists. Instead, this information is gleaned from a manuscript copy located in the Archivio Ricordi di Milano, which was probably copied during the second half of the nineteenth century. That Corri-Paltoni introduced Paisiello's "Nel cor più non mi sento" into this production is confirmed by an article in the *Gazzetta privilegiata di Milano* dated April 22, 1831, also cited by Parker.

5. This second libretto is also extant only in manuscript form and is housed in Paris. Its connections to the premiere in Naples are tenuous, but, Parker comments, "it seems plausible that the form and succession of the musical numbers was similar, if not identical, to those at the first performance in Naples." Ibid.

6. A similar case arises in Pauline Viardot's *Cendrillon.* At the moment when Cinderella presents

Such self-consciousness regarding aria insertion was pervasive. Over the course of the nineteenth century, the suitability and value of these pieces became a matter of discussion throughout the world of Italian opera, and traces of these conversations surface in a variety of documents including contracts, letters, treatises, newspaper reviews, and anecdotal accounts. Oftentimes, this discussion was embedded in complaints leveled against reorchestration, transposition, or other unauthorized alterations to a score, but the practice of aria insertion is singled out in a number of contexts, so much so that it is clear that contemporaries distinguished this type of change from others and thought it a matter of particular interest. This chapter provides a backdrop for nineteenth-century aria insertion by examining this complicated and often contradictory discourse, noting its influence—or lack thereof—over Italian opera production during the nineteenth century. It is not surprising that these conversations became particularly animated during the decades between 1800 and 1850, around the same time, that is, that the understanding of the status of Italian operas as "works"—entities with a structure to which performers should at least attempt to aspire—was beginning to emerge.[7] As we will see, singers of the nineteenth century still used aria insertions during these years, but hints of this new approach began to be felt early on, limiting when they used aria insertions and what arias they chose to perform. Even though singers were still permitted to make these changes, in other words, the ground rules for doing so were shifting subtly beneath them.

ON ARIA INSERTION: SATIRISTS, INSIDERS, SINGERS, AND COMPOSERS

The first weapon wielded in the discourse against "indecencies" committed to opera productions in general, and against aria insertion in particular, was sarcasm, a device that predates by at least a century the first appearance of a work by Rossini. Among the first to brandish this tool was Pier Jacopo Martello, an eighteenth-century librettist, dramatist, and essayist whose vicious satire of opera house abuses, *Della tragedia antica e moderna* (1715), takes aim at aria insertions in the form of a self-conscious dialogue between Martello, the student poet, and "Aristotle," the mentor, who remarks as follows:

> The profession of writing *melodrammi* (my dear Martello) is a school of morals for you which, better than any other, teaches Poets how to conquer themselves and renounce their own wishes. Be prepared cheerfully to change tolerable arias into bad ones if a singer or songstress should wish to tag onto your recitative something that earned

---

herself at the ball, the original score has no aria at all, but rather the instruction that an aria of the singer's choice should be introduced. See Viardot, *Cendrillon, opera comique en 3 tableaux* (Paris: G. Miran, 1904). My gratitude to Will Crutchfield for pointing this out to me.

7. Here and elsewhere throughout this volume, I draw a distinction between a *score* and a *work*. A score is an object; a work, however, is an *experience* of an object. Thus, even though performances might not be faithful to a score, they might have been faithful to some conception of a work as an entity that possesses a beginning, middle, and end. For a discussion of this distinction between score and work, see Fred Everett Maus, "Concepts of Musical Unity," in *Rethinking Music,* ed. Nicholas Cook and Mark Everist (Oxford: Oxford University Press, 1999), 171–92.

them applause in Milan, Venice, Genoa, or elsewhere; and if its sentiment is the very opposite of the one you had at that point—what then? Let them have their way, or they will swarm all over you and pierce your ear with soprano and contralto rebukes. And so I would deem it preferable to let the singers insert their arias wherever they please rather than to share the blame for their failure; enough if they fit properly in the musical fabric, which concern you may safely leave with the *maestro di cappella*.[8]

No less sardonic are remarks leveled a few years later by the Venetian composer and writer Benedetto Giacomo Marcello in his famous satire *Il teatro alla moda* (1733):

> During the rehearsals [the librettist] must not reveal any of his dramatic intentions to the actors since he rightly assumes that they will do as they please anyway.
>
> If the work should be such that certain characters have little to do or to sing, he should immediately comply with the requests of these singers (or of their rich patrons) to add to their parts. He should always keep at hand a supply of a few hundred arias, in case alterations or additions should be wanted.[9]

The use of sarcasm to do battle against aria insertion continues well into the nineteenth century, as Donizetti's parody of theatrical life suggests. Sentiments mirroring Martello's and Marcello's surface, moreover, in a variety of inside accounts of those intimately involved in the production of Italian opera. John Ebers, the embattled impresario of London's King's Theatre for seven years, for example, takes aim at singers and their willingness to expand and alter scores to their own tastes:

> Let a new opera be intended to be brought forward. Signor This will not sing his part, because it is not prominent enough; so, to enrich it, a gathering must be made of airs from other operas, no matter whether by the same composer or not, nor whether there be any congruity between the style of the original piece and the adventitious passages introduced. [Giuseppe d]e Begnis, who, for some cause, or no cause, was disliked by the other performers, chose "Il Turco in Italia" for his own and his wife's debut. Every obstacle was thrown in the way of its representation; at last, all the best parts of "La Cenerentola" were forced into it, to add importance to the parts of other performers.[10]

And as late as 1844, Pier-Angelo Minoli, the author of an exhaustive and often level-headed polemic on operatic reform resorts to irony when describing aria insertion and what he perceives to be carelessness in their selection: "To the prima donna goes, for example, the caprice of removing from the score a cabaletta and in-

---

8. Pier Jacopo Martello, *Della tragedia antica e moderna* (Rome: F. Gonzaga, 1715); translated in Piero Weiss, "Piero Jacopo Martello on Opera (1715): An Annotated Translation," *Musical Quarterly* 66 (1980): 398.

9. Benedetto Marcello, *Il teatro alla moda* (Venice: Aldiviva, 1733); translated in Reinhard Pauly, *Musical Quarterly* 34 (1948): 378.

10. John Ebers, *Seven Years of the King's Theatre* (London: Carey, Lea and Carey, 1828), 116–17. De Begnis and his wife were undoubtedly performing the infamous "Paër" version of the opera, which was presented for the first time at the Théâtre Italien on May 18, 1820. The London production was presented on May 19, 1821. In addition to *La Cenerentola*, numbers from *L'Italiana in Algeri, Torvaldo e Dorliska,* and *Ciro in Babilonia* were introduced into *Il Turco in Italia*. See Gioachino Rossini, *Il Turco in Italia*, ed. Margaret Bent, in *Edizione critica di Gioachino Rossini*, series 1, vol. 13 (Pesaro: Fondazione Rossini, 1988), xxxvii–xxxviii.

serting another by a different author: nothing could be simpler, even though the second is in a dissimilar key and is foreign to the character, to the style of music, and to the meaning of the words."[11] Though these writings and others like them may have convinced some singers to think twice before using insertion arias, the persistence with which such remarks appear over a century of opera history demonstrates their lack of effect. Satire is, at bottom, a weapon of the weak—unable to control their environment, those who employ it do so from the sidelines exerting little power over the structures they wish to change. On its own, this approach is of little practical use to the reformer, something that the eighteenth-century parodists must have been aware of, for their complaints tend to close with gestures of resignation—Martello allowing singers to employ aria insertions rather than taking the blame for a poor performance; Marcello advising librettists to maintain a heavy store of new arias "just in case." On the contrary, fewer compromises exist in the nineteenth-century statements, Ebers and Minoli maintaining resistance to the practice and offering little middle ground. Though this may simply represent a stylistic difference (parody versus polemic), the tougher stance exhibited by the later commentators may also have been feasible because by the time they were writing, irony was no longer the only tool being wielded against aria insertion—Ebers and Minoli had some backup. During the first half of the nineteenth century, a variety of official documents surfaced that sought to limit, if not eliminate, the presence of aria insertions from Italian opera productions.

Among these texts were contracts that bound individual singers to a theater, season, and impresario. Beginning in the eighteenth century and perhaps even earlier, these agreements occasionally included references to aria insertions, as John Rosselli has shown in the case of Virginia Monticelli. A contract this soprano signed with the Teatro del Cocomero, Florence, in 1754 stipulated among other requirements that she carry with her an adequate number of aria insertions to employ when necessary.[12] Decisions concerning which arias she would choose and the operatic contexts into which she would introduce them were left largely up to her. During the nineteenth century, however, such broad liberties were almost always stricken from these official records. In some cases, particularly during the first few decades of the century, many of these documents made no mention whatsoever of aria insertions, leaving open the question of when they would appear and who was in charge of selecting them. A contract signed by the impresario Osea Francia and the singer Caterina Parlamagni for the 1813 carnival season at the Teatro della Pergola, Florence, for example, holds the prima donna responsible for supplying her own costumes (as per long-standing tradition), but is silent on whether or not she should also pack in-

---

11. "Alla prima donna verrà, per esempio, il capriccio di levare dallo spartito una cabaletta ed inserirne altra di altro autore: niente di più facile, benchè la seconda sia in tuono dissimigliante ed estranea al carattere, allo stile della musica, ed al significato delle parole." Minoli's polemic is published in three parts under the general title "Delle cause che conducono a mal partito le opere riprodotte senza l'intervento dell'autore"; this statement appears in the first, subtitled "I maestri-concertatori," *Gazzetta musicale di Milano* 11 (March 17, 1844): 44. The other two installments are "Gl'impresari" 13 (March 31, 1844): 51–52; and "Il pubblico" 16 (April 21, 1844): 64–65.

12. Rosselli, *Singers of Italian Opera: The History of a Profession* (Cambridge: Cambridge University Press, 1992), 161.

sertion arias into her traveling trunk.[13] By the 1830s, this silence was replaced by clauses that sought to regulate when and where singers might alter a score. Giulia Grisi's agreement with the Teatro la Fenice, Venice, for the 1833 carnival season serves as a clear example, containing two clauses that became fixed components of standard contracts regardless of theater, singer, or impresario. Its third article begins, "It is forbidden for Signora Grisi to insert pieces of music without special permission from the impresario,"[14] and the fourth states, "Signora Grisi will be required to execute the parts in the manner in which they will be distributed by the impresario, the ability to vary, diminish, remove them belonging to this person alone; nor may Signora Grisi refuse any of the parts given to her just because they were previously performed by other artists."[15] According to this document the impresario is the person in charge. Aria insertions are not prohibited, but in order to perform them the singer must not only obtain his consent (clause three), she is also obligated—at least as officially stated—to perform whatever music he presents to her (clause four).

Indications that impresarios played active roles in selecting the insertion arias that divas and divos were to sing appear also in contractual stipulations regulating repertory for special occasions, benefit productions in particular. Alessandro Lanari (1787–1852), one of the nineteenth century's most successful theatrical agents whose career overlapped with those of Bellini, Donizetti, Mercadante, and Verdi, included the following language in countless agreements he made with singers between 1840 and 1848 to perform at the Teatro della Pergola: "[Sig.r/ra] will be obligated to lend [his/her] name to those benefit nights that will be produced for the total benefit of the impresario. S/he will have to add some new pieces chosen by the impresario to the score being performed on such occasions. [The impresario] intends to reward [the singer] proportionally according to the income accrued during said benefit nights."[16] Opportunities once left wide open to singers to alter scores and to add whatever music they wished to perform were diminishing. Even in the context of benefit productions, which, as I shall explore further below, were almost always intended as *potpourri* events, official (if not actual) control over alterations was taken out of the hands of singers. Wise impresarios, however, avoided imposing their wills

13. A copy of this contract is found in Giovanni Battista Cavalcaselle, *Tipi di scritture teatrali attraverso luoghi e tempi diversi* (Rome: Athenaeum, 1919), 40–41. For more general information on theatrical contracts and legislation, see Enrico Rosmini, *Legislazione e giurisprudenza dei teatri* (Milan: Ulrico Hoepli, 1893).

14. "È vietato alla Sig.a Grisi d'inserire pezzi di musica senza speciale permesso dell'Impresa." Gran Teatro la Fenice, Archivio [hereafter ATLF], busta 4, fasc. 11.

15. "Dovrà la Sig.ª Grisi eseguire le parti nel modo che le verranno distribuite dall'Impresa, appartenendo a questa sola la facoltà di variarle, diminuirle, levarle; nè potrà la med.ª Sig.ª Grisi rifiutare alcune delle parti, che le verranno date, abbenchè siano state anteriormente eseguite da altri Artisti." Ibid.

16. "Sarà obbligato il [Sig.r/.ra] di prestare il suo nome per quelle Beneficiate, che a totale benefizio dell'Impresa verranno fatte, dovendo in tali occasioni aggiungere dei Pezzi nuovi a quello spartito che sarà in Scena, a scelta dell'Impresa stessa, che si riserva a gratificarlo proporzionatamente agl'Introiti che si faranno con dette Beneficiate." I:Fn, Lanari, 13¹. 11, cc. 1–2. This text is derived from the contract Lanari signed with Giacomo Roppa on June 2, 1840. See Marcello de Angelis, *Le cifre del melodramma: l'archivio inedito dell'impresario teatrale Alessandro Lanari nella Biblioteca nazionale centrale di Firenze,* 2 vols. (Florence: La nuova Italia, 1982), 1: 148.

blindly over performers and rarely demanded that they execute arias unsuited to their voices. It was in their interest, after all, to facilitate the highest quality productions possible, as it was their finances that would suffer if audiences were displeased. These men of the theater worked closely with their prima donnas and leading men, yielding to their opinions and even altering contracts at the behest of singers when they found themselves under pressure to do so. Such was the case when Lanari signed a contract with Marianna Barbieri-Nini to perform at the Teatro della Pergola (dated April 18, 1845) in which the clause concerning benefits was rewritten by hand—with this change, the soprano was still required to add new arias, but the rewording grants her, not the impresario, complete control over selecting what they would be.[17]

Clauses limiting the selection of aria insertions continued to appear in singers' contracts throughout the middle of the nineteenth century, almost always designating the impresario as the arbiter of what were and were not acceptable alterations. This situation shifted slightly, but significantly in the 1870s when the standard clause regulating when and where singers could alter a score was rewritten: "The artist must perform the parts as the authors composed them; he may not transpose them, nor introduce pieces or variants without the authorization of the director of the orchestra. He must perform his part even if it was previously performed by another artist, and he must, if the occasion should arise, yield even those parts that he had previously performed."[18] This clause retains many features found in the older version (exemplified by Grisi's contract cited above). Singers are still permitted to introduce arias or variants of arias into a score, and consent must still be obtained, though now it comes from the director of the orchestra rather than from the impresario. Even as late as the 1870s, in other words, openness toward aria insertion lingered, and yet, the first sentence of this clause indicates that the progression toward stricter control over performers had reached a new level. Unlike contracts printed during the first half of the nineteenth century, this one appeals directly to the "authors" (composer and librettist), requiring that the music be performed as they wrote it. This statement is by no means definitive, but it does suggest a shift of authority away from singers, and a growing awareness of the status of Italian operas as works.

This understanding did not surface suddenly in the second half of the nineteenth century; as early as the 1830s, there are hints that singers themselves were awakening to the notion that operas might pack a greater aesthetic punch when performed according to the composer's design.[19] Indeed, nineteenth-century prima donnas and

---

17. I:Fn Lanari, 13¹. 23, c. 5. In this context, one might take into account Ebers' sentiments on the matter: "The performers of a Theatre can never be induced to observe the necessary subordination of a manager, while an authority exists independent of him, to whom an appeal may, in effect, be carried against his regulations. It then becomes his part to pay immense sums of money, to persons over whom he can exert no efficient control, but whose deficiencies and irregularities are duly placed by the public, before the scenes, to the account of the manager only" (Ebers, *Seven Years at the King's Theatre*, 42).

18. "L'artista dovrà eseguire le parti, come furono scritte dagli autori, né fare trasporti, introdurre pezzi o varianti, senza l'autorizzazione del maestro direttore d'orchestra. Dovrà nel caso eseguire parti anche che sieno precedentemente state eseguite da altro artista, e dovrà all'occorrenza cedere anche le parti da lui già state disimpegnate." Reprinted in Giovanni Azzaroni, *Del teatro e dintorni: una storia della legislazione e delle strutture teatrali in italia nell'ottocento* (Rome: Bulzoni Editore, 1981), 261.

19. Gossett discusses this issue in *Divas and Scholars: Performing Italian Opera.* (Chicago: University of

leading men occasionally voiced this belief explicitly, as did the soprano Teresa Bertonotti Radicati in a letter she published in the periodical *Teatri arti e letteratura* (December 14, 1836). Radicati was writing on behalf of her student, Rita Gabussi, whose performance in the title role of Rossini's *La Cenerentola* had been reviewed the week before by the same newspaper.[20] Overall, the critic's comments were favorable, noting that Gabussi possessed "an extremely beautiful mezzo soprano voice, as strong as it needs to be and sufficiently wide-ranging,"[21] but even so, her performance was not entirely perfect: "she distorts the music, sings as she pleases, and loses herself in misplaced cadenzas, excessive fioritura, and useless affectations (and does so quite poorly)."[22] Radicati strongly disagreed with this assessment of her student's performance, responding heatedly as follows: "The beautiful music of *Cenerentola,* one of the masterworks by the sublime Rossini is known to everyone, and no piano exists that does not have these precious volumes draped upon it. May I verify, therefore, that *Gabussi* performed this music almost exactly as it was written, with the exception of a few passages that lie outside the center of her mezzo soprano voice, not contralto, for which [the role] was composed."[23] These comments do not refer specifically to aria insertion, but Radicati's strident response to the critic's accusations of "excessive fioritura" and "useless habits"—of taking too many liberties—speaks to some broader issues concerning many singers. On the one hand, she might have been defending Gabussi's technical ability, arguing that her student did not need to alter Rossini's music because she was perfectly capable of performing it all well. But Radicati also may have been referring to a larger concern: accusing a prima donna of willfully misinterpreting an operatic work, and of altering the content of those "precious volumes" that appear on all pianos, was tantamount to impugning her integrity as an artist. Many singers paid close attention to what the composer wrote—to the notes printed in scores—Radicati seems to be asserting, and it was a point of honor that this aesthetic approach be recognized by critics and spectators alike.

Aria insertion itself is rarely mentioned in letters or other correspondence by singers, but one particularly poignant example survives, penned by an angry tenor, Napoleone Moriani. Writing in 1841 in reaction to negative experiences performing at the Teatro la Fenice, Venice, Moriani takes aim at his impresario (probably Alessandro Lanari), who clearly misjudged the inclinations of this singer, and pos-

---

Chicago Press, 2006), 211–12. Here, he draws attention to a famous letter written by Giuseppina Ronzi de Begnis to Bellini's best friend and confident Francesco Florimo in which she objects to the tradition that had grown around *I Capuleti e i Montecchi* of replacing Bellini's entire last scene with the dramatically equivalent passage from Vaccai's *Giulietta e Romeo.* I will return to a discussion of this letter in chapter 4.

20. *Teatri arti e letteratura* 667 (December 10, 1836): 109–10.

21. "[U]na belissima voce di mezzo soprano, forte al bisogno ed abbastanza estesa." Ibid.

22. "Ella svisa la musica, e canta a piacere, e si perde in cadenze fuor di luogo, in fioriture soverchie, in inutil vezzi (e qui fa male)." Ibid.

23. "La bellissima musica della *Cenerentola,* uno dei Capo-lavori del sublime *Rossini,* è conosciuta da tutti, e non esiste piano-forte, che non ne abbia indossati li preziosi volumi. Posso dunque accertare che la *Gabussi* eseguisce quella musica pressochè come è scritta, toltone però qualche passaggio, o nota fuori del centro della sua voce di mezzo Soprano sfogato, e non di Contralto per cui è stata composta." *Teatri arti e letteratura* 668 (December 15, 1836): 119.

sibly others as well: "If an ignorant impresario wants to do an opera that is not suited to the means of one such artist, no problem, he alters, transposes, and changes the pieces with damage to the poor composer, and the singer protests, but he must do the opera because the contract obliges him [to carry out] all of the caprices of the impresario, and meanwhile, the booing public degrades [the singer], who is not to blame, and the impresario goes and declares him a dog, an imposter and reproaches him as the cause of his ruin."[24] Moriani's displeasure does not stem exclusively from damage inflicted on "the poor composer." He is angry, above all, that the alterations made were not adequate to his talents and resulted, therefore, in his own bad reception. That he makes reference to the composer at all, however, is significant, for it illustrates that some performers, in some contexts, were growing aware of the stakes involved when arias were introduced without care.

Not surprisingly, composers themselves were instrumental in conveying this point, and their opinions about aria insertions surface occasionally in correspondence with singers, impresarios, and friends. In a famous letter to Francesco Florimo, for instance, Bellini describes a skirmish with the soprano Adelaide Tosi, who was to sing the lead role in *Bianca e Fernando* at the inauguration of the newly refurbished Teatro Carlo Felice, Genoa, in 1828. For this occasion, Bellini agreed to provide the theater with a thoroughly reworked version of the opera (originally *Bianca e Gernando,* premiered at the Teatro San Carlo, Naples, 1826), adding to it a *sinfonia* and three new vocal numbers, including a new cavatina composed specifically for Tosi's voice. During rehearsals, composer and prima donna nearly came to blows over this piece:

> She rehearsed the cavatina with the orchestra and then, after she had sung it like a dog and therefore had not found it effective, she wanted another, and at the same time she did not want [to sing] the *stretta* of the *scena,* which she said lacked any [opportunity for displaying] agility, and she called it music composed for children, saying that if I didn't change it, she would substitute one of her *pezzi di baule* for it. I realized then that we were on the verge of quarreling . . . I replied that I would not change a note; not out of disrespect, but because I wanted my music performed with the tempos that I decided upon, and not at her caprice, and wanted it given exactly the shadings that I had imagined. She struggled for two days—[but] finally sang the pieces as I had handed them to her. My dear Florimo, they were so effective that she came to beg my pardon—and that cabaletta, which she told me I had composed for children, will bring down the house. Now we are the very best of friends, as though nothing took place. She is very happy and sings everything as I wanted it, and therefore the music makes the effect that I had imagined.[25]

24. "Un ignorante impresario vuol fare un opera che non si attaglia ai mezzi di un tale Artista, non importa, si punti si trasporti si cambi i pezzi con danno del povero Maestro, si sgoli il cantante, ma l'opera si deve fare perchè la scrittura lo obbliga a tutte i caprici dell'impresario, e frattanto il pubblico fischia avvilisce l'artista che non ha colpa e l'impresario per giunta lo dichiara un cane un impostora e lo rinfaccia di esser causa della sua rovina." ATLF, busta 4, fasc. 4, "Napoleone Moriani." Letter dated October 9, 1841, Bologna, and sent to B. Caresana, who was the secretary of the Teatro la Fenice during the 1839–1840 carnival season.

25. Reproduced in Luisa Cambi, ed., *Bellini: epistolario* (Milan: A. Mondadori, 1943), 74–75; translated in Herbert Weinstock, *Vincenzo Bellini: His Life and His Operas* (New York: Knopf, 1971), 47.

Having won this battle over a prima donna's threats to introduce an insertion aria rather than perform the "pieces as he had handed them to her," however, it is not at all clear that he was at war with the practice as a whole. For Bellini, aria insertion was more palatable when it was the opera's composer (rather than the singers or other agents) who was making the choices, as a letter concerning one of Pacini's operas suggests. Of an upcoming production of *Gli arabi nelle Gallie,* Bellini wrote once again to Florimo: "Next Monday *Arabi* arrives, which is certain to have a success with [Henriette Méric-]Lalande [in the lead role], for whom Pacini has composed a new cavatina and inserted the *scena* from *Amazilia* [also by Pacini]; as such, the production is sure to succeed."[26] This positive reaction suggests that for Bellini, preserving a single authorial vision may have been more important than protecting the integrity of a work.

Indeed, where his own operas were concerned, Bellini was resigned to the idea that he could not always prevent singers from performing aria insertions, whether they were written by him or by others. For a revival of *Il pirata* staged in Vienna (carnival 1828) that occurred without his direct participation, he was aware (albeit displeased) that Adelaide Comelli-Rubini in the role of Imogene introduced "Oh! come rapida," a cavatina by Meyerbeer;[27] and for the same production he suggested that Antonio Tamburini as Ernesto replace the cabaletta of his cavatina with "O contento desiato," one of the pieces newly composed for the Genoa production of *Bianca e Fernando.*[28] This flexible stance was atypical, however, the actions of a young composer anxious to see his opera received favorably, even when executed by singers whose voices were not ideally suited to the original parts. As Paolo Fabbri has observed, these alterations were acceptable to Bellini for one reason alone: he was the person in charge of dictating what music was to be performed and thus he was responsible for the reception his opera would receive, regardless of whether it was positive or negative. *Bianca e Fernando, Il pirata,* and all of his subsequent operas were tolerable to him only when they were performed according to his decisions and dictates, even though such an ideal was ultimately unattainable.[29]

Donizetti conveyed similar sentiments toward aria insertions, approving of some, and advising performers on others, as chapter 2 will explore in greater detail. But in general, he was deeply opposed to the introduction of arias into his operas without his approval, whether or not they were his compositions. In *Donizetti and His Operas,* William Ashbrook recounts an incident in which an 1843 revival of *Fausta* was tampered with heavily, raising the composer's ire. Donizetti published an article on the matter and expressed his opinion in an angry letter to his friend, Gaetano Melzi of Milan:

---

26. "Lunedí prossimo vanno gli *Arabi* che certo faran furore con la Lalande, a cui Pacini ha fatto una nuova cavatina, e mette la scena dell'*Amazilia;* perciò l'esito è certo." Letter from Milan, February 20, 1828; Cambi, *Bellini: epistolario,* 53.

27. Letter from Genoa, April 19, 1828; Cambi, *Bellini: epistolario,* 86. See also Paolo Fabbri, "Per un'edizione critica del *Pirata,*" *Chigiana* 45 (2004): 191–92.

28. See Bellini's letter from Milan to Florimo (May 12, 1828); Cambi, *Bellini: epistolario,* 93.

29. Fabbri, "Per un'edizione critica del *Pirata,*" 191–92.

I believed that with the letter I published I would open the public's eyes to the direction of the theaters. I believed it would be of use to my colleagues. I hoped to draw away from our shoulders the whirlwind of whistling that oppresses us when pieces by another composer are introduced into an opera, or when they are transposed or altered. All these things are most damaging to poor composers who cannot come out and say: *This is not mine, this was not originally designed like this, this does not go so slow or so fast, this is not suited to the voice of A or B.*[30]

Donizetti's conspicuous frustration is born of a historical moment during which the ideal of authorial control affected how composers perceived their operas, but before efficient regulations were set in place to assure that their works would not be tampered with without their approval. Only a few years later, Giuseppe Verdi formulated just such a regulation. As has been widely noted, the period leading up to the premiere of his *Macbeth* (Florence, Teatro della Pergola, March 14, 1845) was characterized by increased concern on his part for music-dramatic unity and precision on the part of singers.[31] Generally frustrated by alterations made to his scores by theaters, performers, and censors, Verdi insisted that his publisher, Giovanni Ricordi, include the following language in contracts with theaters wishing to stage his works: "In order to prevent the alterations which theaters make to operatic works, it is prohibited to subject the score in question to any addition, any mutilation, transposition, in short to any alteration which requires the smallest change in the orchestration, under threat of 1,000 francs fine which I will extract through you from any theater where alterations are made to the score."[32] As Verdi was well aware, this regulation was utterly unenforceable, a symbolic gesture that had little practical effect. Nevertheless, the clause is significant, representing the earliest official effort by a composer to compel singers, impresarios, theater managers, and censors to respect the integrity of his scores. Like his predecessors, Verdi allowed star performers to influence the shape and contents of his operas, particularly early on in his career. As David Lawton and David Rosen have shown, he often complied when demands for new arias arose, composing pieces anew for almost all of his works up to and including *Attila*.[33] Verdi's language demonstrates, however, that there came a point—one that coincided with his steadily blossoming popularity throughout Europe—when such liberties taken with-

30. Paris, October 31, 1843; reproduced in Guido Zavadini, *Donizetti: vita, musiche, epistolario* (Bergamo: Istituto Italiano d'Arti Grafiche, 1948), 696; translated in William Ashbrook, *Donizetti and His Operas* (Cambridge: Cambridge University Press, 1982), 212. Ashbrook provides no information regarding the article Donizetti published on this subject, nor have I been able to locate it.

31. For correspondence between Verdi and the singers involved in the premier of *Macbeth*, see David Rosen and Andrew Porter, eds., *Verdi's "Macbeth": A Sourcebook* (New York: W. W. Norton, 1984), 3–65.

32. Milan, May 20, 1847, in Gaetano Cesari and Alessandro Luzio, eds., *I copialettere di Giuseppe Verdi* (1913; reprint, Milan: Forni Editore Bologna, 1968), 39. Translated in Roger Parker, *Studies in Early Verdi* (New York: Garland, 1989), 145. This letter is one of many in which the composer demands that singers give his operas the respect he believed they deserved. See, among others, Verdi to Giovanni Ricordi, Milan, December 29, 1846 (*I copialettere,* 34–35); and Verdi to Francesco Lucca, Milan, April 10, 1847 (*I copialettere,* 35–36). For further discussion of this clause and its relevance to censorial practice in nineteenth-century opera production in Rome, see Andreas Giger, "Social Control and the Censorship of Giuseppe Verdi's Operas in Rome (1844–1859)," *Cambridge Opera Journal* 11 (1999): 233–65.

33. "Verdi's Non-Definitive Revisions: The Early Operas," *Atti del IIIo Congresso internazionale di*

out his permission were unacceptable. By 1847, the act of adding or substituting arias into one of his operas was a crime that, in an ideal world, would merit heavy financial penalties—in the real world, of course, such goals were quite a ways off.

Verdi's arias were routinely extracted from their original contexts and used as aria insertions: the tenor Giacomo Roppa introduced Zamoro's "Un Inca . . . eccesso orribile" from *Alzira* into a production of Donizetti's *Maria di Rohan,* for example; Clelia Forti Babacci performed the soprano cavatina from *Ernani* in a performance of Donizetti's *Gemma di Vergy;* and as I will explore in chapter 5, prima donnas selected a variety of numbers by Verdi to insert into the lesson scene of Rossini's *Il barbiere di Siviglia.*[34] Undoubtedly more disturbing to the composer, however, was that his operas were affected by aria insertions, as the performance history of *Attila* illustrates. Scholars have long been aware that for a production of this opera in Trieste in the autumn of 1846, Verdi composed a substitute aria for the tenor Nicola Ivanoff, the romanza "Sventurato! Alla mia vita."[35] This opera also encountered a second alteration, however, one that undoubtedly occurred without Verdi's approval: between 1849 and 1852, sopranos in the role of Odabella excised the character's "Oh! nel fuggente nuvolo" from the first act and replaced it with "Cupa fatal mestizia" from Donizetti's *Maria di Rohan.*[36] This isolated incident does not compare with the hundreds of aria insertions that affected scores by Rossini, Donizetti, Bellini, and their contemporaries. Nevertheless, that Odabellas performed an aria by Donizetti in the context of one of Verdi's operas as late as 1852 is revealing: official sanctions against these pieces were a little more effective than the sarcasm employed by Marcello and Martello, but just as the earlier discourse lacked force, so, too, did the later. Contractual obligations and threatening clauses bound performers to composers' scores only loosely, tenuous markers of change along the path of a tradition in which singers were long accustomed to expressing their own aesthetic choices. Where were the nooks and crannies into which they continued to exert their influence?

---

studi verdiani (Parma: Istituto di studi verdiani, 1972), 189–237. One might also mention in this context Mary Ann Smart's article "Verdi Sings Erminia Frezzolini," *Women and Music* 1 (1997): 13–22, in which she investigates how Erminia Frezzolini may have influenced the way Verdi composed the roles of Giselda in *I Lombardi* and Giovanna d'Arco, both created by the soprano.

34. The production in which Roppa inserted Zamora's aria into *Maria di Rohan* occurred at Rome's Teatro Apollo, carnival 1847 (Alberto Cametti, *Il Teatro di Tordinona poi di Apollo,* 2 vols. [Rome: A. Chicca, 1938], 2: 470–71). The production in which Babacci introduced Elvira's aria from *Ernani* into *Gemma di Vergy* occurred in the spring season 1846 at the theater in the town of Grosetto, located in Tuscany (*Teatri arti e letteratura* 1161 [April 7, 1846]: 80).

35. Julian Budden, *The Operas of Verdi,* 3 vols. (1973–1981; reprint, Oxford: Clarendon Press, 1992), 1: 262–63; Gossett, "A New Romanza for *Attila,*" *Studi Verdiani* 9 (1993): 13–35, and *Divas and Scholars,* 144; and Emanuele Senici, "Per Guasco, Ivanoff e Moriani: le tre versioni della romanza di Foresto nel 'Attila,'" in *Pensieri per un maestro: studi in onore di Pierluigi Petrobelli,* ed. Stefano La Via and Roger Parker (Turin: EDT, 2002), 273–88.

36. The theaters in which this alteration was made, the dates, and the singers who performed the aria were as follows: Siena, Teatro Rinnovati, summer 1849, Metilde Dille; Viterbo, Teatro del Genio, summer 1851, Matilde Dille; and Livorno, Teatro dei Floridi, summer 1852, Fanny Capuani. Librettos for each of these productions are housed in the Cini Foundation, Venice (I:Vgc). I must thank Luigi Ferrara who assisted me in locating these examples.

OPERE DI RIPIEGO **AND BENEFIT PRODUCTIONS**

Practical reasons account, in part, for the continued presence of aria insertions in opera performances during the nineteenth century. Singers, for instance, would often substitute new pieces into operas whose arias were already so well known, having been inserted into other contexts, that there was a danger of boring the audience with yet one more repetition.[37] In a review of Rossini's *Elisabetta, regina d'Inghilterra* (Milan, La Scala, 1828), for instance, the critic berates Giovanni David for interpolating several arias, but he forgives a second singer, Henriette Méric-Lalande, for taking a similar liberty: "One might, perhaps, object that Lalande was no better advised [than David], substituting into the first act an aria by Pavesi for the cavatina. But those who know how much the cavatina from *Elisabetta* resembles another cavatina, which was recently heard in *The Barber of Seville* ["Una voce poco fa"], will find the necessity to change it an important task."[38] In fact, the cabaletta from Elisabetta's aria ("Questo cor ben lo comprende") is nearly identical to the cabaletta of "Una voce poco fa" ("Io son docile"), rendering the critic's observation even more logical.

Aria insertions, moreover, often came to the aid of singers who were required to appear in productions mounted without adequate rehearsal time, a situation that frequently arose when an impresario or theater opted to stage an *opera di ripiego* (a replacement for a failed production; most often an opera that had proven successful during a previous season or seasons). In such a situation, in which a singer might have had only limited exposure to the new production and only a few days to learn his or her role, arias found to be too difficult could be substituted with more familiar ones. The exceptional nature of the *opera di ripiego* and the position that aria insertions held within are codified in Giovanni Valle's *Cenni teorico-pratici sulle aziende teatrali,* a detailed guidebook published in 1823 that outlines a wide range of management procedures for the production of Italian opera: 

> A situation that frequently arises, in which the first production of a season cannot sustain itself [since it is] disliked by the public, demands a speedy replacement with another, an *opera di ripiego;* this new opera is chosen in consultation with the entire company, and that which has already been performed in other theaters either by all, or by the majority of the leading performers, is preferred. In such cases, the impresario expects it to be produced within a few days, and thus, given the urgency, he will permit a few of the virtuosi who have not previously performed this work to insert foreign [*estraneo*] cantabiles with which they are more familiar.[39]

37. There is at least one very well known example of singers interpolating arias to avoid repetition of the most popular pieces. At the French premiere in 1824 of Rossini's *La donna del lago* at the Théâtre Italien in Paris, the prima donna did not sing the entrance aria composed for this work, "Elena! oh tu, che chiamo." She chose to sing instead "Ah! quel giorno ognor rammento" from the same composer's *Semiramide* because Giuditta Pasta had recently interpolated "Elena, oh tu che chiamo" into a performance of *Otello* at the same theater. See Gossett, *Divas and Scholars,* 210.

38. "Qualcuno potrebbe forse obbiettare che non avvisò meglio la *Lalande* sostituendo nel primo Atto alla cavatina dello spartito un'aria di *Pavesi.* Ma quelli cui è noto quanto la cavatina dell'*Elisabetta* ne ricordi un'altra recentissimamente udita *Barbiere di Siviglia,* troverà questa necessità di cambio ben più poderosa." *I teatri* (January 4, 1828): 636.

39. "Il caso che frequentemente accade, che uno spartito di primo spettacolo della stagione non si

One witnesses this theory translated into practice through newspaper reviews, as in this animated description of the semi-disastrous season at the Teatro di Ancona (carnival 1833):

> It is an uncontested truth, confirmed by irrefutable experience, that the fortune or misfortune of a company depends on the choice of scores, and that just as the satisfaction of the public depends on them, so too does the ensemble of artists: this truth was confirmed in Ancona during the current carnival season: the team of singers, which Signor *Marzi* [impresario] prodigiously, and in very little time, shrewdly reunited, produced the score *Violenza e Costanza* [by Mercadante], and it failed: this cast was reanimated somewhat, falling back quickly on *L'Inganno Felice,* and with some pieces from *Semiramide,* sung with distinction by the contralto Signora *Giuseppina Angelini Dossi.*[40]

Though it is unclear whether this was Dossi's first encounter with Rossini's one-act *farsa L'inganno felice,* we know that she was intimately familiar with *Semiramide,* having just the year before appeared as Arsace at the Teatro dell'Aquila in Fermo.[41] She was no doubt happy to enhance the evening's production with a few arias drawn from that score.[42] In this production and in most *opere di ripiego,* singers and impresarios did not necessarily want audience members to recognize the aria insertions (though some spectators undoubtedly did anyway). Rather, in most cases, the new music would have been selected with the goal of blending into the featured opera, providing as few clues as possible that singers were resorting to a "quick fix."

Benefit productions, too, represented theatrical moments when freedoms to cut, alter, and introduce new arias to a score were taken for granted by singers, impresarios, and even by composers. The benefit was a privilege granted to star singers and impresarios from the eighteenth century and extending well into the nineteenth as a means for supplementing their incomes.[43] Though the precise terms for

---

sostenga, e che al pubblico non gradisca, esige la più sollecita sostituzione di altra opera di ripiego; questa viene scelta comunemente di consenso colla Compagnia, e si preferisce già quella che sia stata eseguita o da tutte o dal più delle prime parti in altri teatri. In simili casi un'Impresa pretende che in pochi giorni essa vada in iscena, e perciò permetterà che per l'urgenza alcuni de'virtuosi che non l'hanno fatta, inseriscano qualche cantabile estraneo, e che essi sanno." Valle, *Cenni teorico-pratici sulle aziende teatrali* (Milan: Socoetà tipog. de' classici Italiani, 1823), 90. Contemporary views of the *opera di ripiego* are also explored in a satirical article published in the *Gazzetta musicale di Milano,* "Costumi teatrali. Le opere di ripiego. Riflessioni umoristiche" 48 (November 27, 1842): 205.

40. "È una verità incontrastabile autenticata da mai dismentitasi esperienza, che l'esito fortunato, od infausto di una impresa dipende dalla scelta degli spartiti, e che mentre da questi nasce la soddisfazione del pubblico, ne risulta pur anco l'incontro degli artisti: tale verità venne confermata in Ancona nell'attual carnevale: si produsse la compagnia cantante, che prodigiosamente in angustia di tempo seppe con avvedutezza riunire il signor *Marzi,* con lo spartito *Violenza e Costanza,* e rimase sacrificata: si rianimò alquanto ripiegando subito con *L'Inganno Felice,* e con dei pezzi della *Semiramide* egregiamente cantanti dal contralto signora *Giuseppina Angelini Dossi." Teatri arti e letteratura* 464 (January 31, 1833): 205.

41. See the libretto for the production at the Teatro dell'Aquila, fiera 1832, located in the Biblioteca privata Giochi, Macerata (Misc.14bis E.VI.2).

42. Among the pieces from *Semiramide,* she undoubtedly inserted Arsace's "Ah! quel giorno ognor rammento," an aria used by other singers for insertion. See footnote 37, and Gossett, *Divas and Scholars,* 210.

43. See Rosselli, *Singers of Italian Opera,* 82–84 and 142–43, for descriptions of a few singers' benefits that occurred during the eighteenth and nineteenth centuries.

these evenings differed from city to city, they almost always entitled the honoree to some or all of the proceeds accumulated at the box office on that night.[44] Given these strong financial incentives, singers were encouraged to produce gala events during which spectators would be attracted to the theater in large numbers by the promise of a variety of musical material. It was common, for example, for benefits to consist of a selection of individual acts from a group of operas, each of which featured the singer of honor in the best possible light. For Carolina Ungher's benefit at the Teatro Comunale, Bologna (June 4, 1832), for instance, the company performed the first act of Mercadante's *I normanni in Parigi* and the second of *La straniera;*[45] and for Eloisa Gaggi Storti's benefit at the Teatro di Corte, Modena (November 21, 1832), the first act of *Il barbiere di Siviglia* and the whole of Rossini's *L'inganno felice* were the featured selections.[46]

Almost as familiar were benefits that showcased an opera regularly scheduled for the season, but enhanced by one or more insertion aria. For a benefit staged at the Teatro Valle, Rome, in the spring of 1826, for instance, the soprano Virginia Blasis introduced "Bel raggio lusinghier" from Rossini's *Semiramide* into *Le civette in apparenza* by Luigi Gambale;[47] Teresa de Giuli's evening at the Teatro Comunale, Lugo (September 21, 1841), featured Donizetti's *Lucrezia Borgia,* during which she sang the cavatina from Bellini's *Beatrice di Tenda* ("Ma la sola, ohimè! son io");[48] and for Giuditta Grisi's benefit at the Teatro dei Condomini, Macerata (September 6, 1836), various pieces were added to Bellini's *I Capuleti e i Montecchi,* including "the aria from *Parisina* sung by the bass *Giunti,* an aria by Pacini sung by madama *Grisi;* and the so-called pistol duet from *Chiara di Rosemburg* sung by the above-mentioned *Giunti* and *Guidotti.*"[49] Benefits were announced in advance on posters, flyers, or in local newspapers, where the full opera was announced and where the added attractions were featured prominently. In other words, spectators attended these events fully aware that aria insertions were going to appear, many opera fans buying tickets specifically to hear what were often their favorite numbers performed by their favorite singers. The beneficiary depended on attracting a large crowd, and so it be-

---

44. In chapter IV, article iv, "Serate de beneficio, e mezze serate" of *Cenni teorico-pratici sulle aziende teatrali,* 63–71, Valle outlines five possible payment structures for a singer's benefit evening: (a) *serata intera:* the singer is entitled to all of the proceeds from the evening; (b) *serata a metà coll'impresa:* the singer shares the proceeds with the impresario; (c) *serate franche di spese:* the singer is exempt from all expenses accrued that evening (it is unclear how this model differs from the first); (d) *serate col carico delle spese al virtuoso:* the singer is responsible for all expenses accrued that evening; (e) *serate assicurata in una determinata somma:* the singer is paid in a lump sum determined prior to the evening—this amount is entirely independent of the proceeds accrued during the benefit evening itself.

45. *L'eco* (June 18, 1832).

46. *Teatri arti e letteratura* 454 (November 29, 1832): 113. For an extended discussion of the practice of stringing together a selection of individual acts in performance, see my article, "To the Ear of the Amateur: Performing Operas Piecemeal," in *Fashions and Legacies of Nineteenth-Century Italian Opera,* ed. Roberta Montemorra Marvin and Hilary Poriss (Cambridge: Cambridge University Press, forthcoming).

47. *Le notizie del giorno* (June 15, 1826).

48. *Teatri arti e letteratura* 949 (September 30, 1841): 36.

49. "L'aria della *Parisina* cantata dal basso *Giunti,* un'aria di *Pacini* cantata da madama *Grisi;* e il duetto così detto della Pistola nella *Chiara* cantata dal *Giunti* suddetto, e da *Guidotti.*" *Teatri arti e letteratura* 655 (September 15, 1836): 15–16.

hooved him or her to feature music that was both well known and that featured their voices in the best possible light.

These practical reasons clarify why some aria insertions appeared during the nineteenth century, but they cannot account for the majority. Indeed, when Ester Mombelli introduced "Giusto Dio che umile adoro" from *Tancredi* into a production of Paër's *Agnese di Fitzhenry*,[50] when Fanny Eckerlin sang an aria by Bellini in the context of Luigi Ricci's *L'eroina del Messico*,[51] and when Anna De Lagrange performed the soprano cavatina from Federico Ricci's *Corrado d'Altamura* in a production of Mercandante's *Il bravo,* they all did so under "normal" circumstances, operas regularly scheduled for a given theater and a given season.[52] It is this normalcy that surrounded the practice of aria insertion (as opposed to the circumstances offered by the *opera di ripiego* and the benefit) that this book aims to unpack. Nineteenth-century theatrical manuals contain some clues pertaining to a set of general guidelines that singers followed when making these alterations on a day-to-day basis.

THEATRICAL MANUALS: GIOVANNI VALLE AND NICOLA TACCHINARDI

Giovanni Valle's treatise of 1823 mentioned above contains a discussion of aria insertion that opens with language similar to that found in singers' contracts: "All principal singers are obliged to perform their roles, and those numbers that are original to the score. Absolutely no one may remove or substitute or add a piece without the express approval and understanding of the impresario."[53] Directly following this familiar admonition, however, Valle loosens up, appending a list of exceptional circumstances when instances of aria insertions might be performed:

> [T]here are also several cases in which what has been said should be modified a bit; that is, when the tessitura of the music of one part does not correspond to the voice of the singer, it should be changed or altered if the music so allows, or changed entirely, by substituting it with something else that is more acceptable to the singer himself;—when this piece of music has already been heard and performed at other times at the same theater by other artists who have previously inserted it into other scores to accommodate themselves, especially if this happened only shortly before.[54]

This passage is intriguing, for it effectively delivers control of aria insertions directly back into the hands of the singer. Of greatest consequence is Valle's allowance per-

---

50. Rome, Teatro Valle (carnival 1824). Notice of inserted aria found in *Le notizie del giorno* (January 15, 1824).

51. Rome, Teatro Apollo (carnival 1830). Notice of inserted aria found in *Le notizie del giorno* (February 18, 1830).

52. Piacenza, Teatro Municipale (carnival 1843). Notice of inserted aria found in *Il pirata* 55 (January 6, 1843).

53. "Tutti i virtuosi di canto sono obbligati ad eseguire la loro parte, e que' pezzi che sono originali dello spartito. Nessuno indistintamente può levare o sostituire o aggiungere pezzo alcuno senza il dovuto assenseo ed intelligenza dell'impresario." Valle, *Cenni teorico-pratici sulle aziende teatrali,* 90.

54. "[V]i sono però diversi casi che consigliano un temperamento a quanto si è detto, e cioè, quando la tessitura della musica d'una parte cantante non corrisponde alla di lei voce, per cui conviene o accomodarla se ne è suscettibile, o cambiarla senza eccezione, sostituendone altra che sia di gradimento

mitting performers to alter, or to substitute entirely, arias that do not conform to their vocal ranges and styles. In effect, this provision negates the earlier guideline stating that virtuoso singers are "obligated" to perform numbers that are "original to the score." But how much license did these singers possess in reality?

A second theatrical manual outlines the dangers inherent in pushing seemingly limitless freedoms too far. *Dell'opera in musica sul teatro italiano e de'suoi difetti* offers a particularly valuable commentary on aria insertion primarily because its author, Nicola Tacchinardi (1772–1859), was a well-known tenor who had developed an intimate firsthand knowledge of the practice over the course of his twenty-five-year-long career. When he published this manual in 1833, he had recently retired, having served as *primo uomo* in productions of operas by Paër, Pacini, Rossini, Donizetti, and others, and having appeared in theaters throughout Italy and elsewhere.[55] Though it is unclear how frequently he employed aria insertions himself, he certainly did not shun the practice: according to extant librettos, Tacchinardi introduced what must have been one of his favorite arias, "Ma dov'è? perché fugge i miei sguardi" (Pacini, *La sacerdotessa d'Irminsul*), into at least one production of Pacini's *Alessandro nell'Indie,* two of Rossini's *La donna del lago,* and three of Pacini's *Cesare in Egitto.*[56] One can imagine that these incidents were not isolated. Given, therefore, that he himself made use of aria insertions, it is surprising how vigorously he rebukes them in his manual:

> The contradictions and inconsistencies produced by pastiches, which are commonly made by introducing (so-called) trunk arias, are uncountable. These are inserted wherever caprice dictates; both buffo pieces within serious operas and serious pieces within comic operas reduce the music drama to a parody.
>
> But people like them! some may reply; and the public little notices that there are all these incongruencies and contradictions. Sing your piece well and you will always be successful. The public audience of our operas does not demand exactness and precision where it has never existed. But if the spectators are aware of the contradictions and inconsistencies, look at them watching a comedy or a tragedy where they demand exactness and you will then realize that they will demand, notice, and remark on the same weaknesses, and no error escapes their eyes and ears.[57]

This passage confirms what Valle's description of aria insertions implies: singers enjoyed the freedom to introduce arias when they wanted and they did so "wherever

---

all'attore stesso;—quando quel tal pezzo di musica sia già stato sentito ed eseguito altre volte sull'istesso teatro da altri artisti che lo avessero per loro comodo inserito in diversi spartiti, e massime se questo successe poco tempo prima." Ibid., 90.

55. "Nicola Tacchinardi," in *Enciclopedia dello spettacolo,* 9 vols. (Rome: Casa editrice Le Maschere, 1954–1962), 9: 20–21.

56. *La donna del lago* (Trieste, autumn 1822; Parma, carnival 1823), and *La sacerdotessa d'Irminsul* (Senigallia, fiera 1822; Ferrara, summer 1822; Florence, spring 1825). Librettos for these productions are all located in I:Vgc. I have not seen a libretto for the production of *Alessandro nell'Indie,* but a review of the production, with mention of the insertion, is found in *I teatri* (1827): 696–97.

57. "I controsensi, e le sconnessioni prodotti da pasticci che si fanno comunemente per introdurre i (così detti) pezzi di Baule, sono innumerevoli. Situati questi dove detta il capriccio, e buffi, nell'opera seria, e serj nell'opera buffa, riducono le Drammatiche rappresentazioni in Musica, a sceniche parodie.

"Ma piacciono! da taluni si risponde; ed il pubblico poco s'accorge che vi sono tutte queste incongruenze, e controsensi. Cantate bene i vostri pezzi, e ne otterrete sempre un successo felice. Il pubblico

caprice dictate[d]." But Tacchinardi pushes further than his predecessor, offering a critique of the changes and a deconstruction of the explanation that practitioners used to justify them ("But people like them! [. . .] Sing your piece well and you will always be successful"). He does not deny that beautiful singing can result in a positive reception, but his heavy reliance on sarcasm here conveys his point clearly: replacing one aria with another solely to accommodate one's voice is not a tolerable plan of action. Particularly objectionable to Tacchinardi are insertions that involve generic disruptions (the introduction of a comic aria into a serious opera and vice versa), but his remarks are also aimed generally at alterations that cause noticeable rifts in the musical text (one might imagine that if the aria insertion conformed generically and stylistically to the new opera, his objections might dissipate). At the root of this assertion is an aesthetic dilemma that Susan Rutherford describes as having absorbed and affected "the development of the operatic marketplace" over the course of the nineteenth century. At issue, she writes, was not only the integrity of the artwork, but also "the very *identity* of the artwork: was the artwork the composition, or was it the performance?"[58] Tacchinardi suggests that where aria insertions were concerned, the identity of the artwork was grounded in the "composition," an aesthetic entity whose constituent parts corresponded to and complemented one another. He does not insist that these components originate from a singular authorial voice, but he does imply that avoiding disruptions in the dramatic and musical sense of a production is essential.

Significantly, Tacchinardi does not identify impresarios, publishers, or even composers as the arbiters of this judgment. Rather he points toward spectators as the most influential force in demanding a cohesive composition. "The public," he elaborates further, "tolerates, but does not approve of, comic cavatinas in serious operas; a martial duet arranged with amorous words; a tragic rondò in a comic opera, and many other confused pieces of music."[59] Singers do a disservice to themselves and the operas in which they appear, in other words, when they insert arias without having paid adequate attention to the musical and dramatic features of the new surroundings. Again, the notion of generic mingling stands at the center of his objections. Tacchinardi suggests that mismatched arias were, if not outwardly rejected, at least held in check by spectators who were actively engaged in aesthetic and analytic matters, perhaps because they were more easily recognized. But what does it mean for the public to "tolerate" but not "approve of" such changes? And how did spectators exert their will?

These questions are difficult to engage with directly, because little documentary evidence survives concerning what the "average" operagoer thought about aria in-

---

spettatore alla nostra Opera in Musica, non esige esattezza, e precisione, dove questa non ha mai esistito. Ma se conosce i controsensi, e le incongruenze, esaminatelo spettatore alla Commedia, ed alla Tragedia, e vi accorgerete, se dove l'esige, li conosce, li rimarca, e se le sfugge di vista, e dall'orecchio il minimo errore." Nicola Tacchinardi, *Dell'opera in musica sul teatro italiano e de'suoi difetti* (1833; reprint, Modena: Mucchi Editore, 1995), 56–57.

58. Rutherford, *The Prima Donna, 1815–1930* (Cambridge: Cambridge University Press, 2006), 163.

59. "Il pubblico tollera, ma non approva, la cavatina scherzosa nell'Opera seria; il duetto Marziale ridotto con parole amorose: Il Rondò tragico nell'Opera Buffa, e tanti altri impasticciati pezzi di musica." Tacchinardi, *Dell'opera in musica sul teatro Italiano e de'suoi difetti,* 57.

sertion. We can, however, turn to newspaper criticism from the first half of the nineteenth century to catch a glimpse of the types of insertions that spectators approved of and those they did not. Reviews published in dailies and weeklies, particularly Italian ones, can be quite revealing, for, as William Ashbrook has noted, early-nineteenth-century critics tended to keep close track of how audiences reacted to opera productions as a whole, and to individual numbers within. "The prevailing view" among Italian critics, "seems to have been that an audience, *esperti tutti quanti,* held the fortunes of a particular season in its discriminating hands."[60] Nineteenth-century journalism is not an ideal measure and it is necessary to treat these reviews with circumspection given that some periodicals were closely tied to particular composers and singers. Nevertheless, we can gain at least a general sense of how aria insertions were received through these publications.

THE PRESS

> [Pauline Viardot] Garcia is a worthy Desdemona; she has a fresh, melodious voice of the most beautiful quality, which she modulates with the greatest of agility, and in the famous *Se il padre m'abbandona* she performed the coloratura with much purity and perfection [. . .] She possesses beautiful methods of singing: it is a shame, then, that she wished to add something of her own in some cadences, and even worse, that she thought to change the original cavatina for one by Pacini. The audience warned her of her error, not making one sign of celebration, even though she sang it with much mastery.[61]

This review, penned by the leading voice of Venetian arts and culture from the late 1820s through the early 1860s, Tommaso Locatelli, provides one of the most vivid descriptions of what Tacchinardi alludes to in his theater manual as audience disapproval. Their reaction to Viardot's interpolation of a cavatina by Pacini into the first act of Rossini's *Otello* is swift, unequivocal, and, above all, wrapped in silence. They "warned" this most celebrated of artists against her transgression by withholding any perceptible sign of celebration. The effect must have been chilling, all the more so for the context out of which Viardot's alteration emerged. Since its premiere in 1816, *Otello*'s performance history was mired in alterations, both authentic and otherwise. Most relevant to Viardot's experience with her Venetian critics concerns Desdemona's entrance, for as has been well documented, Rossini intentionally avoided granting sopranos in this role an aria at the opening of the opera for dramatic purposes. By refusing to conform to the well-established tradition of permitting prima donnas a moment of soloistic abandon with which to introduce themselves, Rossini virtually guaranteed those same prima donnas would correct this "oversight" by

60. "Popular Success, the Critics and Fame: The Early Careers of *Lucia di Lammermoor* and *Belisario*," *Cambridge Opera Journal* 2 (1990): 66.

61. "La *Garcia* è una valente Desdemona; ell'ha voce fresca, intonata, di bellissima tempra, che modula con grandissima agilità, e nel famoso *Se il padre m'abbondona* ella eseguì con molta purezza e perfezione que' difficili gorgheggi [. . .] Ella possiede bei modi di canto: peccato ch'abbia voluto aggiunger qualcosa del suo in alcune cadenze di quella, e peggio ancora ch'abbia pensato a mutare l'original cavatina con altra del *Pacini*. Il pubblico l'avvertì del suo errore, non facendole nessun segno di festa, quantunque ella la cantasse con molta maestria." Tommaso Locatelli, *L'appendice della Gazzetta di Venezia,* 16 vols. (Venice: Tip. del Gondoliere, 1837–1880), 11: 236–37.

adding arias of their own, something they did without inhibition almost whenever and wherever *Otello* was staged.[62] Rossini himself participated in this custom, adding an aria for Desdemona in the 1820 Roman production of *Otello,* but he also attempted to put a halt to such changes in 1827, publishing a letter in a Parisian newspaper urging spectators to accept the opera as he had written it.[63] Despite those efforts, the tradition of inserting an entrance aria into Act I of *Otello* remained an integral component of the opera's performance history—the temptation to interpolate was simply too strong for most prima donnas to resist. Indeed, this tradition was so deeply entrenched that Locatelli himself errs in his review, stating that Viardot performed Pacini's cavatina "in place of the original." Which of the dozens of arias introduced into this scene Locatelli assumed was Rossini's "original" can only be guessed.

The Venetian audience's objections are significant not only because they emerged in the face of a custom that had long accepted aria insertion, but also because they confirm Tacchinardi's warnings about relying too faithfully on the power of performance: good singing is really *not* always good enough. In 1846, when this performance occurred, Viardot was nearing the height of her fame; the daughter of Manuel Garcia and the younger sister of Maria Malibran, she was one of the most highly respected performers of the nineteenth century, particularly in France, but beloved throughout much of Europe as well.[64] As Locatelli remarks, moreover, she sang with much "purity and perfection" when she appeared at the Teatro la Fenice. That Viardot's use of an aria insertion was received coldly suggests that public sentiment may have been turning against the practice. It would be an exaggeration to argue that by the mid-1840s audiences and critics throughout Europe were unified in dismissing the value of aria insertions altogether. As we will see shortly, some critics began voicing strong objections earlier, but many others remained sanguine up through and past the middle of the century. Locatelli himself voiced positive opinions about a small handful of aria insertions in reviews published as late as the 1850s and 1860s, and sentiments on these matters altered depending on location— what Venetian audiences rejected might have been loudly applauded in Milan,

62. To take just a few of many instances: Amalia Brambilla interpolated "Se alfin goder mi è dato," from Pacini's *L'ultimo giorno di Pompei* (Senigallia, Teatro Comunale, fiera 1828); Giuditta Grisi interpolated "Della rosa il bel vermiglio," from Rossini's *Bianca e Falliero* (Pisa, Regio Teatro di Pisa, spring 1830); Fanny Tacchinardi-Persiani inserted "Se d'amor fra le ritorte," from Pacini's *Alessandro nell'Indie* (Pisa, Regio Teatro di Pisa, spring 1835); and Carlotta Vittadini sang "L'amor suo mi fe' beata," from Donizetti's *Roberto Devereux* (Verona, Teatro Filarmonico, carnival 1838–1839). The texts for these arias are printed in the librettos for the productions, the first three of which are available at I-Vgc. The libretto for the Verona production is housed at the Biblioteca Nazionale Marciana, Venice (I-Vnm. Dramm. 3339.23).

63. As Philip Gossett has shown, the aria that Rossini added for Desdemona for the 1820 Roman revival was "Esulta, Elisa omai," from *Elisabetta, regina d'Inghilterra.* See "The Operas of Rossini: Problems of Textual Criticism in Nineteenth-Century Opera" (Ph.D. diss., Princeton University, 1970), 316–18. For an account of Rossini's attempt to appease Parisian audiences in 1827, see Rossini, *Otello,* ed. Michael Collins, in *Edizione critica delle opera di Gioachino Rossini,* series 1, vol. 19 (Pesaro: Fondazione Rossini, 1994), xxxvi–xxxix.

64. For information on Viardot's biography and on her widespread influence, see April FitzLyon, *The Price of Genius: A Life of Pauline Viardot* (New York: Appleton-Century, 1964); and Mark Everist, "Enshrining Mozart: *Don Giovanni* and the Viardot Circle," *19th-Century Music* 25 (2001–2002): 165–89.

Naples, London, Paris, or elsewhere.[65] As was the case with composers, as well as with some singers and impresarios, however, audiences were growing more ambivalent toward aria insertions.

From the earliest decades of the nineteenth century, newspaper reviews took stock of a variety of aria insertions. Critics were not always careful to identify when an aria was introduced into a production, but they were consistent in recognizing those that made a strong impression on audiences, whether positive or negative. At times, critics refer only fleetingly to changes, as in this review from an 1830 production of Rossini's *Otello:* "David pleased more and more every evening in his cavatina, *Ah sì per voi già sento,* in an introduced *agitato* [composed] by Cimarosa, *Confusa quest'anima;* in the duet with *Iago* [. . .] in short, they can say: *David was never so grand as in* Otello."[66] As this comment suggests, aria insertions were often treated as ordinary components of a performance, spoken of in the same breath as those pieces belonging to the original score. It illustrates, moreover, that reactions to these alterations were often genuinely enthusiastic. In this case, as in many others, moreover, the critic's benevolence may have stemmed from knowledge of the singers involved—the role of Otello was not composed with David's voice in mind, after all, but rather for Andrea Nozzari's. It may have seemed only natural therefore, that David would introduce music more suitable to his own voice in revivals of the work.

Indeed, critics frequently credited a singer's success in a given production to the superior manner in which he or she sang newly introduced arias: "On the twenty-ninth of what is now last May, *I normanni a Parigi* followed *La straniera* [. . .] The contralto Carobbi, new on this stage, pleased very much with her strong, wide-ranging and agile voice, particularly during her interpolated aria, which was originally written for the tenor in *Arabi nelle Gallie* by Pacini."[67] And, just as frequently, aria insertions are described as the highlights (sometimes as the only redeeming feature) of a performance:

Following the success of *Cenerentola,* one was in doubt about l'*Ajo in Imbarazzo* by *Donizetti,* produced the evening of the ninth of this month [June 1830]. However, the audience greeted it with satisfaction, and signor *Pantaleoni* tenor, signor *Setti* bass, and

65. Any positive, or at least neutral, assessments that Locatelli made regarding aria insertions in the 1850s and 1860s were limited to alterations that had become "standard." Of an 1854 production of Bellini's *I Capuleti e i Montecchi,* for example, he wrote, "Where Corvetti and Orecchia elevated themselves to the highest point in their performances was in the third [act], derived as usual, from Vaccai's score. Corvetti sang with that dramatic expression for which we have praised her on other occasions" (*L'appendice della Gazzetta di Venezia,* 11: 308); and in 1862, he spoke enthusiastically about an insertion aria appearing in a performance of *Il barbiere di Siviglia:* "After all, Pessina is a sweet, gentle and charming Rosina who sustains her part with gracefulness. One forgets the lack of robustness in her voice in favor of her agility, perfect intonation, those beautiful methods that she showed in Arditi's *walzer brillante* in the lesson scene" (15: 96).

66. "David è piaciuto ogni sera di più nella *cavatina, Ah sì per voi già sento,* in un introdotto *agitato* di *Cimarosa, Confusa quest'anima;* nel duetto con *Iago* [. . .] in somma si dice: *David non fu mai sì grande come nell'*Otello." *I teatri* (May 15, 1828).

67. "Il 29 dell'ora scorso Maggio *I Normanni a Parigi* succeddettero alla *Straniera* [. . .] La Carobbi Contralto, nuova per queste scene, piacque assaissimo per una forte, estesa ed agilissima voce, massime nell'intrusa Aria scritta pel Tenore nello spartito degli *Arabi nelle Gallie* di Pacini." *L'eco* (June 6, 1832).

signor *Castaldi* comic buffo, succeeded in a way that they deserved the applause that ensued after each of their respective numbers. And the two pillars which sustain this construction are the *cavatina,* not part of this score, but by the same composer, and the *rondò* by the composer *Nicolini.* These are two inspired pieces, which signora *Lugani* sings with mastery and with a truly enchanting spirit.[68]

Although these and myriad positive reviews like them are revealing, demonstrating that audiences during the first half of the nineteenth century still took pleasure in hearing aria insertions, more enlightening are instances when critics took issue with such alterations. As early as the 1820s, a small handful began calling for a ban, arguing that operas were best performed as their authors had written them. The following description from an 1820 production of Cimarosa's *Il matrimonio segreto* at Rome's Teatro Valle represents one of the earliest examples of a writer referring explicitly to the authority of the composer:

> When Cimarosa wrote il Matrimonio Segreto he elevated for himself an immortal monument to his fame. It would have been desirable, however, had the opera been given complete, and if despite the so-called usual theatrical combinations, the prima donna's aria in the first act, [and] that of the *buffo* in the second had not been eliminated or substituted with other pieces, nor had other pieces been mutilated, particularly the second finale (especially in its most charming stretta), which, when performed in its entirety, is everywhere deemed as sublime as the first [. . .]. In order to bring back good taste in music, we hope that next carnival more of the many excellent *opere buffe* by this well-deserving Author, properly arranged for performance, will be produced on our stages. This is the only means by which to adequately educate the ear of the public in the taste of a moderate harmony, to break the excessive wantonness of modern composers, to honor the greatest *maestri* of art, and to properly serve the glory of Cimarosa.[69]

The author here advocates upholding the honor of the "greatest" composers, taking as his example one of the most famous—Cimarosa—and berating singers for altering the score of his most popular work, *Il matrimonio segreto.* Whether he might

68. "Dopo il furore della *Cenerentola* si dubitava dell'*Ajo in Imbarazzo* di *Donizetti,* che si produsse la sera dei 9. corrente, ma il Pubblico lo ha accolto con soddisfazione, ed il signor *Pantaleoni* tenore, *Setti* basso cantante, e *Castaldi* buffo comico si sono disimpegnati in modo da meritarsi gli applausi che hanno conseguiti in ogni loro rispettivo pezzo. Le due colonne poi, che mantengono l'edificio, sono la cavatina, non già di questo spartito, ma dello stesso maestro ed il rondeau del maestro *Niccolini* [sic]. Questi sono due pezzi di getto, che la signora *Lugani* canta con una maestrìa, e con un anima veramente incantatrice." *Teatri arti e letteratura* 327 (June 23, 1830): 161.

69. "Cimarosa allorchè scrisse il Matrimonio segreto ha sollevato la per se stesso un immortale monumento alla sua fama. Solo sarebbe stato desiderabile che l'Opera si fosse data nella sua integrità, e che, per le solite così dette combinazioni teatrali, non si fossero lasciati fuori o cambiati con altri pezzi l'aria della della prima donna nel primo atto, quella del buffo nel secondo, nè mutilati altri pezzi, e segnatamente il secondo finale (specialmente nella sua vaghissima stretta), che eseguito nella sua totalità da per tutto s'è trovato sublime al pari del primo [. . .] Noi desideriamo che per ricondurre il buon gusto nella musica sia nel prossimo Carnevale riprodotta sulle nostre scene, debitamente predisposta per l'esecuzione, qualche altra delle tante pregevolissime Opere buffe del benemerito Autore. Questo è il solo mezzo di ben educare l'orecchio del pubblico al gusto d'una temperata armonia, di frenare la smodata lascivia de'moderni compositori, di onorare i sommi maestri dell'Arte, e di servir degnamente alla gloria di Cimarosa." *Le notizie del giorno* (November 9, 1820).

be more accepting of the presence of aria insertions in the works of "lesser" composers is unclear.

By the early 1830s, the same years in which Tacchinardi was writing his theater manual, one finds a few critics casting their nets across the entire repertory, condemning the practice outright regardless of which composer or opera was involved. In 1833, for example, the following damning remarks appear in *Il barbiere:*

> I will admit that *Odoardo in Iscozia* was not completely adapted to the singers, and that in many places it required *some innovations and reinforcements:* in this case, however, it would have been better to choose another opera altogether (we have many of them), rather than insisting on performing one score which had to be altered and contrafacted. [. . .] I do not intend here to place blame on this person or that person: The impresario will be right, the singers will be right; but the practice does not cease to be any less barbaric, against any sane laws of justice, and I will even say, of courtesy.[70]

One year later, a second review also published in *Il barbiere* concludes that aria insertions "are the resources of the mediocre; those who possess a true ability sing and act according to what is written and do not need to resort to other composers."[71]

Although these negative sentiments undoubtedly reflect the feelings of some, most criticism of the era suggests that aria insertions inhabited a middle ground where the tension between the identity of the artwork as a performance or as a "composition" was acted out. Time and again, reviews of aria insertions balance the fact of their presence in an opera against the manner in which they were sung, and they accept as components of the work aria insertions that conform well to their new surroundings. The following review presents what might be perceived as a guiding philosophy of aria insertion:

> *La Ginevra di Scozia,* music by Simon Mayr was produced in this theater on the 23rd of this month. There are some who disapprove of so-called "pastiches" but when these are well reasoned, and when the added pieces do not alter the action of the drama, rather than the practice of inserting into an opera pieces by another author being censurable, he who has good sense will only be able to commend it. And indeed, if the pieces in a score either lack that theatrical effect, which today one would demand even from the few notes of the secondary parts, or if they are not fully adapted to the talents of the artists who have to perform them, and if the added pieces bring together these requisites, who can help but approve of them?[72]

70. "Voglio ammettere che l'*Odoardo in Iscozia* non fosse totalmente adattato alla compagnia, e che addomandasse in più luoghi *qualche innovazione e qualche rinforzo:* in questo caso, però era meglio appigliarsi ad altr'Opera (ne abbiamo tante), anzi che ostinarsi a porre in iscena uno spartito, il quale poi dovesse essere avisato e contraffatto. [. . .] Né qui io intendo attribuire la colpa a questo, od a quello: avrà ragione l'impresa, avran ragione gli artisti; ma l'uso non lascia di essere barbaro, contro ogni sana legge di giustizia, e dirò pure di cortesia." *Il barbiere* (October 26, 1833).

71. "Sono le risorse dei mediocri; chi possiede una vera abilità canta ed eseguisce quello che è scritto, né d'uopo ha di ricorrere agli altri Maestri." *Il barbiere* (September 13, 1834). For a thorough discussion of the philosophical underpinnings of the notion of *true ability*—a term similar to the *genius* of performance as described by (among others) Hegel—see Mary Hunter, " 'To Play as if from the Soul of the Composer': The Idea of the Performer in Early Romantic Aesthetics," *Journal of the American Musicological Society* 58 (2005): 357–98. For a handful of other negative reviews, see Theodore Fenner, *Opera in London, Views of the Press, 1785–1830* (Carbondale: Southern Illinois Press, 1994), 259.

72. "Nella sera del 23 corrente fu posta sulle scene di questo Teatro *La Ginevra di Scozia* musica nel

"He who has good sense will only be able to commend it." With these words we locate a space in which singers during the first half of the nineteenth century could continue to perform aria insertions; where, in doing so, they might hope to be well received; where their audiences might both "tolerate" and "accept" alterations made to a score. Not every change conformed to these requirements, as we will see often in the chapters that follow. But just as frequently, if not more, one witnesses singers of the first half of the nineteenth century paying careful attention to the aesthetic appropriateness of the alterations they made to the operatic scores with which they were intimately familiar. An example of how these theoretical principals were applied, and of how individual singers went about selecting their aria insertions, provides a glimpse into the logic and thought processes that often controlled the presence of aria interpolations and substitutions in operatic productions. The protagonist of this example is Carolina Ungher; the opera, Donizetti's *Marino Faliero.*

---

maestro signor *Simone Mayr.* Taluno v'ha, che disapprova i così detti—Centoni—ma quando questi sono ragionati, e quando i pezzi aggiunti non alterano l'azione del dramma, anzicché essere biasimevole l'uso d'inserire in un opera pezzi d'altro autore, chi ha buon senso non può che commendarlo. E difatti se i pezzi dello spartito o mancano di quell'effetto teatrale, che al dì d'oggi si esigerebbe perfino nelle poche note delle seconde parti, o non sono pienamente adattati ai mezzi degli artisti, che li debbono eseguire, e se all'incontro quelli aggiunti hanno i suddetti requisiti, chi v'ha che non abbia d'approvare tali sostituzioni?" *Teatri arti e letteratura* 302 (January 28, 1830): 152–53.

CHAPTER 2

SELECTING A "PERFECT" ENTRANCE: CAROLINA UNGHER AND *MARINO FALIERO*

Extremely intelligent, [Carolina Ungher] understands and plays her roles not in the way that they have been laid out for her, but as they ought to be played [. . .] She is noble, sincere, captivating, and impassioned, and although her exaltation and ardor win us over, it is primarily her great skill, wise heart, and ultimately her art, in the best meaning of the word, that conquer us. From the moment she makes her entrance, the nobility of her bearing and dignity of her actions command attention.
—*Franz Liszt,* L'Artiste

THE PRIMA DONNA ARRIVES

The ability to make a fabulous entrance is one of those critical elements that separates the iconic diva from the rest of the pack, a skill that all actresses and opera singers cultivate, but that only the exceptional ones master. Who could forget Ingrid Bergman swinging open the door to Rick's Cafe in *Casablanca*, illuminated only by the search light that flashes behind her? Or Maria Callas, whose entrances time and again inspired effusive, over-the-top rhetoric in an attempt to replicate the electric aura she generated when audiences first caught sight of her. "Maria, Maria!" one critic recalls, "the thunder-like hand clapping and the clamorous cries, the Callas entrance was sensational, her floor-length dress hugged her slender body, her dark hair pulled back with a cascade of thick curls."[1] Though one can point to many memorable moments in both Callas' and Bergman's careers, their entrances stand out as truly unforgettable.

Twentieth-century spectators were not unique in appreciating this moment above most others. Making a grand entrance has long played a central role in the composition and production of Italian opera, and during the nineteenth century,

---

Epigraph source: "Venice," *L'Artiste* (June 16–August 11, 1839), in five installments: pp. 91–93, 132–34, 220–23, 237–39, and 255–57. Translated and annotated by Charles Suttoni, *An Artist's Journey: Lettres d'un bachelier ès musique, 1835–1841* (Chicago: University of Chicago Press, 1989), 135.

1. Julie Charles, *Hellenic Times* (May 1974); cited on the cover of *The Last of the Red Hot Divas* (Ombra Records, 2002).

prima donnas and leading men were almost always guaranteed a cavatina (as entrance arias were known) with which they could dazzle their spectators. In his 1841 treatise on Rossinian conventions, the critic and opera enthusiast Carlo Ritorni remarked that composers who neglected to include entrance arias did so at their own risk, for although singers might sometimes give up their rondòs (the term given to the concluding aria of an opera), the cavatinas were indispensable.[2] Indeed, throughout the first half of the nineteenth century, the entrance aria served a dual function: not only did it introduce characters into the context of the opera, but it also provided them a solo opportunity with which they could showcase their glorious voices. Making a perfect entrance was perhaps never so highly valued.[3]

Rossini's *Otello* offers the most famous cautionary tale against flouting the convention of the entrance aria, particularly where prima donnas were concerned. As noted in chapter 1, women singing the role of Desdemona emended the score at will, interpolating arias by Donizetti, Pacini, Persiani, Rossini, and many others to compensate for the character's "missing" entrance aria. Twenty years following the premiere of *Otello*, Donizetti dared to make a similarly unusual decision for his forty-sixth opera *Marino Faliero* (Paris, Théâtre Italien, March 12, 1835), eliminating an entrance aria for the prima donna role of Elena where one "should" have been. Just as Desdemonas were loath to accept such an omission, so, too, did Elenas rebel, inserting a variety of arias into the scene as the opera made its way from Paris to London, and then on to Italy and beyond. The first to make such an addition was Carolina Ungher (1803–1877), and it is on her relationship with *Marino Faliero* that this chapter focuses (see figure 2.1 for an image of this prima donna). She first performed the role of Elena in Italy (Teatro Alfieri, Florence, spring 1836), and she sang in the opera on at least six other occasions over the course of her career. In bending this role to her talents, Ungher displayed what might seem to have been indecisiveness when it came to her entrance, selecting three different arias for this scene in the space of little more than a year. For the Italian premiere she interpolated "Io talor più nol rammento" from Donizetti's *Sancia di Castiglia*.[4] A year later, she revived the role at the Teatro della Pergola, Florence, with a different cavatina, "Ah! quando in regio talamo" from the same composer's *Ugo, Conte di Parigi*.[5]

---

2. Carlo Ritorni, *Ammaestramenti alla composizione d'ogni poema e d'ogni opera appartenente alla musica* (Milan: Tipi di Luigi di Giacomo Pirola, 1841), 48. See also Scott Balthazar, "Ritorni's *Ammaestramenti* and the Conventions of Rossinian Melodramma," *Journal of Musicological Research* 8 (1988–1989): 281–311. Many prima donnas were reluctant to forego their rondò finales as well; see Philip Gossett, *Divas and Scholars* (Chicago: University of Chicago Press, 2006), 40 and 616.

3. For a summary of the evolution and significance of the entrance aria in Italian opera from Rossini through Bellini and Donizetti, see William Ashbrook, *Donizetti and His Operas* (Cambridge: Cambridge University Press, 1982), 248–56.

4. Marino Faliero / azione tragica in tre atti / da rappresentarsi nell'imp. e real / Teatro Alfieri / *La primavera del 1836,* / sotto la protezione di S. A. I. Imp. E. R. / Leopoldo II. / Gran-Duca di Toscana / ec. ec. ec. / – / Firenze / nella stamperia di F. Giachetti / *presso il Teatro Nuovo* (I: Vgc). In addition to this alteration, the libretto shows that Paolo Ferretti, the baritone singing the role of Israele, omitted the aria for that character.

5. Marino Faliero / azione tragica in tre atti / da rappresentarsi nell'I. e R. Teatro / in via della Pergola / la quadragesima del 1837. / Sotto la protezione di S. A. Imp. E. R. / Leopoldo II. / Gran-Duca di Toscana / ec. ec. ec. / – / Firenze / presso Giuseppe Galletti / *In Via Porta Rossa* (I:Vgc).

FIGURE 2.1.   Carolina Ungher. *Source:* CAN 1031 Ungher.JPG; Museo Teatrale alla Scala—
Archivio e Biblioteca, Milan.

Finally, only a few months later in the fall of 1837, she prepared a third aria for Trieste's Teatro Grande, "Oh tu che desti il fulmine" from Donizetti's *Pia de' Tolomei,*
although as we shall see below, she did not ultimately perform this last aria due to
illness.[6] Once she left Trieste, she relied exclusively on the second of these arias, "Ah!
quando in regio talamo," as her entrance of choice. For successive productions in
Parma, Reggio, Sinigaglia, and Lucca, she emerged on stage singing only this piece.[7]

6. Marino Faliero / azione tragica in tre atti / del signor / Gio. Emmanuele Bidera / posta in musica
dal sig. maestro / *Cav. Gaetano Donizzetti* [*sic*] / da rappresentarsi / nel Teatro Grande di Trieste / l'autunno del MDCCCXXXVII / – / Trieste / presso Michele Weis tip. teatrale (I:Vnm, Dramm. 3337.1).

7. These productions all occurred in 1838 in rapid succession: Parma, Teatro Ducale (spring); Reggio, Teatro del Comune (fiera); Senigallia, Teatro Comunale (fiera); Lucca, Teatro del Giglio (autumn).
Librettos for all four productions are located in I:Vgc. Ungher also participated in a production of *Marino
Faliero* in Vienna at the Kärntnertortheater on April 20, 1839, but I have been unable to locate any source
that reveals which aria she introduced for her entrance.

Ungher's encounter with this scene is marked by excess, testing, rejecting, and finally accepting an aria for Elena's entrance. The expansiveness of her choices stems in part from her virtuosity and her exceptional familiarity with the repertory. By 1836 when she first performed in *Marino Faliero,* she had achieved a reputation as one of the finest singers in all of Europe. Today her greatest claim to fame is that she was one of the soloists who participated in the premiere of Beethoven's Ninth Symphony (May 7, 1824), but she was better known in her own day as a star of the opera stage. Appearing in Vienna and Paris, she experienced her greatest successes in Italy, delighting audiences in Naples, Florence, Milan, Venice, and a host of smaller cities and towns from 1825 until her retirement in 1843. Rossini famously described her as an artist who embodied "the ardor of the south, the energy of the north, lungs of bronze, a silver voice, and a talent of gold";[8] and to Franz Liszt she was a marvel: "A consummate musician, she is quite prepared to undertake any role. The comic repertory is as familiar to her as the tragic, and the breadth of her talent is as exceptional as its profundity."[9] Indeed, by 1837 Ungher allegedly had a repertory of more than one hundred roles. Though this figure may be inflated, it helps explain her approach to her entrance in *Marino Faliero.* Armed with a wealth of musical material, she could choose from a variety of arias with which she was already familiar, wasting little time and energy learning new parts.

In one sense, then, Ungher's experiment was unusual. It is rare to find a singer rotating so rapidly through a selection of arias for a single scene. And yet, her actions are revelatory of more than a solitary instance of virtuosic *jouissance,* for wrapped up in her encounter with *Marino Faliero* is also an audible struggle, almost a desperate desire, to get Elena's entrance *just right.* Liszt's description of her, quoted in the epigraph to this chapter, implies an awareness on her part that to succeed she had to "command attention" from the very start, no matter what the opera. In wrestling with this scene, however, Ungher exposes concerns that extend beyond individual experience. Her example highlights anxieties generated by the discourse swirling around aria insertion during the first half of the nineteenth century, at the root of which stood the familiar opposition between performance and composition. As discussed in the preceding chapter, the balance between these two poles was shifting during the first half of the nineteenth century, opening up a variety of complicated and interweaving problems.

On the side of performance, Ungher confronted a question as long-standing as it was predictable: which entrance aria would function most effectively as a showpiece for her talents? For a prima donna forging a career during the opening decades of the nineteenth century, the response to this question was anything but straightforward. A successful performance depended not only on the creation and delivery of exceptional sound; the prima donna also had to be willing to expose more to her audiences, to reveal her "expressive self."[10] If Liszt is to be believed,

---

8. "Fuoco del sud, energia del nord, petto di bronzo, voce d'argento, talento d'oro." Guido Zavadini, *Donizetti: vita, musiche, epistolario* (Bergamo: Istituto italiano d'arti grafiche, 1948), 320.

9. Franz Liszt, *An Artist's Journey: Lettres d'un bachelier ès musique, 1835–1841,* trans. and annotated by Charles Suttoni (Chicago: University of Chicago Press, 1989), 174.

10. Here, I borrow language used by J. Q. Davies in "'Velluti in Speculum': The Twilight of the Castrato," *Cambridge Opera Journal* 17 (2005): 276.

Ungher achieved this ideal more poignantly than did most of her contemporaries: "Always sincere, noble, and moving, she penetrates to the heart of her role [. . .] *she becomes sublime where one would have thought it impossible to be anything more than pleasing*" (emphasis mine).[11] Her approach to Elena's entrance might thus be read as more than a singer simply trying to sound good; it also reflects a shared desire among all singers to locate this realm of the sublime.

As she grappled with this issue of performance, Ungher's rotation through a series of entrance arias simultaneously reveals a second concern: the need to determine which aria conformed most effectively to the dramatic and musical shape of *Marino Faliero.* This issue draws closer to the demands that were encountered in Tacchinardi's theatrical manual and echoed by the contemporary critics cited in chapter 1; specifically, it speaks to the difference between an insertion aria that is simply "tolerable" to one that is also "acceptable." To all appearances, Ungher seems to have wrestled with precisely this problem, and as such, her experience illustrates the intricate thought processes that stood behind the selection of many insertion arias. Like many of her predecessors, contemporaries, and successors, Ungher had to resolve several potential difficulties in order to assure that an aria insertion was fully "acceptable" to her spectators. An awareness of these problems makes it possible to identify the tools that she and many other singers, as well as their collaborators, used to assure a cohesive balance between new and old, "foreign" and "original." Understanding how Ungher attempted to achieve such a balance in performances of *Marino Faliero* entails beginning with the opera's genesis and its early reception.

ELIMINATING THE CAVATINA: THE EARLY HISTORY
OF *MARINO FALIERO*

As Donizetti's first commission for the Théâtre Italien, *Marino Faliero* was the product of one of the composer's most fervent career ambitions—to write an opera for Paris. Working in that city offered a wealth of benefits over Italian theaters: higher earnings, less censorship, access to the best orchestra in the world, and greater freedom from convention. "A resounding success upon that city's stages," writes William Ashbrook, "set a special seal upon a composer's reputation," and thus Donizetti was particularly determined to do well with *Marino Faliero.*[12] Events leading to this opera's commission and its complicated compositional history have been well charted, but a few details shed light on the absence of an entrance aria for Elena and are thus worth recounting here.[13]

Donizetti's entrée into the Parisian scene came when Rossini, then serving as artistic consultant to the Théâtre Italien, extended an invitation to compose an

11. Liszt, *An Artist's Journey,* 174.

12. Ashbrook, *Donizetti and His Operas,* 89.

13. The scholarship on this subject includes Ashbrook, *Donizetti and His Operas,* 88–92; Annalisa Bini and Jeremy Commons, eds., *Le prime rappresentazione delle opere di Donizetti nella stampa coeva* (Milan: Skira, 1997), 451–61; Paolo Fabbri, "Fosca notte, notte orrenda," program notes for *Marino Faliero* at the Teatro la Fenice (Venice, 2003), 73–88; Philip Gossett, "Music at the Théâtre-Italien," in *Music in Paris*

opera for the autumn season of 1834.[14] Donizetti accepted enthusiastically, though due to previous commitments to write operas for Naples (*Maria Stuarda*) and Milan (*Gemma di Vergy*), his trip to Paris was postponed until early January 1835 and his opera scheduled for its debut in March.[15] This delay meant that his arrival overlapped with another important premiere occurring at the Théâtre Italien that season: Bellini's *I puritani* (January 24, 1835). Of greater immediate consequence to Donizetti, however, was that the tight schedule required him to work on his first commission for Paris while still in Italy, without the benefit that firsthand exposure to the expectations and tastes of his new French audiences might have offered.[16] He composed *Marino Faliero* during the fall of 1834, writing to Jacopo Ferretti from Naples that the opera was finished with the exception of one duet.[17] The result was what Gossett has described as a "quintessentially Italian opera," consisting of a conventional succession of tonally closed formal numbers.[18] Of greatest significance here is that this early version contains a brief recitative and a single-movement solo aria for Elena in the first act—an entrance aria ("Dì che parta, e che funesta").[19] After arriving in Paris, however, Donizetti undertook a complete revision of *Marino Faliero,* altering more than one-third of the score under Rossini's supervision.[20] Among the changes made, Donizetti eliminated Elena's entrance material, a deci-

---

in the 1830s, ed. Peter Bloom (Stuyvesant, N.Y.: Pendragon Press, 1987), 327–64; Giorgio Pagannone, "Aspetti drammaturgici e formali nel *Marino Faliero* e nell'*Assedio di Calais,*" in *Donizetti—Napoli—L'Europa,* ed. Franco Carmelo Greco and Renato Di Benedetto (Naples: Edizioni Scientifiche Italiane, 2000), 299–321; Francesca Seller, "Il *Marin Faliero* da Napoli a Parigi: raffronti testuali," *Donizetti Society Journal* 7 (2002): 31–46; Dennis W. Wakeling, Review of *Marino Faliero,* Melodram 27030, 2 CDs, *Opera Quarterly* 6 (1988): 121–24; Alexander Weatherson, "Donizetti in Paris," *Donizetti Society Journal* 7 (2002): 3–9; and Herbert Weinstock, *Donizetti and the World of Opera in Italy, Paris and Vienna in the First Half of the Nineteenth Century* (New York: Pantheon Books, 1963), 104–7.

14. On Donizetti's previous attempts to get to Paris and Rossini's invitation, see Weatherson, "Donizetti in Paris," 3–9; and Fabbri, "Fosca notte, notte orrenda," 73. *Marino Faliero* was not the first of Donizetti's operas to be performed in Paris; it was, however, the first production there with which he was directly involved.

15. Donizetti was in Naples beginning in March 1834 composing *Maria Stuarda* for the Teatro San Carlo. Due to difficulties with the censors, he was forced to rework this opera as *Buondelmonte* and it received its premiere as such on October 18. Donizetti left for Milan on November 13, where he composed *Gemma di Vergy* for the Teatro alla Scala. It premiered on December 26, after which he traveled to Paris.

16. At least one contemporary critic who observed the premiere of *Marino Faliero* and *I puritani* at the Théâtre Italien found it significant that Bellini wrote his opera while in Paris and that Donizetti was unable to do so. See *Le courrier français* (March 16, 1835), in Bini and Commons, *Le prime rappresentazioni,* 478.

17. Letter dated October 7, 1834, in Zavadini, *Donizetti: vita, musiche, epistolario,* 361–62.

18. Gossett, "Music at the Théâtre-Italien," 350.

19. A manuscript copy of the libretto for this original version is held in Naples, Conservatorio di musica "S. Pietro a Majella" (I-Nc) (Rari 10.11.30[20]). The corresponding autograph score is also housed there (I-Nc, Rari 3.6.20). A facsimile of the libretto is published in the *Donizetti Society Journal* 7 (2002): n.p.; and it is transcribed in full in the program for *Marino Faliero* at the Teatro la Fenice (Venice, 2003), 135–50.

20. Exactly what sort of assistance Rossini lent to Donizetti, or what *supervision* meant in this context, are questions that have not been fully answered. The libretto for the Neapolitan version of *Marino Faliero* was written by Giovanni Emanuele Bidera, who also wrote the text for *Gemma di Vergy.* For re-

sion that reduced the prima donna's role significantly and that served to emphasize further the very male-centered drama around which this opera's plot unfolds. It is this Parisian version that became standard for subsequent productions of the opera.

The real-life saga of Marino Faliero, the fourteenth-century Doge executed for participating in a conspiracy against the Council of Forty—derived from the tragedy of the same name by Casamir Delavigne, which was in turn loosely adapted from Lord Byron's play—opens in the masculine zone of a shipyard. Israele Bertucci (baritone), captain of the Venetian arsenal, is insulted by the patrician Michele Steno (bass), who recently committed an act of slander. He publicly accused Elena, wife of Faliero (bass), of carrying on an adulterous affair, brazenly scribbling his allegations on the Rialto Bridge. Bruised by Steno's insolence, Faliero is gently persuaded by Bertucci to lead the oppressed plebeians in a scheme to overthrow Steno and the rest of the corrupt council, a plot at once noble and treasonous. Meanwhile, Faliero's beloved nephew Fernando (tenor) has challenged Steno to a duel, in part to reinstate Elena's honor, and in part because he knows Steno's accusations are true, having himself carried on a torrid affair with her. Tragically, Steno proves the better swordsman, killing his opponent, whose sole parting wish is to be buried with Elena's scarf covering his face. Devastated by his nephew's death, Faliero then receives another blow. A traitor among the conspirators has revealed their plot, and Faliero is arrested. Shortly before his beheading, he is granted one more visit with Elena, who confesses her affair with Fernando; forgiving her, he is led off to face his death. The opera concludes as Elena, hearing the axe fall on her husband, screams and falls unconscious.

Though this plot includes a love triangle typical of many Italian operas of the time, the main interest falls not on that private drama but rather on the public events surrounding the conspiracy among the plebian men and the duel between Fernando and Steno. The story turns inward during the third act as Faliero ponders his death, Elena reveals her infidelity, and they say goodbye. Her involvement in the narrative is peripheral until this final act, and the music Donizetti assigns her reflects this condition: in Act I she sings a duet with Fernando and participates in the finale; in Act II she disappears entirely. She must wait until the third act for solo material, the scena and two-movement aria "Dio clemente, ah mi perdona" / "Fra due tombe, fra due spettri." In short, the prima donna has less to do in *Marino Faliero* than most lead female characters in the *bel canto* repertory.[21] Despite the idiosyncratic nature of her role, however, Parisian audiences received *Marino Faliero* warmly, a situation attributable in part to the superior ensemble of star vocalists who participated in the premiere (the same who debuted Bellini's *I puritani*): Giulia Grisi (Elena), Luigi La-

visions undertaken in Paris, alterations to the libretto were made by Agostino Ruffini. That Rossini may have helped Donizetti rewrite his score comes to us from a letter sent from Bellini to Florimo, dated February 27, 1835; Luisa Cambi, *Bellini: Epistolario* (Milan: A. Mondadori, 1943), 528–29. See also Bini and Commons, *Le prime rappresentazione,* 455–57, Fabbri, "Fosca notte, notte orrenda," 77–80, and Gossett, "Music at the Théâtre-Italien," 342–43, for detailed descriptions of the alterations Donizetti made.

21. The part of Antonina in *Belisario,* a role that Ungher debuted, is similarly idiosyncratic—the character sings only in the first act and in the final scene of the third. *Marino Faliero,* in other words, is not the only of Donizetti's operas that places lesser weight on the female lead than on the male roles.

blache (Faliero), Giovanni Battista Rubini (Fernando), Antonio Tamburini (Israele Bertucci), and Nicola Ivanoff (Gondoliere).

I puritani was ultimately more successful than *Marino Faliero* (the first four singers listed here became known as the "*Puritani* Quartet" after all, not the "*Faliero* Quartet"), but Donizetti held his own in the face of stiff competition.[22] Shortly following the opera's third performance, he reported to his childhood friend from Bergamo, Antonio Dolci, that "Bellini's reception with *I puritani* made me tremble more than a little, but as our works are of contrasting genres we have both therefore obtained a fine success without displeasing the public."[23] Most of the roughly three dozen reviews published in Parisian dailies and quarterlies following the premiere recorded positive opinions, the general sentiment summed up by the critic for the *Revue du théâtre:* "On Thursday *Marino Faliero* was applauded as it merited, which is to say a great deal, for it is a very remarkable work."[24] Nevertheless, a variety of complaints surfaced concerning Donizetti's score. A few writers were dissatisfied that Fernando was killed off during the second act, which deprived audiences of Rubini's astounding voice for the opera's entire third act (this complaint arose despite the fact that Donizetti provided his tenor two show-stopping, two-movement arias—more than for any other character); others criticized Donizetti for adhering too faithfully to Rossinian conventions, arguing that *Marino Faliero* was not as imaginative as *Anna Bolena.*[25] About Elena (the character) and Grisi (the singer), the reviews were almost uniformly positive. Observations such as the one from *L'avant-scène* were typical: "There is no praise precise enough to characterize the feeling that Mademoiselle Grisi causes one to experience in this work: it is beyond marvel, beyond enchantment; there is truly something supernatural and magical in the voice and the spirit of this *Diva.*"[26] There were a few misgivings expressed, a handful of critics complaining that Grisi did not appear to be inspired by the role, but significantly, no disparaging remarks regarding the absence of an entrance aria for her character were made.[27]

This situation changed when the identical cast took *Marino Faliero* and *I puritani* on the road less than five weeks later, performing both operas at the King's Theatre, London. "On such occasions, when more than one work makes its first showing,"

22. It is worth stating in this context that it was not immediately evident that Bellini's opera would be more successful in the long run than Donizetti's. Critics were impressed by both works, one commenting, "In sum, *Marino Faliero* is a beautiful and grand success equal to that of the *Puritans* by Bellini." *Le charivari* (March 15, 1835), in Bini and Commons, *Le prime rappresentazioni,* 472.

23. Letter dated March 16, 1835, in Zavadini, *Donizetti: vita, musiche, epistolario,* 368–69.

24. "Jeudi, son *Marino Faliero* a été applaudit comme il méritait, c'est-à-dire, beaucoup, car c'est une oeuvre très-remarquable." "Théâtre de Paris," *Revue du théatre* (n.d.), in Bini and Commons, *Le prime rappresentazioni,* 475.

25. For complaints about Rubini's role, see, for example, *Revue de Paris* 15 (March 12, 1835), in Bini and Commons, *Le prime rappresentazioni,* 464. For complaints about Donizetti's adherence to Rossinian convention, see *Le courrier française* (March 16, 1835), in Bini and Commons, 481, and *Le cabinet de lecture* (March 20, 1835), in Bini and Commons, 492.

26. "Il n'est pas de louange assez vive pour caractériser le sentiment que Mlle Grisi fait éprouver dans cet ouvrage; c'est plus que de l'admiration, plus que de l'entraînement; il y a vraiment quelque chose de surnaturel et de magique dans la voix el la jeu de la *Diva.*" *L'avant-scène* (March 15, 1835), in Bini and Commons, *Le prime rappresentazioni,* 470.

27. See, for instance, *L'entr'acte* (March 12, 1835), in Bini and Commons, *Le prime rappresentazioni,* 462.

wrote the British critic Henry Chorley, "there is always a success and a failure. The public will not endure two favorites."[28] Indeed, in comparison to the brilliant reception of Bellini's opera, Donizetti's paled. Chorley explained why: "In spite of the grandeur of Lablache as the Doge of Venice, in spite of the beauty of the duet of the two basses in the first act of *Marino,* in spite of the second act containing a beautiful moonlight scene with a barcarole, sung to perfection by Ivanoff, and one of Rubini's most incomparable and superb vocal displays, *Marino Faliero* languished, in part from the want of interest in the female character—a fault fatal to an opera's popularity."[29] The unsatisfying reception of this opera in London, in other words, resulted at least partially from the particular nature of Elena's role. When Chorley described a "lack of interest in the female character," he was referring no doubt to a number of factors, among which would have been the absence of an entrance aria. Little surprise, then, that when the opera finally made it to Italy, when a new prima donna—Carolina Ungher—adopted the role, Elena's part expanded during the first act. The character would rarely appear without an entrance aria again.

UNGHER'S CHOICES

Of all prima donnas traveling the operatic circuit in the 1830s, Ungher was more qualified than most to alter Donizetti's scores to her liking. The two had worked together for nearly ten years prior to her appearance in *Marino Faliero,* their first encounter occurring in Naples, where she debuted the role of Marietta in his *Il borgomastro di Saardam* (Naples, Teatro del Fondo, summer 1827). She later took leading roles in the premieres of his *Parisina* (Florence, Teatro della Pergola, carnival 1833), *Belisario* (Venice, Teatro la Fenice, carnival 1836), and *Maria de Rudenz* (Venice, Teatro la Fenice, carnival 1838); and she participated in many revivals of his works, experiencing some of her greatest triumphs in *Maria Stuarda* and *Lucrezia Borgia* as well as *Marino Faliero.*[30] Donizetti alludes to Ungher's familiarity with his music and his faith in her abilities in a letter to the conductor Raffaele Mazzetti concerning an 1837 production of *Maria Stuarda.* This work had long been plagued by censorial difficulties, so much so that the composer grew flexible with it, offering several suggestions concerning the numbers that might be changed or cut entirely. He recommended that the tenor perform an insertion aria, and about Ungher's part in the opera, he provided only these vague instructions: "She can sing her *scena* as she likes, for my Carolina knows exactly what she is capable of doing! Just take care that the repetition of the cabaletta begins in the major and ends in the minor."[31] His

28. Henry F. Chorley, *Thirty Years' Musical Recollections* (1862; reprint, New York: Alfred A. Knopf, 1926), 65.

29. Ibid.

30. Details concerning Ungher's performances in the premieres of *Il borgomastro di Saardam, Parisina, Belisario,* and *Maria de Rudenz* are found in Bini and Commons, *Le prime rappresentazioni,* 146–50, 339–55, 551–80, and 670–94. For biographical details on this singer, see Aldo Reggioli, *Carolina Ungher: virtuosa di camera e cappella di S. A. R. il granduca di Toscana* (Florence: Polistampa, 1995).

31. "La sua scena come vuole, chè la mia Carolina sa cosa far ci si può! Badate che alla seconda ripresa dell'ultima cabaletta entra in maggiore e finisce in minore." Letter dated May 13, 1837, Zavadini, *Donizetti: vita, musiche, epistolario,* 428.

confidence in this performer is unmistakable—she is allowed to choose the aria she would like to perform (within certain limits) because she knows what works best, both for her voice, and above all, for the opera.

The arias Ungher selected for Elena's entrance in *Marino Faliero* demonstrates that this trust was well placed. All three were cavatinas that originated in operas by Donizetti, illustrating a fidelity to the composer that was by no means obligatory in the practice of nineteenth-century aria insertion. All three arias, furthermore, suggest that Ungher was not aiming to draw attention to the fact that she was performing aria insertions, for all three were extracted from operas that would not have been easily recognizable to most audience members. *Pia de' Tolomei, Sancia di Castiglia,* and *Ugo, Conte di Parigi* were all warmly received at their premieres, but of the three, only *Pia* was revived with any regularity, and it had only half a dozen or so Italian productions before disappearing.[32] There was little risk, in other words, that the arias would be identified as Pia's, Sancia's, or Bianca's (in the case of *Ugo*), and thus it is possible that she was attempting to locate an aria that would come to be identified specifically as Elena's. All three insertion arias, moreover, follow Tacchinardi's cardinal rule dictating that inserted music blend generically into its new surroundings. *Marino Faliero* is a *tragedia lirica,* as are *Pia, Sancia,* and *Ugo*—no comic numbers imposing themselves awkwardly on a serious context; Ungher knew better. Even so, the presence of new music creates mild disruptions in the dramatic structure of the opera as Donizetti conceived it for Paris. Observing the types of adjustments made to this libretto and score illustrates some general approaches to mitigating such disruptions by those who participated in the practice of aria insertion.

The addition of an aria for Elena affects the relationship between her and Fernando, the new music appearing after he sings his cavatina, "Di mia patria bel soggiorno" / "Un solo conforto." In this number, he announces that he will exile himself voluntarily from Venice in order to prevent his affair with Elena from being discovered and to protect her from further shame. During the slow movement, Fernando describes his misery at leaving his beloved land, but in the cabaletta, he is comforted that by doing so, he will salvage his beloved's reputation. In the Paris version of *Marino Faliero,* Elena walks on stage directly after this cabaletta concludes and a brief recitative dialogue between the two characters ensues:

Fer.:	Ma giunge alcun? . . . È dessa?	But someone arrives . . . Is it her?
	Felice me!	Happy me!
Ele.:	Fernando!	Fernando!
	Ardisci ancor?	Are you still so bold?
	(in atto di partir)	*(as if to leave)*

---

32. *Ugo, Conte di Parigi* was only a qualified success following its premiere at the Teatro alla Scala on March 13, 1832. Thereafter, it received six revivals, only three of which took place in Italy: Pisa (1835); Trieste (1835); and Ferrara (1839–1840); the other three were in Prague (1837); Madrid (1839); and Lisbon (1846). *Sancia di Castiglia* (Naples, Teatro San Carlo, November 4, 1832) received only six performances at its premiere in Naples, and was never revived in Italy during the nineteenth century. There were, however, two productions in Portugal: Lisbon (1839) and Porto (1842). *Pia de' Tolomei* (Venice, Teatro Apollo, February 18, 1837) received seven revivals in Italian theaters, though it was not a particularly popular work either: Senigallia (1837), Lucca (1837), Rome (1838), Naples (1838), Milan (1839), Florence (1842), and Parma (1858).

Fer.:	T'arresta.	Stop.
Ele.:	No.	No.
Fer.:	Per l'ultima volta . . .	For the last time . . .
Ele.:	Fuggir ti debbo.	You must flee.
Fer.:	Ah, per pietà m'ascolta!	Ah, please listen to me!

They then launch into a duet ("Tu non sai la nave è presta") that witnesses a tumultuous scene between the ex-lovers. Initially, Elena is unresponsive, furious at Fernando for approaching her after their affair has nearly been discovered. She reveals her true feelings of affection only gradually, sending him off regretfully at the conclusion with a tear-soaked scarf (the one he eventually requests be draped over his corpse) as a "memento of sorrow."[33]

When Ungher interpolated her entrance arias, she and her costar Fernandos preserved these portions of the score.[34] According to printed librettos, the alteration was made by inserting the new music into their introductory dialogue, after Fernando sees Elena and exclaims, "Ma giunge alcun? . . . È dessa! / Felice me!" and before she responds "Fernando! / Ardisci ancor?" Regardless of the aria Ungher added, she always prefaced it with a new recitative dialogue in which her lady in waiting, Irene, plays a prominent role. The text of this new dialogue follows (the author of the poetry and the composer of the recitative are unknown):

Ele.:	E narri il vero? io fremo!	Do you speak the truth? I tremble!
	Vergava Steno l'oltraggioso scritto?	Steno etched the outrageous remark?
Ire.:	Tratto al consiglio il confessava ei stesso	Taken before the court, he himself confessed
	E dell'infame eccesso	and for his disgraceful license
	Riceve or forse la dovuta pena.	he now perhaps receives his rightful punishment.
Ele.:	L'onta che il vil recava	The disgrace that villain has brought
	All'onor di Faliero e al mio	to Faliero's and to my honor
	È tal, che niuna pena	is such that no punishment
	Può cancellar. Ahi viva eterna fonte	can erase it. Alas, for me that disgrace
	Sarà per me d'inestinguibil pianto!	will be the live, eternal well of inextinguishable tears!
Ire.:	Il troppo tuo dolore	Let your excessive sorrow
	Alla ragion dia loco.	give way to reason.
	Fia punito fra poco	The wicked one who dared tarnish your reputation
	L'empio che osò contaminar tua fama.	will soon be punished.
	E a te la rende intera	And your repute is being completely restored to you
	Fernando generoso	by generous Fernando

33. It is worth noting that this is the alternate duet from *Anna Bolena* for Anna and Percy that Donizetti composed for his opera. This duet, "Sì, son io che a te ritorno," replaced "S'ei t'abborre, io t'amo ancora." "Tu non sai la nave è presta" is, in short, a borrowed piece that Donizetti revised and inserted from an earlier opera. See Philip Gossett, *"Anna Bolena" and the Artistic Maturity of Gaetano Donizetti* (Oxford: Clarendon Press, 1985), 151–76.

34. In Ungher's first three appearances as Elena, three different tenors sang the role of Fernando: Napoleone Moriani (Florence, 1836), Glibert-Louis Duprez (Florence, 1837), and Antonio Poggi (Tri-

Col volontario esiglio suo . . .	through his voluntary exile . . .
Ele.: Fernando!	Fernando!
Deh taci (oh Ciel) non proferir quel nome!	Oh be silent (oh heavens) do not utter that name!
Cagion d'ogni mia pena (ahi giusta troppo!)	The cause of all my suffering (much too deserved!)
Non più vederlo io mai, odiarlo deggio	I must never see him again, I must loath him
E sveller dal mio cor	and tear from my heart
Ogni memoria d'un incauto amore.	every memory of that imprudent love.

This new material was necessary to justify dramatically the presence of an interpolated entrance aria. Elena could not simply walk on stage and launch immediately into song; this dialogue provides a credible explanation for why she appears. Simultaneously, the text of this recitative conforms closely to the existing drama, summarizing plot features established earlier. When Elena and Irene discuss the slanderous crimes Steno has committed, they merely rehash information provided in the Introduzione of Act I, and although their conversation emphasizes Elena's miserable state, it adds no new information to what the Paris version provides about this character. As such, this *scena* suggests a commitment to maintaining the established narrative balance.

Simultaneously, however, this dialogue exhibits some unusual features that sit rather awkwardly in its new context. Conventionally, for instance, a *scena e cavatina* would begin with an independent recitative for the featured performer, not with a conversation between two or more characters. Thus, as a vehicle for introducing a cavatina, this dialogue represents an atypical design, marking it from the outset as strange or foreign. Its presence, moreover, creates some problems with staging that do not occur in Donizetti's Parisian score. It is unclear, for instance, where Fernando should go when Elena and Irene hold their conversation and when Elena performs her cavatina. He could exit and make a second entrance immediately before their duet, or he could remain hiding somewhere on stage, a witness to her torment. And what of Irene? In the Paris version, this character appears only in Act III, comforting Elena before her final meeting with Faliero. The new dialogue introduces this minor character on stage much earlier, but provides little indication as to what she should do once she is there. She might leave when Fernando makes his presence known, for instance, or she could linger until their duet has reached its concluding cadences. Librettos containing this additional recitative dialogue provide no clues as to how these issues were negotiated, nor are contemporary reviews helpful.[35]

---

este, 1837). The libretto for the Trieste production records a substitute aria for Poggi in the first act. The original "Di mia patria o bel soggiorno" / "Ma un solo conforto" was replaced by a one-movement aria, "Un sol raggio di speranza," the origin of which I have been unable to identify (the text for this new aria is printed in the libretto for this production). Poggi probably made this change because the original, which was composed with the virtuosic talents of Rubini in mind, was too difficult to execute well.

35. Interestingly, there is evidence suggesting that these are precisely the sorts of questions that Donizetti sought to eliminate when he revised his opera for Paris. The libretto preserved from the original Neapolitan version, which contains an entrance aria for Elena (as discussed above), instructs Fernando to hide ("si nasconde") after he performs his cavatina and she sings. Moreover, in this earlier version,

Despite its slightly awkward fit, Ungher retained this new dialogue in all of her appearances as Elena, altering only the aria that followed. This recitative, moreover, maintained a semipermanent presence in *Marino Faliero* beyond Ungher, adopted and performed by a variety of prima donnas. Almost without exception, when the recitative appears in extant librettos of *Marino Faliero,* so, too, does an interpolated aria, its presence offering Elenas an all-purpose starting point from which they could construct their individual entrances and inviting them to introduce arias of their own choice.[36] Many of these prima donnas, moreover, followed Ungher's lead when it came to the arias they selected for Elena's entrance. Observing how this music interacts with the dramatic and musical structure of *Marino Faliero,* as well as with Ungher's particular vocal talents, helps explain why.

A TRIO OF CAVATINAS FOR ELENA

The aria that Ungher introduced into the first Italian production of *Marino Faliero* at the Teatro Alfieri, Florence, "Io talor più nol rammento" from *Sancia di Castiglia,* had much to recommend it as a cavatina for Elena. It is relatively brief, consisting of a thirty-measure slow movement and a concise cabaletta. The singer does not risk exhausting herself by performing it in an act in which she still has a fair amount of musical material to tackle. According to Ashbrook, moreover, the terseness of Sancia's entrance aria was the product of Donizetti's increasing appreciation during the 1830s for the greater dramatic potential that ensembles could offer over arias. In composing two short movements, he deemphasized this soloistic moment and placed greater weight on the duet that succeeded it between Sancia and her trusted minister Rodrigo.[37] Introducing "Io talor più nol rammento" directly before the turbulent duet between Elena and Faliero thus constructs a neat parallel between old and new contexts, whereas its brevity helps preserve the original shape of *Marino Faliero*'s first act as much possible.

Of course, relatively short, two-movement cavatinas are by no means unusual in operas of the *Primo Ottocento*. Rossini's *oeuvre,* for instance, contains many—Rosina's

---

Irene appears in Act I, but sings only one line of text after which she is instructed to exit. Because the Parisian version places Fernando's and Elena's duet directly after his cavatina, there is no need for him to hide or for Irene to appear on stage.

36. This recitative reappears in librettos for the following productions (all librettos are located in I:Vgc or I:Vnm). Productions marked with an asterisk indicate an abbreviated version of the dialogue: Florence, Teatro della Pergola, 1836 (Carolina Ungher); Trieste, Teatro Grande, 1837 (Carolina Ungher); Vicenza, Teatro Eretenio, 1837 (Carolina Carobbi); Padova, Teatro Nuovo, 1838 (Eugenia Garcia); Mantova, Teatro Sociale, 1839 (Desiderata Derancour)*; Cremona, Teatro della Concordia, 1839 (Felicita Forcini)*; Perugia, Teatro del Pavone, 1838 (Giuseppina Aman); Parma, Teatro Ducale, 1838 (Carolina Ungher); Reggio, Teatro del Comune, 1838 (Carolina Ungher); Senigallia, Teatro Comunale, 1838 (Carolina Ungher); Lucca, Teatro del Giglio, 1838 (Carolina Ungher); Fermo, 1838 (Carlotta Zucchielli); Macerata, Teatro dei Signori Condomini, 1839 (Ezebina Ercolani); Pescia, Teatro degli Affilati, 1839 (Carolina Soret); Venice, Teatro la Fenice, 1840 (Emilia Boldrini); and Pisa, Teatro de' Ravvivati, 1842 (Amalia Patriozzi). Only one libretto includes the recitative without a succeeding interpolated aria: Vicenza, Teatro Eretenio, 1837, starring Carolina Carobbi. It is possible, of course, that Carobbi performed an entrance aria as Elena, but that the text was not printed.

37. Ashbrook, *Donizetti and His Operas,* 334.

"Una voce poco fa" (*Il barbiere di Siviglia*), Semiramide's "Bel raggio lusinghier," Malcolm's "Elena! o tu, che chiamo" (*La donna del lago*), and Ninetta's "Di piacer mi balza il cor" (*La gazza ladra*) are the most obvious examples. That Ungher opted to introduce "Io talor non più nol rammento" instead of these alternatives into *Marino Faliero* not only signals a commitment to perform Donizetti's own music, it suggests the possibility that this piece appealed to her for dramatic and musical reasons as well. Indeed, the circumstances under which Sancia sings this aria in its original context are quite solemn, as are Elena's. This widowed queen has just been informed (falsely) that her son Garzia has died in battle, and although she is miserable, she is determined nevertheless to discover happiness in her upcoming marriage to the duplicitous Ircano, a Moorish prince:

San.:	Io talor più nol rammento,	Sometimes I no longer remember him,
	Perchè vince la mia pena,	because my pain has won,
	Ma regnar più in me lo sento,	and yet, I feel him reign over me,
	Se il suo nome ascolto appena.	if only I hear his name.
	A lui solo diè l'amor	To him alone love gave,
	Tanto impero sul mio cor.	so much power over my heart.
	Se contro lui mi parlano	If they speak to me against him
	il ciel, la terra, il regno,	heaven, the earth, the kingdom,
	io quasi allora ho sdegno	I almost, then, doubt
	ch'egli mi sia fedel.	that he is faithful to me.
	Ma s'ei mi parla all'anima	But if he speaks to my soul
	Non va sua voce invano	his voice does not go in vain,
	Per me diventa Ircano	for me Ircano becomes
	E regno e terra e ciel.	kingdom, and earth, and heaven.

As often occurred when arias were inserted into new operatic contexts, the text for "Io talor più nol rammento" was rewritten to help it conform to its new environment. In this case, whoever did the work was careful to follow the original contours of the poetry, a route frequently taken because it marked the path of least resistance. The first and fourth lines of Sancia's slow movement, for instance, are retained, as are a handful of key words scattered throughout the text ("pena," "sento," and "anima"). Direct references to Sancia's particular situation, phrases that would sound odd in Elena's mouth (such as the reference to Ircano), are replaced by generic declarations—a passing remark regarding the passion that "his name" (Fernando's) stirs in her soul, for instance, and a plea to heaven to release her from her torment. Overall, however, the general sentiments that Sancia's aria convey remain largely intact when it becomes Elena's cavatina:

Elena:	Io talor più nol rammento	Sometimes I no longer remember him,
	Del mio cor tace la pena	my heart's pain is silent
	Avvampar gelar mi sento	I feel ablaze, frozen,
	Se il suo nome ascolto appena!	if only I hear his name!
	Tanto ha impero sul mio cor	So much has ruled over my heart
	Il pensier d'un cieco amor!	the thought of a blind love!
	A tante pene e smanie	From so many sorrows and frenzies
	Al fiero mio tormento	From my fierce torment

Di calma un sol momento	Give me just one moment of calm
Doni clemente il Ciel!	Merciful heaven!
Oppressa omai quest'anima	For now this spirit is overwhelmed
Non regge a tanto affanno	Unable to support so much anguish
Troppo è con me tiranno	This terrible, cruel fate
Il rio destin crudel.	is too tyrannical to me.

As was the case with the newly interpolated recitative dialogue discussed above, this text provides only a modicum of fresh insight into Elena's psyche, the poetry merely reinforcing what audiences might already assume about this character. The aria conforms closely to the original narrative while also providing Ungher a soloistic display of these emotions.

Ungher might have selected Sancia's aria, moreover, for a slight resemblance that its cabaletta bears to music that Elena sings later in the opera. The likeness occurs between Sancia's cabaletta ("Se contro lui mi parlano") and a passage of *arioso* in the *scena* to Elena's Act III aria (examples 2.1 and 2.2). Both four-bar phrases are set in different keys and time signatures (Sancia's cabaletta is in G major and 3/4, whereas the Act III *scena* is in A-flat major and common time), but their vocal lines and harmonies are similarly shaped. They each begin on a tonic chord, their melodies ascending from scale degree $\hat{3}$ up through $\hat{4}$ to $\hat{6}$, arriving on the downbeat of the second measure. This appoggiatura first resolves melodically to $\hat{5}$ (followed by a brief rest), and then harmonically to the dominant in the third measure of each example. Both passages conclude on a tonic chord. Though fleeting, this resemblance forms a slight bond linking the music that Ungher interpolated into Act I with music that she sings later in the opera. Of course, there are significant musical differences between the two passages, and their varying contexts (cabaletta versus arioso within a *scena*) would have made a direct connection between them difficult for spectators to discern. This link between the two passages, therefore, was probably not the reason that Ungher selected Sancia's music for Elena's entrance, but the likeness might have seemed fortuitous nevertheless.

By all accounts, this production of *Marino Faliero* was a smash hit with spectators, one critic reporting as follows: "The reception it received is among the most flattering and brilliant that has ever been recorded in the annals of music.—The acclamation and signs of complete enjoyment, with which the artists were distin-

EXAMPLE 2.1.   *Sancia di Castiglia,* cabaletta, "Se contro lui mi parlano"

Source: Milan: Ricordi, 1832, plate no. 6710.

EXAMPLE 2.2.   *Marino Faliero,* Act III, introductory *scena* to Elena's "Dio clemente, ah mi perdona"

Source: Milan: Ricordi, 1835, plate no. 8686.

guished throughout the course of the entire score, are indescribable: it is enough to say that there was continuous applause, and that when the curtain fell, the actors [were called] to the stage a good six times accompanied by the impresario [Alessandro] *Lanari.*"[38] Lanari himself sent a lengthy report to Donizetti regarding the opera's triumph, opening his letter with "*Furore! fanatismo! entusiasmo!* Your Marino Faliero was judged to be your masterpiece," and then providing descriptions of how each individual number was received.[39] According to his report, one of the only disappointing moments of the entire production came with Elena's entrance: "Ungher placed [her hopes] in the cavatina from your *Sancia di Castiglia,* but she could not sing it like she knew she could have, due, she said, to a very fierce tremor in her heart that arrived suddenly on account of her intense desire to perform it well."[40] Given that she never again interpolated "Io talor più nol rammento" into *Marino Faliero,* and given that there is no evidence she ever performed this aria in public after this production, her reservations about the music as she could sing it must have been quite serious.

Ungher's concerns likely arose from a disparity between her vocal strengths and the demands that the aria imposes on the singer who attempts it. Ungher performed

38. "L'accoglienza che n'ebbe è fra le più lusinghiere e brillanti che mai si conosca nè fasti musicali.—Le acclamazioni e i segni di pieno aggradimento, onde vennero via via distinti quegli artisti in tutto il corso dello spartito, sono indescrivibili: dir basti che fu un applauso continuo, e che, calata la tela, i primari attori si vollero sul proscenio per ben sei volte in compagni dell'impresario *Lanari.*" *Teatri arti e letteratura* 642 (June 16, 1836): 137.

39. "Furore! fanatismo! entusiasmo! Il tuo Marino Faliero fu giudicato il tuo Capo Lavoro." Jeremy Commons, "Una corrispondenza tra Alessandro Lanari e Donizetti," *Studi Donizetti* 3 (1978): 22.

40. "La Ungher ripose la Cavatina delle tua Sancia di Castiglia, ma non la potè cantare come sapeva, e poteva stante, dice Lei un fierissimo palpito di cuore che gli sopravvenne p[er] la smania di voler far bene." See Jeremy Commons, "Una corrispondenza tra Alessandro Lanari e Donizetti." Ibid. There was one other moment in this opera that Lanari reports was not well received: the Act I duet between Elena and Fernando, he writes, was "sufficiently applauded, but the public recognized in its first two tempos those from the *Anna Bolena* duet many times performed here." This refers, of course, to Donizetti's reuse of "Sì, son io che a te ritorno" from *Anna Bolena* (see footnote 33).

soprano, mezzo-soprano, and contralto roles over the course of her career, but she was strongest in her low and middle ranges and thus was more comfortable in mezzo and contralto parts.[41] According to contemporary reports, her notes above G^5 tended to sound harsh. Bellini, in fact, called them "dagger-thrusts," and in 1834 he complained to Florimo about her insistence on performing roles that he thought were out of her range (especially when his own operas were affected): "To me, it is such terrible news that Ungher will do *Il pirata*! My dear, this woman cannot sing soprano at all: I wish she could be persuaded of this once and for all."[42] Donizetti composed "Io talor più nol rammento" for a prima donna with a different set of skills. Giuseppina Ronzi de Begnis (1800–1853) possessed a vocal range that extended higher than Ungher's and she luxuriated in coloratura display. The role of Sancia—for whom Donizetti wrote two duets and a rondò finale in addition to the cavatina—was a vehicle for de Begnis's vocal acrobatics, and the music thus contains traces of what Ungher may have found problematic.

The *larghetto* in G major opens with a passage that matches Ungher's vocal strengths precisely (example 2.3). Sitting comfortably in the center of her range (from $F\#^4$ to E^5), these initial measures move in leisurely stepwise motion, circling gently around the tonic, and reserving ornamentation for the conclusion of the phrase. Starting in measure twenty one, however, and continuing throughout the remainder of the movement, the vocal line insists on a relentless string of ascending and descending scales, wide leaps, and arpeggios. One contemporary critic complained bitterly at the premiere of *Sancia* that "De-Begnis's cavatina is overwhelmingly diminished, so that the primo tempo is run through with scales and *gorgheggi* rendering it impossible to comprehend the principal motive."[43] This was not the type of music with which Ungher was most at ease.

The cabaletta, "Se contro lui mi parlano" (*allegretto*, G major, 3/4) contains similar features. The vocal line is built primarily of jaunty arpeggios and skips that let up only momentarily during the "b" section of its standard lyric form (aa′ba″);[44] the cadential figures are punctuated by high, syncopated B- and C-naturals approached by leap, notes that would have sounded forced in Ungher's throat if she sang them precisely as written; and a set of rapid, sixteenth-note passages that dominate the conclusion might have been responsible for creating the "tremor" in her heart that Lanari described.

Why did Ungher select this music for Elena's entrance? Why not choose a number with which she was comfortable and that she knew would flatter her voice? The

41. For an assessment of Ungher's vocal range and talents, see Reggioli, *Carolina Ungher*, 31.

42. "Che cattiva notizia mi è quella che la Ungher farà il Pirata! Mio caro non può quella donna cantare il soprano affatto affatto: vorrei che ella se ne persuadesse una volta per sempre." Bellini's letter to Florimo is dated October 10, 1834; Cambi, *Bellini: epistolario*, 452.

43. "La Cavatina della De-Begnis è soverchiamente diminuita, cosicché il primo tempo è una infilacciata di scale e gorgheggi senza che se ne comprenda il motivo principale," in *Il Raccoglitore*, Naples, n.d. This review is reproduced in Bini and Commons, *Le prime rappresentazione*, 318.

44. For detailed discussions of lyric form, see Scott Balthazar, "Rossini and the Development of Mid-Century Lyric Form," *Journal of the American Musicological Association* 41 (1988): 102–25; Joseph Kerman, "Lyric Form and Flexibility in *Simon Boccanegra*," *Studi Verdiani* 1 (1982): 47–62; and Robert Moreen, "Integration of Text Forms and Musical Forms in Early Verdi" (Ph.D. diss., Princeton University, 1975).

EXAMPLE 2.3.   *Sancia di Castiglia,* "Io talor più nol rammento," mm. 15–29

Source: Milan: Ricordi, 1832, plate no. 6710.

traditional wisdom on aria insertion assumes that this (or any) prima donna would
have had on hand a collection of favorite, tried-and-true arias that she could introduce regardless of the operatic context (her so-called trunk arias). That this was
only one of many models that nineteenth-century performers followed when selecting their insertion arias will be explored in further detail in the next chapter.
Here it suffices to recognize that Ungher's discomfort with this aria signals that her
motivations for choosing it might not have stemmed exclusively from a desire to
dazzle her spectators, but also from an attempt to locate music that would avoid the

sort of jolting inconsistencies between opera and aria insertion that Tacchinardi cited as particularly objectionable to the practice. In "Io talor più nol rammento," she found an aria that was generically, dramatically, and musically consistent with *Marino Faliero,* perhaps explaining why she opted to sing it, even in the face of potential vocal discomfort.

Vanity, moreover, was likely not pushed entirely to the side. Ungher undoubtedly chose to interpolate "Io talor più nol rammento" into *Marino Faliero* because she thought she *could* sing it well, as Lanari suggests in the letter cited above. Sancia's cavatina, after all, was not at all out of her technical reach, and she was eminently capable of attempting all the coloratura passages that this aria contains. Indeed, "Io talor più nol rammento" offers challenges identical to those in Elena's Act III aria, particularly in its cabaletta, "Fra due tombe, fra due spettri." Elena performs this music after Fernando's murder and before Faliero is sent to the gallows. Despondent at the tragic loss of both men in her life, she sings of a sea of blood swelling up around her feet, an image that Donizetti complements with virtuosic ascending leaps of a tenth that would have landed directly in the "harsh" region of Ungher's register; and this movement ends with a set of sixteenth-note passages that resemble the delicate runs concluding Sancia's aria. If Ungher was able to perform "Fra due tombe, fra due spettri"—something she presumably did quite well given her continued success in *Marino Faliero*—then there would have been every reason to believe that she could sing Sancia's cavatina equally as well. When she could not, she chose Bianca's entrance aria from *Ugo, Conte di Parigi* for her next appearance as Elena. Before moving to a discussion of this piece, however, a consideration of "Oh tu che desti il fulmine" from *Pia de' Tolomei* completes the picture of the music that Ungher considered, and ultimately rejected, for Elena's entrance.

Ungher arrived in Trieste in October of 1837 for a full season of opera that included performing the lead roles in *Lucia di Lammermoor, Beatrice di Tenda,* and *Marino Faliero.* Contemporary newspapers report that she was taken ill unexpectedly at the end of November, however, two-thirds of the way through her scheduled time in the city, and that, as a result, she had to back out of her commitment to appear in *Marino Faliero.*[45] Fortunately, the libretto for this production was completed before Ungher's illness struck, leaving behind evidence of what she had planned to do had she been able. Because the text for Pia's cavatina was printed in this libretto, there is no question that she prepared it for her entrance.

Unlike *Sancia di Castiglia* or *Ugo, Conte di Parigi, Pia de' Tolomei* premiered after *Marino Faliero.* The first performance was at the Teatro Apollo on February 18, 1837, where it had a successful run, and it was revived during the summer of 1837 in Senigallia.[46] Among the numbers singled out for praise at both productions, "Oh tu che desti il fulmine" proved to be a favorite with spectators. A critic for *Il*

45. *Teatri arti e letteratura* 719 (December 7, 1837): 115, and 722 (December 28, 1837): 142. The part of Elena was taken by the lesser known Antonietta Vial.

46. Giorgio Pagannone, *La Pia de' Tolomei di Salvadore Cammarano* (Florence: Olschki, 2006). See also Bini and Commons, *Le prime rappresentazioni,* 622–35, for a detailed account of this opera's genesis and first production in Rome; see pp. 640–43 for a discussion of the revisions Donizetti made for the Senigallia production.

censore universale dei teatri who witnessed the Venetian production remarked that it was "clamorously celebrated with three uproarious encores";[47] and a critic in attendance at the Senigallia production commented that the aria was applauded loudly following both the slow movement and the cabaletta.[48] "Oh tu che desti il fulmine" was a crowd-pleaser, a characteristic that must have played a role in selecting it for Elena's cavatina. Its currency, coupled with the fact that it had not yet been heard in Trieste, helps explain why she opted to interpolate it into her third appearance in *Marino Faliero* at the Teatro Grande (fall 1837). This aria, however, does not conform as neatly to the new surroundings as Sancia's did, at least not without alterations. Pia's cavatina contains a *tempo di mezzo,* as well as *pertichini* for chorus and a secondary character, all of which had to be cut for use as Elena's entrance. More perplexing, however, was that with this aria Ungher would have encountered vocal challenges similar to those she faced with "Io talor più nol rammento."

Just as Sancia's aria was tailored to the talents of a soprano with distinct vocal strengths, so, too, was the music Donizetti composed for the character of Pia, Fanny Tacchinardi-Persiani (1812–1867). Like de Begnis, Tacchinardi-Persiani was renowned for her remarkable ability in coloratura roles, and her range extended higher than Ungher's (her voice had a compass of Bb^3 to F^6). She was known for her exceptional agility and her talent for executing chromatic scales and rapid trills flawlessly.[49] The slow movement of "Oh tu che desti il fulmine" (*larghetto,* Ab major, 2/4) is thus saturated with vocal filigree—rapid-fire *passaggi,* an abundance of ornamental material, and high notes extending well outside Ungher's comfort zone.[50] This extravagant display of technique was undoubtedly part of the aria's appeal to spectators, for such vocal pyrotechnics were growing more popular during the 1830s. If Ungher faced difficulties performing Sancia's aria, however, it is difficult to imagine that she would have found Pia's any more gratifying. Why, then, would she have chosen it? There is no clear-cut answer, but just as was the case with "Io talor più nol rammento," it is perhaps safe to assume that as one of the most powerful prima donnas touring the operatic circuit, Ungher believed that she could sing it and that Pia's aria would bring her the same sort of acclaim that it had brought to other singers. At bottom, the practice of aria insertion was very much rooted in the desire to please the ticket-buying public, and Ungher's selection of Pia's aria was undoubtedly based on a confidence in her abilities to perform it spectacularly.

47. ". . . esaltata al furore con tre chiamate strepitosissime." *Il censore universale dei teatri* 18 (March 4, 1837): 69. In Bini and Commons, *Le prime rappresentazioni,* 639.

48. *Teatri arti e letteratura* 702 (August 10, 1837): 197. In Bini and Commons, *Le prime rappresentazioni,* 644.

49. Paola Ciarlantini, "Fanny Tacchinardi Persiani: Biographical and Artistic Portrait of the First Lucia," in *Il teatro di Donizetti. Atti dei convegni delle celebrazioni,* ed. Francesco Bellotto and Paolo Fabbri (Bergamo: Fondazione Donizetti, 2001), 125–52, and *Giuseppe Persiani e Fanny Tacchinardi: due protagonisti del melodramma romantico* (Bologna: Lavoro Editoriale, 1988).

50. It is perhaps no coincidence that when Donizetti revised *Pia de' Tolomei* a second time for a production in the fall of 1838 at the Teatro San Carlo, Naples, Giuseppina Ronzi de Begnis took the title role. See Bini and Commons, *Le prime rappresentazioni,* 640–43.

EXAMPLE 2.4.   *Pia de' Tolomei,* "Oh tu che desti il fulmine" / "Di pura gioja in estasi," mm. 124–42

Source: Milan: Ricordi, 1837.

The cabaletta (*moderato,* G major, 4/4), moreover, presents challenges that have more to do with dramatic than with musical concerns. Constructed in lyric form (aa′bc), its melody is characterized by uncomplicated rhythms and melodic contours shorn of virtually all ornament. Hovering primarily in Ungher's middle range, there is no doubt that she would have been able to sing it well (example 2.4).

Doing so, however, might have offered few rewards, for whoever rewrote the text of this section neglected to pay careful attention to its new dramatic surroundings. When Pia sings this aria, she has just purchased her brother Rodrigo's freedom from prison, and she rejoices as she awaits his arrival. The cheerful text reflects her happy mood.

Pia: Di pura gioia in estasi   In pure joy and ecstasy,
            è l'alma mia rapita!   my spirit is enraptured!
            A lui dirò: sei libero,   to him I will say: you are free,
            io ti salvai la vita . . .   I have saved your life for you . . .
            E amplessi, e baci, e palpiti   Embraces, and kisses, and sighs,
            confonderemo intanto . . .   will overwhelm us meanwhile . . .
            E verserem quel pianto   and we will pour forth those tears
            che di dolor non è!   that are not born of sorrow!

As was the case for Sancia's aria, the poetry was rewritten for Elena's entrance, but here the new text maintains the jovial spirit inherent in the original that obscures the melancholic sentiments this character might more convincingly convey at this moment in the drama:

Elena: Non più rimorsi e lagrime   No more remorse and tears
            Sgombrate da quest'alma,   Escape from this soul,
            I lieti dì ritornino   May the happy days
            Di pura gioja e calma: of pure joy and calm return:
            Per la virtù che m'anima   I will breathe
            Respirerò soltanto,   Only for the virtue that animates me,
            E verserò quel pianto   And I will pour forth those tears
            Che di dolor non è!   That are not born of sorrow!

This cabaletta text demonstrates an interesting point regarding the practice of aria insertion: newly selected music did not always conform flawlessly to the plot of its new context. Indeed, sometimes it was quite out of sync, and yet these arias still possessed the potential to function quite successfully, pleasing audiences even as they caused inconsistencies in the narrative. Aria insertion was by no means a precise science, nor can rational explanations account for why each and every aria was selected. At bottom, some singers may have consistently attempted to locate numbers that were ideal both for their voices and for the operas in which they were performing, but many prima donnas and leading men were also willing to compromise when the spirit moved them to do so. In the end, Ungher rejected "Oh tu che desti il fulmine," never using it as an entrance aria for Elena, though the reason is uncertain—perhaps because it did not conform well to the shape of her voice; perhaps because it did not mesh well with the plot of *Marino Faliero;* or perhaps for another motive entirely. All that is known is that after regaining her health and returning to the stage, she did not opt to give Pia's aria a try in subsequent performances of *Marino Faliero.* Instead, she relied exclusively from that point forward on the aria she had discovered a few months earlier during her second appearance as Elena at the Teatro della Pergola, Florence. It was in "Ah! quando in regio talamo" from *Ugo, Conte di Parigi* that she located an ideal solution both for her and for the opera.

Donizetti originally composed this aria for a character whose temperament stands worlds apart from Elena's. Bianca of Aquitaine is a treacherous, unstable woman who loathes her fiancé, the newly crowned King Luigi V of France. She is secretly in love with the soldier Ugo and reveals her feelings publicly when she learns that he is engaged to her sister, Adelaide, an admission that lands the unwitting Ugo in prison. Sharing none of Bianca's amorous feelings, Ugo is thoroughly repulsed when she visits and pleads with him to launch a revolt against Luigi, an idea he flatly refuses out of loyalty to the king. When Luigi learns of his fiancée's machinations, he restores Ugo to his rightful position, and then brings the soldier and Adelaide to the chapel where they are happily married. News of this festive event sends Bianca into a mad rage—she downs a vial of poison with which she had originally intended to kill Luigi and dies, leaving those around her both stunned and mildly relieved.

The plot has only begun to unfurl when Bianca sings "Ah! quando in regio talamo"; she is not yet aware of the budding romance between Ugo and Adelaide as she waits for her sister to arrive. The original aria contains a brief *scena* and a *tempo di mezzo*, which were cut for use as Elena's aria. The slow movement and cabaletta remain, their poetry altered to eliminate details specific to the original setting (a reference to Adelaide, for example, is removed), and to emphasize the feelings of anxiety embedded in the earlier text. The rewritten version conveys Elena's desperate state of mind:

Elena: Ah! quando in regio talamo	Ah! when in the royal bridal bed
Felicità credei,	I believed in happiness,
Io non sapea che vittima	I did not know that as a victim
Pianger dovuto avrei.	I would have to cry.
Nò, che infelice appieno	No, you didn't want me
Non mi volesti, o fato,	So thoroughly unhappy, o fate,
Se ritrovar mi è dato	If I am allowed to find
Il mio coraggio ancor,	My courage once again,
Ah riedi pace in seno	Ah, peace, return to my breast,
Ah riedi speme al cor.	Ah, hope, return to my heart.[51]

This aria differs from the previous two in many respects, one of the most significant being that Donizetti composed it for Giuditta Pasta, a performer whose vocal strengths, unlike those of de Begnis and Tacchinardi-Persiani, mirrored Ungher's closely. Descriptions of Pasta's and Ungher's talents bear striking similarities, commentators remarking that neither singer was gifted by nature, but that each was required to undergo assiduous training in order to succeed on stage (much like descriptions of Callas later on). Pasta's voice was stronger in the lower and middle registers, and both prima donnas were praised for their histrionic talents, often more so than for their singing.[52] Little surprise, then, that an aria written for Pasta would hold greater appeal to Ungher than would music from *Pia* or *Sancia*.

***

51. The original text for this aria is as follows (the portions altered for Ungher's 1837 appearance in Florence are italicized):

Ah! quando in regio talamo / felicità credei, / no, non sapea che vittima / *a splendid'ara andrei;* / no, non sapea che piangere / dovuto avrei così.

No, che infelice appieno / non mi volesti, o fato, / se ritrovar mi è dato / il mio coraggio ancor. / *Vola d'Adelia in seno, / vola alla speme, ancor.*

52. Rupert Christiansen summarizes Pasta's career in *Prima Donna: A History* (New York: Viking, 1985), 63–76. For a contemporary account of the singer, see Stendhal, *The Life of Rossini*, trans. Richard N. Coe (London: John Calder, 1985), 371–86. For a modern assessment of Pasta's voice and histrionic strengths, see Susan Rutherford, "'La cantante delle passioni': Giuditta Pasta and the Idea of Operatic Performance," *Cambridge Opera Journal* 19 (2007): 107–38.

EXAMPLE 2.5. *Ugo, Conte di Parigi,* "Ah! quando regio in talamo," mm. 42–68

The slow movement of "Ah! quando in regio talamo" (*larghetto,* Ab major, 6/8)
opens with a passage that bears a striking resemblance to that of Sancia's cavatina,
once again sitting firmly in the center of Ungher's vocal range and circling almost
as smoothly around the tonic (example 2.5). Unlike "Io talor più nol rammento,"
however, this movement is never overrun by coloratura; rather, ornamentation is
limited almost exclusively to cadences and expressive moments. The brief flourish
concluding the first phrase (m. 46) is as complicated as one finds, and the chromatic
descending scales of measures 62 and 64 delicately paint the word *piangere* in addition to emphasizing the prima donna's particular virtuosic abilities. The descending
gestures in these two measures characterize much of the vocal part throughout the
movement. In measures 49–50, the cadential material is approached in the voice

Source: Milan: Ricordi, 1832, plate no. 6028.

through downward motion, for example, and the entire central portion of the movement (mm. 52–58) is built of a series of consecutive descending lines. Though cliché, this sloping melody might be interpreted as conveying a sense of sadness, a performance by a character overwhelmed by despair. Within this middle section, furthermore, the balance between voice and accompaniment shifts slightly, the prima donna yielding melodic control to the orchestra, almost as if she were too weak, too dispirited by her circumstances, to manage more than an extended group of sighs.

This melancholic mood is amplified in the cabaletta "Nò che infelice appieno" (*andante*, C major, 4/4), much of the vocal part mimicking that of the slow movement (example 2.6). Its initial phrases, for example, consist almost exclusively of gentle sigh figures that twice trace a descending line down to G natural; and the scales in mm. 130 and 132 are reminiscent of the gestures that decorated the word *piangere* in the *larghetto*. The inflection to E minor that occurs at the moment when the character begs for peace and hope to return to her heart (mm. 121–124), moreover, emphasizes a sense of deep remorse that Elena might wish to convey.

What distinguishes this cabaletta from the others, what may have been the feature most responsible for Ungher's decision to use the aria time and again as Elena's

EXAMPLE 2.6.   *Ugo, Conte di Parigi,* "Nò che infelice appieno," mm. 112–34

Source: Milan: Ricordi, 1832, plate no. 6028.

entrance, is the manner in which it toys with generic expectations. In a piece such as this, constructed on the double-aria model that was standard during the first half of the nineteenth century, the expectation is for the cabaletta to be set in a rapid tempo, or at least that its pace move faster than the first movement's. But this movement flouts such convention, adopting instead a stately *andante,* signaling that something is wrong with, or at least different about, the character performing it. This is not the first aria that Donizetti composed with a *moderato* cabaletta—Edgardo's "Tu che a Dio spiegasti l'ali" (*Lucia di Lammermoor*), Antonina's "Egli è spento" (*Belisario*), and Elisabetta's "Vivi, ingrate" (*Roberto Devereux*) are three of the best-known instances, all appearing at the conclusion of their operas, all sung by characters who have already suffered the tragic deaths of loved ones. When sung by Elena, therefore, "Ah! quando in regio talamo" not only calls attention to her misery. The bleak mood this aria projects also foreshadows that worse is to come, its tone prefiguring a tragic outcome for her, Fernando, and Faliero. With this cavatina, Ungher located a musical vehicle that was ideal not only for her own voice, but for the drama itself. Her search for Elena's entrance was over.

PARAMETERS OF CHOICE

This exploration of Ungher's experiments with Donizetti's opera might end here, perhaps with a triumphant conclusion extolling the virtues of "Ah! quando in regio talamo" and congratulating the prima donna for her good work. And work it was indeed. As we have seen, inserting an aria into an opera production was no simple task when approached thoughtfully: arias of appropriate generic matter needed to be identified; scores located; poetry rewritten; sometimes, though not always, introductory recitatives composed in order to smooth over narrative disjunctions that the presence of inserted arias generated; and glitches that were created by the newly interpolated material had to be negotiated. At its best, aria insertion entailed searching for music that accommodated the singer's voice, but that also conveyed the "expressive self" of both the prima donna and the character she portrayed. Ungher accomplished these tasks when she performed "Ah! quando in regio talamo," and as such, it is tempting to claim that she located the perfect entrance for Elena, that through her painstaking efforts, she effectively "authored" this scene. The implications of this line of reasoning would be sweeping, extending up through the present day when one could insist that if a modern revival of *Marino Faliero* were to include an interpolated cavatina for Elena, then the aria from *Ugo* would represent the only "responsible" piece to introduce.

To conclude with such unabashed confidence in Ungher's authorship, however, would only place unnecessary limits on an operatic moment that was never so carefully policed during the nineteenth century; it would, to put it a different way, assert a notion of *Werktreue* that simply did not exist. If a modern-day prima donna were to consider adding an entrance aria for Elena, there are many others who performed the role during the 1830s and 1840s who staked out their own choice for Elena's entrance whose lead might also be followed. To name only a few: Emilia Boldrini and Eugenia d'Alibert, both well-respected prima donnas of their time, chose entrance arias from operas by Donizetti—Boldrini interpolated "O nube!

che lieve per l'aria ti aggiri" from *Maria Stuarda,* and D'Alibert sang "Perché non ho del vento" from *Rosmonda d'Inghilterra;*[53] and Amalia Mattoli selected "Par che mi dica ancora" from Donizetti's *Il castello di Kenilworth.*[54] Depending on the performer and on her voice type, all three pieces might make welcome additions to *Marino Faliero.* If these choices prove unsatisfying, Giuseppina Strepponi, who took on the role of Elena while at the height of her fame, left behind yet another viable option. For performances of *Marino Faliero* at the Teatro Comunale, Bologna (fiera 1837), she selected as her cavatina the aria that Donizetti composed for Elena while still working on the opera in Naples, "Dì che parta; che funesta."[55] Given that this piece represented a vital component of Donizetti's early conception of the character, albeit one that he excised for Paris, a modern-day reconstruction of the aria might yield rewarding results. These and other nineteenth-century prima donnas, in other words, laid out a broad parameter of choice for Elena's entrance, seeking, like Ungher, their own form of expression for this scene.[56]

Ungher's impact, however, was significantly more powerful than that of her contemporaries, her choices for Elena's entrance lingering well beyond her own performances. Whereas the alterations made by D'Alibert, Boldrini, Mattoli, and Strepponi represented unique occasions, arias they alone used for Elena's cavatina, Ungher's choices were closely observed and imitated by many of her contemporaries. Extant librettos reveal that during the ten years following her appearances as Elena, a host of prima donnas who sang the role interpolated either "Io talor più nol rammento" from *Sancia* or "Ah! quando in regio talamo" from *Ugo* (no one seems to have introduced "Oh tu che desti il fulmine" from *Pia*).[57] Although the

53. Boldrini made this change at the Teatro la Fenice (carnival 1840), and D'Alibert made her alteration at the Teatro alla Scala (spring 1840). The texts for these arias were printed in librettos for those productions, both available at I-Vgc. "Perché non ho del vento" became important as a substitute aria in the context of *Lucia di Lammermoor,* where it frequently replaced Lucia's entrance and was published in the French version of the score that Donizetti sanctioned.

54. "Par che mi dica ancora" was not an entrance aria, but rather a solo aria sung by Amelia in Act III of *Il castello di Kenilworth,* after the character has already spent much time on stage. It was a popular substitute aria, inserted into a variety of operas including Mayr's *Rosa bianca e la rosa rossa* (Trieste, Teatro Grande, 1832); Donizetti's *Maria de Rudenz* (Turin, Teatro Regio, 1841); and Donizetti's *Fausta* (Venice, Teatro la Fenice, 1859). Its cabaletta, "Fuggi l'immagine," was even more popular making its way into several additional productions including Bellini's *Il pirata* (Venice, Teatro la Fenice, 1837) and Donizetti's *Alina, regina di Golconda* (Bologna, Teatro Comunale, 1842). Librettos for these productions are available at I-Vgc.

55. Marino Faliero / azione tragica / e / Il candidate cavaliere / ballo eroico / da rappresentarsi in Bologna / nel Gran Teatro della Comune / la primavera del 1837 / – / pei Tipi Governativi della Volpe al Sassi / nelle spadiere (I-Vgc).

56. The term *parameter of choice* is John Mauceri's ("Working with a Living Composer: Multiple Versions of *Candide* and *A Quiet Place,*" paper read at the Annual Meeting of the American Musicological Society, Houston, Texas, November 2003). In addition to those listed above, I have located the following examples of prima donnas inserting cavatinas into *Marino Faliero:* Emilia Hallez, "Solo per lui quest'anima" / "Sol ti chieggo oh Dio se avviene," origin unknown (Ferrara, Teatro Comunale, 1839); Ester Corsini, "Ah! chi mi tolse all'estasi," from Alessandro Nini, *Marescialla d'Ancre* (Pavia, Teatro de' Signori, 1840–1841); Jenny Oliver, "O caro oggetto," origin unknown (Macerata, Teatro dei Signori Condomini, spring 1841); and Felicita Rocca, "Quando il core a te rapito," from Persiani, *Inès de Castro* (Granata, theater unknown, spring 1843) (*Il pirata* [May 16, 1843], 372).

57. The following prima donnas interpolated "Io talor più nol rammento" from *Sancia di Castiglia*

1830s and 1840s gave rise to a variety of "authors" for this scene, Ungher was the one whose authority was held in highest regard—it was she who became the standard bearer of Elena's entrance. This tendency to look toward one performer for leadership where aria insertions were concerned was not limited to this scene or to these arias, representing instead a central component of aria insertion throughout the first half of the nineteenth century. It is to a wider consideration of this phenomenon that the next chapter is dedicated.

---

into *Marino Faliero* (unless stated otherwise, the following information was gleaned from librettos located in I-Vgc or I-Vnm): Eugenia Garcia (Genoa, Teatro Carlo Felice, 1838; Padua, Teatro Nuovo, 1838; and Rome, Teatro Apollo, 1839); Carlotta Zucchieli (Fermo, 1838); Felicita Forcini (Cremona, Teatro della Concordia, 1839); and Ezebina Ercolani (Macerata, Teatro dei Signori, 1839). Prima donnas who interpolated "Ah! quando in regio talamo" from *Ugo, Conte di Parigi* were: Desiderata Derancour (Mantua, Teatro Sociale, 1839); Carolina Soret (Pescia, Teatro degli Affilati, 1839); Ottavia Malvani (Modena, Teatro Comunale, 1839–1840); Sofia Grevedon (Pisa, Teatro de' Ravvivati, 1842–1843); Ademaide Moltini (Ravenna, Teatro Comunitativo, 1844); Elisabetta Parepa (theater and date unknown, Lib. Burcardo [Lib. Mus. 103.3]); and Giulia Sanchioli (Messina, Teatro S. Elisabetta, 1852 [*Gazzetta musicale di Milano* (February 29, 1852), 39–40]).

CHAPTER 3

MAKING THEIR WAY
THROUGH THE WORLD:
ITALIAN ONE-HIT WONDERS

Carolina Ungher's experience with choosing a cavatina for Elena in *Marino Faliero* illustrates one extreme to which prima donnas and leading men might go when selecting insertions for their operatic appearances. The trials and tribulations that Ungher faced when selecting an appropriate insertion aria for Donizetti's opera were unusual, however—most singers simply did not engage in such complex decision-making processes, adopting instead a more straightforward approach. If changes were to be made, prima donnas and leading men tended to select one aria for a given scene and, with some exceptions, they stuck with that alteration for all subsequent productions of the opera in which they appeared.

The most common explanation for how singers went about choosing their substitutions and interpolations relies on the concept of the trunk aria. This model assumes a one-to-one relationship between a movable aria and an individual singer, and it implies that performers carried along with them from town to town a small collection of their favorite arias, introducing them into operatic productions whenever whim or necessity dictated. This individualistic and limited notion of how aria insertions were transmitted has helped create an exaggerated picture of performers unwilling to learn music that was new to them and intent only to show off their voices with their tried-and-true favorites. Most important, this concept has obscured many other aesthetic and cultural forces that encouraged the presence of aria insertions. In this chapter, I seek to problematize the concept of the trunk aria, but in doing so my intent is not to argue that such a tradition did not exist. My purpose, rather, is to introduce a second model that played an equally powerful role during the first half of the nineteenth century and perhaps earlier: the "favorite insertion."[1] Favorite insertions embodied a communal quality, performed as substitutes and/or interpolations by a host of different singers in an assortment of operatic contexts. "Non che felice appieno," the cabaletta of Bianca's "Ah! quando in regio talamo" from *Ugo, Conte di*

---

1. In an earlier version of this chapter, I referred to favorite insertions as "favorite substitutes." I have adopted this new term to acknowledge that these arias were used not only as substitutions, but also as interpolations. See Poriss, "Making Their Way through the World: Italian One-Hit Wonders," *19th-Century Music* 24 (2001): 197–224.

Parigi, provides a good example. As observed in chapter 2, this aria appeared in a variety of productions of *Marino Faliero,* first performed by Ungher, and then by a series of other prima donnas. This cabaletta did not remain tethered only to this one opera alone, however, traveling also through a number of productions of Donizetti's operas including *L'elisir d'amore, Alina, regina di Golconda,* and *La favorita.*[2]

I begin this discussion of trunk arias and favorite insertions by contextualizing both concepts in the "long history" of aria insertion, peering back onto evidence of the practice during the seventeenth and eighteenth centuries. During this time, singers selected much of their borrowed musical material from a shared repertory in addition to relying on a set of personal favorites. Against this background, I situate the aria insertion habits of one of the most famous prima donnas of the nineteenth century, Giuditta Pasta (1797–1865), whose career reveals a host of motivations for participating in the practice of aria insertion, some quite similar to those of her predecessors. Most germane to this discussion is the presence in Pasta's repertory of a pair of favorite insertions, one of which—Pacini's "Il soave e bel contento / "I tuoi frequenti palpiti"—reveals a fascinating history. This aria, as well as a host of other favorite insertions, not only destabilizes the assumption that singers inserted only their preferred numbers into new operatic contexts, but it also serves to expand traditional notions of the work concept, opening up a new theoretical space for thinking about issues surrounding canon formation during the *Primo Ottocento.*

PAST MODELS OF ARIA INSERTION

I know that you are having some troubles in Brescia . . . Listen to the advice of a friend: if you are disposed to making some sacrifices in order to obtain calmness (the greatest of all possessions) then do it, but take care to have at least one aria that is suited to you and in which your abilities may shine; if you turn down this necessary privilege, I would label your docility foolishness.[3]
— *Violante Camporesi to Giuditta Pasta, July 16, 1819*

Camporesi's advice to her younger and less experienced colleague conjures up images of trunk arias, and it is worthwhile considering what have long been believed to be their most distinguishing characteristics. Trunk arias were an individual singer's "hits"—pieces that may have been composed with their talents in mind, but which definitely had proven exceptional vehicles for their voices in the past. Both principal and secondary performers are thought to have traveled with these arias as a type of insurance against failure, and they introduced them into any scene in any opera, regardless of the generic, musical, or dramatic nature of that new context. By

---

2. The productions in which these insertions occurred were *L'elisir d'amore* (Naples, 1834), *Regina di Golconda* (Venice, 1842; Este, 1842; and Bologna, 1842); and *La favorite* (Turin, 1842). Librettos for these productions are available at I-Vgc.

3. "So che hai qualche dispiacere a Brescia [. . .] senti il consiglio di un'amica, qualora tu sii disposta a fare dei sagrifici per ottener la quiete (sommo dei beni) fallo pure, ma bada di avere almeno un'aria che ti sia adattata e nella quale possa brillare la tua abilità; se ricusasti anche a questo per te necessario vantaggio, chiamerei schiochezza la tua condiscendenza." Pasta Collection of the New York Public Library of the Performing Arts at Lincoln Center. Cited in Kenneth Stern, "A Documentary Study of Giuditta Pasta on the Opera Stage" (Ph.D. diss., City University of New York, 1983), 41.

encouraging Pasta to select "at least one" preferred number, Camporesi suggests that the trunk aria was still an important component of *ottocento* production, a "privilege" that only a foolhardy prima donna could refuse.

And yet, musicological investigations of seventeenth- and eighteenth-century aria insertion suggest that, historically, the trunk-aria paradigm was only one of a few modes of transmission. Among the finest of these studies is the rather dated, but still quite significant, exploration by Robert Freeman of the life and repertory of the eighteenth-century castrato Carlo Broschi Farinello, better known as Farinelli.[4] Through an examination of extant librettos and scores dating from 1720 to 1737, Freeman identified a total of 350 aria texts (and 250 musical settings of those texts) sung by the castrato throughout his meteoric career. "Given the pressure that Farinello's enormous popularity must have enabled him to assert over impresarios," Freeman remarks, "and given the ease with which the great majority of the arias he sang might in fact be transferred [from opera to opera], one would expect that his collected repertory would in the end contain a considerable number of substitute arias."[5] What he found, however, was surprisingly different. He was able to locate only fourteen arias that Farinelli performed in more than one opera throughout his lengthy career.[6] This collection, moreover, exhibited few of the characteristics commonly associated with a singer's "trunk." Specifically, rather than reusing the arias in multiple opera productions, Farinelli varied his repertory, preferring to interpolate or substitute new material rather than old. In fact, of the fourteen numbers contained in what might be called his trunk, only two remained there for longer than five years. He introduced only four of these pieces into more than one opera, and he never sang the same aria in more than two operas.[7] In addition to these fourteen trunk arias, Freeman identified more than three dozen arias that Farinelli seems to have used as insertion arias only once.[8] Repetition of the same arias, in other words, was rare for this singer.

Freeman concludes that Farinelli's approach to selecting and performing insertion arias was anomalous—that his exceptional abilities as a singer and composer made it possible for him to learn a larger quantity of music and to master a greater variety of styles more rapidly than his contemporaries could.[9] Indeed, the article concludes with a compendium of eighteenth-century reports suggesting that less capable singers were more dependent on the trunk-aria model. The most interesting is an account by Ranieri de' Calzabigi of the preparations typical for a contemporary opera production: "It happens rather often that the virtuosi—the principal male and the principal female singer—who determine the fashion of their colleagues, present the composer, the impresario, and the public with arias which they

---

4. Robert Freeman, "Farinelli and His Repertory," in *Studies in Renaissance and Baroque Music in Honor of Arthur Mendel,* ed. Robert L. Marshall (Kassel: Bärenreiter, 1974), 301–30.

5. Ibid., 315.

6. Ibid., 316.

7. Ibid. The two arias that Farinelli kept in his repertory for longer than five years were "Navigante che non spera," from Vinci's *Medo,* and "Serbami o cara," from *Ezio* by Farinelli's brother, Riccardo Broschi.

8. Ibid., 319.

9. Ibid., 320–23.

have sung with success in other operas; they compel the composer to adjust these at once to their present roles, in order, as they say, to assure the opera's success. One must subordinate oneself to their directions, for there is no court of higher authority than these people, of whom the maxim says, 'Impertinent as a singer.'"[10] Here Calzabigi implies that singers—principal singers in particular—made ample use of the trunk-aria tradition, demanding that music they had performed successfully in the past be readjusted for insertion into new contexts. But what does the author mean when he writes that these singers "determine the fashion of their colleagues"? Given that aria insertion was fully ensconced in eighteenth-century practice, Calzabigi may have intended something beyond the act of trading one aria for another. The "fashion" to which he alludes, in other words, may have had to do with the music itself, with the determination of which arias were "fashionable" as insertions, and which ones were not. A second study—this one focusing on late-seventeenth-century examples of aria insertion—enhances this possibility.

In her investigation of Venetian operas produced toward the end of the seventeenth century, Jennifer Williams Brown located evidence suggesting that the trunk-aria model was not the only one that singers followed when selecting their aria insertions.[11] To be sure, the sample from which she was working was confined: due to limited cast information provided in seventeenth-century librettos, Brown was able to assemble a total of only twenty-two borrowings in which the singer was known on one or both sides of the "transaction." Even so, this collection yielded some provocative findings. First, singers at this time did travel occasionally with their own substitution arias: two of the examples that Brown identified were performed by the renowned soprano Margarita Salicola in both "donor" and "recipient" operas.[12] Such continuity, however, was rare. Instead, it was more common for an aria performed by one singer in the donor opera to be adopted by a different person in the recipient work. The majority of arias from Brown's sample bore this trait, and from this information she concluded that many late-seventeenth-century aria insertions were members of a larger, central repertory—a set of pieces shared among performers throughout Italy and beyond.[13] Rather than depending on a limited quantity of familiar numbers, individual singers may have selected their borrowed material from a central pool of arias commonly used for this purpose by other performers as well.

This "recycling-box" model, as Brown calls it, has ramifications for the way in which aria insertions are perceived, not only as they occurred in seventeenth-century operatic productions, but also later ones as well. Most significant, the recycling-box

<hr>

10. Cited and translated in Freeman, "Farinelli and His Repertory," 321–22. Until recently, this letter has been attributed to Josse de Villeneuve. See Daniel Heartz, *Haydn, Mozart, and the Viennese School* (New York: W. W. Norton, 1995), 158–64.

11. "On the Road with the 'Suitcase Aria': The Transmission of Borrowed Arias in Late Seventeenth-Century Italian Opera Revivals," *Journal of Musicological Research* 15 (1995), 3–23. I have adopted here the terminology Brown adopts in her article regarding "transaction," "donor," and "recipient" operas.

12. Ibid., 7. The two arias were "Prio ch'io lasci," first identified in a libretto for *Ottaviano* (Mantua 1682); the second was "Sì bacia, stringa, e godi," first performed in *Re infante* (Venice 1683). Both pieces migrated into the 1683 production of *Il talamo preservato* in Reggio.

13. Ibid., 8.

model shifts motivations for aria insertion away from the desires of singers themselves toward audience demand, something that remains critical in nineteenth-century productions. A shared repertory of borrowed numbers would have constituted a collection of works that had proven popular with spectators, rather than pieces booed unceremoniously off stage or those received only neutrally. The compelling factor behind the insertion of a recycling-box number, then, was not necessarily an individual's attachment to it, but rather its reputation as music that had the potential to please.

Because the recycling-box model was influential during the late-seventeenth century, it may have carried over as a component of early- and mid-eighteenth-century production. As such, it helps explain what Freeman perceived as the anomalous character of Farinelli's "trunk." If the castrato had selected his borrowed arias from a set of popular numbers rather than from a group of his own favorites, then the rapidity with which they fell from his repertory makes sense: basing his choices on changing fashions would have required flexibility, allowing those currently in style to replace those that had become passé. Such flexibility was almost certainly not characteristic of all Farinelli's contemporaries. The better the singer, the quicker she or he was able to learn new music, and the more possible it was for him or her to remain flexible when it came to selecting aria insertions (a phenomenon observed quite clearly in the example of Ungher working with Elena's cavatina). Secondary singers, on the other hand, may not have had the same luxury because they depended on a smaller selection of aria insertions by virtue of their own limitations—relying, in other words, on a set of trunk arias.

In his biography of Rossini, Stendhal suggests that such a distinction between first-rate and mediocre singers was prominent during the first decades of the nineteenth century. In a chapter provocatively titled "Excuses," Stendhal presents a lengthy and ambivalent exegesis on trunk arias, describing them first as "one of the huge standing jokes of the Italian stage!"[14] but also acknowledging that "there is nothing better calculated to satisfy an audience than an *aria di baule*."[15] The most significant aspect of Stendhal's description is that he identifies *who* is most likely to make use of trunk arias. It is, he writes, most common for "a second-rate singer to travel about the countryside completely equipped with a special set of arias, usually referred to as *arie di baule* or *baggage-arias,* which are carried around permanently, as it were, like a change of underwear."[16] These pieces were the province, in other words, of singers who ranked as prima donnas and leading men, but who were mediocre nevertheless and who found employment only in the opera houses of small cities and towns. Stendhal expands on this point at length:

> The *baggage-aria* tradition is admirably devised, not only with regard to the undeniable mediocrity of the average performer—a mediocrity which is scarcely to be wondered at in an art so supremely difficult—but also with respect to the extreme poverty which haunts the resources of so many of the smaller Italian towns; for such places, despite the grotesque insufficiency of the municipal purse, still manage to achieve two

14. Stendhal, *The Life of Rossini,* trans. Richard N. Coe (London: John Calder, 1985), 360.
15. Ibid., 361.
16. Ibid., 360.

or three extremely adequate productions every year, a miracle which is only made possible by the exploitation of the *baggage-aria,* and by the engagement of two or three exceedingly mediocre artists, each one of whom is nevertheless capable of giving a really brilliant performance of *not more than two or three arias* (original emphasis).[17]

Absent from Stendhal's account are indications of whether first-rate singers participated in this practice as well. He did not indicate, for instance, whether they, too, resorted to trunk arias, selecting insertion arias anew for each operatic context; nor does he reveal whether there were any connections between the manner in which star singers and their lesser-known contemporaries selected their aria insertions. A glimpse at the arias that Giuditta Pasta (one of Stendhal's favorite singers) used as substitutions and interpolations, and a discussion of her motivations for choosing them, helps bring some of these issues into sharper focus (see figure 3.1 for an image of Pasta).[18]

GIUDITTA PASTA'S TRUNK AND FAVORITE INSERTIONS

In his biography of Pasta, Kenneth Stern writes that "by [the autumn of 1820] Pasta was following Violante Camporesi's advice and substituting *arie di baule* in operas not specifically written for her voice."[19] An analysis of the array of arias Pasta employed as aria insertions, however, reveals a situation far more complicated (see table 3.1).[20] Immediately noticeable are the features that Pasta's aria insertions share with Farinelli's. Her substitutions and interpolations, though more numerous than the castrato's, were also fairly limited in scope: for a singer who took the stage in hundreds of productions throughout her twenty-five-year-long career, this relatively small collection of arias suggests that insertion was probably not a primary component of her approach to individual performances. Indeed, with only slightly more than thirty productions represented, many of which are clustered around the early part of her career, aria insertion appears more the exception than the rule.

Packed into this "trunk," moreover—woven into the fabric of each of its arias— is a rich amalgam of motivations for the appearance of substitutions and interpolations, reasons that affected Pasta, as well as many of her contemporaries, throughout the first half of the nineteenth century. The first instance of aria insertion listed

17. Ibid., 361–62.

18. In "'La cantante delle passioni': Giuditta Pasta and the Idea of Operatic Performance," *Cambridge Opera Journal* 19 (2007): 107–38, Susan Rutherford expands on Stendhal's relationship with Pasta.

19. Stern, "A Documentary Study of Giuditta Pasta," 57–58. Pasta made her debut at the Teatro degli Accademici Filodrammatici, Milan, in 1816 and spent the following four years in Italy, London, and Paris performing secondary and leading roles in works such as Zingarelli's *Giulietta e Romeo,* Cimarosa's *Penelope,* and Mozart's *Don Giovanni.* Her first major public success came in 1821 at the Théâtre Italien, where she sang Desdemona in Rossini's *Otello.* Thereafter, she established herself as Europe's premiere singer, excelling in roles such as Mayr's Medea and Paisiello's Nina. She appeared also in many operas by Donizetti and Bellini, creating the title roles in *Anna Bolena* (Milan 1830), *Norma* (Milan 1831), and *Beatrice di Tenda* (Venice 1833). She retired from the stage in 1835, appearing only occasionally thereafter in concert recitals.

20. Unless specifically noted, my source for the information in table 3.1 was Stern, "A Documentary Study of Giuditta Pasta."

FIGURE 3.1.   Giuditta Pasta. *Source:* CAN 195 Pasta.JPG; Museo Teatrale alla Scala—Archivio e Biblioteca, Milan.

in table 3.1 is a case in point. On the night of November 30, 1818, the final evening of the autumn season at Padua's Teatro Nuovo, the company mounted a special performance of *I virtuosi,* Mayr's one-act *farsa,* in addition to the regularly scheduled *La Cenerentola.* As a special feature, Pasta interpolated Rossini's "Tu che accendi" / "Di tanti palpiti" from *Tancredi* into Mayr's work.[21] The motivations behind this alter-

21. Notice of this production is found in *Il nuovo osservatore,* December 3, 1818. Cited in Stern, "A Documentary Study of Giuditta Pasta," 30–31.

TABLE 3.1. Giuditta Pasta's Aria Insertions, 1818–1833

Interpolated Aria	Original Opera	Host Opera	City / Theater / Season or Date
"Tu che accendi" / "Di tanti palpiti"	Gioachino Rossini, *Tancredi* (1813)	Mayr, *I virtuosi*	Padua, Teatro Nuovo, November 30, 1818
		I virtuosi	Trieste, Teatro Nuovo, carnival 1819–1820
"Perché straziarmi tanto"	Giusepppe Nicolini, *Giulio Cesare nelle Gallie* (1819)	*I virtuosi*	Trieste, Teatro Nuovo, carnival 1819–1820
"Fatale imagine d'un primo affetto"	Unidentified	Giovanni Pacini, *Adelaide e Comingio*	Rome, Teatro Valle, April 1819
"Frenar vorrei le lagrime"	Marcos António Portogallo, *La morte di Semiramide* (1801)	Ferdinando Paër, *Agnese di Fitzhenry*	Trieste, Teatro Nuovo, carnival 1819–1820
		Giuseppe Farinelli, *I riti d'Efeso*	Turin, Teatro Regio, carnival 1822
"Prima s'avvezzi al lampo"	Ferdinando Orlandi, *Fedra* (1820)	Paër, *Sargino, ossia L'allievo dell'amore*	Turin, Teatro Carignano, autumn 1820
"Lungi dal caro ben"	Pacini, *La sposa fedele* (1819)	Bellini, *Il pirata*	Vienna, Kärntnertortheater, spring 1830
"Elena! oh tu, che chiamo"[a]	Rossini, *La donna del lago* (1819)	Rossini, *Otello*	Paris, Théâtre Italien, spring 1821
		I riti d'Efeso	Turin, Teatro Regio, carnival 1822
		Otello[b]	Paris, Théâtre Italien, 1823
		Otello	London, King's Theatre, 1825
		Otello[c]	Paris, Théâtre Italien, 1826
		Otello[d]	Milan, La Scala, 1832
"Ah! si per voi già sento"	Rossini, *Otello* (1816)	Rossini, *Eduardo e Cristina*	Turin, Teatro Regio, carnival 1822
"Sommo ciel"	Niccolò Antonio Zingarelli, *Giulietta e Romeo* (1796)	*Eduardo e Cristina*	
"Bell'alme avventurose"	Rossini, *Elisabetta, regina d'Inghilterra* (1815)	*Eduardo e Cristina*	
"Dolci d'amor parole"	Rossini, *Tancredi*[e]	Mayr, *La rosa bianca e la rosa rossa*	Paris, Théâtre Italien, May 1823

(continued)

TABLE 3.1. (continued)

Interpolated Aria	Original Opera	Host Opera	City / Theater / Season or Date
"Ah! quel giorno ognor rammento"	Rossini, *Semiramide* (1823)	*La donna del lago*[f]	Paris, Théâtre Italien, autumn 1824
"Ah, come rapida fuggi la speme" / "L'aspetto adorabile"[h]	Meyerbeer, *Il crociato in Egitto* (1824; rev. 1825)	*Otello*[g]	Verona, Teatro Filarmonico, carnival 1829–1830
		Otello[i]	Mantua, Teatro Sociale, quaresima 1830
"Il braccio mio conquisse" / "Or che son vicino a te"	Nicolini, *Il Conte di Lenosse* (1820)	Mayr, *La rosa bianca e la rosa rossa*	Paris, Théâtre Italien, November 1825
		Tancredi[j]	Milan, La Scala, spring 1829
		Tancredi	Bologna, Teatro Comunale, November 1829
		Tancredi[k]	Venice, La Fenice, Carnival 1833
"Il soave e bel contento" / "I tuoi frequenti palpiti"	Pacini, *Niobe* (1826)	Mercadante, *Didone*	London, King's Theatre, summer 1827
		Otello	Milan, Teatro Carcano, autumn 1829
		Otello	Milan, La Scala, carnival 1832
		Otello	Venice, La Fenice, carnival 1833
"Or sei pago, o ciel tremendo"	Bellini, *La straniera* (1829)	*Il pirata*	Vienna, Kärntnertortheater, spring 1830

[a] Pasta also included the recitative "Mura felice." The texts for both recitative and aria were changed to account for the new context. "Mura felici" became "Mura infelici," and "Elena! oh tu, che chiamo" became "Palpita incerta l'alma." See Gossett, *Divas and Scholars,* 210.

[b] Libretto, Bn: Yth. 50571

[c] Libretto, Bn: Yth. 50572.

[d] Libretto, I:Vgc.

[e] This aria was composed by Rossini for the first Tancredi, Adelaide Malanotte, to sing instead of the famous "Tu che acendi" / "Di tanti palpiti."

[f] Gossett, "The Operas of Rossini," 445.

[g] The version of "Ah, come rapida fuggi la speme" that Pasta introduced into *Otello* was the version that Meyerbeer composed for her for the revised production of *Il crociato in Egitto* at the Théâtre Italien (Paris 1825). The origin of the cabaletta, "L'aspetto adorabile," is unknown, though it may have been written by Giuseppe Nicolini. See Helen Greenwald, Review of Giacomo Meyerbeer, *Opern-Arien: Sopran.,* ed. Peter Kaiser, *Notes* 58 (2002): 946.

[h] Libretto, I:Vgc.

[i] Libretto, I:Vnm, dramm. 856.24.

[j] Libretto, Op. Liv. 3007.

[k] Libretto, Bn: Yth. 51375.

ation were twofold: first, it was Pasta's benefit evening, and therefore she would have been expected to take liberties with the score, as observed in chapter 1; second, Mayr's *I virtuosi* (like Donizetti's *Le convenienze ed inconvenienze*) is an opera about an opera in which the prima donna is encouraged to interpolate arias of her own choice. Indeed, by selecting "Tu che accendi" and its cabaletta—an aria that Stendhal describes as having "enjoyed a wider and more universal popularity than perhaps any other aria in the world"[22]—Pasta undoubtedly sought to make an ostentatious display of the insertion. Everyone in the audience would have recognized the aria, and they would have been aware of what she was doing and why.

Practical concerns account for many other arias she inserted into her operatic appearances. The tradition of making a powerful entrance, for instance, compelled a second group of Pasta's alterations. When she performed the lead female role in Pacini's *Adelaide e Comingio* at the Teatro Valle, Rome (1819), for instance, she replaced the original cavatina, "Alma bella, che spiegate," with a different aria "Fatale immagine d'un primo affetto."[23] Her motivation for making this alteration likely stemmed from the poor reception that *Adelaide e Comingio* encountered a year earlier at the Teatro San Benedetto, Venice, a production in which Pasta also participated. The Venetian audience so despised the first act of this opera that following its premiere, the theater management cut the entire act and replaced it with a one-act *farsa, Quanti casi in giorno!* by Vittorio Trento.[24] Because the production of *Adelaide e Comingio* in 1819 in Rome was mounted in honor of a special occasion—the arrival of Francis I of Austria in Rome—Pasta sang a new entrance aria in an attempt to stave off at least some of the negative sentiment experienced in Venice.

Into Act I of Rossini's *Otello,* moreover, Pasta interpolated no fewer than three cavatinas for Desdemona. Though reminiscent of Ungher's tinkering with *Marino Faliero,* the circumstances under which Pasta made her alterations were different, occurring over the space of twelve years rather than just one. Whereas Ungher's choices illustrated an attempt to identify the aria that was the most musically dramatically appropriate for the scene, Pasta's reflected the changing tastes of her spectators (and possibly herself) over a long stretch of time. Fashion and variety, in other words, were likely the factors dictating which arias she selected and when. It is almost certain that many spectators in attendance at Pasta's performances in *Otello* would have recognized her aria insertions. In these two cases, in other words, Ungher and Pasta represent the extremes of this practice: on the one hand, a prima donna might attempt to disguise her aria insertions from spectators in order to create the illusion that all of the music performed originated at the same time and place; on the other, a prima donna might flaunt her aria insertions, rendering it obvious to one and all that she was singing music that did not belong to the opera in which she was appearing.

Different concerns determined the presence of three interpolated arias in the 1822 production of Rossini's *Eduardo e Cristina* in Turin, stemming from the opera's unique compositional history. This work originated as a *pasticcio* of sorts, an opera that Rossini cobbled together from a trio of his earlier operas that were unfamiliar

22. Stendhal, *The Life of Rossini,* 57.
23. Stern, "A Documentary Study of Giuditta Pasta," 38.
24. Ibid., 28.

to the Venetian public for whom the opera was fashioned.[25] Perhaps as a consequence of this early history, revivals of *Eduardo e Cristina* frequently hosted additions and substitutions, and the production in which Pasta participated was no exception. She was not the only performer in that company to sing inserted material. Also added were the duet "Fra i teneri amplessi" from Rossini's *Ricciardo e Zoraide,* which she sang with Elisabetta Ferron, and the trio "Crudele sorte" also from *Ricciardo e Zoraide,* performed with Ferron and Nicola Tacchinardi.[26] Pasta's additions, therefore, were merely part of a broader pattern of change into which *Eduardo e Cristina* often fell.

Situated alongside these examples are a set of arias that do not reveal practical motivations for insertion. On the contrary, some of the pieces listed in table 3.1 were numbers that Pasta probably performed in new contexts because they had proven exceptional vehicles for her voice in the recent or distant past—*trunk arias,* in other words. Giuseppe Nicolini's "Perché straziarmi tanto," for instance, originated in his *Giulio Cesare nelle Gallie,* a work that premiered at the Teatro Argentina, Rome (January 17, 1819), with Pasta singing the trousers role of Clodomiro. She likely found the aria flattering to her vocal talents, for it was this piece she chose to introduce only a few months later into Mayr's *I virtuosi.* Similarly, Giovanni Pacini wrote "Lungi dal caro bene" for her to perform in a revival of his opera *La sposa fedele* (Turin, Teatro Carignano, 1820), and ten years later she selected this number to replace Imogene's entrance aria in Bellini's *Il pirata.*[27] These pieces relied exclusively on Pasta for their exposure as insertions.

Particularly illuminating is the possibility that Pasta selected some of her aria insertions because other singers before her had performed them successfully and that she may have been attempting to imitate, even surpass, their success. Writing about Portogallo's "Frenar vorrei le lagrime," for instance, Stern explains, "[Pasta] had noted the effect [Josephina] Grassini made with this music during performances of Cimarosa's *Gli Orazi e i Curiazi* and expected similar results."[28] Pasta looked toward her famous predecessor in search of effective material to insert, an action that might be understood as borrowing, or even sharing. In the cases of "Or che son vicino a te" and "Il soave e bel contento," two other pieces that sit prominently among Pasta's repertory of substitutions and interpolations, the idea that aria insertions were shared among many singers takes on even greater force, extending beyond a pair of closely acquainted prima donnas. Indeed, these two arias are representative

25. *Eduardo e Cristina* was premiered at the Teatro San Benedetto, April 24, 1819. The three operas from which Rossini drew musical material were *Adelaide di Borgogna, Ricciardo e Zoriade,* and *Ermione.* See Reto Müller and Bernd-Rüdiger Kern, *Rossinis "Eduardo e Cristina": Beiträge zur Jarhundert-Erstaufführung* (Leipzig: Leipziger Universitätsverlag, 1997).

26. Stern, "A Documentary Study of Giuditta Pasta," 82.

27. Ibid., 55 and 203.

28. Ibid., 51. Josephina Grassini (1773–1850) was an Italian contralto who made her operatic debut in Pietro Alessandro Guglielmi's *La pastorella nobile* (Parma, Teatro Ducale, 1789) and went on to an international career, performing in cities throughout Italy, France, and Great Britain, that lasted nearly three and a half decades. She was a contemporary of Elizabeth Billington, and the aunt and teacher of Giuditta and Giulia Grisi. See Arthur Pougin, *Une cantatrice "amie" de Napoléon: Giuseppina Grassini 1773–1850* (Paris: Fischbacher, 1920), and Rupert Christiansen, *Prima Donna: A History* (New York: Viking, 1984), 84.

of a group of pieces that functioned as aria insertions for numerous performers throughout the first half of the nineteenth century.

Table 3.2 presents a set of the nineteenth century's most active favorite insertion arias, selected because their texts appear in ten or more extant librettos.[29] In addition to those listed, there are many other arias that traveled almost as frequently from singer to singer, and from opera to opera.[30] As this table illustrates, some favorite insertions appeared only in a small number of operas: Fioravanti's "Era notte scura scura" is the best example, limited almost exclusively to productions of Pacini's *Il barone di Dolsheim* and his *Adelaide e Comingio.* Most, however, traveled through a wider variety of works, and some were performed with equal frequency by both men and women. For the most part, these favorite insertions originated in operas that had only limited presence in Italian theaters, works that had failed either at their premieres or soon thereafter. Just as a sort of "homelessness" characterizes the arias Ungher selected for her entrance as Elena, these, too, were "free," able to circulate throughout the repertory with little risk that spectators would associate them with their original contexts.

The exception, of course, is "Tu che i miseri conforti" from Rossini's *Tancredi,* an opera that had an exceptionally wide circulation in the decades following its premiere. This aria, however, has an odd history that might help explain its use as a favorite insertion. "Tu che i miseri conforti" exists in two distinct musical settings, both of which were performed in the context of *Tancredi,* but only one of which was definitely composed by Rossini: the "authentic" setting is in E-flat major; the second version, in G major, was introduced into several productions of *Tancredi,* starting as early as 1814 in performances of the opera in Padua.[31] Because the words are identical for both versions, it is not apparent from librettos which version singers selected when they introduced this aria into operas other than *Tancredi.* Given, however, that the G-major version had an enormous diffusion in revivals of *Tancredi* (preferred to the original, perhaps, because of its higher tessitura); and given that the dissemination of the G-major setting in sheet music vastly exceeds the original, it is likely that this second version, not the first, served as the favorite insertion.[32]

29. I am indebted to Luigi Ferrara, whose catalogue of the librettos housed in the Rolandi Collection, Fondazione Cini, Venice, has proven invaluable to this research. His database allowed me to identify a group of the most active favorite substitutes and to trace their path through a variety of operatic contexts.

30. "Dagli affanni ogn'alma oppressa" from Nicolini's *Annibale in Bitinia,* for example, appears in librettos for seven productions: Rossini's *Otello* (Pavia 1829) and *Elisabetta* (Perugia 1830), Pacini's *La sacerdotessa d'Irminsul* (Ferrara 1822; Senigallia 1822; Florence 1823), and Meyerbeer's *Donna Caritea* (Turin 1828; Livorno 1831). Similarly, Pacini's "Se alfin goder mi è dato" from *L'ultimo giorno di Pompei* appears in seven librettos: Rossini's *Otello* (Senigallia, 1828), *Tancredi* (Genoa 1828), *Le Comte Ory* (Pavia 1830), *Eduardo e Cristina* (Pavia 1831), Pacini's *Gli arabi nelle Gallie* (Ascoli 1830; Mahone 1832), and Morlacchi's *Tebaldo e Isolina* (Rome c. 1829). A handful of other arias also follow extended paths: "Soave imagine," from Mercadante's *Andronico,* "Elena! oh tu, che chiamo," from Rossini's *La donna del lago,* and "Smarrita quest'alma," from Cimarosa's *Penelope,* are a few examples. A few others reveal a slightly less impressive presence: "Come mai calmar le pene" from Pacini's *Amazilia,* for instance, surfaces as an interpolation in only four productions: *Otello* (Pisa 1830), *I Capuleti e i Montecchi* (Lisbon 1835; Lisbon 1856), and Morlacchi's *Gianni di Parigi* (Varese 1829).

31. Rossini, *Tancredi,* ed. Philip Gossett, reduction for voice and piano (Milan: Ricordi, 1991), xxi.

32. My gratitude to Will Crutchfield for pointing out this possibility to me.

TABLE 3.2. Favorite Insertions

Interpolated Aria	Original Source	Productions during Which Aria Was Performed				Voice Type
"Tu che i miseri conforti"	Rossini, *Tancredi* (Venice, La Fenice, 1813)	*Il ritorno di Serse*	Portogallo	Florence	1815	Mezzo-soprano
		Demetrio e Polibio	Rossini	Padua	1815	
		Demetrio e Polibio	Rossini	Palermo	1819	
		I baccanali di Roma	Generali	Reggio	1819	
		Otello	Rossini	Rome	1820	
		Il gioventù di Enrico V	Pacini	Lucca	1821	
		La gazza ladra	Rossini	Zara	1821	
		L'italiana in Algeri	Rossini	Turin	1823	
		Semiramide	Rossini	Rome	1826	
		Clotilde	Coccia	Cremona	1826	
		Otello	Rossini	Rome	1827	
		Gli arabi nelle Gallie	Pacini	Ascoli	1830	
		Tebaldo e Isolina	Morlacchi	Venice	1830	
		Semiramide	Rossini	Fermo	1832	
		Tebaldo e Isolina	Morlacchi	Udine	1832	
"Era notte scura scura"	Fioravanti, *Contessa di Fersen* (Rome, Valle, 1817)	*Il barone di Dolsheim*	Pacini	Monaco	1819	Baritone
		La pietra del paragone	Rossini	Pavia	1820	
		Il barone di Dolsheim	Pacini	Trieste	1820	
		Adelaide e Comingio	Pacini	Verona	1820	
		Adelaide e Comingio	Pacini	Florence	1820	
		Il barone di Dolsheim	Pacini	Florence	1821	
		Adelaide e Comingio	Pacini	Pavia	1821	
		Il barone di Dolsheim	Pacini	Modena	1824	
		Adelaide e Comingio	Pacini	Oporto	1825	
		Il barone di Dolsheim	Pacini	Novara	1829	
		Il barone di Dolsheim	Pacini	Varese	1830	

		Adelaide e Comingio	Pacini	Florence	1830
		Adelaide e Comingio	Pacini	Milan	1831
		Il barone di Dolsheim	Pacini	Ravenna	1833
		La figlia del reggimento	Donizetti	Bologna	1844
"Or che son vicino a te"	Nicolini, *Il Conte di Lenosse* (Trieste, Teatro Nuovo, 1820)	*La rosa bianca*	Mayr	Paris	1828	Mezzo-soprano and soprano
		Il borgomastro di Saardam	Donizetti	Milan	1828
		Otello	Rossini	Genova	1828
		Clotilde	Coccia	Milan	1828
		I baccanali di Roma	Generali	Reggio	1829
		Tancredi	Rossini	Milan	1829
		Bianca e Falliero	Rossini	Lucca	1829
		Tancredi	Rossini	Bologna	1829
		Bianca e Falliero	Rossini	Parma	1830
		L'ajo nell'imbarazzo	Donizetti	Ferrara	1830
		Elisa e Claudio	Mercadante	Modena	1831
		Olivio e Pasquale	Donizetti	Verona	1832
		La straniera	Bellini	Castello	1832
		Ciro in Babilonia	Rossini	Perugia	1832
		Gli arabi nelle Gallie	Pacini	Mahone	1832
		Tancredi	Rossini	Venice	1833
		La straniera	Bellini	Florence	1833
		Semiramide	Rossini	Novara	1833
		L'inganno felice	Rossini	Venice	1841
		Il barbiere di Siviglia	Rossini	Corfù	1847

(*continued*)

TABLE 3.2. (continued)

Interpolated Aria	Original Source	Productions during Which Aria Was Performed				Voice Type
"Ma dov'è? perchè fugge i miei sguardi"	Pacini, *Cesare in Egitto* (Rome, Argentina, 1821)	*La donna del lago*	Rossini	Trieste	1822	Tenor
		La sacerdotessa d'Irminsul	Pacini	Sinigaglia	1822	
		La sacerdotessa	Pacini	Ferrara	1822	
		La sacerdotessa	Pacini	Florence	1823	
		La donna del lago	Rossini	Parma	1823	
		Aminta ed Andromico	Mercadante	Reggio	1823	
		La gioventù di Enrico V	Pacini	Siena	1823	
		Temistocle	Pacini	Lucca	1823	
		La donna del lago	Rossini	Reggio	1825	
		L'italiana in Algeri	Rossini	Venice	1826	
		Didone abbandonata	Mercadante	Venice	1827	
		Matilde di Shabran	Rossini	Faenza	1830	
		Il falegname di Livonia	Pacini	Varese	1831	
		Semiramide	Rossini	Sessari	1837	
"l soave e bel contento"/ "I tuoi frequenti palpiti"	Pacini, *Niobe* (Naples, Teatro San Carlo, 1826)	See table 3.3				Soprano, mezzo-soprano, and tenor
"Nell'ebbrezza dell'amore"	Persiani, *Ines de Castro* (Naples, San Carlo, 1835)	*Otello*	Rossini	Milan	1835	Soprano
		Lucia di Lammermoor	Donizetti	Pavia	1837	
		Zaira	Mercadante	Lisbon	1837	
		Lucia di Lammermoor	Donizetti	Novara	1838	

		Lucia di Lammermoor	Donizetti	Varese	1838
		Otello	Rossini	Pavia	1838
		Il bravo	Mercadante	Sinigaglia	1843
		Elena da Feltre	Mercadante	Trieste	1844
		Pia de' Tolomei	Donizetti	Lisbon	1846
		Otello	Rossini	Venice	1848
		Otello	Rossini	Venice	1852
"Alla gioia, ed al piacer"[a]	Bellini, *Bianca e Fernando*	*Bianca e Falliero*	Rossini	Trieste	1829	Soprano
		Tancredi	Rossini	Milan	1829
		Gianni di Parigi	Morlacchi	Varese	1829
		Arminia	Pavesi	Cremona	1829
		La sposa fedele	Pacini	Lodi	1830
		Bianca e Falliero	Rossini	Milan	1831
		Bianca e Falliero	Rossini	Perugia	1831
		L'esule di Roma	Donizetti	Marcerata	1833
		Edoardo	Coccia	Bologna	1833
		La sonnambula	Bellini	Modena	1834
		Otto mese in due ore	Donizetti	Aquila	1840

[a]This cabaletta also seems to have been introduced frequently into Act I of *Il pirata,* with or without Imogene's original music for that moment, "Lo sognai ferito." I have not seen librettos that demonstrate its presence in this scene, but multiple musical prints assert *Il pirata* as one of the many contexts for "Alla gioia, ed al piacer." Personal communication with Will Crutchfield.

What is most striking about the collection listed in table 3.2 is the strong resemblance it bears to the "recycling-box" model that Jennifer Williams Brown identified in late-seventeenth-century productions. This connection between earlier and later practices merits attention, but before turning to this matter, we might first consider, through the example of Pacini's "Il soave e bel contento" from *Niobe,* the unique role that favorite insertions played in productions of Italian operas during the first half of the nineteenth century, and why they may have become favorites in the first place.

"IL SOAVE E BEL CONTENTO"

In 1855 one of Pacini's earliest biographers declared, "Pacini gave to us *Niobe* whose famous cabaletta made its way through the world."[33] *Niobe* premiered at the San Carlo in Naples on November 19, 1826, with an all-star cast that included Giuditta Pasta in the title role, Giovanni Battista Rubini (Licida), Carolina Ungher (Asteria), and Luigi Lablache (Anfione). The plot concerns the goddess Niobe, mother of twelve, who prepares for the marriage of her eldest daughter Asteria to Prince Licida of Thessalia. The matriarch's fierce pride compels her to declare superiority over the goddess Latona, who, in turn, demands repentance. When Niobe does not comply, Latona strikes Niobe's twelve children dead and then turns her enemy into stone.[34] This opera had a respectable run of approximately eight or nine performances during this season in Naples, and it garnered some enthusiastic notice in the press.[35] Despite one critic's characterization of the work as one of Pacini's masterpieces, however, there is no evidence that it was ever again performed in a major opera house.[36]

The "famous cabaletta," on the other hand, followed a very different path. Pacini, who wrote "Il soave e bel contento" for Rubini's entrance as Licida and tailored it to the tenor's legendary vocal skills, told a story about this aria in his memoirs. He recalled that when Rubini first attempted to perform the music, he became displeased, complaining that it was unfit for the human voice. Pacini was so confident that "Il soave e bel contento" would be popular with audiences, however, that

33. Cited in Giovanni Pacini, *Le mie memorie artistiche,* introduction by Rafaelo Colucci (Florence: Tipi dei Successori le Monnier, 1875), xvii.

34. I have paraphrased Philip Gossett's synopsis in Giovanni Pacini, *L'ultimo giorno di Pompei and Excerpts* (New York: Garland, 1986), n.p.

35. It is not clear precisely how many times *Niobe* was performed that season. Stern writes, "*Niobe* was sung eight times; the first act only was performed on three other occasions," *A Documentary Study of Giuditta Pasta,* 171. But in a detailed chronology of Rubini's career, the opera is listed as having had nine performances, during two of which only the first act was heard. See Bruce Brewer, "Il cigno di Romano—Giovan Battista Rubini: A Performance Study," *Donizetti Society Journal* 4 (1980): 142. Reviews of the production were published in *Teatri arti e letterature* 135 (December 7, 1826): 116–17, and *Giornale del regno delle due Sicilie* (November 20, 1826).

36. Oscar Chilesotti, "Giovanni Pacini," *I nostri maestri del passato* (Milan: Ricordi, 1882), 423. In this brief biographical sketch, Chilesotti writes only this about the opera: "This opera, which grew to be considered one of Pacini's masterpieces, was performed at the San Carlo on 19 November 1826, and had as its interpreters Pasta, Ungher, Rubini and Lablache; it was very warmly applauded." ("Quest'opera, che viene considerata come uno dei capolavori di Pacini, fu rappresentata al San Carlo il 19 novembre 1826, ed ebbe ad interpreti la Pasta, la Ungher, Rubini e Lablache; essa fu calorosamente applaudita.")

he refused Rubini's desperate pleas to alter the score. In the end, Pacini's obstinacy was rewarded, for "Il soave e bel contento" was a tremendous success with Neapolitan audiences, so much so that Rubini begged forgiveness, admitting that he had been a fool to complain.[37] According to one biographer, it was from this point forward that Rubini's reputation as "the greatest tenor in the world" was established.[38] This story may be apocryphal—or at the very least exaggerated, but even if Pacini embellished his narrative, the mythical flavor he bestowed on the story probably reflects some elements of the truth. More important, it conveys a retrospective understanding of how celebrated this aria became following *Niobe's* demise.

"Il soave e bel contento" was ubiquitous in European theaters, gaining a high profile in a variety of contexts, sung in transposition by sopranos and contraltos, as well as by tenors. It quickly became popular in benefit productions both inside and outside Italy. In the fall of 1830 at the Teatro dei Rinnovati, Siena, for example, the soprano Marianna Brighenti was honored. The featured opera was Pacini's *Gli arabi nelle Gallie,* followed by a sort of "mini concert" consisting of three popular numbers sung by Brighenti and a pair of her colleagues: the duet "Serbami ognor sì fido" from Rossini's *Semiramide,* the tenor cabaletta "Amor dirada il nembo" from *Otello,* and the grand finale, "Il soave e bel contento," sung by the beneficiary herself.[39] Three years later, moreover, the soprano Carolina Pedrotti was given a benefit at New York's Bowery Theatre, during which she introduced Pacini's number into a production of Mercadante's *Elisa e Claudio;*[40] and at Parma's Teatro Ducale in 1838, the soprano Eugenia Garcia inserted "Il soave e bel contento" into a production of Rossini's *Otello* for a benefit dedicated to the tenor Angelini Dossi.[41] These examples represent only the tip of the iceberg. That singers often selected "Il soave e bel contento" for these evenings is significant, for as discussed in chapter 1, the financial stakes involved in benefits were high. A performer's reliance on this number indicated a confidence in its ability to attract and please an exceptionally large group of spectators.[42] Its widespread appeal undoubtedly compelled singers to program "Il soave e bel contento" for their recitals and academies as well.[43]

37. Pacini, *Le mie memorie artistiche,* 45–47.

38. Eugenio Gara, *Giovan Battista Rubini nel centenario della morte* (Bergamo: Industrie Grafiche Cattaneo, 1954), 6–7.

39. Brighenti's colleagues were contralto Adele Cesari and tenor Andrea Peruzzi. A review of this benefit is published in *Teatri arti e letteratura* 337 (September 2, 1830).

40. *Gazzetta privilegiata di Venezia* (March 1, 1833).

41. The poster advertisement for this benefit production, which took place on January 24, 1838, announces in advance that Garcia was planning to make this alteration to Rossini's score. This announcement is located in the Archivio storico Teatro Regio, Parma (hereafter ASTR).

42. It is worth noting, however, that the appearance of this piece did not guarantee large box-office intakes. According to extant ticket-sales records for the Teatro Ducale in Parma, for example, the receipts for Dossi's benefit in 1838 fell well below the average for the entire 1837–1838 carnival season (ASTR, Introit. Ser., anno 1833–1846). The average intake each evening that year was approximately 504 lire, whereas Dossi's benefit earned only 383. This amount, compared to the 515 lire brought in during the benefit for ballerina Fanny Mabel, the 1331 lire for Eugenia Garcia's and the 1268 for Orazio Cartegenova's benefits, moreover, indicates that Dossi's evening was not an overwhelming success despite the presence of "Il soave e bel contento."

43. An extant program of one such performance at the Teatro Ducale featuring the singer Pietro

Like many popular *bel canto* tunes, "Il soave e bel contento" attained vast exposure on European stages and in private salons in the form of instrumental transcriptions. Composers whose names are hardly recognized today transformed the melody into such diverse incarnations as a caprice for solo cello, a fantasy for clarinet, and a setting for piano four hands.[44] In addition, Franz Liszt adopted the cabaletta tune in his *Divertissement sur la cavatine "I tuoi frequenti palpiti"* (1835–1836), a work for piano solo that he included on his European concert tours throughout the 1830s and 1840s.[45] Although he presented many memorable performances of this piece, the most famous occurred on the evening of March 31, 1837, in the salon of the Princess Belgiojoso, in front of an elite group of Parisians who were interested in getting to the bottom of one question: who was the greatest piano virtuoso in the world, Liszt or his rival Sigismond Thalberg? For this celebrated duel, on which both of their reputations depended, each musician presented his own composition: Thalberg played his *Moses* Fantasia and Liszt, his *Divertissement*. About Liszt's performance, Heinrich Heine had this to say:

> I no longer know what he played, but I could swear that it was variations on a theme out of the Apocalypse. At first I could not see them distinctly, those four mystic animals, I could hear their voices only, especially the roaring of the lion and the screeching of the eagle [. . .] What Liszt played best of all was his rendering of the Valley of Jehoshaphat. There were lists as at a tournament, and around the immense enclosure the people pressed as spectators, deathly white and trembling. [. . .] A storm of applause was awarded to this performance of the valiant Liszt, who rose from the piano exhausted, and bowed to the ladies.[46]

Clearly, Heine and the other spectators were powerfully moved by Liszt's performance, ultimately crowning him the unquestioned victor in this competition. Even so—or perhaps especially for this reason—his decision to perform his transcription of "Il soave e bel contento" has perplexed many music historians: why did Liszt select this work for an event so crucial to the future of his career? Why not choose

---

Rimercata lists this aria among a group of others by Rossini and Bellini, for instance (ASTR, serie carteggio, anno 1842, scat. 19, fasc. III.2).

44. A fascinating study could be made of these transcriptions alone. I have identified the following composers and their interpretations of the aria from printed scores: Friedrich Burgmüller, *Cavatine de la Niobe: Fleurs mélodiques*, op. 82, 1re suite, no. 1 (piano solo); Giuseppe Cecchini, *Il soave e bel contento* (piano solo); Edward Hesselberg, *Niobe valse* (piano solo); Franz Hunten, *Trois airs italiens varies pour le piano-forte;* Henri Lemcke, *Variations brillantes sur un thème de Niobe* (piano solo); Domenico Liverani, *Fantasia sulla cavatina della Niobe di Pacini* (clarinet and piano); Nicolas Mori, *Il soave e bel contento* (violin and piano); Ignaz Moscheles, *Gems à la Pasta: a dramatic fantasia in which are introduced the favorite airs "Ombra adorata," "I tuoi frequenti palpiti," "Che farò," and "Ah come rapido"* (piano solo); Alfredo C. Piatti, *Caprices pour violoncelle seul;* and Camille Schubert, *2 rondeaux brillans pour le piano à quatre mains.* Furthermore, concert reviews attest to the existence of other instrumental transcriptions. Pianist Francesco Schoberlechner, for instance, presented his variations on "I tuoi frequenti palpiti" in concert at the Teatro Massimo, Bologna, a piece that was reviewed quite favorably in *Teatri arti e letteratura* (November 24, 1840).

45. Michael Saffle, *Liszt in Germany, 1840–1845: A Study in Sources, Documents, and the History of Reception* (Stuyvesant, N.Y.: Pendragon Press, 1994). See especially appendix C: "Sources and Evidence for Individual Concerts," 227–78.

46. Elizabeth A. Sharp, ed. and trans., *Heine in Art and Letters* (London: U. Scott, 1895), 23–24. Cited in Adrian Williams, *Portrait of Liszt: By Himself and His Contemporaries* (Oxford: Clarendon Press, 1990), 90.

one of his transcriptions of material drawn from a more popular opera such as his *Réminiscences des Puritains* (1836) or his *Marche e cavatine de Lucie di Lammermoor* (1835–1836)?[47] Having traced "Il soave e bel contento" through a variety of contexts, an answer begins to emerge: this piece may have been just as familiar to Liszt's spectators as any of the tunes he drew from Bellini's and Donizetti's works. Just how popular this music was only becomes clear with a survey of its travels as a favorite insertion.

Extant librettos, newspaper reviews, secondary sources, and miscellaneous documents reveal that singers introduced Pacini's aria into dozens of productions (see table 3.3). As this table illustrates, Pacini's aria had an enormous appeal to performers. Its textual and musical characteristics help explain why.

The aria's text consists of one double and one triple quatrain, (4 + 4) + (4 + 4 + 4). The initial lines, in *ottonario* (eight-syllable lines) furnished the text for the first movement of this double aria, the cantabile. The concluding lines shifted to *settenari* (seven-syllable lines) for the contrasting cabaletta. As a whole, the original text conveys the feelings of Licida happily anticipating the arrival of his lover, Asteria.

Il soave, e bel contento	The grateful words from my lips
Di quest'alma appien felice	cannot express all
Del mio labbro il grato accento	the sweet and beautiful happiness
Tutto esprimere non sa.	of this all-contented soul.
A' miei voti, al mio desire	On my wishes, on my hopes,
Fausto arrida il Nume Imene!	may the god Hymen smile propitiously!
Fiano eterne le catene	Let them be eternal, the chains
E di amore, e di amistà!	of love and of friendship!
I tuoi frequenti palpiti	O loving heart,
Deh frena o core amante!	restrain your frequent beating!
Or rivedrai l'amabile	Soon you will see the lovable
Oggetto del tuo ardor.	object of your passion once more.
La fiamma tua vorace	My eyes will express
Esprimerà il mio sguardo . . .	your ardent flame . . .
Dirò . . . mia bella face!	I will say . . . "my beautiful light!
Per te divampo ed ardo!	for you I smolder and burn!"
Vedrò quel vago ciglio,	I will see the pleasing mien
Che amor, candore addita . . .	that bespeaks love and innocence . . .
Tutto a goder m'invita!	Everything invites me to enjoy!
Pago sarai mio cor!	You will be content, my heart!

Most of this text is generic, making its introduction into a variety of dramatic situations a simple matter. Still, one line links it to its ancient Greek setting: the invocation of Hymen's good will in the second quatrain of the cantabile. To prevent disjunctions when inserting the number into new contexts, this line was often adjusted to something less specific—"Fausto arrida amore intanto" ("May love also smile happily")[48] or "Fausto arrida il dio del bene" ("May the God of love smile

---

47. My thanks to James Parakilas for pointing this matter out to me. See also Charlotte N. Eyerman and James Parakilas, "1820s to 1870s: The Piano Calls the Tune," in *Piano Roles,* ed. James Parakilas (New Haven, Conn.: Yale University Press, 1999), 193.

48. *La donna del lago* (Bologna, 1830) (I:Vgc).

TABLE 3.3.   Opera Productions in Which "Il soave e bel contento" / "I tuoi frequenti palpiti" Appeared

Opera	City	Theater	Season	Singer	Source
Didone abbandonata Mercadante	London	King's Theatre	July 1827	Giuditta Pasta	Libretto, I-Vgc
Sigismondo Rossini	Bologna	Teatro Comunale	Autumn 1827	Luigi Ravaglia	Libretto, I-Vgc
L'ultimo giorno di Pompei Pacini	Milan	Teatro alla Scala	Autumn 1827	Giovanni Battista Rubini	Libretto, I-Vgc and Vnm
Semiramide Rossini	Florence	Regio Teatro degl'Intrepidi	Autumn 1828	Giuditta Grisi	Libretto, I-Vgc
Otello Rossini	Milan	Teatro Carcano	Autumn 1829	Giuditta Pasta	Libretto, I-Vgc and Vnm
La donna del lago Rossini	Bologna	Teatro Comunale	Autumn 1830	Giovanni Battista Rubini	Libretto, I-Vgc
La straniera Bellini	Bologna	Teatro del Corso	Spring 1831	Carolina Ungher	*Teatri arti e letteratura* (June 23, 1831)
I normanni in Parigi (act I) Mercadante *La straniera* (act II)	Bologna	Teatro Comunale	Spring 1832	Carolina Ungher	*L'eco* (June 18, 1832)
La straniera	Paris	Théâtre Italien	Summer 1832	Giovanni Battista Rubini	Johnson[a]
L'ultimo giorno di Pompei	Genova	Teatro Carlo Felice	Carnival 1832	Francesco Pedrazzi	Libretto, I-Vgc
Gli arabi nelle Gallie Pacini	Spoleto	Teatro dei Nobili	Carnival 1832	Domenico Moretti	*Teatri arti e letteratura* (March 15, 1832)
La donna del lago	Genoa	Teatro Carlo Felice	Carnival 1832	Giovanni David	Libretto, I-Rsc
Otello	Milan	Teatro alla Scala	Carnival 1833	Giuditta Pasta	*L'eco* (January 20, 1832)
Elisa e Claudio Mercadante	New York	Bowery Theater	January 1833	Madame Pedrozzi	*Gazzetta privilgiata di* *Venezia* (March 1, 1833)

Opera / Composer	City	Theater	Date	Singer	Source
Otello	Venice	Teatro la Fenice	Carnival 1833	Giuditta Pasta	Libretto, I-Vnm
Il borgomastro di Saardam Donizetti	Turin	Teatro Carignano	Autumn 1833	Natalina Tassistro	Libretto, I-Vgc and I-Vnm
Mosè in Egitto Rossini	Sinigaglia	Nuovo Teatro di Sinigaglia	Fiera 1833	Giovanni Batista Rubini	Libretto, I-Vgc
Ricciardo e Zoraide Rossini	Bergamo	Teatro Riccardi	Fiera 1833	Giovanni David	Libretto, I-Vgc and Vnm
L'elisir d'amore Donizetti	Brescia	Teatro di Brescia	Carnival 1834	Fanny Corri-Paltoni	Libretto, I-Vnm
L'elisir d'amore	Mantua	Teatro Nuovo della Società	Spring 1834	Chiara Albertini	Libretto, I-Vnm
Le convenienze ed inconvenienze teatrale Donizetti	Cagliari	Civico Teatro di Cagliari	Carnival 1835	Luigi Rigamonti	Libretto, Biblioteca e Raccolta Teatro del Burcardo, Rome
La straniera	Lisbon	Teatro di S. Carlos	1835	Joao Storti	Libretto, I-Vgc
Otello	Venice	Teatro la Fenice	Spring 1835	Maria Malibran	Libretto, I-Vgc, Vnm, and Vlevi
Il pirata Bellini	Bergamo	Teatro Riccardi	August 24, 1837	Giovanni Battista Rubini	Kaufman[b]
Semiramide	Sassari	Teatro Civico di Sassari	Autumn 1837	Antonio Michelini	Libretto, I-Vgc
Otello	Cremona	Teatro della Concordia	September 1837	Elisa Taccani	Libretto, I-Vgc
Gemma di Vergy Donizetti	Trieste	Teatro Grande	Carnival 1839–1840	Sofia Schoberlechner	Libretto, I-Vgc
Otello	Venice	Teatro Apollo	Autumn 1840	Giuseppina Strepponi	Libretto, I-Rsc
Otello	Lucca	Teatro Giglio	Autumn 1841	Fanny Maray	*Teatri arti e letteratura* (September 30, 1841)
Belisario Donizetti	Verona	Teatro Filarmonico	Carnival 1842	Enrico Bonfigli	Libretto, I-Vgc

(continued)

TABLE 3.3.   (continued)

Opera	City	Theater	Season	Singer	Source
Otello	Perugia	Teatro Civico	Carnival 1842	Marietta Napoleona Albini	*Teatri arti e letteratura* (February 24, 1842)
Saffo Pacini	Fermo	Teatro dell'Aquila	August 1842	Clara Novello	Libretto, I-Vgc
L'ajo nell'imbarazzo Donizetti	Novara	Teatro di Novara	Autumn 1844	Eugenia Albani	Libretto, I-Vgc
Otello	Milan	Teatro alla Scala	Carnival 1846	Caterina Hayez	Libretto, I-Vgc
Otello	Venice	Teatro la Fenice	Spring 1846	Eugenia Garcia	Libretto, I-Vgc and Vnm
Il barbiere di Siviglia Rossini	Venice	Teatro San Benedetto	Spring 1846	Teresina Karker	*Gazzetta di Venezia* (May 11, 1846)
Il barbiere di Siviglia	London	Royal Italian Opera	Spring 1847	Maria Alboni	*Illustrated London News* (June 19, 1847)

[a]Janet Johnson, "Donizetti's First 'Affare di Parigi'," 169.
[b]Thomas G. Kaufman, "Giovan Battista Rubini," 153.

happily")[49]—or the entire stanza (and presumably the corresponding musical material) was eliminated altogether.[50] There were a few instances in which the sentiment of the text was revised, as in the 1827 Bolognese production of *Sigismondo*, in which Luigi Ravaglia, singing the role of the evil Ladislao, performed Pacini's aria in the middle of the second act. Here the character is in turmoil: once deeply in love with King Sigismondo's wife Aldamira, Ladislao conspired to have her killed when she rejected his amorous advances. Due to a twist of fate, she survived and returned to the kingdom disguised as the "look-alike" Egelinda, a presence who summons up guilt and longing in Ladislao's heart. Because a character wracked with such emotions would sound foolish uttering the optimistic sentiment of "Il soave e bel contento," small alterations appeared that turned around the meaning of the text. The first stanza, for example, became the following:

Il soave e bel contento	The sweet and beautiful happiness
Di quest'alma appien felice	of this all-contented soul,
È cangiato in rio tormento	is transformed into a river of torment
Da crudel fatalità.	of cruel fate.

Similarly drastic changes were made to the remainder of the poetry. Thus, although interpolating "Il soave e bel contento" occasionally required some effort to make it conform to its new dramatic surroundings, the text itself did not represent an obstacle.

Pacini's musical setting may also have facilitated the incorporation of "Il soave e bel contento" into a variety of operatic contexts: at the most superficial level, its double-aria structure parallels that of many other arias composed at this time, thus allowing it to function well as a replacement. Further, the presence of standard musical formulae—stock figures and gestures that became familiar to spectators either through Pacini's own work or through that of his contemporaries—may help explain why this aria had such a ubiquitous presence during the first half of the nineteenth century. Both the cantabile and the cabaletta bear some of these characteristics.[51]

Pacini gained his national reputation as a composer in the 1820s in a theatrical climate entrenched in the works of Giochino Rossini; in his memoirs, Pacini openly admits the profound effect this artist had on his own compositional development: "If I was the follower of the great man of Pesaro, so were all the others [. . .] At that time everyone followed the same school, the same style, and thus were imitators, like me, of the Great Star. But heavens! what was one to do if there was no other way

<hr>

49. *Il Mosè in Egitto* (Senigallia, 1833) (I:Vgc).

50. The following librettos for productions contain examples: *Semiramide* (Florence, 1828); *Saffo* (Fermo, 1842); *Ricciardo e Zoraide* (Bergamo, 1833); and *Gemma di Vergy* (Trieste, 1839). These librettos are all housed at I:Vgc.

51. Following *Niobe*'s run in Naples, Ricordi published five of its numbers in piano-vocal score: *Il sogno di Anfone*, "Fra le notturne tenebre"; *cavatina e duettino* [Niobe and Asteria], "Invan tuoi pregi ostenti"; *cavatina* [Licida], "Il soave e bel contento"; *preghiera di Anfione*, "S'è primo tuo vanto"; and *scena and aria* [Niobe], "Tuoni a sinistra il cielo." These are all available in Giovanni Pacini, *L'ultimo giorno di Pompei and Excerpts*, 257–321. The score of "Il soave e bel contento" (pp. 283–92) is introduced with the following note, indicating its popularity among prima donnas as well as tenors: "CAVATINA / *Il soave e bel contento* / Cantata dal Sig.ᵣ Rubini / *E trasportata per voce di Soprano* / *Con accompt.ᵗᵒ di Piano-Forte.*"

EXAMPLE 3.1.   Pacini, *Niobe,* "Il soave e bel contento," mm. 1–27

to make a living?"[52] Rossini's influence emerges most vividly in the slow movements of Pacini's arias, and "Il soave e bel contento" is no exception (see example 3.1).

The proliferation of vocal embellishments punctuating cadential points and the middle of phrases suggests a dependence on the tradition of florid writing popularized by his predecessor. In addition, Pacini adopted standard melodic structures from Rossini: "Il soave e bel contento" begins with a four-line primary section, di-

52. Cited and translated in Michael Rose, "A Note on Giovanni Pacini," *Musical Times* 124 (1983): 163.

Source: Milan: Ricordi, 1827, plate no. 3015.

vided between a florid opening with cadenza (mm. 1–9; each vocal phrase ends with a half cadence) and a lyrical continuation concluding with a perfect authentic cadence (mm. 10–19). This is elided with a secondary cantabile section (mm. 19–27)—the second quatrain preparing the cabaletta—acting as a kind of transition, underscoring an active dominant (mm. 23–27). His reliance on these, as well as other tried-and-true stylistic traits, however, did not make Pacini a slavish imitator. On the contrary, he consistently wove into each of his slow movements a mixture of convention and originality. The manner in which he toys with the melodic gesture of "Il soave e bel contento" is illustrative: this figure, first anticipated in the orchestra (mm. 2–4) and then heard in the vocal line (mm. 5–7), returns a final time (metrically displaced) toward the conclusion of this primary section (mm. 14–15). In its final appearance, Pacini altered its function considerably: although the first two incarnations are somewhat isolated, set slightly apart from what follows by firm half cadences, Pacini here expanded the phrase and this time led it to a conclusive perfect authentic cadence in m. 19. He began by reharmonizing the opening gesture with a $\text{vii}^{\circ 6}_{5}/\text{vi}$ diminished seventh that moves toward the submediant chord (m. 15). He then extended this inconclusive gesture by fragmenting the opening motive and placing it into a sequential pattern that broadens out to the dominant ($V^{6\text{–}7}_{4\ 3}$) in measure 16. An imperfect authentic cadence in measure 17 is immediately reactivated and led to full closure, via a cadenza, in measure 19. Although Pacini was certainly not the only composer to develop his melodic ideas in this manner, his talent for incorporating unexpected turns into his music consistently resulted in works that were at once derivative of his predecessor and yet unique. This achievement can be traced through his fast movements as well.

It was in his cabalettas that Pacini's reputation as a composer was most firmly established: during his lifetime he was known as the "maestro delle cabalette." The cabaletta of the present aria, "I tuoi frequenti palpiti," embodies features that he typically included within these movements (see example 3.2).

Here, for instance, the last movement opens with a playful, almost trivial quality: the rapid-march *topos* and the straightforward sixteenth notes in the melody, each separated by a sixteenth-note rest, create a steady pulsation analogous to excited heartbeats. The rhythmic energy is both underscored and intensified through the triplet sixteenths in the accompaniment. Set directly alongside this self-evidently imitative device, moreover, is an example of Pacini's characteristic attempts to break with standard, verse-bound rhythmic formulae. The "hook" of the opening phrase is the triplet repetition of the words, "deh frena" ("oh restrain"—or better, "oh *brake*"), in which the first repetition (flung forth, trilled in mm. 42–43) itself represents a sudden "braking" action within the melody, underpinned by a wrenching V^{4}_{3}/ii—ii chordal motion underneath. (The melody of the initial phrase then reproceeds, march-like, to its inconclusive "cadence" in m. 45.)

Together, these opening measures represent the first limb of a cabaletta whose theme as a whole foreshadows mid-century lyric form, a structure that Pacini typically employed in his early cabalettas, although he usually included some variations the standard aa′ba″ (or aa′bc) structure. Here the second, a′ section, for instance, slumps downward to a perfect authentic cadence in the "melancholy" submediant, G minor (m. 53). In addition, the b section of "I tuoi frequenti palpiti"—as usual,

Allegro
pp
I tuoi fre - quen - ti pal - pi - ti deh fre - na o - co - re a - man - te! deh
fre - - na deh fre na o cor - re a - man - te or ri - ve - drai l'a -
ma - bi - le og - get - to del tuo ar - do - re og - get - - to og-
get - to del tuo ar - dor. La fiam - ma tua vo - ra - ce es - prim - me - rà il mio
sguar - do di - rò mia bel - la fa - ce! per te di vam - po ed ar - do! di vam - po ed
ar - do! di vam - po ed ar - do ve - dro quel va - go ci - glio, che a - mo - re, ar - do re ad-

continued

EXAMPLE 3.2.   (continued)

Source: Milan: Ricordi, 1827, plate no. 3015.

prolonging the active dominant—sets four full lines of text rather than two (mm. 54–63). In the b section, moreover, we find an example of Pacini's gift for composing disjunct contours and abrupt rhythmic motives into his melodies. This central portion is built from two phrases over a dominant pedal. The second begins like the first but soon collapses with intermixture from B-flat minor (beginning with the unexpected D flats in m. 60), underscoring "divampo ed ardo!" and expanding the idea further with the gasping ascending sequential pattern in measures 61–63—articulating to the end of the B section with the common harmonic interruption on V. Nor is the concluding A section, the reprise (mm. 64–77) merely formulaic. Here, the return of the opening material begins predictably with a literal repetition of the music from measures 38–41, but this phrase takes an altogether different and more conclusive path to its final cadence in measure 77. In sum, Pacini's achievement in both the cantabile and cabaletta was his ability to play with more flexible listener expectations, setting up seemingly predictable patterns and then shifting away from them in a manner that provides a sense of breathless energy. (A "ritornello" interlude follows—not shown in the example—leading to a full repetition of the cabaletta, text and music, and a follows, rounding out the whole piece.)

At bottom, then, "Il soave e bel contento" / "I tuoi frequenti palpiti" illustrates how Pacini relied on musical conventions while simultaneously incorporating into these established structures a host of unusual twists and trajectories that surely contributed to the novelty and attractiveness of this piece. This explanation, however, does not tell the whole story. "Il soave e bel contento" was only one of many arias in Pacini's oeuvre to display the characteristics discussed here; furthermore, there was certainly an endless supply of pieces by his predecessors, contemporaries, and successors that embodied some or all of these features as well. It remains, then, to understand how and why "Il soave e bel contento" developed such strong currency as an insertion aria.

A COMMUNAL EXPERIENCE

When the curtain was drawn on *Niobe* for the final time at the end of 1826, neither Rubini nor Giuditta Pasta had forgotten about "Il soave e bel contento." Aware of the success this aria had brought, Rubini introduced it into at least five other productions throughout the remainder of his career and sang it in numerous concerts.[53] Each time he performed it, spectators went wild, as illustrated in a review of the 1830 production of *La donna del lago* at Bologna's Teatro Comunale: "And here we will limit ourselves to assuring our readers that the cavatina by Pacini from *Niobe,* sung by [Rubini] in Act II, is a piece of pure magic, so much so that it injects into you an electric fire that seeks out the innermost recesses of your heart, and stirs every fiber, leading you toward rapture, enthusiasm, delirium. Such is the art, the skill, and the force with which he performs [the aria]. Therefore . . . therefore, it is better to keep silent, and not to stretch too far for words with which to explain his worth."[54] By 1831, when another tenor, Francesco Pedrazzi, inserted Pacini's aria into a production of Pacini's *L'ultimo giorno di Pompei,* it had become so closely associated with Rubini that a critic reviewing the performance could simply refer to it as "Rubini's famous aria."[55] Similarly Pasta, who had been a firsthand witness to the number's success in Naples, quickly adopted it as one of her own warhorses. She used it as an insertion aria throughout her career, and featured it in a series of concert recitals following her retirement.[56] In a letter to her daughter, Pasta credited "Il soave e bel contento" as one of the three pieces ultimately responsible for elevating her to stardom.[57] It was an aria for which both of these singers had received countless ovations and ecstatic praise from audiences and critics alike.

Common sense might dictate, then, that singers whose careers had not scaled the heights of Pasta's and Rubini's would steer clear of "Il soave e bel contento" to

53. Rubini traveled widely, singing in concerts in addition to fully staged opera productions. Reviews published in *Teatri arti e letteratura* attest to the fact that as late as 1841, he was singing "Il soave e bel contento" in concerts in cities throughout Europe, including Amsterdam, Rotterdam, Utrect, and Wiesbaden. *Teatri arti e letteratura* 921 (October 14, 1841), and 922 (October 21, 1841).

54. "E solo ci limiteremo a far certi i nostri lettori che la cavatina di *Pacini* nella Niobe da esso lui cantata nel second'atto è un pezzo di musica affatto magico, e tale che t'insinua un fuoco elettrico che ti ricerca tutte le più riposte latebre del cuore, che ti scuote tutte le fibre fino a condurti all'ebbrezza, all'entusiasmo, al deliro, tanta è l'arte, il magistero, la forza con la quale per lui si eseguisce. Dunque . . . Dunque è meglio usare silenzio, e non estendersi in più lunghe parole a far chiaro il di lui valore." *Teatri arti e letteratura* 346 (November 4, 1830).

55. "The tenor Pedrazzi has a beautiful voice and he accents with much grace; he wished to sing the famous aria by Rubini, 'I tuoi frequenti palpiti,' and those who had not heard Rubini found Pedrazzi to be excellent." ("Pedrazzi tenore ha una bella voce ed accenta con molta grazia: esso volle cantare l'aria famosa di Rubini, *I tuoi frequenti palpiti,* e chi non aveva sentito Rubini, trovò eccellente il Pedrazzi.") *L'eco* (January 8, 1831).

56. Stern, *A Documentary Study of Giuditta Pasta,* 245, 253–54, and 257.

57. Letter dated October 1840 and cited in Maria Ferranti Giulini, *Giuditta Pasta e i suoi tempi: memorie e lettere raccolte* (Milan: Cromotipia E. Sormani, 1935), 180. In this letter Pasta writes, "You wanted to know which was the piece that brought the highest praise, and I wouldn't know if [it was] . . . 'I tuoi frequenti palpiti,' or the romanza 'di notte tremenda' or 'di tanti palpiti.'" ("Tu vuoi sapere qual fu il pezzo che portò la palma, e io non saprei se . . . 'I tuoi frequenti palpiti,' o la romanza 'di notte tremenda' oppure 'di tanti palpiti.'")

avoid inevitable, and perhaps unfavorable, comparison. But the reverse was true. Contemporary reviews suggest that performers often chose insertion arias intentionally to emulate these two legends and to encourage associations with them. In 1832, a critic covering an early production of Bellini's *I Capuleti e i Montechi,* during which the soprano Elisa Taccani introduced a different aria associated with Pasta, wrote the following: "Taccani, who sang the role of the lovely Giulietta, moved and surprised [. . .] the Turinese public showered her with applause, especially in the second-act aria, and in the interpolated cavatina of the first act, which is from *Sonnambula* ['Come per me sereno'] also by Maestro Bellini, written for Pasta, *and sung by Taccani in imitation of her*" (emphasis mine).[58] Taccani's choice of which aria to interpolate, in other words, was based on a conscious effort to align herself with Pasta's stardom and to compete with her voice.

A similar desire to associate themselves with Pasta and Rubini—to absorb some of their luster—was responsible, at least in part, for contemporaries' and successors' tendency to adopt "Il soave e bel contento" as an insertion aria. What better way to prove one's worth, after all, than to perform the signature tune of a star and to do so, perhaps, even better than the star him- or herself? Indeed, the potential rewards were many, as Carolina Ungher's experience illustrates. When Pasta's slightly younger colleague and the *seconda donna* in the premiere of *Niobe* introduced "Il soave e bel contento" into a pair of performances of *La straniera* in 1831, she received the highest praise: "It is no exaggeration to say that we were able to forget both Signora *Pasta* and *Rubini.*"[59] Ungher was no mere imitator, as witnessed in chapter 2— she followed the lead of her more illustrious predecessors, but transformed the music into something that could be identified as her own, and in doing so, she bolstered her reputation. Only a few years later, prima donnas were following *her* lead in selecting aria insertions. These associations with famous predecessors, and the potential rewards that performing their signature tunes could bring, help explain the popularity of some of the other favorite insertions listed in table 3.2 as well. In almost all cases, these arias can be traced back to one of the most renowned opera stars of the day. The practice of interpolating Pacini's "Ma dov'è? perché fugge i miei sguardi," for example, began with Nicola Tacchinardi, the popular tenor and author who spoke so defensively against aria insertion in his theater manual; and the first to employ Fioravanti's "Era notte scura scura" was Rossini's good friend and the first Figaro in *Il barbiere di Siviglia,* Luigi Zamboni. As far as I have been able to discern, moreover, the singers who initiated the trend of using "Or che son vicino a te" and "Nell'ebbrezza dell'amore" as borrowed material were Pasta and Maria Malibran, respectively.

Favorite insertions, therefore, often had direct links to one or two famous singers. These prima donnas and leading men set the "fashion" for their contempo-

58. "La Taccani, che sostiene la parte dell'amabile *Giulietta,* commosse e sorprese [. . .] ed il Pubblico Torinese la coprì d'applausi, massime nell'Aria dell'atto secondo, e nella intrusa Cavatina del primo, che è quella della *Sonnambula* dello stesso Maestro Bellini, scritta per la Pasta, e cantata dalla Taccani ad imitazione di lei." *L'eco* (May 28, 1832).

59. "Non è esagerato il dire che abbiamo dovuto dimenticare e la signora *Pasta* e *Rubini.*" *Teatri arti e letteratura* 379 (June 23, 1831). These performances took place at the Teatro Comunale, Bologna, in the spring season of 1831.

raries, authoring not only particular operatic moments, but also popularizing a sample of arias from which other singers occasionally drew. Although imitation was not the only factor determining which arias a singer would insert, it was a powerful one with some powerful implications, the most important having to do with the issue of canon formation.

The shift toward the modern repertory system of operas occurred gradually, and the task of identifying starting and ending points is complicated by the range of habits and customs that permeated every country (not to mention individual towns and cities) throughout Europe. Even so, most musicologists engaged with this issue map out a broad period between 1800 and 1875 as the time during which the practice of restaging older works replaced the continual and rapid production of new ones.[60] The stabilization of this repertory did not arise from a vacuum, but rather was founded on specific notions of value: coherence, originality, and dramatic truth—qualities thought to be inherent in the operatic works that made up this newly established repertory. What has not been fully recognized, however, is that at the same time that a canon of complete operas was being constituted, so, too, was a steady constellation of aria insertions. At bottom, the situation is ironic: the presence of favorite insertions in nineteenth-century productions suggests that the practice of aria interpolation and substitution—something that music historians have come to perceive as a destabilizing element within operatic texts—was made up, at least in part, of a stable group of works. The idea of a *repertory,* in other words, may have surfaced in the realm of the insertion aria concurrently with (or perhaps prior to) the time that the same concept was becoming associated with whole operas.[61] But if a sense of continuity permeated favorite insertions during the first half of the nineteenth century, what are we to make of repertories of aria insertions that appear during earlier periods? Might spectators who crowded into opera houses in the late-seventeenth century, for example, have perceived what Jennifer Williams Brown labeled recycling-box arias as a stable repertory as well?

Maybe, but this was probably not the case. The reason why may be attributed to an issue of frequency: Brown's recycling-box numbers did not surface as often as did such arias as "Il soave e bel contento," or others listed in table 3.2. At most, Brown identified the migration of a single piece through three operatic productions. Thus, although performers at that time were in the habit of sharing arias, the level of consistency was likely far lower than during the nineteenth century. The reception of favorite insertions and recycling-box arias, therefore, was diverse, for the earlier set could not have engendered the same sort of audience recognition as

---

60. See, for instance, Lydia Goehr, *The Imaginary Museum of Musical Works: An Essay in the Philosophy of Music* (Oxford: Clarendon Press, 1994); Joseph Kerman, "A Few Canonic Variations," *Critical Inquiry* 10 (1983): 107–26; Emmanuele Senici, "'Adopted to the Modern Stage': *La Clemenza di Tito* in London," *Cambridge Opera Journal* 7 (1995): 1–22; William Weber, *The Rise of Musical Classics in Eighteenth-Century England: A Study in Canon, Ritual, and Ideology* (Oxford: Clarendon Press, 1992); and Luca Zoppelli, "Intorno a Rossini: sondaggi sulla precezione della centralità del compositore," in *Gioachino Rossini 1792–1992: Il testo e la scena,* ed. Paolo Fabbri (Pesaro: Fondazione Rossini, 1994), 13–24.

61. See William Weber, *The Great Transformation of Musical Taste* (Cambridge: Cambridge University Press, 2008), 34, where he writes, "If aesthetic thinkers attributed canonic status to symphonies, musicians endowed opera selections and popular songs with canonic identity as they kept them in repertory."

did the later—spectators simply had fewer opportunities to become familiar with them.

This issue, however, was determined by more than events occurring within the opera house; it also resulted from differing modes of private music making. Thomas Christensen has explored how such public genres as operas and symphonies began to be appropriated into the private realm toward the end of the eighteenth century by means of the keyboard arrangement.[62] One of the primary catalysts for this development was the burgeoning presence of the piano in European parlors and living rooms starting around 1770. The popularizing of this instrument brought with it an unprecedented demand for musical scores of all sorts, which included not only works composed specifically for the piano, but also transcriptions of symphonies and arrangements of operatic works in piano-vocal format. The growing market for these scores throughout the nineteenth century, Christensen argues, created a radical and irrevocable alteration of the identity of operatic works. What had once been tethered to the theater could now be experienced, learned, contemplated, and criticized within the private sphere. This new intimacy altered the manner in which operatic works could be received; and conversely, spectators, newly able to play through their favorite operas at home, demanded the presentation of these works in the theater as well. A new sort of permanence was established that relied on a fluid interaction between public and private, and that served as one of the principal means by which the modern system of a stable repertory was constituted.

It is in a similar sense that individual extracts—arias and ensembles—could have gained a canonic persona as well. It was common practice throughout Europe for publishers to release the most popular numbers from an opera in piano-vocal arrangement as soon as possible after the premiere.[63] Thus numbers such as "Il soave e bel contento" and "Or che son vicino a te" had the potential to develop active followings outside the opera house as well as within. Favorite insertions, therefore, represented more than the preferred music of individual singers—they were also arias popularized in the private arena: they represented *everyone's* favorites. Such participation among audiences was impossible until the sort of domestic consumption enabled by piano-vocal transcriptions existed. Consequently, the recycling-box arias that Brown identified could not have obtained the status of repertorial works that favorite insertions were able to attain.

The presence of a repertory of substitute arias in nineteenth-century productions illustrates one more irony: the aesthetic forces that encouraged a stable set of interpolations to coalesce were precisely those that hastened their demise. Along with the canonization of operatic works came the conviction that they should be performed according to the author's design—that is, without aria insertions. Thus

62. He has investigated these arrangements in two separate articles, both of which I gloss here: "Four-Hand Piano Transcriptions and Geographies of Nineteenth-Century Musical Reception," *Journal of the American Musicological Society* 52 (1999): 255–98, and "Public Music in Private Spaces: Piano-Vocal Scores and the Domestication of Opera," in *Music and the Cultures of Print,* ed. Kate van Orden (New York: Garland, 2000), 67–93.

63. In fact, the publication of excerpts preceded that of whole operas in Italy: Ricordi began publishing individual numbers in 1808, but he did not acquire the rights to publish whole operas until 1823. See Philip Gossett, "The Ricordi Numerical Catalogue: A Background," *Notes* 42 (1985): 25.

by the close of the century, the function of the favorite insertion had virtually disappeared. This evaporation explains why numbers like "Il soave e bel contento" and "Or che son vicino a te" are no longer heard in today's theaters—without revivals of *Niobe* and *Il Conte di Lenosse,* the possibility of experiencing their most popular arias during an operatic performance is small. Once pushed to the sidelines on stage, favorite insertions became obscured from all other realms of musical performance as well. Recordings, for instance, are practically nonexistent; and even though modern scores are available for a few of these works, there are others (such as Fioravanti's "Era notte scura, scura") for which it is difficult to locate even nineteenth-century editions. The loss of function within the public realm was fatal for these numbers. Even though they represented some of the most popular tunes of the nineteenth century, they could not survive in the private sphere alone. Their livelihood depended on their ability to travel back and forth between these distinct musical geographies, and their extinction became inevitable when such interplay was no longer possible. The idea that the nineteenth century witnessed the establishment of a "canon" of aria insertions thus hits a serious snag, caught up on those notions of value cited above (coherence, originality, dramatic truth) that serve as the centralizing forces in the establishment of any musical repertory. Aria insertions are, by their very nature, entities that eschew these characteristics, and thus the parallel between a repertory of operatic works and a repertory of aria insertions falters. And yet, it is not severed entirely, for, as this chapter has illustrated, there is reason to believe that favorite insertions such as "Il soave e bel contento" may have been perceived as coherent, original works unto themselves, rooted in their own dramatic truths. This mode of reception was ephemeral, of course, but for a brief period of time, these arias carried with them the same ideals of coherence and originality— even when performed in the context of a variety of operatic works—as did many full-length operas.

Although such composers as Pacini, Fioravanti, and Persiani were not known as one-hit wonders to many nineteenth-century audiences, it may be useful to think of them in such terms today, at a time when one of the central tasks of Italian opera scholars is the piecing together of critical editions. We cannot recover all of the music of all of the nineteenth-century Italian opera composers—the time and resources necessary are well beyond our means and the outcome probably not very useful. But identifying their favorite insertions—their hit (or hits)—provides an interesting and economical way of getting at those pieces that had the strongest impact on nineteenth-century audiences and that have until now remained largely overlooked. Most of Pacini's, Fioravanti's, and Persiani's operas will never make it back onto our operatic stages—but perhaps a few of their arias should.

CHAPTER 4

MARIA MALIBRAN,

I CAPULETI E I MONTECCHI,

AND A TALE OF SUICIDE

By now it is evident that Italian operas were wide open to the presence of fa-vorite insertions and trunk arias regardless of what theaters hosted the produc-tion, which impresario was in charge, and which cast of singers was participating. Virtually no *bel canto* work composed prior to 1840 or so, whether by Rossini, Don-izetti, Bellini, or one of their many contemporaries, was immune, and even music now most fondly associated with an opera was susceptible to replacement. Take the mad scene of Donizetti's *Lucia di Lammermoor,* that explosive moment of romantic *jouissance* when the title character, having brutally stabbed her new husband in their wedding chamber and drenched herself in his blood, performs a double aria ("Ardon gli incesi" / "Spargi d'amaro pianto") before collapsing to the ground and dying of grief. Today, staging this opera without this music would be unthinkable, robbing Donizetti's work of what is widely perceived to be its *raison d'être.* But such was not always the case: shortly following the opera's premiere, Lucia's famous aria was replaced by the rondò finale from one of Donizetti's earlier operas, *Fausta* (Naples, Teatro San Carlo, January 12, 1832). At least four productions were af-fected, and this alteration was performed by some of the most well respected prima donnas of the time including Eugenia Tadolini and Giuseppina Strepponi.[1] The mad scene quickly recuperated its original shape as audiences, critics, and singers alike grew to perceive "Ardon gli incensi" and its cabaletta as integral components of *Lucia di Lammermoor,* but not every scene and every opera "bounced back" in a similar fashion.[2]

1. The rondò finale was "Tu che voli già spirito beato" / "Non, qui morir degg'io." The four pro-ductions I have identified that include this substitution are as follows: Parma, Teatro Ducale, carnival 1836–1837, Mathilde Palazzesi as Lucia (Libretto: I:Vgc); Bologna, Teatro Comunale, spring 1837, Giuseppina Strepponi as Lucia (Letter: Lanari to Donizetti, Bologna, May 22, 1837, in Jeremy Com-mons, "Una corrispondenza tra Alessandro Lanari e Donizetti," *Studi donizettiani* 3 [1978]: 47); Florence, Teatro della Pergola, autumn 1837, Eugenia Tadolini as Lucia (Libretto: I:Vgc); and Turin, Teatro Regio, carnival 1837–1838, Mathilde Palazzesi as Lucia (Libretto: I:Vgc).

2. I have explored the topic of Lucia's mad scene at length in Poriss, "A Madwoman's Choice: Aria Substitution in *Lucia di Lammermoor,*" *Cambridge Opera Journal* 13 (2001): 1–28. Although Donizetti's original aria became a fixed component of the opera quickly following its premiere, the music itself was

Some operas circulating in the repertory were subject to excessive change, singers substituting and interpolating arias and even ensembles at various and seemingly random moments in the scores. Not surprisingly, the older the opera, and the longer it lingered on European stages, the more likely this sort of extreme manipulation was apt to occur: Mayr's *La rosa bianca e la rosa rossa* (Genoa, San Agostino, 1813), for example, included multiple numbers by multiple composers during the same production more frequently than did Rossini's *La donna del lago* (Naples, Teatro San Carlo, 1819), which in turn hosted more than Ricci's *Chiara di Rosemberg* (Milan, La Scala, 1831).[3] Although, as we will see, some works composed as late as the 1830s were subject to extreme alteration as well, timing had much to do with how freely singers treated a score.

Whether the opera was tragic, semi-serious, or comic, on the other hand, seems to have mattered little: some serious works were inundated by aria insertions just as were those in the comic realm. Thus, to take one example, Rossini's *L'assedio di Corinto* (the Italian translation of *Le Siège de Corinthe* [Paris, Opéra, 1826], which the composer adapted from *Maometto II* [Naples, Teatro San Carlo, 1820]), was frequently treated to revivals such as the one that occurred at the Teatro Apollo, Rome in the spring of 1830. For this performance, not only did Filippo Galli (Maometto) and Matilde Kyntherland Cascelli (Pamira) perform the duet cabaletta "Pietoso all'amor mio" that Donizetti composed in 1828 as a replacement for Rossini's original music; so, too, did Isabella Fabrica Montrésor (Neocle) insert two arias; and Cascelli made the daring choice of adding a buffa aria to the score.[4] Despite what was undoubtedly a noticeable clash between serious and comic, a disparity that Tacchinardi warned no audience would tolerate, spectators received the production enthusiastically, one critic commenting that "From the *sinfonia* until the third [-act] finale all of the pieces were energetically applauded, and the primary singers were called to the stage many times to share with the audience their mutual satisfaction."[5]

Though other operas such as Rossini's *Aureliano in Palmira* and Donizetti's *Le con-*

---

by no means immutable, most notably in the famous cadenza for flute and voice. As Romana Margherita Pugliese has shown, this cadenza was most likely written by the German mezzo-soprano and singing teacher Mathilde Marchesi and was first introduced into the mad scene by Nellie Melba at the Opéra Garnier, Paris in 1889. See Pugliese, "The Origins of *Lucia di Lammermoor*'s Cadenza," *Cambridge Opera Journal* 16 (2004): 23–42.

3. The popularity of *La rosa rossa* and *La donna del lago* is well known. Marcello Conati has demonstrated that Ricci's *Chiara di Rosemberg* was the fifth most frequently revived opera on Italian stages during the decade spanning 1830–1839. See Conati, "Presenze delle opere di Donizetti nei teatri italiani nella prima metà dell'Ottocento," in *L'opera teatrale di Gaetano Donizetti. Atti del Convegno Internazionale di Studio, Bergamo, 17–20 settembre 1992,* ed. Francesco Bellotto, (Bergamo: Comune di Bergamo, 1993), 435.

4. Alberto Cametti, *Il teatro di Tordinona poi di Apollo,* 2 vols. (Rome: A. Cicca, 1938), 2: 435–36. For information on "Pietoso all'amor mio," see Weinstock, *Donizetti and the World of Opera in Italy, Paris and Vienna in the First Half of the Nineteenth Century* (New York: Pantheon Books, 1963), 61–62, and for a detailed account of cuts and other alterations to *L'assedio di Corinto,* see Philip Gossett, Review of Gioachino Rossini, *L'assedio di Corinto,* recording on Angel Records SCLX–3819, *Musical Quarterly* 61 (1975): 626–38.

5. "Dalla sinfonia sino al terzo finale furono vivamente applauditi tutti i pezzi, e i primarj Cantanti vennero più volte sul proscenio a dividere col Pubblico il reciproco gradimento." *Teatri arti e letteratura* 16 (April 22, 1830): 4.

venienze ed inconvenienze teatrali were treated in a fashion similar to that of their eighteenth-century counterparts, extreme tampering with any one score on a regular basis became more the exception than the rule. Increasingly throughout the first half of the nineteenth century, singers tended to perform insertion arias at specific moments in an opera, rather than randomly throughout the work. Again, *Lucia* provides a vivid example: although the mad scene was briefly a site of aria substitution, the only moment in the opera that was affected regularly by such changes was the Act I fountain scene, in which Donizetti's original aria ("Regnava nel silenzio") was replaced with numbers by Giuseppe Persiani, Nicola Vaccai, as well as those drawn from Donizetti's other operas.[6] We have seen, moreover, how prima donnas in the role of Elena in *Marino Faliero* interpolated numbers into the opera, but only at their entrance. And performances of *L'elisir d'amore,* to take a less familiar example, frequently included substitutions, but only in the second act, in which Adina's final aria, "Prendi per me sei libero" / "Il mio rigor dimentica," was frequently replaced by other pieces.[7]

Notable in these and similar changes is that explanations for their appearances can be located not directly with the desires and demands of individual singers, but with what was perceived broadly—by critics and audiences, as well as by singers—as inadequacies with the scores themselves. "Regnava nel silenzio," for example, was an idiosyncratic number, built of a loose additive structure that might have made it seem disorganized; almost immediately following the opera's premiere, prima donnas sought to replace it with more conventional arias.[8] The reason that sopranos frequently changed their final aria in *L'elisir d'amore* has an equally understandable explanation. The cabaletta ("Il mio rigor dimentica") was an old-fashioned piece for 1832, using the kind of triplet figuration that Rossini employed in several of his cabalettas and consisting almost entirely of monotonous repetitions of ascending and descending scalar passages. It comes as little surprise, therefore, that sopranos re-

6. In the spring of 1837 at the Teatro Compadroni, Pavia, for example, Adelaide Mazza replaced Lucia's original cabaletta, "Quando rapito in estasi," with "Nell'ebbrezza dell'amore" from *Ines de Castro* by Giuseppe Persiani (I:Vgc). Emilia Kallez made the same alteration a year later in the town of Novara (I:Vgc). In the fall of 1837 at the Teatro della Pergola, Florence, Eugenia Tadolini omitted all of Donizetti's original music and replaced it with the double aria, "Io talor più nol rammento" / "Se contro lui mi parlano" from Donizetti's *Sancia di Castiglia* (I:Vgc). At least two sopranos replaced "Regnava nel silenzio" with "Al pensier m'appare ognora": Eugenia Garcia (Teatro Riccardi, Bergamo, summer 1838, I:Vgc) and Benedetta Coleoni Cori (Teatro Eretenio, Vincenza, autumn 1838, I:Vnm, dramm. 891.10). Mathilde Palazzesi replaced Lucia's cabaletta during a performance at the Teatro Regio in Turin, carnival 1837–1838. She sang "Al sol pensiero del mio contento" from *Il precipizio, o Le fucine di Norvegia* by Nicola Vaccai (I:Vgc).

7. Arias that sopranos introduced into this moment included "Il soave e bel contento" (Adina: Fanny Corri-Paltoni, Brescia, Teatro di Brescia, carnival 1834; Adina: Chiara Albertini, Mantua, Teatro Nuovo della Società, spring 1834); "Contenti e placidi," from *Aver moglie è poco* by Bornacini (Adina: Adelaide Maldotti, Cremona, Teatro della Concordia, carnival 1834), and "Nò che infelice appieno," from *Ugo, Conte di Parigi* by Donizetti (Adina: Fanny Tacchinardi-Persiani, Naples, Teatro del Fondo, spring 1834; Adina: unidentified, Verona, Teatro Filarmonico, carnival 1840). Malibran performed a setting of "Prendi per me sei libero" composed either by her or her husband, Charles de Bériot (see Remo Giazotto, *Maria Malibran (1808-36): Una vita nei nomi di Rossini e Bellini* [Turin: ERI, 1986], 364–66).

8. For a discussion of this aria and its connections to Lucia's unstable mental state, see Mary Ann Smart, "The Silencing of Lucia," *Cambridge Opera Journal* 4 (1992): 119–41.

placed this rather uninspiring piece (and sometimes the slow movement as well) with something more apt to please, especially since it follows Nemorino's show-stopping "Una furtiva lagrima."

The presence of regular patterns of substitution and interpolation by no means constituted a set of fixed and unbreakable rules; quite often singers chose to perform these scenes as the composer wrote them, and on occasion, aria insertions appeared at moments in an opera that were not typically affected by such pieces. Nevertheless, these changes tended to gravitate more and more toward one or two particular sites within individual scores, rendering aria insertion more predictable than it had been during the eighteenth century, and suggesting an interesting possibility: during the nineteenth century, the practice of aria insertion mirrored changes that had been taking place in Italian opera as a whole. Just as a consolidated international repertory of works was being established, and just as a repertory of aria insertions was forming (as we saw in the previous chapter), so, too, was a confined number of scenes in which aria insertion was most likely to occur beginning to form. Stability, in other words, was becoming more prevalent not only in the operas that were performed, but in the manner in which they tended to be altered.

One of the most "canonic" alterations to a nineteenth-century score occurred in revivals of Bellini's *I Capuleti e i Montecchi* (Venice, Teatro la Fenice, March 11, 1830), and it is on this opera, its performance history, and most centrally, its close association with one prima donna, Maria Malibran (1808–1836), that this chapter focuses (see figure 4.1 for an image of Malibran). In the autumn of 1832, when this mezzo-soprano was at the height of her fame—recognized widely as one of the most accomplished and exciting prima donnas touring the international operatic circuit—she arrived at Bologna's Teatro Comunale, where she took on the trousers role of Romeo for the first time. No different from other celebrated singers of the first half of the nineteenth century, Malibran was accustomed to approaching unfamiliar scores with a sense of freedom, making use of aria insertions when necessary. What she and her fellow costar Giuliettas did with the final scene of *I Capuleti e i Montecchi,* the "tomb scene," however, was extraordinary (indeed, the term *aria insertion* is hardly sufficient): they eliminated all of Bellini's music and replaced it with the corresponding scene from the older, but still popular, *Giulietta e Romeo* by Nicola Vaccai (Milan, Teatro della Cannobiana, October 31, 1825). Like many other substitutions that occurred within the *bel canto* repertory, this one did not disappear when the final curtain of the season was drawn. Following the Bologna production, Malibran took on the role of Romeo on at least five other occasions, each time trading in Bellini's music for Vaccai's.[9] What is more, beginning as early as

9. This information was obtained from librettos published for each of the productions in which Malibran participated, and verified in some cases by newspaper reviews. For the Bologna production, the soprano in the role of Giulietta was Sofia Schoberlechner; the libretto is housed in I:Vgc. As I will discuss below, the fact that these two singers performed Vaccai's music in place of Bellini's is corroborated by a lengthy review published on the occasion of the opening night in *Teatri arti e letteratura* 450 (November 3, 1832): 71–74. The second time Malibran sang in this opera was two years later, also at the Teatro Comunale in Bologna (May 1834), but I have not seen a libretto for this production. Instead, evidence appears in another review published in *Teatri arti e letteratura:* "Bologna—Gran Teatro della Co-

FIGURE 4.1.   Maria Malibran. *Source:* CAN 30 Malibran.JPG; Museo Teatrale alla Scala—Archivio e Biblioteca, Milan.

1833 other divas began to follow her lead, performing the opera "alla Malibran" rather than "alla Bellini." Extant librettos reveal that nearly two-thirds of all productions that occurred between 1833 and 1857 featured the Vaccai ending.[10] The practice of replacing Bellini's music with Vaccai's had become so common, in fact, that a piano-vocal score published by Ricordi includes Vaccai's scene in an appen-

---

mune—*Giovedì 8 maggio*—*Secondo atto della* Sonnambula. *Seconda, terza e quarta parte dei* Capuleti e i Montecchi" (530 [May 10, 1834]: 97). The soprano in the role of Giulietta for this production was Giuseppina Ruiz-Garcia. Ruiz-Garcia costarred with Malibran in her next three appearances as Romeo as well. These productions were as follows: Senigallia, Teatro Comunale, summer 1834 (libretto: I:Vgc); Lucca, Teatro del Giglio, summer 1834 (libretto: I:Vgc); and Milan, Teatro alla Scala, autumn 1834 (libretto: I:Vnm, dramm. 3326). The last time Malibran sang in *I Capuleti e i Montecchi,* Schoberlechner was once again her costar: Milan, Teatro alla Scala, carnival 1836 (libretto: I:Vnm, dramm. 3333.13).

10. These figures were gathered through a survey of forty-nine extant librettos for productions of *I*

dix. A note prefacing it reads, "To be substituted, if desired, as is generally done, for the last scene of Bellini's opera."[11]

The ubiquity of this change and its institutionalization has compelled nearly every commentator since 1832 to weigh in on its merits.[12] A resounding testament to the fascination that the alteration continues to exert is the recent publication of two new scholarly explorations of the topic: the first, an expansive article by Michael Collins sketching out the production history of *I Capuleti e i Montecchi;* the second by Claudio Toscani, a detailed exploration of the reception of the tomb-scene alteration throughout European centers during the nineteenth century.[13] Although Collins focuses some attention on the Vaccai substitution, dealing briefly with its reception, the scope of his study extends beyond this singular alteration, his goal being to follow Italian productions of the opera from 1830 through 1871, identifying and analyzing any additions or substitutions made to Bellini's score during those years.[14] Toscani's essay, on the other hand, was written in conjunction with his work as editor of the critical edition of *I Capuleti e i Montecchi,* and as such, his mission falls primarily with reconstructing the "authentic" performance history of this work. The Vaccai substitution, inauthentic yet integral to the opera's identity, is the only such alteration to Bellini's work that he treats in detail. Even though

---

Capuleti e i Montecchi housed in Venice (Biblioteca Nazionale Marciana [I:Vnm] and the Fondazione Giorgio Cini [I:Vgc]). See Poriss, *Artistic License: Aria Interpolation and the Italian Operatic World, 1816–1850* (Ph.D. diss., University of Chicago, 2000), 184.

11. "Da sostituirsi, volendo, come generalmente si practica, all'ultimo pezzo dell'opera di Bellini." Vincenzo Bellini, *I Capuleti e i Montecchi* (Milan: Ricordi, 188–). The appendix is located on pp. 137–53 of this score.

12. See, for example, Julian Budden, Elizabeth Forbes, and Simon Maguire, "I Capuleti e i Montecchi," in *New Grove Online,* ed. Laura Macy, http://www.grovemusic.com (accessed March 4, 2007); Winton Dean, "Shakespeare and Opera," in *Shakespeare in Music,* ed. Phyllis Hartnoll (London: Macmillan, 1964), 148; Francesco Florimo, "*La Giulietta* del Vaccaj e *i Capuleti* del Bellini," in *La scuola musicale di Napoli e i suoi conservatorii,* 2nd ed. (Naples: Stabilmento tip. V. Morano, 1880–1883), 3: 252–55; Philip Gossett, introductions to Bellini, *I Capuleti e i Montecchi* (New York: Garland, 1981), n.p., and Vaccai, *Giulietta e Romeo* (New York: Garland, 1989), n.p.; Charles Osborne, *The Bel Canto Operas* (Portland, Ore.: Amadeus Press, 1994), 329–31; Roberto di Perna, "Forgetting Shakespeare," in Bellini, *I Capuleti e i Montecchi* (Nuova Era 7020–21), liner notes, 8; Giulio Vaccaj, *Vita di Nicola Vaccaj* (Bologna: Nicola Zanichelli, 1882), 142–47. Accounts of this alteration also appear in every biography of Maria Malibran. See, for instance, Howard Bushnell, *Maria Malibran: A Biography of a Singer* (University Park: Pennsylvania State University Press, 1979), 144–47 and 163; April FitzLyon, *Maria Malibran: Diva of the Romantic Age* (London: Souvenir Press, 1987), 177; and Remo Giazotto, *Maria Malibran,* 228. At least one modern recording includes a performance of Vaccai's last act in addition to Bellini's original (see *I Capuleti e i Montecchi,* BMG/RCA Vic 68899).

13. Michael Collins, "Bellini and the *Pasticcio alla Malibran:* A Performance History of *I Capuleti e i Montecchi,*" *Note su note* 9–10 (2002): 109–52; and Claudio Toscani, "Bellini e Vaccaj: peripezie di un finale," in *Vincenzo Bellini nel secondo centenario della nascita,* ed. Graziella Seminara and Anna Tedesco (Florence: Leo S. Olschki, 2004), 535–67. Much of what Toscani discusses in his article is also included in his introduction to the critical edition of *I Capuleti e i Montecchi.* See Vincenzo Bellini, *I Capuleti e i Montecchi,* ed. Claudio Toscani, in *Edizione critica delle opere di Vincenzo Bellini,* vol. 6 (Milan: Ricordi, 2003), xi–xxix. In addition, Philip Gossett discusses this alteration and its aftermath in *Divas and Scholars: Performing Italian Opera* (Chicago: University of Chicago Press, 2006), 211–12.

14. Collins, "Bellini and the *Pasticcio alla Malibran,*" 109.

both studies mention that Malibran played a central role in the reception of this alteration, neither explores why or how, which is what I intend to do here.

Distinct though Collins's and Toscani's studies are, each introduces a pair of important overlapping details, the first of which can be addressed right away, the second of which merits fuller discussion below. Both articles present the fairly startling discovery that Maria Malibran was not, in fact, the first singer in the role of Romeo to perform Vaccai's tomb scene in place of Bellini's. That "honor," as it were, goes to the prima donna Santina Ferlotti, who introduced the new music during a benefit production of *I Capuleti e i Montecchi* at the Teatro della Pergola, Florence, on February 26, 1831 (there is no evidence that the alteration was performed during the normal run of the opera).[15] Collins interprets this information as highly significant, arguing that Malibran "must cede precedence regarding the substitution of the Vaccai tomb scene," but how she would do this, or why, is unclear.[16] Toscani makes no such pronouncement, remarking only that "her example became a school of thought" ("il suo esempio fece scuola"), and in leaving it at that, he edges closer to a vital point: regardless of whether Malibran was the first to make this alteration, there can be no doubt that it was she—not Ferlotti, not her cooperating costar Giuliettas, not any other prima donna—with whom it became intimately associated.[17] The question more fruitfully posed, therefore, is why did it become known as the "pasticcio alla Malibran"? Her unparalleled fame certainly played a role. As our discussion of favorite insertions in chapter 3 demonstrated, alterations to operatic scores that took on a canonic persona can typically be traced back to a first-rate performer. What remains to be explored are the means by which Malibran exerted agency over this scene and over its continuation within the repertory. This example helps explain more generally how singers' fame and personas become wrapped up in the alterations they made to operatic scores, and how those connections helped to generate, or at least perpetuate, a fashion for change.

The second detail revealed by Collins and Toscani regarding Malibran's performances in this opera is that—contrary to what most secondary sources lead one to believe—substituting the Vaccai ending was not the only alteration that she and her costar Giuliettas made.[18] Librettos and newspaper reviews reveal two additional major changes to Bellini's score that have received only passing attention. The first, in fact, merits brief mention because it probably occurred only once, at Malibran's initial appearance as Romeo in Bologna. During this production, she and Sofia Schoberlechner eliminated the Act I *scena e duetto* between Romeo and Giulietta, "Sì, fuggire: a noi non resta," in favor of a new duet: "Tremante, palpitante," composed by Filippo Celli for his little known and little performed opera *Ezio* (Rome,

---

15. Both authors glean this information from an article published in *Il censore universale* 22 (March 16, 1831): 86–87. See Collins, "Bellini and the *Pasticcio alla Malibran*," 133; Toscani, "Bellini e Vaccaj," 546. Also, see Heather Hadlock, "On the Cusp between Past and Future: The Mezzo-Soprano Romeo of Bellini's *I Capuleti*," *Opera Quarterly* 17 (2001): 420, where she cites the article.

16. Collins, "Bellini and the *Pasticcio alla Malibran*," 134.

17. Toscani, "Bellini e Vaccaj," 547.

18. The identification of and information regarding these additional changes contained in this paragraph are also found in Poriss, *Artistic License,* 171–82.

Teatro Argentina, 1824).[19] This duet was well received at the Teatro Comunale, the critic for *Teatri arti e letteratura* commenting that "the duet by Cavalier *Celli* from *Ezio,* which possesses many good qualities, above all in the largo, was performed with the most exquisite perfection that it would be absolutely impossible to surpass it, and even one might say, to equal it."[20] Regardless of this praise, there is no evidence that any Romeo and Giulietta performed it in the context of Bellini's opera ever again.[21] The second alteration also involved a duet: for every production in which Malibran participated, she and whoever performed the role of Giulietta (either Schoberlechner or Giuseppina Ruiz-Garcia) interpolated Mercadante's "Vanne: se alberghi in petto" from *Andronico* (Venice, La Fenice, December 26, 1821), this time replacing none of Bellini's music. Unlike Celli's duet, Mercadante's had a long-lasting impact on the performance history of *I Capuleti e i Montecchi* that—like the tomb-scene alteration—was also tied to Malibran's unique biographical story, or, rather, to one of its most interesting facets: her premature death following a violent horse-riding accident in 1836 at the tragically young age of twenty-eight. These connections emerge gradually, beginning with the early reception of the opera.

BELLINI VERSUS VACCAI

Unfairly condemned by critics during the nineteenth century and much of the twentieth century for its unfaithfulness to Shakespeare, Romani's libretto for *I Capuleti e i Montecchi* diverges significantly from the story of Romeo and Juliet narrated by the famous playwright. As is now well known, Romani's immediate source for Bellini's opera was not Shakespeare, but rather the libretto he wrote for Vaccai's version of the opera in 1825, a work he based on retellings of the tragedy by the French playwright Jean François Ducis (*Roméo et Juliette,* 1772), the Italian playwright Luigi Scevola (*Giulietta e Romeo,* 1818), and on the synopsis for a ballet choreographed by Antonio Cherubini and first performed at the Teatro Concordia in Cremona in 1820 (*Le tombe di Verona, ossia Giulietta e Romeo*).[22] One of many points during which plot

19. Evidence for only two productions of this opera exists: the premiere, and a second that occurred at the Teatro della Pergola, Florence, carnival 1830 (libretto, I-Fm [Mel.2062.20]).

20. "Il duetto del Cav. *Celli* nell'*Ezio,* che sopra tutto nel largo ha molto pregio, fu eseguito colla perfezione la più squisita, ed impossibile assolutamente a superarsi, e quasi direbbesi ad uguagliare." *Teatri arti e letteratura* 450 (November 3, 1832): 72.

21. As Collins points out, the text for Celli's duet appears in two more librettos associated with Malibran's appearances as Romeo: those for Senigallia 1834 and Lucca 1834. A few pieces of circumstantial evidence suggest that the duet was not sung during these productions, however: first, the Senigallia and Lucca librettos were reprints of the Bologna libretto, and thus they may not reflect what was actually performed. Second, the Giulietta for these two productions was Giuseppina Ruiz-Garcia, not Schoberlechner. In the libretto printed specifically for the production of *I Capuleti e i Montecchi* performed at La Scala in 1834, in which Ruiz-Garcia also sang the role of Giulietta, the text for Celli's duet does not appear suggesting that she never sang the piece. Collins, "Bellini and the *Pasticcio alla Malibran,*" 136.

22. Romani's sources and their influence on his librettos, both for Vaccai and Bellini, have been charted meticulously by Michael Collins, "The Literary Background of Bellini's *I Capuleti e i Montecchi,*" *Journal of the American Musicological Society* 35 (1982): 532–38.

differences emerge between Bellini's and Vaccai's works and Shakespeare's play is in the concluding scene of the operas: Romeo arrives at Giulietta's tomb, and believing her to be dead, poisons himself. She awakens to find him fading away, and the two enjoy a brief reunion before the drug takes its fatal toll.

At its Venetian premiere, *I Capuleti e i Montecchi* was an unmitigated success, both music and cast—which included Giuditta Grisi as Romeo and Maria Caradori-Allen as Giulietta—receiving rave reviews. Remarks published in *L'eco,* for instance, bestowed particular praise on Tebaldo's "truly beautiful" entrance aria ("È serbato a questo acciaro"), the first-act duet between Giulietta and Romeo ("Sì fuggire: a noi non resta"), and the cabaletta of Giulietta's second-act aria ("Ah! non poss'io partire"), among other pieces; but the most fervent admiration was reserved for Bellini's tomb scene:

> Now we come to the grand scene in which the singers and the maestro displayed themselves in a manner superior to any praise. Romeo, alone at the tomb in which he believes he sees his beloved Giulietta dead, sings a tender prayer, after which the liveliest applause was heard. But Giulietta arises from her fatal sleep, and clamorous voices of praise rang out after the interesting recitative between her and Romeo. In the final duet, and with grief over the death of the two unfortunate lovers, the [audience's] enthusiasm knew no restraint, and the delight for these mournful and truly rational, philosophical ensembles sent forth to the brow of he who listened tears of such effect that one almost wished the agony would have endured for longer in order to experience these sweet sensations for longer.[23]

Excitement for the work increased during subsequent performances, and following the third repetition, Venetian spectators paid the composer the ultimate homage of accompanying him home with torches blazing brightly and a military band performing a group of favorite selections from his operas.[24]

Despite this overwhelmingly warm reception, unfavorable comparisons began to emerge between Bellini's opera, Vaccai's, and a third operatic version of the Romeo and Juliet story that had recently reasserted its popularity in productions starring Giuditta Pasta—Niccolò Antonio Zingarelli's *Giulietta e Romeo* (Milan, La Scala, January 30, 1796).[25] The first stone was cast in the form of a letter written by an anonymous season ticket holder at the Teatro la Fenice, published in *I teatri,* and

---

23. "Eccoci giunti alla gran scena nella quale cantanti e maestro si mostrarono superiori a qualunque elogio. Romeo solo fra quelle tombe, in una delle quali crede vedere estinta l'amata Giulietta, canta un'affettuosa preghiera, dopo cui si udirono i più vivi applausi. Ma Giulietta si desta dal fatal sonno ed all'interessante recitativo fra questa a Romeo si odono voci clamorose di lode. Nel duetto finale, ed alle ambascie di morte dei due sventurati amanti; l'entusiasmo non ha più ritegno, e la delizia di quei mesti e veramente ragionati filosofici concerti, sprigiona dal ciglio di chi ascolta le lagrime con tanto effetto che quasi si vorrebbe che più lungamente durasse quella agonia per più lungamente provare quelle dolci sensazioni." *L'eco* 34 (March 19, 1830); cited in Cambi, ed., *Bellini: Epistolario* (Milan: Mondadori, 1943), 244–45; and in Toscani, *I Capuleti e i Montecchi,* introduction, xix. Toscani provides an excellent overview of the reception of this opera's premiere, as well of its subsequent productions. I am indebted to his work for many of the reviews I cite here.

24. Florimo, *La scuola musicale di Napoli e i suoi conservatorii,* 3: 191.

25. For a comparison of these three operas, see Hadlock, "On the Cusp between Past and Future," 399–422.

aimed directly at Bellini's tomb scene: "Fourth part. Composed primarily for Grisi (Romeo). Many elements are included to display the excellence of this distinguished singer, but at bottom this scene leaves cold even he who does not know *Giulietta e Romeo* by *Zingarelli* and by *Vaccaj.*"[26]

As Toscani notes, such negative sentiments only grew more pronounced as *I Capuleti e i Montecchi* began to travel through Italian and European opera houses, a situation illustrated by a handful of reviews published on the occasion of the opera's first revival at the Teatro alla Scala in Milan (carnival 1831).[27] Though some critics were as complimentary as those who witnessed the premiere at La Fenice, others such as Francesco Pezzi writing for the *Gazzetta privilegiata di Milano,* were decidedly disenchanted by Bellini's opera in general, and by his final scene in particular:

> We have three operas about the catastrophe of the two unhappy lovers of Verona— one by Zingarelli, one by Vaccaj, and one by Bellini. These three compositions stand in order of date as well as of merit; in terms of their effect [on the audience], if one judges by the facts, they are listed in inverse order. Without speaking of the oldest one, which only Pasta has been able to revive last year, we will say that the one by Vaccaj loses to Bellini's in the preciousness of *detail,* but on the whole, it wins. As far as the last scene is concerned, there is not the least bit of comparison. Vaccaj emphasizes the full drama of the calamity with melodies that ravish; Bellini, who had won in the final act of *Straniera,* has to accept defeat in the final aria of Giulietta's lover.[28]

The critic for the *Allgemeine musikalische Zeitung* was more succinct: "There was very little satisfaction with the music of this opera mainly because *Romeo e Giulietta* by Vaccai is preferred by a long shot."[29] Given such negative comparisons, it is perhaps not surprising that Malibran and others would have opted to trade in Bellini's conclusion for the corresponding section of Vaccai's score. Just as the reception of *I Capuleti e i Montecchi* was mixed, however, so, too, was the reception of this alteration.

Early reviews suggest that productions that included Vaccai's ending were often greeted enthusiastically. Of particular interest is a lengthy article published in *Teatri arti e letteratura* on the occasion of Malibran's debut in the role of Romeo, a detailed

---

26. "Quarta parte. Consiste questa nella scena della *Grisi* (Romeo). Moltissime cose vengono porte per eccellenza da questa esimia Cantante, ma in pieno questa scena riesce fredda anche per chi non conosce le *Giuliette e Romeo* di *Zingarelli* e di *Vaccaj.*" *I teatri* a. IV, fasc. X, 1830. Cited in Cambi, *Bellini: Epistolario,* 247, and Toscani, *I Capuleti e i Montecchi,* xix.

27. The cast for this production was slightly different than that for the premiere at La Fenice. Grisi and Bonfigli retained their roles, but the Giulietta was Santina Ferlotti.

28. "Tre opere abbiamo sulla catastrofe dei due infelici amanti di Verona. Quella di Zingarelli, quella di Vaccaj, e quella di Bellini. Queste tre composizioni stanno in ordine di data pel merito; in quanto all'effetto, se si giudichi dal fatto, stanno in ordine inverso. Senza parlare della più vecchia, che la Pasta sola ha potuto ringiovanire l'anno scorso, diremo che quella di Vaccaj, cede a quella di Bellini nei pregi di *dettaglio,* ma che nell'insieme la vince. In quanto all'ultima scena non regge la menoma idea di paragone. Vaccaj vi fece spiccare tutto il drammatico della sciagura con melodie che rapiscono; Bellini che aveva saputo vincerlo nell'aria finale della *Straniera* dee darsi per vinto in quella dell'amator di Giulietta." *Gazzetta privilegiata di Milano* 364 (December 30, 1830); cited in Toscani, *I Capuleti e i Montecchi,* xxi.

29. "Della musica di quest'opera si è molto poco soddisfatti, e a ragioni si preferiscono di gran lunga *Romeo e Giulietta* di Vaccai." *Allgemeine musikalische Zeitung* XXXIII/11 (March 16, 1831): col. 170; cited, along with the original German, in Toscani, *I Capuleti e i Montecchi,* xxi.

report chronicling the Bolognese spectators' reaction to each of the numbers performed, including those that were not composed by Bellini. The critic is thrilled with the entire evening, introducing his remarks about the production with, "The great *Malibran* and the grand *Schoberlechner,* the first in the character of *Romeo,* and the second in that of *Giulietta,* generated much excitement with Bellini's melodies during the first three parts, Vaccai's in the fourth, [and] *Mercadante*'s and *Celli*'s in two inserted duets."[30] The language he employs throughout most of the review is, in large part, typical of nineteenth-century reviews: "objective" reporting on the music that was sung and the manner in which it was received. Of the Act II duet between Romeo and Tebaldo ("Stolto! ad un sol mio grido"), for instance, the critic remarks plainly that it is "masterfully written" and that both Pedrazzi and Malibran deserved to be congratulated for singing it beautifully, even though the score was new to them and they had only two days of rehearsal. This balanced stance, however, tips noticeably when he writes about the tomb scene. In this fascinating description, the critic adopts an elevated rhetorical tone, focusing not only on typical matters such as music and audience reception, but also on issues that rarely arise in these types of reviews—gesture, action, and emotion:

> *Romeo* presents himself with his faithful and he commands them to open the tomb. He embraces her immediately and he abandons his whole spirit over the one he believes to be dead, whose cold limbs he caresses tenderly, and over this, he sings with so much sweetness that if she were not dead, she would have to wake up by means of the incantation, "Ah se tu dormi, svegliati." So prodigiously sung!! That finely detailed touch, the way in which *Romeo* abandons the hand of his *Giulietta,* expressing a tender irritation at not seeing it reciprocated! [. . .] All of *Romeo*'s visible expressions explain to you the movements of his spirit, and *Giulietta* reciprocates. But why does *Giulietta*—the loving and desperate *Giulietta* who sees her lover near death, and his limbs falter—twice pull back from him? She can invoke help without moving. No *Giulietta,* don't move a single step away from your dying *Romeo;* don't you see with how much passion he holds your head between his hands, weakly caressing your sentimental face? But already his [melodic] lines become truncated . . . *Romeo* declaims rather than sings . . . he lacks breath—to the ground, he is already dead. Stupor dominates all the senses; but a little later the spectators' lethargy ceases in order to see *Romeo* again, and to assure themselves that they have not lost him, and that he will return to delight them subsequently. After the incessant yells and [curtain] calls, one abandoned that enclosure of joy with difficulty.[31]

30. "Fu nella notte antecedente alla decorsa che la somma *Malibran,* e la grande *Schoberlechner,* in figura di *Romeo* la prima, e di *Giulietta* la seconda, ne fecero giustamente entusiasmare colle melodìe di *Bellini* nelle prime tre parti, di *Vaccai* nella quarta, di *Mercadante,* e del Cav. Maestro *Celli* con due duetti innestati." *Teatri arti e letteratura* 450 (November 3, 1832): 71.

31. "[. . .] presentarsi *Romeo* coi suoi fidi, e comandar loro di aprire il sepolcro. Già la abbraccia[o] e tutta l'anima sua abbandona sulla creduta estinta, di cui teneramente accarezza le fredde membra, e vi canta sopra con tanta dolcezza, che se non spenta dovrà svegliarsi per l'incantesimo *"Ah se tu dormi, svegliati"* come prodigiosamente cantato!! Qual tocco di finissima miniatura, l'abbandono che fa *Romeo* della mano della sua *Giulietta* esprimendo un tenero irritamento per non vedersi corrisposto! [. . .] Quei lineamenti nella fisionomia di *Romeo* tutti ti spiegono i moti dell'anima, e *Giulietta* gli corrisponde. Ma, e perchè, *Giulietta,* l'amorosa, e disperata *Giulietta* che a morte vede vicino l'amante, e le sue membra vacillanti, per due volta da lui si allontana? Soccorso può invocarlo senza muoversi. No *Giulietta,* non ti

Discussion of the music plays a role in this précis of the tomb scene. The critic notes, for instance, that Vaccai's aria for Romeo, "Ah se tu dormi, svegliati," was sung "prodigiously." But vocal matters are not what interest him most here. Instead, this reviewer attempts to convey verbally the raw emotional force generated not just by Vaccai's music, but—more important—by Malibran and Schoberlechner as actresses. Their performances are so overwhelming, so persuasive, that over the course of this description the critic loses his grip not only on what they sing, but also on their individual identities—their names, mentioned frequently throughout the preceding parts of the review, disappear from this passage, replaced by references to Romeo and Giulietta. In an effective turn, moreover, the critic addresses the characters directly ("No *Giulietta,* don't move even a single step from your dying *Romeo*"), and toward the end, the text ruptures in imitation of Romeo's faltering breath ("they halt their voices . . . *Romeo* declaims rather than sings . . . he lacks breath—to the ground, he is already dead"). So convinced are spectators by this performance, the critic reports, that they need to be reassured Romeo/Malibran is not literally dead (significantly, a similar reassurance is not called for in the case of Giulietta/Schoberlechner). This association between Malibran and death is vital, as we will explore further below; for now it is enough to note that such overwhelmingly positive reactions among critics and audiences to this performance played a significant role in perpetuating the practice of substituting Vaccai's music for Bellini's.

The emotional response to the substitution witnessed in this review is reflected in later ones as well, critics conveying the new tomb scene's affect through similar rhetorical means—fragmented utterance and a reliance on ellipses. When Giuditta Grisi (Bellini's original Romeo) performed *I Capuleti e i Montecchi* in Madrid in the summer of 1834, for instance, she, too, had made the switch from Bellini to Vaccai, a fact duly noted in the press (the ellipses are original):

> Our pen could contribute an extremely pallid sketch of such a marvelous performance, because only in seeing it can one comprehend how she was. Her manner of taking the poison. . . . . her manner of raising her head to hear *Giulietta'*s breath. . . . . the stupor she feels at seeing [Giulietta] descend into the tomb. . . . . her agony in the arms of her beloved. . . . . the kiss that she, dying, impresses on [Giulietta]. . . . . the profound and pathetic expression that she gives to such simple melodies. . . . . all of these things we would endeavor in vain to describe to those who did not have the fortune of seeing her themselves.[32]

---

scostare di un sol passo dal moriente tuo *Romeo;* non vedi con quanta passione fra le sue mani stringe il tuo capo blandemente accarezzando il sentimentale tuo volto? Ma già si fan tronche le sue voci. . . . *Romeo* declama piuttosto che cantare . . . manca il respiro—a terra è già spento. Lo stupore domina tutti i sensi; ma poco dopo cessa il letargo degli spettatori per rivedere quel *Romeo,* ed assicurarsi che non l'hanno perduto, e che tornerà a formare la delizia loro in appresso. Dopo le grida incessanti, e le chiamate, a stento si abbandonò quel recinto del godimento." Ibid., 73–74.

32. "La nostra penna darebbe un assai pallido abbozzo di esecuzione tanto meravigliosa; chè solamente vedendola può concepirsi com'è. Il modo di pigliare il veleno. . . . il modo di levare la testa a sentire il respiro di *Giulietta.* . . . la stupore che prova al vederla discendere nella tomba. . . . la sua agonia fra le braccia dell'amante. . . . il bacio che spirando le imprime. . . . il profondo e patetico colorito che dà a quelle così semplici cantilene. . . . tutte codeste cose invano ci sforzeremmo di dipingerle a chi non ebbe la sorte di vederle." This was excerpted from a "Spanish newspaper," and published in *Teatri arti e letteratura* 535 (June 12, 1834): 141–42.

Once again, this review focuses attention on gestures and acting, illustrating how the performative element in Italian opera often pushed into virtual insignificance all other aspects of the experience. Indeed, this ending seems to have had this sort of visceral effect on audiences time and again, a reaction still evident as late as the 1840s, as a review of a revival at the Teatro la Fenice illustrates. Here the critic Tomasso Locatelli points to the substituted scene as the highlight, not only of the evening, but of the entire season: "Here, Vaccai's strings were added to Bellini's lyre, and the final scene of his score was thrown out. In one stroke and without any adjustment, one passed from the mediocre to the sublime, from boredom or from commiseration to the most complete delight and true enthusiasm. It was like a sudden ray of light fallen over the horror of night, an oasis in the desert, an unexpected harbor in the eye of a storm [. . .] for the first time this year, the theater was filled with true enthusiasm."[33] Though decidedly more detached than the earlier reviews, Locatelli nevertheless speaks to the emotional power this scene held over audiences whether or not Malibran was on stage.

Equally, if not more, significant are the negative notices the Vaccai substitution received, particularly for the manner in which they tended to vilify Malibran. Bellini's own words on the matter do not survive, but those of the opera's librettist, Romani, were recorded in the *Gazzetta ufficiale Piemontese* on January 18, 1836, a very sarcastic, almost bitter, account of what he perceived was going on. After describing how two "good friends," a musician (Bellini) and poet (Romani), worked together to create *I Capuleti e i Montecchi,* he describes the activities of two other "friends," Malibran and a fictional personification of the idea of caprice:

> Another beautiful day, two other good friends were spotted working together. Malibran and Capriccio wished to revise the work of the poet and the musician, and embroidered it in such a way that one could no longer recognize the original. Mme. Malibran suggested one course, and Signor Capriccio approved; Signor Capriccio suggested a revision, and Mme. Malibran welcomed it; and Malibran did her best by one part, and Capriccio did his best by another; and finally, Capriccio and Malibran blended together, blended, blended, in such a manner that their suggestions, their proposals, their manipulations served up a dainty dish, a sauce, a fricassee that was a wonder to see. A weak broth by Celli, gelatin by Pacini, spices by Ricci, carrots by Rossi [. . .] there was a little bit of everything. To top it all off, the fourth act was substituted by the third act of Vaccai.[34]

33. "Quivi alla malinconica lira del Bellini, s'aggiunsero per più effetto le corde del Vaccaj, e se ne tolsero le ultime scene del suo spartito. D'un tratto e senza transazione veruna si varcò dal mediocre al sublime, dalla noia o dal compatimento, al più compiuto diletto e vero entusiasmo. Fu come un improvviso raggio caduto nell'orror d'una notte, un'oasi nel deserto, un porto non isperato nella procella [. . .] il teatro per la prima volta in quest'anno s'accese di vero entusiasmo." Tomasso Locatelli, *L'appendice della Gazzetta di Venezia. Prose scelte di T. L.* (Venice: Tip. Del Gondoliere, 1837–1880), 7: 241–42.

34. "Un altro bel giorno si trovarono insieme altri due buoni amici, la Malibran e il Capriccio, ai quali venne il ticchio di rifare il lavoro di quel poeta e di quel maestro, e di raffazzonarlo in modo che più non si avesse a ravvisare. E la Malibran proponeva una cosa, e il Capriccio l'approvava; e il Capriccio suggeriva un ripiego, e la Malibran l'accoglieva; e la Malibran si adoperava da una parte, e il Capriccio da un'altra; e finalmente il Capriccio e la Malibran manipolavano insieme, manipolavano, manipolavano, di maniera che da cotesti suggerimenti, da coteste proposte, da coteste manipolazioni ne venne imbandito un manicaretto, un intingolo, un cibreo che fu meraviglia a vedersi. Brodo lungo di Celli,

Most damaging to Malibran's reputation is the existence of a letter supposedly written by another leading mezzo of the time, Giuseppina Ronzi de Begnis, and sent to Bellini's friend and biographer Francesco Florimo. In this missive (dated June 18, 1834) the singer describes a difficult struggle that she underwent when she took on the role of Romeo in Florence. She explains that she had resolved to perform Bellini's original final scene rather than Vaccai's, but she was afraid that the Florentine spectators, anticipating the "pasticcio alla Malibran," would complain. In the end, however, she writes that the entire performance was an extraordinary success and her efforts to restore *I Capuleti e i Montecchi* to its "true" form were rewarded: "To tell you the truth, I would have been very unhappy if this opera had failed; and I am the more content because it is all Bellini's work. There were people to say:—how does Malibran happen to change the third act? It seems to me that, as a singer who is said to be such an actress, she should be content. Does this seem to you a small triumph?"[35] This letter is compelling for its account of a singer wrestling with a larger tension at play during the first half of the nineteenth century: de Begnis's story illustrates the resistance faced by those who were among the first to translate the new aesthetic of the work-concept into practice on the Italian operatic stage. Since 1871, when Florimo published this missive, scholars and critics have treated it as gospel and she as an intrepid heroine. In his study of Bellini, for example, Michele Scherillo writes, "In 1834, invited to sing the opera again at the Pergola in Florence at a time when Malibran's dainty dish had had great success, [de Begnis] had the courage and the intelligence to perform the Bellinian opera integrally and to open the public's eyes."[36]

In light of this and similar responses, it is important to recognize that de Begnis's letter may have been a fake. Florimo was notorious for forging letters, or for distorting those he received in order to enhance the image of Bellini he wished to project, and there is no reason to believe that he treated it any differently than the others he forged—no original survives, and thus we have only Florimo's word on which to rely.[37] Whether it was penned in 1834 by a singer on the front lines of this performance tradition, or in 1871 by Bellini's best friend and posthumous champion makes a significant difference, for in the former case, the letter represents a legitimate firsthand account of the Vaccai alteration and its reception among some prac-

---

gelatina di Pacini, droghe di Ricci, carote di Rossi [. . .] ci fu un po' di tutto. Per ultimo al quart'atto fu sostituito il terz'atto di Vaccai." Florimo, *La scuola musicale di Napoli e i suoi conservatorii,* 3: 192. Excerpts from Romani's article are also published in Maria Rosario Adamo and Friedrich Lippman, *Vincenzo Bellini* (Turin: ERI, 1981), 137–38, and Giampiero Tintori, *Bellini* (Milan: Rusconi, 1983), 131–34. See also Toscani, *I Capuleti e i Montecchi,* xxiii, and Gossett, *Divas and Scholars,* 211–12.

35. Cited and translated in Herbert Weinstock, *Vincenzo Bellini* (New York: Knopf, 1975), 249.

36. "Invitata, nel 1834, a ricantare quell'opera alla Pergola di Firenze, quando già il manicaretto del Maliban aveva fatto fortuna, ebbe l'ardire e l'ingegno di rappresentare integralmente l'opera belliniana, e di far ricredere il pubblico." Michele Scherillo, *Belliniana: Nuove note* (Milan: Ricordi, 1885), 35.

37. See Rosselli, *The Life of Bellini* (Cambridge: Cambridge University Press, 1996), 6–11. In *Divas and Scholars* Gossett alludes to the fact that this letter might be a forgery: "One would not like to think it inauthentic, but Florimo was sometimes a less than reliable witness" (see 556n27). The earliest evidence of this letter appears in Florimo, *La scuola musicale di Napoli e i suoi conservatorii (1880–1883),* 3: 192–93.

titioners and spectators; in the latter, it stands as a fabricated document that falsely projects later nineteenth-century ideals of aesthetic coherence onto the first half of the century. Even if the letter were a forgery, however, it has always been treated as legitimate, and as such, it has had an undeniable impact on both Malibran's and de Begnis's reputations, allowing a seemingly clear distinction to emerge in reconstructions of *I Capuleti e i Montecchi*'s performance history: as the "rescuer" of Bellini's music, de Begnis serves as a metonym for his will; Malibran symbolizes exactly the opposite—the desires and demands of the singer. There is no question as to who represents the more virtuous player.

The risks of accepting this interpretation of the tomb-scene alteration without exploring its larger contexts are many. The most significant is that it has allowed a rather simplistic dichotomy between good and bad, artistic integrity and lack thereof to dominate the discourse surrounding the change. Stepping back and exploring the compositional and performance history of *I Capuleti e i Montecchi* brings to light a more complex picture of a work that was saturated by many diverse changes in addition to the Vaccai substitution. Indeed, singers perceived this opera, more than any other that Bellini composed, as a score that called for manipulation of all sorts.

ARIA INSERTION IN THE OPERAS OF VINCENZO BELLINI

Extant librettos from productions of *I Capuleti e i Montecchi* indicate that it was almost as common to perform the opera with interpolated and substituted numbers as it was to present it "as written."[38] On occasion, these alterations were localized, affecting only one moment in the opera. In an 1831 production in Udine, for example, Rafaele Scalese singing the role of Capellio interpolated an aria of unidentified origin titled "Crudi affetti di vendetti" into the second act;[39] and during an 1832 Turinese production of *I Capuleti e i Montecchi,* the soprano Elisa Taccani sang "Come per me sereno" from Bellini's *La sonnambula* instead of Giulietta's entrance aria, "Oh quante volte."[40] Alongside these productions of *I Capuleti e i Montecchi,* during which only one moment was altered, there were others that made quite a mess of the score, altering three, four, and as many as five different sections, including the tomb scene. In 1833 in Trieste, for example, spectators were treated to music by Luigi Ricci, Saverio Mercadante, as well as Bellini's and Vaccai's; and a few years later in Siena, Giulietta and Romeo performed almost as much music that was not a part of *I Capuleti e i Montecchi* as they did music from the score.[41]

38. Out of the forty-nine librettos I have consulted (all dated between 1831 and 1857), twenty-three included significant changes (not including the tomb scene). See also Collins, "Bellini and the 'Pasticcio alla Malibran,'" 109–52.

39. Udine, Teatro della Nob. Società, autumn 1831 (libretto: I:Vnm, dramm. 888.13). See also Collins, "Bellini and the 'Pasticcio alla Malibran,'" 115–16.

40. Turin, Teatro d'Angennes, spring 1832 (libretto: I:Vgc). According to Collins, she also made this substitution in Novara (autumn 1831), and in Bologna (carnival 1832). Collins, "Bellini and the *Pasticcio alla Malibran,*" 123.

41. Trieste, Teatro Grande, autumn 1833 (libretto: I:Vnm, dramm. 3325.19); Siena, Teatro dei Rinnovati, carnival 1841–1842 (libretto: I:Vgc). See Collins, "Bellini and the *Pasticcio alla Malibran,*" 116–17, for a discussion of the Trieste production.

Such massive reworkings are not at all unheard of, as we have already noted. What is unusual, though, is that these liberties were taken with one of Bellini's operas, for none of his other scores was affected by aria insertion to the same extent as was *I Capuleti e i Montecchi*. This is not to say that performances of his works presented faithful reproductions of his scores, but in comparison to operas by Rossini, Donizetti, Pacini, and other contemporaries, Bellini's works were less often punctuated by arias and ensembles that he himself did not authorize. When substitutions and interpolations did appear in his operas, moreover, they typically did so at specific moments rather than randomly. For instance, his third opera, *Il pirata* (Milan, La Scala, 1827)—the first for which he achieved true commercial success—hosted new arias in roughly one-third of its revivals. As frequently as this opera was performed with substitutions, however, they appeared almost exclusively during two moments within the first act: either as replacements for Imogene's treacherous cavatina ("Lo sognai ferito esangue"), composed for the virtuoso soprano Henriette Méric-Lalande;[42] or for Ernesto's entrance aria ("Sì vincemmo, e il pregio io sento"), which even the opera's first bass in this role, Antonio Tamburini, found unrewarding.[43] *Norma* (Milan, La Scala, 1831), which received more revivals on more stages than any other *opera seria* of the 1830s, moreover, was produced with far fewer aria insertions than *Il pirata,* and when such pieces appeared, they almost always did so during the second act as showpieces for Oroveso.[44] A logical explanation exists for why singers in this role might have opted for such a change: the aria Bellini composed for this character in Act II ("Ah! del Tebro al giogo indegno") is only one movement, a cantabile without a cabaletta, and therefore bulking this moment up

42. Among the first to make such a change was Adelaide Comelli-Rubini, who performed Meyerbeer's "Oh! come rapida" rather than "Lo sognai ferito esangue" in Vienna in 1828 (see Fabbri, "Per un'edizione critica del *Pirata,*" 192); according to the libretto for a production in Bologna in which Comelli-Rubini participated a few years later (Bologna, Teatro Comunale, autumn 1830), she took this opportunity to sing another aria, "Ah! non giova al cielo innante," the identity of which I have been unable to identify (I:Vgc). Other singers made a variety of choices for this scene. Some examples include Catterina Lipparini, who performed Percy's much more modest "Ah! così ne' dì ridenti" from Donizetti's *Anna Bolena* (Padua, Teatro Nuovo, autumn 1831 [I:Vnm, dramm. 888.16]); and Elisa Sedlach replaced Imogene's cabaletta ("Sventurata, anch'io deliro") with "Fuggì l'imagine," the cabaletta that Amelia sings in Act III of Donizetti's *Il castello di Kenilworth* (Turin, Teatro d'Angennes, spring 1833 [I:Rsc, Carv. 12265]). The most interesting alteration, however, was made by Adelina Spech (Udine, Teatro della Nobile Società, fiera 1832 [I:Vgc]), and by Annette Maraffa (Verona, Teatro Filarmonico, carnival 1833 [I:Vgc]): both sopranos sang "Casta diva," Norma's *aria di sortita,* with a text fully rewritten to conform to its new context.

43. The most common aria to substitute into this scene was "Sì, miei prodi, questo sole" / "Paventi il perfido" from Pacini's *Amazilia.* The basses who I have identified as making this alteration are Massimiliano Orlandi (Rovigo, Teatro di Società, fiera 1830 [I:Vgc]); Luigi Maggiorotti (Cremona, Teatro della Concordia, fiera 1830 [I:Rsc, Carv. 12253]); and Guido Lusanti (Padua, Teatro Nuovo, autumn 1831 [I:Vnm, dramm. 888.16]).

44. Six librettos reveal this to have been the case. Among other examples, during the 1832–1833 carnival season at the Teatro Carlo Felice, Genoa, Felice Bottelli removed Oroveso's aria and performed a double aria from Pacini's *Amazilia* instead (I:Vgc). Two years later, the same singer introduced an unidentified aria into the second act of *Norma* titled "Di terror, di strage armato" at the Teatro Ducale, Parma, carnival 1834–1835 (I:Vnm, dramm. 3332.10). The identical alteration was made by two other singers: Giovanni Schover, Teatro degli Avvalorati, Livorno, carnival 1833–1834 (I:Vnm, dramm. 3326.19), and Luigi Alessandrini, Teatro Comunale, Guastalla, autumn 1840 (I:Vnm, dramm 3343.22).

with something more impressive would have been the obvious ploy for a singer more capable of virtuosic expression.[45] *La sonnambula* (Milan, Teatro Carcano, 1831), to take one final example, developed a tradition of aria substitution in which the secondary character, Lisa, frequently excised her one-movement *aria di sorbetto,* "De' lieti augurj a voi son grata," in favor of two-movement arias, pieces that served to differentiate her role from that of the prima donna (Amina) more effectively than does the original.[46] No other moment in this score received similar treatment. During the nineteenth century, stability was far off for Bellini's oeuvre, but *I Capuleti e i Montecchi* seems to have been further than most. The opera's compositional history provides some clues as to why.

The circumstances under which Bellini came to write *I Capuleti e i Montecchi* for the Teatro la Fenice were unusual for the composer. He arrived in Venice in December 1829 with the intention of mounting a revival of his third opera, *Il pirata,* while Giovanni Pacini had been hired to compose the new work for that season. Overwhelmed by prior commitments, however, Pacini never showed up in Venice. In a panicked rush, the theater management contracted Bellini to fill in, giving him six weeks to produce a full-length opera. The notoriously "slow" composer agreed to this arrangement for a few reasons: first, Romani did not delay, as he often did, in delivering the libretto to the composer. Rather than write a new one, he revised what he had prepared five years earlier for Vaccai's *Giulietta e Romeo.* Bellini did not work from scratch either: instead, he borrowed extensively from two of his earlier operas—*Zaira,* which had failed at its premiere in May 1829, and his student work *Adelson e Salvini.*[47] (For the tomb scene, Bellini borrowed the melody for Romeo's aria, "Deh! tu bell'anima," from the cavatina for Zaira, "Non è tormento" [*Zaira,* Act I]).

Despite the opera's initial success, neither composer nor librettist was comfortable with the rapid pace at which they were forced to work. In the preface to the printed libretto, in fact, Romani admitted that they both felt "constrained by the pressure of time to an extreme brevity and were persuaded to omit many recitative scenes which would have justified the continuity of the drama."[48] Perhaps it was this very discomfort that encouraged singers to manipulate this score—its origins as a

45. As Weinstock explains, the original Oroveso, Vincenzo Negrini, "suffered from a weak heart and had to conserve his strength," and it was for this reason that Bellini "jettisoned some of his original conception of the role of Oroveso." *Vincenzo Bellini,* 488n111.

46. This aria is rather thankless, lasting a little over two minutes, its key of B-flat major placing it high in the soprano range, and featuring descending arpeggios that begin on high C, which render the melody rather repetitive. Sopranos who traded it in for others include Rosina Ferrari who sang "È tale in dolce incanto" from Pacini's *I fidanzati, ossia Il contestabile di Chester* (Udine, Teatro della Nobile Società, fiera 1835 [I:Vnm, dramm. 889.17]). I have been unable to identify the origin of the other arias introduced at this point in the drama, but librettos indicate that such a change was made on at least five other occasions between 1834 and 1840.

47. Weinstock, *Vincenzo Bellini,* 253–59. For a discussion of Bellini's self-borrowings throughout his entire oeuvre, see Charlotte Greenspan, *The Operas of Vincenzo Bellini* (Ph.D. diss., University of California, Berkeley, 1977), and Mary Ann Smart, "In Praise of Convention: Formula and Experiment in Bellini's Self-Borrowings," *Journal of the American Musicological Society* 53 (2000): 25–68.

48. Liner notes accompanying *I Capuleti e i Montecchi* (BMG/RCA Vic 68899), 13.

pasticcio paving the way for the extreme elaborations we find only shortly following the opera's premiere. What is more, when the opera was revived at La Scala in 1831, Bellini rewrote the part of Giulietta for Amalia Schütz, whose range was lower than that of the first Giulietta, Caradori-Allan. These alterations were extensive, involving the transposition downward of her vocal lines and of any corresponding *puntature,* the revision of several connecting passages, and retouching of the orchestration. As a result, this opera existed in two "authentic" versions, a situation that may have added some incentive for singers to make alterations on their own.[49] This history provides some perspective on why Bellini's score was manipulated as often as it was, but it still does not fully explain the allure that Vaccai's scene held over Bellini's.

Scholars have approached the issue of why singers chose to perform the Vaccai ending in place of Bellini's with a mixture of clarity and bewilderment, concluding simply that the earlier setting was more conventional and that it offered prima donnas in the role of Romeo greater opportunity for solo singing than the original. In fact, a comparison of the two scenes reveals as much opportunity for vocal display for Romeo in Bellini's version as in Vaccai's, and in neither case is the prima donna in that role provided with the opportunity to conclude the opera with elaborate solo music. Both versions follow a similar design: they each open with a chorus of Montagues who mourn for Giulietta, which is followed by a recitative and aria for Romeo (Bellini's is "Deh! tu bell'anima" [*andante sostenuto,* F major, common time]; Vaccai's is "Ah! se tu dormi, svegliati" [*andante trattenuto,* E-flat major, common time]). After Romeo concludes, Giulietta wakes, and from this moment forward the texts for both operas are virtually identical, a frantic dialogue between the two characters in which they come to understand Romeo's fatal mistake and bid one another farewell. Both Bellini and Vaccai set this section as a duet built of fragmented utterances in which Romeo and Giulietta are provided an equal amount of musical material—in neither case is his role emphasized over hers.[50]

The argument that Vaccai's musical setting was more conventional than Bellini's has a bit more traction, as the recitative preceding Romeo's solo aria demonstrates. In Bellini's version, the assembly of Montagues remains onstage as the distraught character arrives, the music from the preceding chorus ("Siam giunti") separated by

49. Toscani, *I Capuleti e i Montecchi,* xx. See also Friedrich Lippmann, "Pagine sconosciute de 'I Capuleti e i Montecchi' e 'Beatrice di Tenda' di Vincenzo Bellini," *Rivista italiana di musicologica* 2 (1967): 140–51. Many operas of the *Primo Ottocento* existed in more than one authentic version, and thus it would be overstating matters to argue that if an opera existed in more than one guise, singers were automatically encouraged to make further alterations. As Margaret Bent suggests in the case of *Il Turco in Italia,* however, multiple versions may have been one of a variety of factors leading to such changes: "In the decades following its composition, there were many performances of *Il Turco in Italia.* Often the opera was subjected to significant modifications, arising in part out of issues already mentioned: the presence of music not by Rossini in the original version, the existence of a second version (probably authentic), and the desire to expand the part of Narciso." Gioachino Rossini, *Il Turco in Italia,* ed. Margaret Bent, piano-vocal reduction (Milan: Ricordi, 2000), xxxvii.

50. Vaccai's version of the opera concludes with an additional scene for Giulietta during which she performs a solo aria over Romeo's lifeless body. That final section of *Giulietta e Romeo* was never introduced into Bellini's score. For full libretto texts of Bellini's and Vaccai's tomb scenes, see Toscani, "Bellini e Vaccaj," 559–67.

only two measures of orchestral accompaniment that flows seamlessly into his solo statements.

It is in this recitative that Romeo discovers Giulietta's body and as he does, his utterances become as unhinged as his mental state, shifting rapidly between plain recitative and lush ariosos that are in turn interrupted by occasional choral responses. The moment he first sees Giulietta lying in her tomb, for instance, opens with the driest of recitatives, only minimally accompanied by the orchestra (example 4.1,

EXAMPLE 4.1.   Bellini, *I Capuleti e i Montecchi,* Act II, Romeo's *scena,* mm. 92–113

Source: I Capuleti e i Montecchi. Piano-vocal score. Milan: Ricordi, 2006, p. 128.

mm. 92–102). Romeo, however, is unable to maintain this cold, rational discourse for long, and at the moment he states his own name, he bursts into eight measures of deep pathos that could not contrast more starkly with what came before (mm. 103–11). Over a rolling accompaniment, Romeo performs a plaintive, broken melody accompanied by full orchestra in which his trauma is depicted in his desperate repetition of key words ("sorgi, mio ben" and "ti chiama"). Almost as soon as this arioso begins, however, it is cut off by the chorus, which begs Romeo to come away and leave the morose tomb behind. Vaccai's recitative for Romeo also contains shifts between recitative and arioso, but the emotional swings so palpable in Bellini's version are only minimally audible in this far more staid setting.

This is not to say, however, that Vaccai's tomb scene lacks musical interest. On the contrary, his aria for Romeo, "Ah! se tu dormi, svegliati," contains moments of startling beauty, and it is in this piece that we begin to understand the allure this music held over audiences, critics, and singers alike.

Introduced by a lengthy orchestral prelude featuring solo harp, this aria invokes an earlier and more famous expression of suffering, Desdemona's Willow Song ("Assisa a piè d'un salice") from Rossini's *Otello,* an unmistakable reference that would have stirred sympathy for the impetuous Romeo, at least among some spectators. Vaccai's primary melodic material consists of four distinct sections of varied length and character, an additive structure that eschews predictability (example 4.2). Throughout this aria Romeo vents his anguish in a vocal line overflowing with expressive leaps and contours. The first phrase (mm. 136–39), for instance, opens with a two-measure gesture in which the stepwise, descending motion is interrupted by a dramatic jump up on the strong beat to a dissonant C natural. Vaccai resolves this disruption immediately, but not stepwise to B flat as one might predict; instead, the voice leaps downward to D natural, completing the descending line initiated at the beginning of the measure. The overall effect of approaching and resolving this non-chord tone by such wide leaps is striking, a gesture Vaccai winds up in the next measure with another descending leap, a major sixth (G natural to B flat). Similarly disjunct lines are characteristic of much of the remainder of the aria, as when Vaccai sets the text "amore ci condurrà" (mm. 143–45) and then "sorgi, mio bene, mia speme" (mm. 145–47). Despite the melody's impulsive character, however, it is surprisingly easy to sing, a function of its slow tempo, minimal coloratura, and most important, its tessitura. The vocal line falls comfortably within the mezzo-soprano range, extending upwards to E flat[5], but only at climactic moments—the majority of the vocal line hovering between B flat[3] and C[5].

Compare this with Bellini's "Deh! tu bell'anima," which sits higher in the soprano range, extending to G[5] at climactic points and circling throughout most of the aria between G[4] and E[5] (example 4.3).

Given that many prima donnas in the role of Romeo were mezzo-sopranos, it is possible that this difference alone would have attracted them to Vaccai's aria over Bellini's.[51] Range and difficulty aside, however, Bellini's aria lacks much of the immediate appeal that characterizes Vaccai's. "Deh! tu bell'anima" is composed in a

51. Julian Budden has made a similar observation, though he interprets this as Malibran's sole motivation for making the alteration: "a glance at Vaccai's final scene will show why [Malibran] did it: the

EXAMPLE 4.2.   Vaccai, *Giulietta e Romeo,* "Ah! se tu dormi, svegliati," mm. 136–54

standard aa′bc structure, and its sections are divided into neat, four-bar phrases. There are some striking moments, as in the B section (mm. 161–68), when Romeo repeats the same descending gesture three times on "così lasciarmi" and then again four bars later on "nel mio dolore," as if in imitation of real sobs. Overall, however, Bellini's is more conventional in melodic design and formal structure than Vaccai's, features that render it a more challenging vehicle for displaying Romeo's despair. This point illustrates that prima donnas did not always opt for music that was more

---

earlier setting throws the mezzo-soprano part far more strongly into relief than do Bellini's simple melodies. Vaccai gives effective prominence to the lower notes; Bellini does not" (*The Listener* [August 11, 1966]: 216). Cited in Collins, "Bellini and the 'Pasticcio alla Malibran,'" 135.

Source: I Capuleti e i Montecchi. Piano-vocal score. Milan: Ricordi, 2006, pp. 144–45.

difficult when selecting their aria insertions. In this case, Malibran and her contemporaries selected Vaccai's aria not because it provided a singing *tour de force,* but rather because it granted them more expressive opportunity for the dying hero.

It is interesting to note, moreover, that Bellini may have drawn inspiration for some of his tomb scene from Vaccai's. A faint resemblance, for example, appears in Bellini's arioso passage for Romeo reproduced in example 4.1 and Vaccai's "Ah! se tu dormi, sveglati" (example 4.2). The similarity concerns the most effective passage in Vaccai's aria, the second phrase where he sets the text "vieni, fuggiamo insieme" over a harmonic progression leading from the tonic to a secondary dominant (vii^{o7} of vi), and then to vi (example 4.2, mm. 140–41). The voice descends gracefully from scale degree $\hat{4}$ to $\hat{1}$, the appoggiaturas on "vieni" and "insieme" lending an air of pathos to the scene. Bellini uses a parallel gesture in his arioso when he sets the text "ti chiama il tuo Romeo" (example 4.1, mm. 107–109): here he begins on the dominant of A flat instead of the tonic, but then moves to a secondary dominant (this time V of vi) and then to vi. As in Vaccai's aria, Bellini's vocal line moves from $\hat{4}$ to $\hat{1}$, and it opens with a suspension on the word "chiama" that recalls the appoggiaturas in the earlier version. Rhythmically, moreover, the two passages are nearly identical, the vocal lines each consisting primarily of eighth notes and set off at their openings by prominent rests.

A second, more suggestive resemblance appears at the conclusion of the tomb scenes when Romeo utters his final words. Romani's text follows the same outline in both Vaccai's and Bellini's librettos: right before Romeo dies, this character manages only fragmented expressions, "io manco . . . , addio . . . ," and finally only the first two syllables of Giulietta's name, "Giu_liet . . ." As illustrated in examples 4.4 and 4.5, Bellini followed Vaccai's lead in setting this text over a dominant prolon-

EXAMPLE 4.3.   *I Capuleti e i Montecchi,* "Deh! tu bell'anima," mm. 152–80

gation and moving the voice in descending motion from scale degrees $\hat{3}$ to $\hat{1}$ on "io manco" and "addio." In both cases, moreover, the final two syllables ("Giu_liet. . .") are set in an ascending gesture. Vaccai's leaps from scale degrees $\hat{1}$ to $\hat{1}$, whereas Bellini's moves from $\hat{1}$ to $\hat{5}$ but the result is analogous, each version conveying a lack of harmonic resolution that mirrors the inconclusive nature of the dramatic situation. In both cases, the tonic is reached only after Romeo has died.

My claim here is by no means that Bellini stole the best portions of his prede-

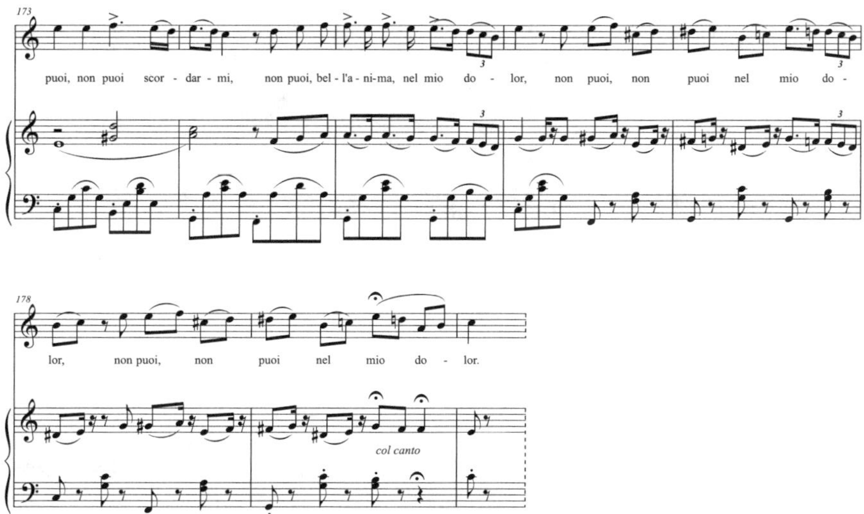

Source: I Capuleti e i Montecchi. Piano-vocal score. Milan: Ricordi, 2006, pp. 144–45.

cessor's score. What I would suggest, however, is that Romeos and Giuliettas may have felt comfortable singing Vaccai's music in place of Bellini's not only because it offered significant differences, but also because the two scenes bore some striking similarities. Rather than this tomb-scene alteration representing an unequivocal dismissal of Bellini's score, singers may have perceived in it far more continuity than have critics of the substitution. This musical explanation helps account, at least in part, for why performers substituted Bellini's music with Vaccai's, but it is only one piece of a much larger puzzle that is solved by returning to a question posed at the opening of this chapter, why and how—when Malibran was not the first prima donna to make this alteration—did it come to be so firmly associated with her, known as the "pasticcio alla Malibran"?

EXAMPLE 4.4.   Vaccai, *Giulietta e Romeo,* final duet, mm. 321–25

Source: I Capuleti e i Montecchi. Piano-vocal score. Milan: Ricordi, 2006, p. 153.

EXAMPLE 4.5.   Bellini, *I Capuleti e i Montecchi,* final duet, mm. 288–93

Source: I Capuleti e i Montecchi. Piano-vocal score. Milan: Ricordi, 2006, p. 135.

MALIBRAN AND MYTH

It is no exaggeration to say that during her brief lifetime, Malibran's reputation loomed larger than her contemporaries'. From 1827, when she returned to Europe from New York City—where she was participating in the first original-language productions of Italian opera in the United States—until her death in 1836, she was the most hotly demanded prima donna touring the operatic circuit, commanding huge fees and in turn attracting record-breaking box-office sales. Described by Alessandro Lanari as an artist who "alone is enough to make the fortune of an enterprise,"[52] she spent the final nine years of her life appearing in every important operatic center in Europe, where time and again she set the standard for artistic excellence. So firmly impressed was the effect of her musicianship and acting abilities on the minds of critics and spectators that prima donnas often found themselves placed in direct competition with her. When Giulia Grisi took on the role of Amina in Bellini's *La sonnambula* at the King's Theatre, London (July 1834), for instance, one critic evaluated her performance based on how she measured up to what Malibran could do:

> It was the first time that [Grisi] appeared in the role from *Sonnambula,* which, being the same performed last season by madama MALIBRAN, generated the greatest interest [among spectators] wanting to see whether madamigella GRISI could hold up under comparison. The result demonstrated that she had not overestimated her abilities, and in spite of the preoccupation in favor of madama MALIBRAN, madamigella GRISI added fresh laurels to the crown with which the public has already ordained her the greatest singer of our time. Not only did she equal, but she also exceeded, if possible, the effect produced by madama MALIBRAN in all of the passionate passages.[53]

52. "Quell'Artista da bastar sola a farla fortuna di un'Impresa." Letter from Lanari to Pacifico Balducci (Naples, July 29, 1834). I:Fn, Lanari 5¹.142.

53. "Era la prima volta che si produceva nella parte della *Sonnambula,* che essendo quella medesima sostenuta nella scorsa stagione da madama MALIBRAN, eccitò grandissimo interesse, volendo pur vedersi se madamigella GRISI reggeva al confronto. L'esito dimostrò ch'essa non aveva troppo presunto delle proprie forze, e ad onta delle preoccupazioni in favore di madama MALIBRAN, madamigella GRISI aggiunse nuovi allori alla corona che già la pubblica opinione aveva decretata come prima can-

Grisi must have been doubly gratified by this reception, for not only did she sing well, she proved herself to be on par—if not superior—to Malibran. Such comparisons were made explicitly when prima donnas took on roles with which Malibran was closely associated. Romeo in *I Capuleti e i Montecchi* was one such part, her appearances as that character so highly admired that one critic reviewing a production of the opera starring a different Romeo, Corinda Corradi Pantanelli (Jesi, Teatro Concordia, 1834), referred to Malibran but without mentioning her by name:

> The impresario, sig. *Malzi,* was worried on account of close comparison with the *Capuleti e i Montecchi* in Senigaglia, where it is well known who was performing the role of *Romeo.*
>
> Signora *Corradi Pantanelli,* well known in Italy's principal theaters, is the *Romeo* of this [production]. She descended into the dangerous arena, where awaiting her were comparisons to the colossal fame [and] the unparalleled skills of she who all of Europe has deemed sublime and unbeatable, and whose inimitable notes still resound in the ear with memories that are still warm today.[54]

Corradi Pantanelli, like Grisi, was able to succeed in the face of this stiff competition, the critic remarking later in the review that she neither "vacillated nor retreated." As such, her performance was received as a far greater triumph than if she had simply sung well—she held up admirably under Malibran's weighty image, and in doing so earned enthusiastic applause.

I would suggest that the opportunity to elicit and contend with Malibran's reputation was one of the primary factors encouraging prima donnas to take on the role of Romeo, the potential rewards of beating this unbeatable singer on her own turf, or merely being recognized as having performed the part as well as her, too tempting to resist. This cultivation of comparison, moreover, may have stood at the core of the popularity of the tomb-scene alteration, for competing with Malibran would have required singing the role as she had chosen to perform it. However, unlike the favorite insertions explored in the last chapter, whose fashion also originated with one or two famous virtuosi, this and one additional alteration Malibran made to Bellini's score resonate with important features of her life story, particularly the tragic tale of her death. To uncover these connections between Malibran and her impersonation of Romeo is to understand why the Vaccai alteration came to be so thickly associated with this singer and no other.

In the anecdotes that follow concerning Malibran, her life, and her death, myth and reality mingle freely, and though I attempt to separate the two, I do not entirely detach fact from fiction, in large part because neither Malibran's public nor Malibran herself made such firm distinctions. Indeed, the stories of her life and

---

tante dei nostri giorni. In tutti i tratti di passione non solo eguagliò, ma superò, se è possibile, l'effetto prodotto in essi da madama MALIBRAN." *Teatri arti e letteratura* 542 (July 31, 1834): 202.

54. "L'appaltatore sig. *Marzi* trepidava a cagione del vicinissimo confronto de' *Capuleti e i Montecchi,* che si sierono in Senigaglia, ove ben sapete chi era colei che la parte eseguiva di *Romeo.*

"La signora *Corradi Pantanelli,* ben nota ai principali teatri d'Italia, è il *Romeo* di questo. Ella discese nella pericolosa arena, ove l'attendevano al paragone la colossale fama, i mezzi insuperabili di quella, che tutta Europa sublime ed insuperabile ha sanzionato, e le cui inimitabili note ancor ne suonano all'orecchio, e con tutt'ora calda rimembranza." *Teatri arti e letteratura* 548 (September 11, 1834): 16.

death became deeply engrained in the popular imagination, and it is the power that these tales held over Malibran's contemporaries and successors, and the effect they may have had on contemporary opera productions, that I would like to explore.

By the 1830s, Malibran was renowned not only as an artist, but also for a reputation for unconventional living, anecdotes concerning her offstage demeanor describing a litany of misbehaviors that might be characterized as self-destructive: she stayed out late; she survived on a meager, unhealthy diet; she drank heavily; she engaged in rigorous physical activity without proper rest; she treated her body ruthlessly.[55] She acted, in other words, like a man—or, more precisely, like a reckless boy—and according to contemporary accounts, she cultivated this image by appearing in public dressed in male garb. She embraced in real life a guise that she so often personified onstage—the trousers role—the most famous of which, of course, was Romeo.

Beyond the physical, Malibran allegedly identified with this character on a darker, more metaphysical level, depicting herself as destined for an early and tragic death. According to her early biographer Ernest Legouvé, she "always said that she would die young [. . .] Sometimes, as if she had felt all at once I don't know what cold breath, as if the shadow of the other world had fallen across her imagination, she would fall into frightful fits of melancholy, and her heart would be plunged into a deluge of tears."[56] Given the retrospective nature of his account, Legouvé may very well have fabricated the story, carving its content from events long past. Indeed, much of Malibran's biography speaks to a tremendous joy and energy in life—her love of nature, her passionate affair with the violinist Charles De Beriot, whom she married in March 1836, and, most of all, her fiery appearances on the operatic stage. Even so, images of death, or rather of a life destined to end too soon, pursued her. Most revealing are journalistic descriptions of Malibran that were published *prior* to her death depicting her as fated. In 1831, a full five years before she passed away, for instance, a critic for London's *Fraser's Magazine* reflected ominously as follows:

> She is one of those, fashioned from that porcelain clay which is so ill calculated to re-sist the shocks of life, and the anxious admirer of her genius cannot oftentimes fail to mark—
>
> —"A gloom
> In her dark eye, prophetic of doom
> Heaven gives its favourites—early death!"
>
> This is, however, too sad a theme to dwell upon.[57]

Not surprisingly, a passing interest in Malibran and death transformed into an obsession once these dire predictions proved correct. Indeed, her posthumous image embodied a mystique that captured the popular imagination during the nineteenth

---

55. Bushnell, *Maria Malibran*, 77–78 and 117; FitzLyon, *Maria Malibran*, 116–18. In her early biography of Malibran, Countess de Merlin discusses and refutes some of these rumors and corroborates others. See *Memoirs of Maria Malibran*, 2 vols. (London: Henry Colburn, 1840), 1: 264–68.

56. Cited and translated in Bushnell, *Maria Malibran*, 129. Legouvé, *Soixant Ans de Souvenirs* (Paris: J. Hetzel, 1880), 100. Remo Giazotto also comments on Malibran's preoccupation with her own death. See his *Maria Malibran*, 176.

57. *Fraser's Magazine* 3 (June 1831): 589.

century in much the same way that Marilyn Monroe's or Princess Diana's do today. Perpetuating this mystique was the operatic story that surrounded her death. This tale has been told and retold by all of her biographers, often with varying details, but with the central elements remaining intact. It begins with a horse ride.

In July 1836, Malibran joined a hunting party with friends in London against the wishes of her husband. She was pregnant, and he did not want her to participate in rigorous activities. The horse she chose to ride was slightly wild, and despite her experience as an equestrian, she was unable to control the animal that broke into a frighteningly rapid gallop as soon as she mounted. She attempted to break free but managed instead to entangle herself in the stirrups. As a result, Malibran was dragged behind for a distance, banging her head repeatedly against the stony road. Her friends rescued her and returned her to her hotel, but once there, Malibran refused to remain in bed. Instead, she got up, cleaned her bruises, and made all witnesses promise to keep the afternoon's events hidden from her husband. She insisted on proceeding with the evening's performance as originally planned. Over the course of the next few months she honored her theatrical commitments in England, Germany, and France, but her health deteriorated rapidly. Her husband and friends encouraged her to consult a doctor, but she shrugged off these suggestions. Following a recital in Manchester in mid-September, Malibran collapsed. She died a few days later at her hotel.[58]

Malibran most likely died of brain damage resulting from her injuries, but this narrative might also be interpreted as revealing a suicide, or at least suicidal tendencies, on her part: her refusal to rest, her insistence on maintaining all performance commitments, her reluctance to consult a physician—all of these elements conspired to rob her of life at too young an age. Of course, Malibran did not literally commit suicide; her refusal to consult a doctor was almost certainly borne of distrust for medical professionals, something shared by many people of the time. Nevertheless, in retellings of this story, Malibran's actions are reported as reckless and ultimately responsible for her death. Read as a suicide, the connections between Malibran and Romeo become quite compelling. Both lived daring—some would say foolhardy—lives; both risked everything for their passion (Romeo's was Juliet; Malibran's was music); and both sacrificed themselves needlessly early for the sake of these loves. In this context, Malibran's famous alteration to *I Capuleti e i Montecchi* adopts a special significance: by selecting her own conclusion for this story—by "rewriting" it with Vaccai's music—the singer strengthened the link between herself and her operatic counterpart: now, not only do they die, but they also do so on her own terms. The evidence here is circumstantial, but during her lifetime, when spectators believed that Malibran actually killed herself during performances of the tomb scene—as witnessed in the review cited above—this connection may have resonated with some audience members. After 1836, the link between Romeo and Malibran was fixed. Performing Vaccai's ending thereafter became a gesture that extended beyond competing with her—it triggered a nostalgia for a performer and creator lost too soon; a perpetual symbol of remembrance.

The connections between Malibran, her posthumous mystique, and the alter-

---

58. See Bushnell, *Maria Malibran,* 216–25, and Merlin, *Memoirs of Maria Malibran,* 249–53, for more detailed accounts of these events.

ations she made to Bellini's score do not end with the tomb scene. One remaining facet of her treatment of *I Capuleti e i Montecchi* renders the links between singer and character, death and suicide, indelible. This connection is rooted in the second major alteration that she and her costar Giuliettas regularly made to the opera, and uncovering its significance requires returning momentarily to a portion of Malibran's death narrative that was omitted above. This part finds her at her final public performance, a concert recital in Manchester, England.

Malibran arrived completely drained from her extended illness. Neither her husband nor her doctors believed she would be capable of performing, but her voice proved as powerful and striking as ever. The final number on the program was the duet from Mercadante's *Andronico,* which she sang with Maria Caradori-Allan. Rather than perform the embellishments as they had rehearsed them, however, Caradori-Allan added more elaborate ones, forcing Malibran to keep pace. The audience's uproarious applause at the conclusion signified that they were thrilled and wanted to hear the whole thing again. Malibran leaned over to the conductor, Sir George Smart, and warned, "If I sing it again it will kill me." "Then don't do it again," he responded. "No," she whispered, "I will do it again, and this time I'm going to annihilate her." Malibran's performance the second time around was twice as virtuosic, and the crowd dissolved into a frenzy. She collapsed almost immediately thereafter and was carried off to her deathbed.[59]

If Malibran can be held responsible for her own death, if this was a metaphorical suicide, then music was the weapon with which she committed the act. What is more, this story reveals the precise identity of the piece that "killed" her: it was the duet from Mercadante's *Andronico,* "Vanne: se alberghi in petto," the other music that she and her costar Giuliettas consistently inserted into their performances of *I Capuleti e i Montecchi.* In the opera, they performed this duet during the Act I finale, interpolating it into the middle of the scene at the moment when Romeo begs Giulietta to run away with him and she resists. "Vanne: se alberghi in petto" is a four-movement duet lasting close to twelve minutes in performance, and thus it would have been challenging, though not unreasonable, to insert into an act during which each character already had to perform their own solo arias, another duet between the two characters, as well as the final ensemble.[60] It would be nearly impossible to perform (twice) in concert while fatally ill.

It is a simple matter to identify where Malibran attempted to "annihilate" Caradori-Allan: the moment arrived with the cabaletta of "Vanne: se alberghi in petto," the text of which is reproduced here:

Giu.:	Quanto è barbaro il mio fato!	How barbarous is my fate!
	Ah! restar più non degg'io.	Ah! I must not stay longer.
	Da te grazia implora, oh Dio!	He who only lives and hopes in you, oh God!
	Chi sol vive e spera in te.	implores mercy from you.

<hr>

59. Paraphrased from Bushnell, *Maria Malibran,* 221–22, and Merlin, *Memoirs of Maria Malibran,* 1: 274–75. A firsthand account by Sir George Smart is reproduced in H. Bertram Cox and G. L. E. Cox, eds., *Leaves from the Journals of Sir George Smart* (London: Longmans, Green, 1907), 282–83.

60. Indeed, the "duet" within the Finale Primo had a long history—Rossini's *Ermione* contains a wonderful one, and it was given new life with Donizetti's *Anna Bolena.*

Rom.: Quanto è barbaro il mio fato!   How barbarous is my fate!
    Ah! lasciarti ohimè! degg'io;   Ah! to leave you, ah! I must;
    Ma non ultimo è l'addio,   but this is not the final farewell,
    Che tu, amata, or hai da me.   that you, love, now have from me.[61]

Like many duet cabalettas, this one contains a built-in competition (example 4.6; the text in the example is Mercandante's original).

It opens in the soprano part with two eight-bar phrases (mm. 106–13 and 114–21), divided evenly into two four-bar units, and concluding with a four-bar cadential passage (mm. 122–25). The mezzo (Malibran's part) takes over in measure 175 and performs the same tune. The pace and excitement then increase as the soprano returns with a four-measure antecedent phrase (m. 146), which she passes on immediately to the mezzo, who answers with a four-bar consequent (m. 150). This tossing back and forth occurs once more until the singers come together to conclude in parallel motion in measure 162 (not included in the example). The whole unit recurs only moments later with the repeat of the entire cabaletta tune. Traditionally, the performers would have waited for this repeat to embellish their vocal lines, but given the special circumstances, both Caradori-Allan and Malibran might have opted to add intricate ornaments right away, especially the second time around. Significantly, Malibran would have maintained the crucial advantage: because she always followed the soprano she could listen to her opponent's ornaments and then exceed them in difficulty.

Though there is no question that the encore occurred, the rivalrous nature of the relationship between these two singers has taken on a significance that, perhaps, exceeds the true nature of actual events. "The possibility of a pair of exceptional singers playing improvisation games with each other live on stage should not be entirely ruled out," writes Damien Colas in his study of *bel canto* ornamentation. But, he warns, "the only trace of it is the testimony of the singers in question—testimony we may suspect of having itself been the object of a certain embellishment."[62] In the case of Malibran and Caradori-Allan, we lack the testimony of both singers, but newspaper reviews confirm that an encore took place—an article in *The Times,* for instance, states that following their first performance of Mercadante's duet, "a complete storm of applause testified the enthusiasm of the audience, and the rapturous *encore* which succeeded was instantly responded to. The repetition was greeted with equal enthusiasm."[63] Some contemporary accounts of the concert, however, make no mention of the fateful contest between the two prima donnas, suggesting that if the two singers were engaged in brutal battle, some in the audience might not have noticed. Indeed, a review published in *Teatri arti e letteratura* does not even mention that an encore occurred: "She sang in the quartet of Fidelio, and she consented to sing in a duet with Carradori [*sic*] Allan. As soon as the tempest of applause which she drew had calmed, the great artist, one moment ear-

---

61. Bologna, Teatro Comunale, autumn 1832 (libretto, I:Vgc).

62. Damien Colas, "Melody and Ornamentation," in *The Cambridge Companion to Rossini,* ed. Emanuele Senici (Cambridge: Cambridge University Press, 2004), 123.

63. *The Times,* September 16, 1836.

EXAMPLE 4.6. Mercadante, *Andronico,* "Vanne: se alberghi in petto," mm. 105–61

Source: Paris: Carli, 18—; plate no. 2431.

lier so brilliant, so animated, fainted out of her senses."[64] This critic alludes to the possibility that Malibran was weakening when she agreed to perform "Vanne: se alberghi in petto," moreover, and if such was the case, it is difficult to believe that Caradori-Allan would have insisted on a rigorous contest. The two women had a long history of performing together, and according to contemporary accounts they were close associates and friends, Caradori-Allan reportedly falling seriously ill on hearing the news of Malibran's death.[65] Another friend and associate, the tenor John Braham, who performed in the same concert, sent news on to his wife three days after Malibran died, remarking only, "I have no doubt the first cause of her death was the dreadful fall she had from her horse in the Park some weeks since."[66] Had he any reason to suspect that her performance of the Mercadante duet was the direct cause of her death, surely he would have said so in this letter.

Though this tale might be slightly exaggerated, its significance to Malibran's biography and to the performance history of Bellini's opera is critical, and its import is illuminated when situated against the broader context of operatic rivalries in general. These narratives tend to pit two singers (at least one of whom is typically a prima donna) against one another, and as Suzanne Aspden has pointed out, they are often exaggerated (or fabricated) as a means to condemn, and thus contain, the threat of powerful women.[67] If quantity is a revealing factor, then the sheer volume of narratives that situate Malibran in rivalrous relationships with other singers suggests that hers was an image that desperately required containment. In addition to the contest between her and Caradori-Allan, tales of competitions with Henriette Sontag, Miss Paton, and Giovanni Battista Velluti all circulated liberally through biographical and journalistic accounts, all equally dubious in their content.[68] The

64. "Essa aveva cantato nel quartetto del Fidelio, ed aveva acconsentito a cantare in un duetto colla Carradori [*sic*] Allan. Appena si era calmata la tempesta di applausi che ella riscosse, che la grande artista, un momento prima così brillante, così animata, cadde priva di sense." *Teatri arti e letteratura* 658 (October 6, 1836): 40.

65. Their association began early in Malibran's career, at the King's Theatre, London, where she appeared as Felicia in Meyerbeer's *Il crociato in Egitto,* which also featured Giovanni Batista Velutti as Armando and Caradori-Allan as Palmide (see *New Monthly Magazine and Literary Journal* 48 [1836]: 302). Malibran and Caradori-Allan appeared together in concert at least one other time in the months leading up to Malibran's death. According to a review in *The Times* the concert was also at the King's Theatre, where, among other pieces, they sang a duet that "afforded a rare specimen of rivalry between two of the finest voices" (see *The Times* [May 5, 1836]). A report of Caradori-Allan falling ill upon learning that Malibran had died is found in *Teatri arti e letteratura* 660 (October 20, 1836): 56.

66. Letter from John Braham to his wife Fanny dated September 26, 1836. Somerset Archive, Taunton, England (DD/SH 60 JB1/21). My thanks to Rachel Cowgill for informing me of this letter's existence.

67. See "'An Infinity of Factions': Opera in Eighteenth-Century Britain and the Undoing of Society," *Cambridge Opera Journal* 9 (1997): 7–10.

68. For anecdotes regarding the rivalry between Malibran and Sontag, see Anonymous, *Life of Henriette Sontag* (New York: Stringer and Townsend, 1852), 15 and 42, Bushnell, *Maria Malibran,* 88, Giazotto, *Maria Malibran,* 102–4, and Francis Rogers, "Henriette Sontag in New York," *Musical Quarterly* 28 (1942): 101. For the anecdote regarding the rivalry with Miss Paton, see "Scene della vita: un tratto singolare della vita della Malibran," *Teatri arti e letteratura* 691 (May 27, 1837): 105–106. For anecdotes regarding the rivalry with Velluti, see Bushnell, *Maria Malibran,* 11, and Merlin, *Memoirs and Letters of Maria Malibran,* 65. Giazotto investigates the dubious nature of the Velluti rivalry (see his *Maria Malibran,* 43).

alleged battle between Malibran and Velluti, the last of the great castratos, is particularly striking for the precision with which it mirrors her contest with Caradori-Allan, both accounts constructed around the same essential plot detail: one singer surprises the other by improvising live in concert ornamentation that was far more complicated than what was planned during rehearsals.

It is the differences between these two tales, though, that are truly revealing. The competition with Velluti supposedly occurred in 1824 when Malibran was still a teenager, long before she achieved fame or recognition, a dwarf to his giant; more important, it was *she* who vanquished in the earlier tale, establishing a triumphant (even heroic) entrée onto what was to become a spectacular career. It is perhaps no coincidence, moreover, that the duet with which she allegedly dealt him his final blow was from Zingarelli's *Romeo e Giulietta.*[69] Once again, the story of this fated couple weaves its way into Malibran's biographical narrative, only this time it is she who sings the part of Giulietta to Velluti's Romeo. In depicting Malibran as the winner in this contest, therefore, this story does more than establish her as the superior artist; it literalizes the transfer of the heroic role of Romeo from a castrato to a mezzo-soprano part. Both the first and the last rivalry thus function as bookends neatly encompassing this singular career: it is in the Romeo and Juliet story that Malibran achieves her first success, and it is in the context of this same tragedy that she is ultimately destroyed. Narrative efficacy gave rise to these tales of rivalry and encouraged them to flourish long after Malibran had passed away.

The story of Malibran and Mercandante's duet may have had a particularly important impact on the performance history of *I Capuleti e i Montecchi,* moreover, for like the alteration to the tomb scene, the addition of "Vanne: se alberghi in petto" into Bellini's opera also made a long-lasting impression: no fewer than five pairs of singers introduced it into later productions of the opera, four of whom did so following Malibran's death.[70] Perhaps it was the duet alone that appealed to these singers, compelling them to introduce it into Bellini's opera, but it is also possible that this piece was attractive to later performers for its connection to Malibran: "Vanne: se alberghi in petto" gained an aura of fatality that was capable of bringing down the strongest, most vibrant performer of the day. By executing it successfully in the context of *I Capuleti e i Montecchi,* her successors may have been trying to convey a simple idea: what Malibran could not withstand, they could overcome.

To perform *I Capuleti e i Montecchi* "alla Malibran," therefore, ultimately meant far more than simply trading in Bellini's tomb scene for Vaccai's. It meant tapping into the reputation that clung to Malibran while she was alive, and into the powerful mystique that surrounded her memory following her death. The narratives of her death fascinated spectators and critics alike not only for their sensationalist over-

69. Merlin, *Memoirs and Letters of Maria Malibran,* 65.

70. The singers who performed the duet, cities, theaters, and years during which these productions occurred are as follows: Chiara Albertini and Lucrezia Sangiorgi (Modena, Teatro del Corte, 1835); Adelaide Morelli and Rosa Camilletti (Urbino, Teatro de' Nobil. Sigg. Pascolini, 1837); Carolina Cuzzani and Serafina Tocchini Alderani (Siena, Teatro dei Rinnovati, 1842); Giulia Sanchioli and Marietta Gubbiani (Ascoli, Teatro di Ventidio Basso, 1856); and Giulia Sanchioli and Marietti Corticelli (Pisa, Teatro di Pisa, 1857). Librettos for all five operas are located in I:Vgc.

tones, but for the image of the Romantic artist that they conjured up. Malibran became more than just a singer who died young—she personified the doomed and tortured Romantic spirit, a haunted figure animated by art. She killed herself with music (or so the story goes), and as such, she became a real-life incarnation of a character drawn from a second piece of popular fiction: Antonia from E. T. A. Hoffmann's short story "Councillor Krespel" (ca. 1817). As many opera goers would have been well aware, Antonia embodies a tragic paradox: gifted with the most magical vocal powers ever heard, she is prohibited from using them by a mysterious medical affliction that will kill her if she sings. Conscious as she is of her condition, she is ultimately unable to deprive herself and her lover of her artistry, and so one fateful night she breaks down and performs gloriously—more beautifully than ever before. By the next morning she is dead. Once again, the connections that one might draw are irresistible: like Antonia, Malibran knew that if she sang it would kill her; like Antonia, she went ahead and did it anyway.[71]

To speak of Malibran, the alterations she made to *I Capuleti e i Montecchi,* and the ideals of Romanticism in the same breath lays bare one final paradox: if altering Bellini's score in imitation of Malibran meant associating oneself with the Romantic components of her story, it also meant participating in the practice that was coming to be perceived as most antithetical to Romantic ideals. She meddled with Bellini's work, and in doing the same her imitators demonstrated a flagrant disrespect for the author and for his opera. Such accusations, however, might have been beside the point, for Malibran, too, played a role in "authoring" *I Capuleti e i Montecchi,* though her contributions were performative rather than textual. To emulate her was to tap into Romantic ideals, regardless of the form they took. Perhaps Malibran herself was aware of the sway she held over others; perhaps we might even believe Legouvé when he tells us in his biography that in the midst of a desperately melancholic mood, Malibran placed pen to paper and set down these tormented words: "How many women envy me! What do they envy me for? It is this unfortunate happiness. Do you understand? My happiness is Juliet! It is dead like her, and me, I am Romeo, I mourn it."[72]

71. For a detailed discussion of Antonia in the context of the Romantic imagination, see Hadlock, *Mad Loves,* chapter 3, "Song as Symptom: Antonia, Olympia, and the Prima Donna Mother" (Princeton, N.J.: Princeton University Press, 2000), 67–85.

72. Letter dated April 1831. Cited and translated in Bushnell, *Maria Malibran,* 129. Legouvé, *Soixante Ans de Souvenirs,* 2: 110–11.

CHAPTER 5

CHE VUOL CANTARE? THE LESSON SCENE OF IL BARBIERE DI SIVIGLIA

The second act of Rossini's *Il barbiere di Siviglia* opens amid confusion, the easily frazzled Dr. Bartolo shaken by an unexpected and unwelcome knock at his door. The culprit is a stranger, "Don Alonso," who proudly introduces himself as professor of music and student of Don Basilio. Alonso explains that Basilio has taken ill unexpectedly and has sent the young man to give Rosina a singing lesson in his place. Bartolo is reluctant to agree to this abrupt change of plan, but his reservations dissipate when Alonso describes the "real" reason for his presence: he claims to have intercepted a letter from Count Almaviva, and if allowed a moment to converse with Rosina alone, he will use it to convince her of the Count's supposed dishonesty. Bartolo is duped, and the ruse begins. As Rosina is aware, Alonso is none other than "Lindoro," the poor student with whom she has fallen in love—he has come not as an ally of her jealous guardian, but rather to steal a few amorous moments in private with her in order to arrange her plan of escape; what she does not know is that Lindoro is actually a grandee of Spain, the Count Almaviva, a character thus presenting himself in double disguise. Though the unveiling of his various masks will eventually come to pass, at the moment Almaviva's multilayered identity is of secondary interest. Rosina's music lesson is about something else—an act of performance initiated by a simple question: "Che vuol cantare?" ("What do you want to sing?") No other question in the operatic repertory has ever received a greater variety of responses.

Almost since the premiere of *Il barbiere di Siviglia* at Rome's Teatro Argentina on February 21, 1816, Rosina's choice for her music lesson has depended on the prima donna cast in the role. The first to eliminate the aria Rossini composed for the scene, "Contro un cor che accende amore," in favor of another was the original Rosina, Geltrude Righetti-Giorgi. In its place she performed "La mia pace, la mia calma" (origin unknown) at the opera's first revival (Bologna, Teatro Comunale, summer 1816), and then she introduced yet another piece, Stefano Pavesi's "Perché non puoi calmar le pene" in her third appearance (Florence, Teatro della Pergola, autumn 1816).[1] Fast forward to the late twentieth century and one still finds prima

1. Philip Gossett has discussed "La mia pace, la mia calma" in detail in "The Operas of Rossini:

donnas taking liberties, though far less frequently than was once the case. Both Marilyn Horne and Cecilia Bartoli have performed "Tanti affetti in tal momento" from Rossini's *La donna del lago* in productions of *Il barbiere di Siviglia;* and as recently as November 1998, Lesley Garrett sang "Bel raggio lusinghier" from *Semiramide* to critical acclaim.[2] Unlike the handful of other *bel canto* operas that have maintained an uninterrupted presence in the repertory, and unlike the scenes in those works that were once regularly affected by substitutions and interpolations, the lesson scene of *Il barbiere di Siviglia* has never completely shed its identity as a site for aria insertion. As the widespread practice of removing one aria in favor of another faded precipitously during the second half of the nineteenth century, the tradition of substituting a new aria (or arias) into the lesson scene paradoxically flourished well into the first half of the twentieth, regardless of the country in which the opera was produced, the decade in which it was heard, or the performer who took on the role of Rosina. As such, this scene provides one of the only examples of how aria insertion altered and adjusted over more than a century and a half of countless productions. Even more important, it allows a unique glimpse into the post-history of this practice. The lesson scene carries us from the beginning of the time period under consideration up to the present day. In this context, the central question occupying the previous chapters in this volume takes on new weight: now not only is it necessary to ask how and why prima donnas continued to use aria insertions as they were drifting out of style, it also becomes necessary to ask how these singers continued to alter a composer's score once the practice of doing so had become virtually extinct.

Several straightforward responses exist. The lesson scene's status as an "opera within an opera," for one, allowed prima donnas to manipulate Rossini's text more freely than was often possible, even at a time when aria insertions were still fairly typical; and throughout much of the nineteenth and twentieth centuries, a myth positing a "lost original" justified the tendency to interpolate music into this scene.[3]

Problems of Textual Criticism in Nineteenth-Century Opera" (Ph.D. diss., Princeton University, 1970), 291–93, and some details concerning this aria will receive attention below. At the time of writing this book, Patricia B. Brauner is preparing the critical edition of *Il barbiere di Siviglia,* the introduction to which will undoubtedly contain much of enormous interest concerning the lesson scene, as well as about the compositional and performance history of the opera in general (Gioachino Rossini, *Il barbiere di Siviglia,* in *Works of Gioachino Rossini,* gen. ed. Philip Gossett [Kassel: Bärenreiter-Verlag, 2008]). See, too, Gioachino Rossini, *Il barbiere di Siviglia,* facsimile of the autograph manuscript, ed. Philip Gossett (Rome: Libreria Musicale Italiano, 1993).

2. See Robert Jacobson, "Viewpoint," *Opera News* 46 (1982): 7. For a review of Bartoli's performance, see Charles Ward, "He Said, She Said: Bartoli Reviews Are In," *The Houston Chronicle* (April 30, 1993). For a review of Garrett's performance at the London Coliseum, see Rodney Milnes, "Singing Lesson from a Soprano," *The Times* (November 28, 1998).

3. The myth that Rossini originally composed a trio for the lesson scene instead of an aria, and that this ensemble was lost, originated in the mid-1860s. Alexis Azvedo, one of Rossini's earliest biographers, makes this claim (*G. Rossini: sa vie et ses oeuvres* [Paris: Heugel, 1864], 112n). Rossini himself alludes to original "concerted pieces for the Lesson" in a letter to his friend Domenico Liverani, though not specifically to a trio (dated June 12, 1866, and translated in Weinstock, *Rossini: A Biography* [New York: Alfred A. Knopf, 1975], 56). Though unfounded, this myth was used throughout the first half of the twentieth century to justify the presence of insertion arias. See, for example, "Music and Music Makers," *New York Times* (March 4, 1906): 11, where Richard Aldrich writes, "Whether or not the trio from

Like many instances of substitution discussed thus far, moreover, the original aria was perceived by prima donnas as dispensable, particularly so in this case because of its utter inability to compete in popularity with Rosina's famous cavatina "Una voce poco fa." The lesson scene alterations are significant not for what they share with changes made to other scenes in other operas, however, but rather for the manner in which they stand apart: more than was the case with any other opera, prima donnas brazenly disregarded stylistic consistency when selecting their substitute arias for Rosina's music lesson, often introducing arias that were wholly—even comically—incompatible with the texture of Rossini's score. Rather than seeking to veil (if only thinly) potential disjunctions by selecting aria insertions that could blend into their new surroundings, performing them with poetry rewritten to conform to the new dramatic context, Rosinas emphasized, sometimes even celebrated, the diversity of their choices, shirking gestures toward unity or conformity. Traces of this tendency can be detected as early as the second and third decades of this opera's performance history, and the situation grew markedly more pronounced as the nineteenth century progressed and the twentieth unfolded.

Critics occasionally complained about, or at least alluded to, what they perceived to be weak connections between Rossini's work and the arias substituted into the lesson scene. Such was the case for a production of *Il barbiere di Siviglia* at the Teatro San Samuele in Venice (October 31, 1830), for instance, about which the critic for *Teatri arti e letteratura* wrote, "[Teresa Croce] *Zacchielli,* who sustained the role of the student, is certainly a fine performer of *gorgheggi,* having sung [*solfeggiate*] well the variations from *Donna del Lago,* which she introduced without even taking the trouble of changing the words."[4] And two decades later, a critic for the *Illustrated London News,* commenting on a production at London's Royal Italian Opera, observed, "Madame [Angiolina] Bosio made quite a sensation: if she had not sung a mawkish air with variations, by Vaccaj, her triumph would have been complete."[5] More typically, however, praise was lavished on these prima donnas, regardless of whether the arias they introduced into the lesson scene were composed by Rossini, a contemporary, or a successor, and regardless of how well (or inadequately) the new music conformed to its surroundings. When Chiara Gualdi sang Pacini's "Ah sì di nuova speme" during an 1832 production at Lugo's Teatro Comunale, for example, the critic for *Teatri arti e letteratura* wrote that she was "greeted with the most universal and lively applause," particularly in the inserted number, "in which she delivered the highest mastery of singing, and force of expression";[6] when Marietta Ar-

---

the lesson scene was deliberately discarded by prima donne [*sic*] who wanted to sing brilliant solo interpolations, it was lost, and for all subsequent time prima donne have had to sing such interpolations for their music master."

4. "La *Zacchielli* che vi sostiene la parte della Pupilla è certamente una buona esecutrice di gorgheggi, ha ben solfeggiate le variazioni della *Donna del Lago* che vi ha intruse senza nemmeno prendersi la pena di cangiar le parole." *Teatri arti e letteratura* 348 (November 18, 1830): 89. This review is published in the form of a letter dated Venice, November 4, 1830.

5. *Illustrated London News* 22, no. 616 (April 9, 1853): 271. According to the *Gazzetta musicale di Milano* (anno 11, no. 16 [April 17, 1853]: 69), this air was probably from Vaccaj's *Pietro il grande* (Teatro Ducale, Parma, 1824).

6. "Ogni sera viene salutata di universali vivissimi applausi, e specialmente nel rondeau finale—*Ah*

mandi introduced "Com'è bello" from Donizetti's *Lucrezia Borgia* at Modena's Teatro Comunitativo (carnival 1848), one critic described the music and her performance as appreciated above all else;[7] and when Regina Pinkert inserted "Ombre légère qui suis mes pas," otherwise known as the Shadow Song from Meyerbeer's *Dinorah* at a production at Trieste's Teatro Fenice in 1894, the *Gazzetta musicale di Milano* reported that she received "clamorous and universal applause" ("applausì calorosi ed unanimi"), the cheering spectators forcing her to repeat the number before the production could move on.[8]

The carnivalesque character of the lesson scene and the variety of arias introduced over the opera's performance history is hardly unfamiliar terrain, yet commentary on the phenomenon has extended little further than inventorying the arias that a handful of prima donnas performed. In his monumental biography of Rossini, Giuseppe Radiciotti supplies one of the most detailed lists:

> Up until 1819, Ronzi de Begnis sang in this scene "La biondina in gondoletta," a Venetian barcarolle with variations; and later, Sontag sang the Rode variations; Fodor sang the aria "Di tanti palpiti," Pauline Garcia sometimes sang a romanza by Malibran, *La fiancée du bandit,* sometimes one of the rondòs in Spanish composed by her father; Borghi-Mamo sang the waltz by Arditi, the far too famous *Bacio;* Patti sometimes sang the waltz, *Di gioia insolita,* sometimes the Spanish canzone titled *La Calessera,* sometimes the rondò from *Manon* by Auber; other singers have introduced the variations by Proch, etc.![9]

Accounts of the lesson scene by H. Sutherland Edwards, Riccardo Bacchelli, Robert Jacobson, and others have followed along similar lines.[10] Given the volume and variety of arias introduced, the temptation to list (almost as if this history were a *buffo* aria in and of itself) is somewhat irresistible, and this chapter will be devoted, in part, to expanding the catalogue of who sang what and when. In participating in the long-established urge to take account of how prima donnas have altered the lesson scene, however, my goal is not merely to offer a new-and-improved inventory. Rather, my aim is to recall and reevaluate the celebratory spirit that surrounded these changes during the nineteenth and early twentieth centuries, to understand whence it emerged, how it was justified, and which prima donnas were most centrally responsible. Today it might seem strange to encounter a production of *Il bar-*

---

sì di nuova speme—del maestro *Pacini* in cui essa spiega tutta la maestrìa del canto, e la forza dell'espressione." *Teatri arti e letteratura* 411 (February 3, 1832): 185.

7. "Sommamente poi riesce gradita la romanza della *Lucrezia Borgia* intrusa nell'opera." *Teatri arti e letteratura* 1256 (March 2, 1848): 211.

8. *Gazzetta musicale di Milano* anno 49, no. 42 (October 21, 1894): 669.

9. "Così, fin dal 1819, la Ronzi de Begnis cantava in quella scene 'La biondina in gondoletta,' barcarola veneziana con variazioni; e, più tardi, la Sontag le variazioni di Rode; la Fodor l'aria 'Di tanti palpiti,' Pauline Garcia ora una romanza della Malibran, *La fiancée du bandit,* ora uno dei rondò in lingua spagnola, composti dal padre; la Borghi-Mamo il valser dell'Arditi, il troppo famoso *Bacio;* la Patti ora il valser, *Di gioia insolita,* ora la canzone spagnola dal titolo *La Calessera,* ora il rondò della *Manon* dell'Auber; altre cantanti v'intercalavano le variazioni di Proch, ecc!" *Gioacchino Rossini: vita documentata, opere ed influenza sul'arte,* 3 vols. (Tivoli: Arti grafiche Majella di A. Chicca, 1927–1929), 1: 232.

10. H. Sutherland Edwards, *The Life of Rossini* (London: Hurst and Blackett, 1869), 149; Riccardo Bacchelli, *Rossini* (Turin: Tipografia Torinese, 1945), 141; Jacobson, "Viewpoint," 7.

biere di Siviglia in which a prima donna eliminated "Contro un cor" in favor of "Deh! torna mio bene" (also known as "Proch's Variations"). And yet, when the American soprano Suzanne Adams made this change for an 1886 production at the Teatro Massimo Bellini in Catania, Sicily, she was applauded so rapturously that rather than move on with the performance, she stepped to the front of the stage and "rewarded" her spectators with an encore of the Sicilian canzone "Non t'arricordi quann'eri malata."[11] This chapter explores the cultural forces that gave rise to this and other spectacles that took place in the lesson scene of *Il barbiere di Siviglia,* looking in particular at what such traditions divulge about performers and their spectators from particular times and places. Addressing these issues requires a full understanding of the historical background of these changes as well as an appreciation of what was at stake when the original aria was removed.

LOSING "CONTRO UN COR"

> The lesson scene was awaited with impatience; the placement of the piano here, long since furniture of Bartolo's salon, was carried to the front of the stage. Don Alonzo, making his selection from among the pieces of music spread over the instrument proposed an air by the composer García to Rosina; this souvenir of one of our most beloved virtuosi, which the talents of his daughter [Maria Malibran] renders even more delightful, was heard favorably, and the name of García received the applause which [spectators] once bestowed on the singer himself.[12]

As this review from an 1828 performance of *Il barbiere di Siviglia* suggests, early-nineteenth-century audiences expected new music to appear during the lesson scene. It represented a moment of anticipation, and waiting to hear which aria the Rosina of the evening would sing quickly established itself as part of the fun, regardless of whether the prima donna was a star or a novice. This situation is not without historical precedent. Lesson scenes appeared in many eighteenth-century *opere buffe,* where it was common for prima donnas to omit composers' original music in favor of arias that, for better or for worse, demonstrated that the last thing they required was a singing lesson. Mayr's *Che originali* (also known as *Il fanatico per la musica*)—which premiered in 1798 and was revived frequently throughout the first quarter of the nineteenth century—was one such opera. Its plot, centering on an arrogant nobleman, Don Febeo (the eponymous "musical fanatic") and his daughter Aristea (a singer and keyboardist), permitted ample opportunities for aria insertions, including a lesson scene during the first act. When Angelica Catalani (1780–1849), the most renowned (many would say notorious) soprano of her generation, took on the role of Aristea at the King's Theatre in 1824, for instance, she

---

11. *Gazzetta musicale di Milano* anno 41, no. 12 (March 21, 1886): 92.

12. "On attendoit avec impatience la scène de la leçon; le simulacre de piano qui, depuis longtemps, meuble le salon de Bartolo, a été porté sur l'avant-scène. D. Alonzo, faisant un choix parmi les morceux de musique étalés sur l'instrument, a proposé à Rosina un air del maestro Garcia; ce souvenir d'un de nos virtuoses favoris, que le talent de sa fille nous rend encor plus cher, a été vivement senti, et le nom de Garcia a reçu les applaudissemens que l'on donnoit autrefois à celui qui le porte." *L'eco* (May 5, 1828). This review was reprinted in the original French in *L'eco* and according to the introductory remarks it first appeared in *Le figaro,* but the exact date of that publication is unknown.

sang Rode's variations in place of Mayr's music.[13] This aria, as Radiciotti's inventory cited above has already suggested, and as I will discuss in greater detail below, came to figure prominently in performances of Rossini's lesson scene as well.

Equally significant were productions of Paisiello's *Il barbiere di Siviglia* (St. Petersburg, Hermitage, 1782). This opera, which famously preceded Rossini's and shared with it many details of plot, may have also influenced the way that prima donnas treated the lesson scene, for Rosinas occasionally replaced Paisiello's original aria, "Già riede primavera," with other numbers. In the autumn of 1785 at Padua's Teatro Obizzi, for example, Teresa Oltrabelli substituted Luigi Caruso's aria "Resta in pace amato bene";[14] and in the spring of 1808 at Verona's Teatro Filarmonico, Adele Delmani sang "Perché mai tiranni Dei" (origin unknown).[15] Though many other prima donnas undoubtedly treated Paisiello's lesson scene in a similar manner, the majority of extant contemporary librettos retain the original text, suggesting that aria substitution may not have been as common in the earlier work as it was in Rossini's.[16] Thus, although precedent may have played some role in compelling Rosinas to add their own choice of arias into *Il barbiere di Siviglia,* other forces were also at play.

Dramatically, the lesson scene of Rossini's opera shares a narrative catalyst encouraging prima donnas to insert arias of their own choice: specifically, it is a moment of "realistic" singing (to borrow the term coined by Edward Cone), during which the participating characters perceive what occurs on stage as an actual musical performance, as opposed to a mundane ("verbal") conversation.[17] Carolyn Abbate clarifies the distinction between this type of music and more ordinary "operatic" singing when she writes that realistic singing "might be loosely defined as musical or vocal performance that declares itself openly, singing that is heard by its singer, the auditors on stage, and understood as 'music that they (too) hear' by us, the theater audience."[18] The recitative dialogue directly preceding "Contro un cor," which the opera's librettist Cesare Sterbini based on the corresponding scene from

13. *Quarterly Musical Magazine* 6, no. 21 (1824): 62.

14. "Resta in pace amato bene" is from Caruso's opera *Scipione in Cartagena* (Venice, Teatro San Samuele, autumn, 1779). The text for the aria is found in Il barbiere di Siviglia / dramma per musica / in quattro atti / da rappresentarsi / nel Reale Teatro Obizzi / di Padova / nel corrente autunno 1785 / [ ] / in Padova / nella Stamperia Penada / con Lic. de' Sup. (I:Vgc).

15. Il barbiere / di Siviglia / ovvero / La Precauzione Inutile / dramma giocoso per musica / da rappresentarsi / nel Teatro Filarmonico / La primavera dell'anno 1808. / [ ] / Verona / Presso Pietro Bisesti Stampatore, e Librajo in Via Nuovo alla Speranza. (I: Vgc).

16. To take two examples, the librettos from productions at Genoa's Teatro del Falcone (spring 1796) starring Francesca Ricardi as Rosina, and from the Teatro alla Scala (autumn 1811) starring Lorenza Corrèa both retain the original text for the lesson scene. Librettos located in the archives of the Fondazione della Scala (Mus. P. VII. 2 and Mus. P. VII. 4).

17. Edward Cone, *The Composer's Voice* (Berkeley: University of California Press, 1974), 29–37, and "The World of Opera and Its Inhabitants," in *Music: A View from Delft,* ed. Robert P. Morgan (Chicago: Chicago University Press, 1990), 13–28. See also Carolyn Abbate, *Unsung Voices* (Princeton, N.J.: Princeton University Press, 1991), 5, who refers to this type of operatic utterance as "phenomenal" song. Another way to define this type of operatic utterance is as "stage music" (see Luca Zoppelli, "'Stage Music' in Early Nineteenth-Century Italian Opera," trans. Arthur Groos and Roger Parker, *Cambridge Opera Journal* 2 [1990]: 29–39).

18. Abbate, *Unsung Voices,* 5.

Beaumarchais's play *Le barbier,* is significant, moving the succeeding musical material swiftly out of the "operatic" world and into the "realistic":

Con.:	Che vuol cantare?	What do you want to sing?
Ros.:	Io canto, se le aggrada,	I will sing, if it pleases you,
	Il rondò dell'inutil precauzione.	The rondò from the Useless Precaution.
Bar.:	E sempre, sempre in bocca	It is always, always on her lips
	L'inutil precauzione.	The Useless Precaution.
Ros.:	Io ve l'ho detto	I told you
	È il titolo dell'opera novella	It's the title of a new opera
	(cercando varie carte sul Pianoforte.)	*(looking through various sheets on the piano.)*
Bar.:	Or bene; intesi: andiamo.	Fine, understood. Let's go.
Ros.:	Eccolo quà.	Here it is.
Con.:	Da brava; incominciamo.[19]	Good; let's begin.

With the Count's question, "Che vuol cantare?" the plane of communication shifts. Rosina will now sing—as opposed to speak—and by announcing her intentions as such ("Io canto"), she establishes that what follows will be a genuine performance of a musical work. The scene is transformed into an opera-within-an-opera, the plot of *Il barbiere di Siviglia* is frozen momentarily, and into this rift a prima donna might conceivably, even comfortably, introduce an aria of her own choice.[20]

It is important to observe in this context an interesting note that appears in Rossini's autograph score. The composer marked an "X" directly after the music lesson's recitative, following which he wrote, "Ovunque si dasse quest'opera è pregata il Sig.e copista dopo s'incominciamo segnar il segno sopra indicato. Rossini" ("Wherever this opera is given, the copyist is requested, after let's begin to mark the sign indicated above. Rossini").[21] The "X" appears once more, following "Contro un cor," within the word "segno."[22] As Gossett explains in his introduction to the facsimile of this score, this notation's meaning is not entirely clear, but it might indicate that Rossini knew that singers playing the role of Rosina would replace "Contro un cor" with alternate musical numbers.[23] Perhaps, in other words, this scene embodied a measure of freedom that was unusual, even at a time when aria insertion throughout the repertory was still quite common.

There are, however, a few important catches, elements dampening the sense that this scene represented a site of unfettered freedom. The first concerns the content of this prefatory dialogue in which Rosina proposes to sing not any old aria, but

19. This text is drawn from the libretto published for the opera's premiere. Alma Viva / o sia / L'inutil precauzione / *commedia* / del signor Beaumarchais / *Di nuovo interamente versificata,e* / *ridotta ad uso dell'odierno teatro* / *Musicale Italiano* / da Cesare Sterbini Romano / *da rappresentarsi* / nel Nobil Teatro / di Torre Argentina / nel carnevale dell'anno 1816 / Con Musica del Maestro / Gioacchino Rossini. / – / Roma / presso Giunchi, e Mordacchini / *Con permesso* (Fondazione della Scala [Mus. R. XXVII.3]).

20. For a similar argument made about Cherubino's aria in Act II of *Le nozze di Figaro,* see Steven Huebner, "Operatic Texts: Ours, Yours, and Mine," *Current Musicology* 84 (2007): 121–22.

21. Gioachino Rossini, *Il barbiere di Siviglia,* ed. Philip Gossett, 2 vols. (Rome: Libreria Musicale Italiano, 1993), 42 of the introduction and 2: 9v.

22. Ibid., 42.

23. Information on this notation in Rossini's score will also be available in the forthcoming critical edition of the opera (*Il barbiere di Siviglia,* ed. Patricia B. Brauner).

rather something from *L'inutile precauzione,* an imaginary opera that is not at all imaginary. This is, of course, the title Rossini originally gave to *Il barbiere di Siviglia* (*Almaviva, o L'inutile precauzione*).[24] The precedent for *L'inutile precauzione* extends back even further to Beaumarchais's play in which Rosine announces that she will sing music from *La précaution inutile.* Dialogue that might have turned spectators' attention outward—say, by naming a nonexistent opera—thus not only refers them directly back to the internal workings of the opera, but also to the play that preceded it, hinting that the following aria will undoubtedly be integral to the surrounding narrative and musical structure. Prima donnas were not deterred by this measure to link "Contro un cor" firmly to the edges of the opera, but there are signs that beginning early on in the performance history of *Il barbiere di Siviglia,* they became aware that replacing "Contro un cor" with a substitute aria called for at least a superficial break from *L'inutile precauzione.*

Extant librettos from the first twenty-five years of *Il barbiere di Siviglia*'s performance history illustrate that as early as the Bologna and Florence revivals of 1816, references to *L'inutile precauzione* were cut throughout the entire opera, including in the lesson scene. The introductory text for "Contro un cor," moreover, was transformed to render the upcoming presence of a substitute aria explicit, alerting listeners to the fact that change was afoot. When Malibran appeared as Rosina at La Scala (autumn 1835) and performed "Di tanti palpiti" during the lesson scene, for example, the text introduced the new aria by name, while simultaneously poking fun at the prima donna's imperious personality:

Con.:	Che volete cantar?	What do you want to sing?
Ros.:	Ora vedremo! (*cercando sul piano-forte*)	Now, let's see! (*looking on the piano*)
	Ecco appunto.—"*Ombra mesta e lagrimosa—*	Ah yes, this exactly.—"*Ombra mesta e lagrimosa—*
Bar.:	Ohibò! troppo nojosa.	Oh no! Too boring.
Ros.:	Questa. "*Di tanti palpiti . . .*	This one. "*Di tanti palpiti . . .*
Bar.:	Neppure.	Not that one either.
	Ci è troppo tenerume e a me non piace.	It is too tender and I don't like it.
Ros.:	Eppur, con vostra pace,	Well, with your blessing,
	Io questa cantar voglio o più non canto	I will sing this one or I won't sing at all.
	Sapete come sono.	You know how I am.
Bar.:	Sì, briccona, lo so.	Yes, you rogue, I know.
Ros.:	Datemi il tono.[25]	Give me the pitch.

In most cases, however, Rosina merely states that she will perform a "piccola arietta," a nonspecific announcement that allows her the freedom to introduce any aria

24. Though it has long been believed that Rossini and Sterbini chose the title *Almaviva, o l'inutile precauzione* to avoid unwanted comparison with Paisiello's opera of the same subject, Saverio Lamacchia has argued convincingly that the link with Paisiello had very little to do with their decision. Much more significant was that the premiere featured Manuel Garcia as Almaviva; he was the real star of the show. See *Il vero Figaro o sia il falso factotum* (Turin: EDT, 2008), 32–39.

25. Il barbiere / di Siviglia / melodramma buffo in due atti / da rappresentarsi / nell'I.R. Teatro alla Scala / l'Autunno 1835 / - / Milano / Per Luigi di Giacomo Pirola / M.DCCC.XXXV (Fondazione della Scala, Mus. R. XXVII. 136).

into the music lesson. This example from an 1818 production of *Il barbiere di Siviglia* at Lucca's Teatro del Giglio is typical:

Ros.:	Io canto se le aggrada	If it pleases you I will sing
	una piccola arietta, colla quale	A little aria,
	esercitar mi soglio	which I usually use
	a temperare il fiero mio cordoglio.	to appease my fierce suffering.
Bar.:	Sarà una bella cosa.	That will be a beautiful thing.
Con.:	Andiamo . . . andiamo.	Let's go . . . let's go.
Ros.:	Eccola qua.	Here it is.
Con.:	Da brava incominciamo.[26]	Good, let's begin.

Rewriting the recitative represented the first step in creating a rift between the lesson scene and the remainder of *Il barbiere di Siviglia;* the second was in eliminating "Contro un cor" itself.

Rossini's original number consists of three parts: a cantabile, *tempo di mezzo,* and cabaletta:

CANTABILE

Ros.:	Contro un cor che accende amore	Against a heart aflame
	Di verace, invitto ardore,	With truthful love and unconquered ardor,
	S'arma invan poter tiranno	The tyrannical power of severity and cruelty
	Di rigor, di crudeltà.	arms itself in vain.
	D'ogni assalto vincitore	Against every assault, love will win
	Sempre amor trionferà.	It will always triumph.
	(*Bartolo s'addormentata.*)	(*Bartolo falls asleep*)

TEMPO DI MEZZO

Ros.:	Ah Lindoro, mio tesoro,	Ah Lindoro, my treasure,
	Se sapessi, se vedessi!	If you only knew, if you could only see!
	Questo cane di tutore	This dog of a tutor, oh how enraged
	Ah che rabbia che mi fa!	He makes me!
	Caro, a te mi raccomando,	Beloved, I beg you,
	Tu mi salva per pietà.	Save me, please.
Con.:	Non temer, ti rassicura,	Do not fear, I assure you,
	Sorte amica a noi sarà.	Fate will be with us.
Ros.:	Dunque spero?	And so I can hope?
Con.:	A me t'affida.	You can trust in me.
Ros.:	E il mio cor?	And my heart?
Con.:	Giubilerà.	It will rejoice.
	(*Bartolo si va risvegliando*)	(*Bartolo is awakened*)

26. Il barbiere di Siviglia / dramma buffo per musica / da rappresentarsi / nel Regio Teatro Pantera / di Lucca / nel carnevale dell'anno 1818 / sotto la protezione / di S. M. Maria Luisa / Infanta di Spagna / Duchessa di Lucca / ec. ec. / Lucca / dalla Tipografia Ducale / con approvazione (I:Vgc). This change, or a slight variant of it, also appears in librettos for the following productions: Bologna, Teatro Contavalli, spring 1816 (I:Bc 4700); Florence, Teatro della Pergola, autumn 1816 (I:Vgc); Milan, Teatro Carcano, quaresima 1819 (I:Bc 4701); Trieste, Teatro Nuovo, carnival 1821 (I:Vgc); Lucca, Teatro del Giglio, spring 1821 (I:Bc 8824); Florence, Teatro della Pergola, autumn 1831 (I:Vgc); Casalmaggiore, Teatro della Società, autumn 1843 (I: Rsc Carv. 1865); Venice, Teatro Apollo, autumn 1843 (I: Vnm, dramm. 1395.14).

CABALETTA

Ros.:   Cara immagine ridente,   Sweet smiling image,
             Dolce idea d'un lieto amore,   Charming idea of a joyful love,
             Tu m'accendi in petto il core,   You make my heart rise in my breast,
             Tu mi porti a delirar.   You make me delirious

As its text suggests, "Contro un cor" is not, in fact, a straightforward example of "realistic" song, but rather a complex blend of "realistic" utterance, and "operatic" speech that refers directly to the narrative at hand. The cantabile (*maestoso,* D major, 4/4) contains the most ambiguous material in the aria, hovering between realistic and operatic realms. On the one hand, it might have originated in any number of *opere serie,* the verse reflecting generic sentiments concerning the power of true love over brutal tyranny. Sung in the context of *Il barbiere di Siviglia,* however, its meaning could not be plainer—Rosina will not allow Bartolo to prevent her from marrying Lindoro. Musically, moreover, the vocal line embodies a double significance: filled with rapid-fire arpeggios and scalar passages, it is simultaneously a parody of an *opera seria* aria and an imitation of the sorts of *esercizi* that a prima donna might practice in the context of a singing lesson.[27]

Bartolo, the cad, fails to grasp this movement's complexity; pleasantly lulled by what he takes to be a simple presentation of a randomly chosen operatic air, he falls fast asleep. At this point, during the frantic *tempo di mezzo* of "Contro un cor," the careful balance between "realistic" and "operatic" collapses, for while Bartolo naps, Rosina and Lindoro hold a conversation in which they exchange information critical to the plot of *Il barbiere di Siviglia.* This is "operatic" singing, plain and simple, in which Rosina expresses the hope that Lindoro will save her from her "dog of a tutor." This shift into the purely operatic realm is reflected in a change within the music itself, Rosina's heavily embellished lines giving way to a series of statements that are almost entirely syllabic—there is no time to waste on ornament. Once Bartolo wakes up, however, their amorous conversation must come to a halt and the cabaletta begins. In this movement Rosina reinitiates the florid singing that she employed in the cantabile, and here, too, the verse can be interpreted as either generic sentiment or plot-specific message. It seems, in other words, that the cabaletta signals a shift back toward a realistic mode of communication, Rosina "performing" her emotions rather than expressing them directly through "speech." Something occurs in this section, however, that indicates a stronger link to the "operatic" world than what appears in the cantabile: in between statements of the cabaletta theme, and again in the final measures, the text from the middle section and its syllabic setting (though not its melody) return. Within the space of a few measures, Rosina must alternate rapidly between her own persona, as plainly exhibited in the plot-specific middle section, and that of an imaginary heroine. Operatic utterance intrudes directly onto the realistic, and as such the cabaletta becomes thickly woven into the plot of the opera.

At bottom then, even though "Contro un cor" is introduced as realistic song, it is in fact anything but, each of its sections fleshing out Rosina's character as well as

27. See Janet Johnson, "*Il barbiere di Siviglia,*" in *The Cambridge Companion to Rossini,* ed. Emanuele Senici (Cambridge: Cambridge University Press, 2004), 172.

providing information that propels the plot of the opera forward. Rossini and Sterbini created an aria rich with musical and dramatic potential, and replacing it with another invariably results in significant changes to the structure of *Il barbiere di Siviglia*. Even so, no singer ever selected an aria insertion for this scene that has struck the same nuanced balance between realistic and operatic singing. Indeed, only a few instances reveal evidence of any attempt to retain the links to the scene's surrounding plot. The most straightforward and well known appears early in the opera's history with "La mia pace, la mia calma," the aria that Righetti-Giorgi substituted into the opera's first revival. This aria is constructed in aba' form, its outer sections containing new musical material that may or may not have been composed by Rossini himself.[28] The b section, however, is familiar, consisting of the original *tempo di mezzo* from "Contro un cor," the portion of the aria most deeply rooted in the "operatic" realm. It is conceivable, then, that at this very early moment in *Il barbiere's* history, the singer (or whoever wrote the new aria for her) deemed it necessary to retain the link between "realistic" and "operatic," between performance and plot.[29]

Such careful attention to the aria's original function, however, evaporated almost immediately. Instead, the lesson scene became witness to aria insertions that had little to do—either musically or dramatically—with the dilemma facing Rosina and Lindoro, and everything to do with drawing attention to the prima donna herself. For the first forty-five years of this opera's life, the majority of these changes consisted of the performance of a single aria, a one-to-one approach to substitution that is typical of the practice throughout most of the *bel canto* repertory. Around 1860, however, an unusual and far more flamboyant tradition began to dominate: in place of "Contro un cor," prima donnas introduced two, three, and sometimes as many as four arias. This break between a conventional mode of aria substitution and what I have come to call the "mini-concert approach" corresponds directly with the ascendancy of one peerless soprano: Adelina Patti (1843–1919). No other singer held more sway over this opera, and beginning with her, the meaning of Rosina's lesson shifted conspicuously. Overlap between the two traditions certainly existed: there are isolated instances prior to 1860 when a prima donna introduced more than one substitution aria into the lesson scene; and the practice of performing only one aria in place of Rossini's original lingered beyond Patti's ascendancy. Nevertheless, it makes sense to speak of a "pre-Patti" and a "post-Patti" approach toward performing the lesson scene. The remainder of this chapter will be devoted to exploring each in turn.

PRE-PATTI TRADITIONS

Beginning with the earliest revivals of *Il barbiere di Siviglia* the lesson scene served as a receptacle for music currently in vogue, and any prohibitions against introducing music that was immediately recognizable to audiences were abandoned gleefully in

---

28. Gossett, "The Operas of Rossini," 291–93.

29. "La mia pace, la mia calma" is included in the new critical edition of *Il barbiere di Siviglia* along with a note that makes the point that the *tempo di mezzo* could be integrated into other substitute arias such as "Di tanti palpiti."

favor of showcasing the favorite arias of the day. The choice of which number a singer performed was often individual, but there were some traditions and habits that accrued around the lesson scene that were followed by a variety of the century's Rosinas.

Many prima donnas stuck close to home, trading in "Contro un cor" for one of Rossini's other arias. Not surprisingly, the most popular was Tancredi's famous cavatina "Tu che accendi" / "Di tanti palpiti," which toured internationally in *Il barbiere di Siviglia:* it was sung by Joséphine Fodor-Mainvielle in Paris (Théâtre Italien, 1821), Rita Gabussi in Milan (Teatro Re, 1837), Giuseppina Ruiz-Garcia in Vienna (Hofoper, 1844), and Teresa Parodi in New York City (Astor Place, 1851).[30] These instances only scratch the surface of this aria's widespread use in Rosina's lesson scene. It was nearly as common for spectators to hear the showpiece *scena* and rondò finale from *La Cenerentola,* "Nacqui all'affanno e al pianto," first introduced by Maria Malibran in 1834, and later by Elena Angri, Adelaide Borghi-Mamo, and many others.[31] Prima donnas mined Rossini's other operas as well. Carolina Pellegrini, for example, chose "Oggetto amabile" from *Sigismondo* for an appearance at Teatro alla Scala (autumn 1820); and Margherita Venturi performed "Quel dirmi, oh Dio!" from *La pietra del paragone* at the Teatro Comunale, Ravenna (carnival 1831).[32] On those occasions when only the second act of *Il barbiere di Siviglia* was performed (such as benefit productions), moreover, prima donnas occasionally chose "Una voce poco fa" as their lesson music rather than depriving audiences of one of the most popular pieces in the opera.[33]

Prima donnas also looked beyond Rossini's *oeuvre,* arias by Pacini, Donizetti, Bellini, their contemporaries, and predecessors appearing as frequently in the lesson scene as Rossini's. Those in attendance at the opera's premiere in Lucca (carnival 1818), for instance, heard Anna Parlamagni sing Pietro Generali's "Deh consola i voti miei" rather than "Contro un cor"; spectators present at the summer 1834 production at Bologna's Teatro Comunale witnessed Gualdi Zinghari introduce the

---

30. Evidence for these performances was gleaned from a variety of sources. For Fodor-Mainvielle, text for "Di tanti palpiti" is printed in the libretto for the 1821 production at the Théâtre Italien (F:Pn Yth 50072); and for Rita Gabussi, the libretto for the 1837 production at the Teatro Re also contains this text (I:Vnm, dramm. 896.14). Information for Ruiz-Garcia's and Parodi's appearances as Rosina are found in reviews. For Ruiz-Garcia, *Teatri arti e letteratura* 1056 (May 2, 1844): 70–71; and for Parodi, *The Literary World* 8, no. 211 (February 15, 1851): 135. See also Mark Everist, "Lindoro in Lyon: Rossini's *Le Barbiere di Séville,*" *Acta Musicologica* 64 (1992): 67–70.

31. Malibran made this alteration in a production at the Teatro Comunale la Fenice, Senigaglia during the summer of 1834 (*Teatri arti e letteratura* 542 [July 31, 1834]: 202). Angri made the alteration at least twice, the first time at Teatro alla Scala in the summer of 1846, and the second at the Hofoper, Vienna, in the summer of 1846 (*Gazzetta musicale di Milano* anno 4, no. 42 [October 19, 1845]: 179–80, and anno 5, no. 32 [August 9, 1846]: 255). Borghi-Mamo also made this change at least twice, the first time at the Teatro alla Scala, during the carnival of 1861, the second at the Teatro Armonia, Trieste in the spring of 1862 (*Gazzetta musicale di Milano* anno 19, no. 9 [March 3, 1861]: 36, and anno 20, no. 20 [May 18, 1862]: 81).

32. Librettos for the productions at the Teatro alla Scala and the Teatro Comunale, Ravena, starring Pellegrini and Venturi respectively, are both housed in I:Vgc.

33. Marietta Alboni performed "Una voce poco fa" instead of "Contro un cor," for example, in a production at the Royal Italian Opera, London (June 1847). *Illustrated London News* 10, no. 268 (June 12, 1847): 379.

rondò finale from Pacini's *Gli Arabi nelle Gallie;* and audiences in British, Italian, Austrian, and French theaters heard the globe-trotting Fanny Tacchinardi-Persiani sing "Forse un destin che intendere" / "V'era un dì" from Donizetti's *Parisina.*[34] As Verdi's star rose during the 1840s and 1850s, his arias were occasionally featured in the lesson scene as well: during a benefit evening at Modena's Teatro Comunitativo in 1848, for instance, Marietta Armandi interpolated "Ernani! . . . Ernani involami"; and a highly praised production at Niblo's Garden in New York City featured Mme. Bertucca-Maretzek performing "an aria from Verdi's *Macbeth*" (probably Lady Macbeth's cavatina, "Vieni, t'affretta").[35]

In his biography of Rossini, Stendhal claims that "in a properly-organized production, Rosina would be given a different song for the music scene every two or three performances."[36] There is little evidence to support this claim, though the sources available prevent us from grasping the whole story—librettos were not reprinted in the event that a prima donna opted to change her aria after opening night, and as a general rule, newspapers published only one review per production, per season. Slightly more apparent is that over many years, a prima donna might vary which aria she sang in the lesson scene, perhaps as a way of accommodating her changing voice, or as a way of catering to the shifting tastes of her spectators. Here, too, evidence is spotty, but we know, for instance, that Elisa Lipparini began her career as Rosina in 1830 substituting "an aria by Donizetti" into the lesson scene; twenty years later, she chose Bellini's "Ah! non giunge," and five years after that, "Della rosa il bel vermiglio" from Rossini's *Bianca e Falliero.*[37] Elena Angri sang Cenerentola's rondò finale at Milan's Teatro Re in the fall of 1845, and then one year later, she introduced two songs "in the Hungarian language by Bartay" when she performed the role at the Hofoper in Vienna. These songs, as one critic notes, "produced a *national enthusiasm*" (emphasis original), an effect that was no doubt carefully planned.[38]

34. A copy of the libretto for the production starring Anna Parlamagni in Lucca is housed in I:Vgc. A review noting that Gualdi Zinghari performed Pacini's aria in the lesson scene is found in *Teatri arti e letteratura* 549 (September 18, 1834): 29. And evidence of Tacchinardi-Persiani's activities is located in a review of her performance at the Théâtre Italien, Paris, in the fall of 1841 (*Teatri arti e letteratura* 930 [December 16, 1841]: 126–27).

35. A review of Armandi's lesson scene appears in *Teatri arti e letteratura* 1256 (March 2, 1848): 211; and a review of Bertucca-Maretzek's performance appears in *The Albion* 12, no. 41 (October 8, 1853): 488.

36. Stendhal, *Life of Rossini,* ed. and trans. Richard N. Coe, 2nd ed. (London and New York: John Calder and Riverrun Press, 1985), 197.

37. The production during which she performed "an aria by Donizetti" took place at the Teatro di Padova (autumn 1830) (*Teatri arti e letteratura,* 351 [December 9, 1830]: 113). She sang "Ah! non giunge" at Milan's Teatro Re (spring 1851) (*Gazzetta musicale di Milano* anno 9, no. 18 [May 4, 1851]: 84). And she performed "Della rosa il bel vermiglio" at Genoa's Teatro Carlo Felice (spring 1856) (*Teatri arti e letteratura* 1658 [October 9, 1856]: 45).

38. A review of Angri's performance appears in the *Gazzetta musicale di Milano* anno 5, no. 32 (August 9, 1846): 255. Introducing arias and songs in the language of the audience was a common ploy, a situation referred to by H. Sutherland Edwards in his biography of Rossini, where he writes that Rosinas "have preferred to substitute a violin concerto, or a waltz, *or a national ballad,* or anything else that the daughter of *Bartholo* [sic] would have been very likely to sing to her music-master" (emphasis mine) (*The Life of Rossini,* 149).

Even when prima donnas chose a new aria every few years, however, they risked accusations of rigidity, of boring audiences by performing the same piece too often. Marietta Alboni, one of mid-century's greatest contraltos and most popular Rosinas, for example, sang the role frequently over the ten-year period spanning 1847 to 1857, during which time she introduced at least two arias into the lesson scene: first Pacini's "Il soave e bel contento" and then later "Carina senti un poco," also known as the "Air à la tyrolienne" by Johann Nepomuk Hummel (1778–1837).[39] According to one critic who heard her at the Théâtre Italien, she should have chosen a third:

> We would like to find a few things to praise in Alboni beyond everything we have already repeated a thousand times:—Fresh, sweet, mellow, velvety voice; easy and extremely efflorescent singing, etc., etc. But, for heaven's sake, couldn't signora Alboni, when she takes her lesson from Don Alonzo, give us an aria other than the eternal *Senti un poco mio carino,* which she has sung for three years without, it seems, changing even one phrase, one note, one cadenza?[40]

This same critic expressed relief when, one season later, Emilie Nantier-Didiée selected another piece in place of Hummel's air: "in the lesson scene, we are finally able to listen to something instead of the same old lullaby with which [Alboni] has tired us: Nantier-Didiée sang an Andalusian *bolero* with some success."[41] What compelled Alboni to choose Hummel's aria and to continue performing it even as critics (at least this one) became restless? Indeed, what was behind any of the choices that prima donnas made for the lesson scene?

Individual preference was unsurprisingly at the root of many of their decisions. When Adelaide Cresotti, a mezzo-soprano about whom virtually nothing is remembered today, selected "Dolenti e care immagini," for example, she was no doubt seeking an alternative to "Contro un cor" that was technically uncomplicated.[42] This aria originated as an insertion aria, composed by Paolo Bonfichi for the Naples

39. She inserted "Il soave e bel contento" into a production at the Royal Italian Opera, London in June 1847 (*Illustrated London News* 10, no. 267 [June 19, 1847]: 394). Hummel's "Air à la tyrolienne" became her lesson-scene "warhorse" beginning as late as February 1854 when she performed it in a production of *Il barbiere di Siviglia* at the Théâtre Italien (*Spirit of the Times* 24, no. 1 [February 18, 1854]: 3). She also inserted "Air à la tyrolienne" at least once in a production at Her Majesty's Theatre, London, in the spring of 1856 (*Illustrated London News* 28, no. 801 [May 24, 1856]: 551). According to Frank Dawes, Hummel's *Tyrolien* was, "a set of vocal variations . . . with orchestral accompaniment, composed for the famous Malibran." See review of *Eleven Piano Duets by the Masters* in *Musical Times* 106, no. 1467 (May 1965): 370.

40. "Voremmo ritrovar nell'Alboni qualche cosa da lodare al di là di quanto abbiam ripetuto le mille volte:—Voce fresca, soave, pastosa e vellutata, canto facile, fioritissimo, ecc., ecc.—Ma non potrebbe di grazia la signora Alboni, quando prende lezione da Don Alonzo, farci dono d'un'altra canzone invece dell'eterna aria, *Senti un poco mio carino,* che canta da tre anni senza forse cangiarvi una frase, una nota, una cadenza?" *Gazzetta musicale di Milano* anno 15, no. 44 (November 1, 1857): 350.

41. "Alla scena della lezione abbiam finalmente potuto intendere altra cosa fuori della solita nenia che ci ha ristucchi: la Nantier-Didiée cantò con abbastanza successo un *bolero* andaluso." *Gazzetta musicale di Milano* (anno 15, no. 46 [November 15, 1857]: 364–65).

42. Cresotti made this alteration in the autumn 1818 at the Teatro di Varese. Evidence for this alteration is located in the libretto: Il barbiere / di / Siviglia / dramma buffo per musica / da rappresentarsi / nel Teatro di Varese / l'Autunno dell'anno 1818 published for this production. / - / Milano / Dai torchj di Gio. Bernardoni, Corsìa di S. Marcellino, / No. 1799 (I: Mr Libr-BAR-10-05).

1817 revival of Carlo Evasio Soliva's *La testa di bronzo* (Milan, Teatro alla Scala, 1817). There is no evidence that anyone else inserted this piece into the lesson scene after Cresotti did at the Teatro di Varese in the autumn of 1818, and the music survives only in manuscripts tucked away in a few Italian archives.[43] In other words, it is arguably only of peripheral importance to the reception history of *Il barbiere di Siviglia*. Nevertheless, it is worthwhile reintroducing here as an example of one extreme—a simplistic one—to which a handful of prima donnas resorted when selecting music for this scene.

The aria's text consists of one quatrain of *settenari,* followed by only seven lines of *quinari* (eight lines would be more common), and the subject matter remains consistent throughout, a gentle plea to a nameless lover. Though shorn of any direct reference to the plot of *Il barbiere di Siviglia,* it might, like "Contro un cor," be read as a performance that takes place on two levels: a generic *seria* aria that is simultaneously capable of delivering a secret message to Lindoro:

Dolenti e care immagini	Sorrowful and dear images
D'un innocente amore	Of an innocent love
Non accrescete i palpiti	Don't increase the throbs
Del misero mio cor.	Of my wretched heart.
Se ancor tu m'ami,	If you still love me,
Mio caro bene,	My beloved,
Alfin dimentica	Finally forgetting
Di tante pene	So many sorrows
Vedrai quest'anima	You will see this soul
Per gioja insolita	Celebrate in this
A giubilar.	Unusual joy.

Musically, this aria could not be simpler, consisting of two sections—a brief 21-measure cantabile followed by a lengthier, though still pithy, 71-measure cabaletta—both in F major. Unlike "Contro un cor," Lindoro does not participate, a characteristic shared by all other arias substituted into the lesson scene. The tessitura of "Dolenti e care immagine" falls within a more restricted range than "Contro un cor" (from B^3 to E^5, as opposed to the original aria's span of A^3 to A^5). What distinguishes the substitution most noticeably, however, is that its melodic line is almost completely void of ornament, a feature exemplified quite clearly in the first statement of the cabaletta theme:

EXAMPLE 5.1.   Paolo Bonfichi, "Dolenti e care immagini," cabaletta theme, mm. 27–38

continued

43. The manuscript copy that I have consulted for this study is a piano-vocal score that contains the

EXAMPLE 5.1.   (continued)

Source: Transcribed from manuscript: "Rondò / Dolenti e care immagini / introdotta / Nell'opera il Barbiere di Siviglia / del Sig. Rossini." Biblioteca del Conservatorio di musica Giuseppe Verdi, Milan (Noseda C.64.15).

With this substitution, Cresotti made little attempt to select an aria that might blend into the fabric of the original, opting instead for music that provided her the best opportunity for a successful performance. This blatant break from Rossini's score, the tendency to forgo "text" in favor of "performance," is amplified and taken to a different extreme when first-rate singers took on the role of Rosina.

As the inventory above suggests, the majority of prima donnas opted for arias that were quite virtuosic, able to showcase their ability for coloratura display. "Oggetto amabile," "Ah! non giunge," "Il soave e bel contento," and so on, all mirror "Contro un cor" in their *fioritura*-rich melodic lines, and it is this feature that undoubtedly appealed more than any other when it came to making a choice for the music lesson. One subset of arias introduced regularly into the scene went further than most in foregrounding virtuosity above drama and poetry: theme-and-variation arias (the vocal equivalent of the instrumental genre in which a simple melody is presented and then adorned in subsequent repetitions). This form emerged on opera and concert stages prior to the premiere of Rossini's *Il barbiere di Siviglia,* and it became an international sensation due to the single-handed efforts of a prima donna who never sang the role of Rosina, Angelica Catalani. During the first quarter of the nineteenth century, Catalani was Europe's premiere soprano, dazzling specta-

---

following written on its cover page: "Rondò / Dolenti e care immagini / introdotta / Nell'opera il Barbiere di Siviglia / del Sig. Rossini." It is located at the Conservatorio di musica Giuseppe Verdi, Milan, where it is catalogued under Soliva's name. A fully orchestrated version of this aria, located at the Conservatorio di musica S. Pietro a Majella, Naples, is correctly attributed to Bonfichi.

tors with a voice that, in the opinion of most contemporaries, was unequaled. Her career spanned two and a half decades, during which time she became a figure of much contention, notorious for her exploits and diva-like behavior: she appeared almost exclusively, for instance, in substandard operas by second-rate composers; she demanded exorbitant fees for her services; and most distastefully, she insisted on singing arias that were perceived by many to be void of aesthetic value. She was, to borrow the words of one of her many detractors past and present, "one of the greatest operatic tyrants of all times."[44]

Despite this tainted reputation, Catalani was a perpetual favorite with European audiences for nearly thirty years and a model to contemporary and successive prima donnas.[45] The music for which she became most highly renowned was her theme-and-variation arias, which she performed both as insertions in various operas and independently in concert. Her repertory contained many, but two in particular became her "signature" tunes: "Rode's variations" (adopted from Pierre Rode's *Air varié* in G major for violin and piano, Op. 10 [1808]), and variations on Paisiello's "Nel cor più non mi sento" (from *La molinara* [1788]).[46] It is no coincidence that these were the two arias that Catalani's successors adopted and performed most frequently in the context of Rossini's lesson scene.

The vogue for introducing these arias into *Il barbiere di Siviglia* began with Henriette Sontag (1806–1854). For her triumphant debut at the Théâtre Italien (May 15, 1826), she introduced Rode's variations, which she continued to use as Rosina's music lesson throughout the remainder of her career.[47] She was not alone in selecting this aria, for the music was so well received in Paris that other prima donnas, including Amalia Schütz, Giulia Grisi, and Anna De Lagrange, followed her lead and performed it on stages in Italy, Great Britain, Mexico, and elsewhere.[48] Through-

44. Stendhal, *Life of Rossini,* 517. The characterization of Catalani as tyrant is Coe's.

45. Hilary Poriss, "Angelica Catalani, Ensemble, and the King's Theatre, 1806–1813," paper read at the annual meeting of the American Musicological Society, Washington, D.C., November 2005. I am currently preparing this study for publication.

46. Catalani's repertory of arias also included variations based on "Das klinget so herrlich" from Mozart's *Die Zauberflöte,* Pacini's "Stanco di pascolar le pecorelle," and "La biondina in gondoletta." According to George Hogarth, she enjoyed entertaining her public, "by way of novelty, with variations, composed for the violin, on popular airs, *God save the King, Rule Britannia, Cease your funning,* and other English songs" (*Memoirs of the Musical Drama,* 2 vols. [London: Richard Bentley, 1838], 2: 376).

47. See "Henriette Sontag" in *Enciclopedia dello spettacolo,* 9 vols. (Rome: Casa editrice Le Maschere, 1954–1962), 9: 125–27, for a description of her first performance as Rosina. Though it is not feasible to account for all of her appearances in this role, we know through printed reviews that she performed Rode's variations during the following productions: King's Theatre, London (summer 1828) (*The New York Mirror* 6, no. 2 [July 19, 1828]: 10); Paris, Théâtre Italien (December 1850) (*Gazzetta musicale di Milano* anno 8, no. 50 [December 15, 1850]: 220); and London, Her Majesty's Theatre (August 1851) (*Illustrated London News* 19, no. 511 [August 23, 1851]: 234).

48. The following list of productions in which Rode's variations were introduced and the singers responsible was gleaned from reviews printed in *Il barbiere di Siviglia, L'eco, Gazzetta musicale di Milano,* and *Teatri arti e letteratura:* Amalia Schütz (Trieste, Teatro Grande [carnival 1830]); Henriette Méric-Lalande (Perugia, Teatro Civico [summer 1834]); Giulia Grisi (Dublin, Theatre Royal [September 1841]); Anna De Lagrange (Trieste, Teatro Grande [carnival 1846], Venice, Teatro la Fenice [carnival 1848], and London, Her Majesty's Theatre [summer 1852]); Sophie Cruvelli (Milan, Teatro alla Scala [carnival 1850]); and Elisa Taccani (Mexico, theater unknown [February 1857]).

out the next three decades, few other arias served as regularly or as widely as replacements for "Contro un cor" (the one possible exception is "Di tanti palpiti"). Variations on "Nel cor più non mi sento" were not as popular as Rode's, but they made occasional appearances in the lesson scene as well, sung by Catalani's student Fanny Corri-Paltoni (Turin, Teatro Carignano, autumn 1829), and later by Fanny Tacchinardi-Persiani (Paris, Théâtre Italien, autumn 1842).[49] The vogue established by these arias in the 1820s and 1830s was perpetuated over the next one hundred years by a few other variation sets. The most prominent were Adolphe Adam's variations on the melody "Ah! vous dirai-je maman" (a.k.a. "Twinkle, Twinkle Little Star") from his opera *Le toréador* (Paris, Opéra Comique, 1849); Hummel's "Air à la tyrolienne" (Alboni's preferred lesson-scene music); and Heinrich Proch's variations, "Deh torna mio bene," which became one of the arias most frequently introduced into the lesson scene during the first quarter of the twentieth century.[50]

A glance at Rode's variations provides some clues as to why theme-and-variation arias were so enthusiastically embraced by Rosinas and their spectators. Pierre Rode (1774–1830), a contemporary of Niccolò Paganini, was considered "the most finished representative of the French violin school," and he composed his *Air varié* to display his unique virtuosic strengths.[51] The original theme is thus unusually ornate for the basis of a variation set (see example 5.2): the opening triplet turn of the first measure, the descending leaps in measure 7 (which are mirrored in the ascending leaps of mm. 17–18), and the sixteenth-note figurations in measures 10 and 15 are all gestures that betray this melody's origins as a work for violin. His variations, moreover (not included here), contain melodic figuration that, predictably, is impossible to sing. His second variation, for example, is constructed almost entirely of double stops, and the fourth contains arpeggios that extend upward to D^7.

Though we cannot know precisely how individual prima donnas varied Rode's music, several surviving nineteenth-century piano-vocal scores contain ornaments attributed to Catalani, providing a sense of how she (and possibly some of her successors) transformed this into a vocal work.[52] According to these sources, several

49. *Teatri arti e letteratura* 297 (December 24, 1829): 102 contains a review of Corri-Paltoni's performance; *Teatri arti e letteratura* 978 (November 10, 1842): 85, contains a review of Tacchinardi-Persiani's. "Nel cor più non mi sento" was among the most frequently published and arranged tunes of the first quarter of the nineteenth century. For an overview of the various versions in which it circulated, see Richard M. Long, " 'Nel cor più non mi sento': Notes on Paisiello's Aria and a Few of Its Interpreters," in *The Consortium on Revolutionary Europe Proceedings,* ed. Donald D. Horward, Harold T. Parker, and Louise Salley Parker (Athens, Ga.: The Consortium on Revolutionary Europe, 1986), 417–23.

50. Adam's theme-and-variation set was first introduced into the lesson scene by Henriette Sontag at Niblo's Garden in New York City in January 1853 (*Spirit of the Times* 22, no. 49 [(January 22, 1853]: 588). Hummel's aria was performed frequently by Alboni, as we have seen, and also by Maddalena Casaloni on at least one occasion (Milan, Teatro Carcano, summer 1862) (*Gazzetta musicale di Milano,* no. 28 [July 13, 1862]: 109). Evidence of prima donnas introducing Proch's variations into the lesson scene comes from Gerald Fitzgerald, ed., *Annals of the Metropolitan Opera: Chronology 1883–1985* (Boston: G. K. Hall, 1989). According to this chronology, Marcella Sembrich sang Proch's variations on February 6, 1899, after which many others, including Elvira De Hidalgo, Lily Pons, and Patrice Munsel followed her lead.

51. Boris Schwarz and Clive Brown, "Pierre Rode," *Grove Music Online,* ed. L. Macy, http://www .grovemusic.com (accessed May 4, 2007).

52. Three piano-vocal scores were consulted for this study: "Rode's celebrated air . . . for the piano

EXAMPLE 5.2.   Pierre Rode, *Air varié* in G major, theme

Source: Air varié: andante con variazioni, op. 10. New York: G. Schirmer, 1900.

forte . . . with Madame Catalani's variations . . . arranged by Pio Cianchettini, etc. [The words adapted by Madame Catalani.]" (Liverpool: Yaniewicz and Weiss, 1822); "Variazione di bravura per soprano di P. Rode," in *Celebri Romanze ed altri pezzi vocali da concerto con accompagnamento di pianoforte esiguiti dalle signore Artôt, Patti, Sembrich, etc.* (Berlin: Schlesinger, n.d.); and "Al dolce canto del Dio d'amore," in *Sammlung der beliebtesten Coloratur-Arien herausgegeben von Mathilde de Castrone Marchesi* (Leipzig: C. F. Peters, n.d.). A fully orchestrated manuscript of this aria is housed at the Conservatorio di musica Giuseppe Verdi, Milan (Mus. Tr. ms. 1097). That these scores record a close approximation of what Catalani sang in concert is verified in a letter from Paganini to Luigi Guglielmo Germi (Milan, June 18, 1823). The violinist describes her performance of Rode's variations and transcribes eight measures of her ornaments, which correspond roughly to the published versions. See Roberto Grisley, ed., *Niccolò Paganini: Epistolario* Vol. 1: 1810–1831 (Milan: Academia Santa Cecilia, 2006), 217.

modifications were introduced: the melody was set to a newly written text; the key transposed down; the number of variations reduced from four in Rode's version to two; and the ornaments for violin replaced or modified to accommodate the voice. The text contains three quatrains (one each for the theme and two variations) of varying metric structure. The first two quatrains are provided here:

Il dolce canto—del dio d'amore	The sweet song of the god of love
Il nostro core—serenerà	Will calm our hearts
A tal concento—sento che l'alma	Through its harmony, I sense that the soul
Trova la calma,—la pace al core.	Finds calm, the heart finds peace.
Sento che al dolce incanto del Dio d'amore	I sense that at the sweet song of the god of love
Dolce soave al core—la calma ritorna	Calm returns, sweet and tender to the heart
Cetra del dio di Delo—nel rinascente ardore	Lyre of Apollo, in ardor reborn
La fiamma del mio core—deh vieni a consolar.	Ah, come console the flame of my heart.

This text may have been written after the ornaments were decided upon, and without any regard for the rules of versification, mere syllables on which to drape the melismas that grow lengthier with each variation. Despite the rather poor correspondence between musical and textual accentuation, its often unrecognizable meter (as in the second strophe), and the overly sentimental tone, these verses contain some clever end-line to *rimalmezzo* rhymes, and a butted rhyme-bridge (-cento/sento) that suggest some care might have gone into writing them.

The new vocal embellishments retain the air's instrumental quality (see example 5.3). Rather than perform Rode's theme as written, for example, the melody is adorned from beginning to end with elaborate turns and a series of 32nd notes that only the most accomplished performer could execute cleanly. On the page, moreover, the variations still appear as if they were intended for violin. The first, in fact, is derived almost note for note from Rode's first variation, and though the second has no counterpart in the earlier version, its arpeggiated leaps, followed by ascending and descending scales, resemble an étude designed to hone a violinist's left-hand technique.

Rode's variations, as well as the other theme-and-variation sets, may have exerted a powerful appeal over Rosina's lesson scene because of their suitability to the new dramatic background, their arpeggios and scalar passages resembling the *esercizi* that characterized the melodic line of "Contro un cor." Dramatic consistency, however, was not the primary reason that prima donnas selected these arias time and again. At bottom, this genre was attractive for its flexibility, a situation made apparent in the case of Rode's variations: Catalani sang two sets of variations, but there was nothing holding others back from adding a third or fourth if their audiences wanted the performance to continue; and even though Catalani sang a particular set of ornaments that were undoubtedly imitated by some of her successors, they were by no means sacred and could be altered at will. The same parameters hold true for other theme-and-variation sets. These arias offered prima donnas the ultimate freedom to place their individual talents on display. A critic present at one

EXAMPLE 5.3.   Rode's variations with ornaments by Angelica Catalani

Source: "Rode's celebrated air for the piano forte with Madame Catalani's variations arranged by Pio Cianchettini, etc. [The words adapted by Madame Catalani.]" Liverpool: Yaniewicz and Weiss, 1822.

of Sontag's earliest appearances as Rosina, for instance, notes that it was "the introduction of the music lesson in the second act, when she sang some of Rode's variations on a theme for the violin, with an unrivalled distinctness of articulation, and brilliancy of tone, that she was most triumphantly successful."[53] Dramatic consistency was irrelevant; the only factor that counted was the prima donna's voice.

53. This production occurred in July 1828 at the King's Theatre, London (*New York Mirror* 6, no. 2 [July 19, 1828]: 10).

There may have been risks involved in selecting Rode's variations or any other theme-and-variation set, for by the late 1820s, these arias had become loaded with negative connotations, critics attacking them as affronts to "sensitive" musical expression. The English critic Mount Edgcumbe was among the most vocal, arguing in his *Musical Reminiscences of an Old Amateur* that Rode's variations were "absolute nonsense, a lamentable misapplication of the finest of instruments, the human voice, and of the delightful faculty of song."[54] These complaints are typical of criticism commonly fired at coloratura arias in general, musical utterances that transform "the singing voice" into what Abbate characterizes as the "voice-object."[55] This music, in other words, represents little more than empty virtuosity that draws attention away from words, plot, and character, leaving only an unsettling presence in its wake. The net result was that these and other aria insertions caused a rift between opera and singer that was, in the end, enormously pleasurable for spectators, becoming one of the most celebrated aspects of the lesson scene. In selecting theme-and-variation arias, prima donnas explicitly resisted the aesthetic nuances of Rossini's score, threw away any pretense of acting a part, and stepped forward as themselves. Just as Almaviva participates in this scene in double disguise, so, too, did these performers—prima donnas acting the part of Rosina who, in turn, acted like themselves. It was the promise of witnessing the spectacle of this doubling that kept audiences coming back, and it is this promise that opens up even wider during the 1860s when Adelina Patti began to make her sensational appearances as Rosina.

THE LESSON SCENE AS SHOW-STOPPING CABARET

I like the Barbiere best of all my operas. I love the comedy and the constant fun.
I can laugh and feel joyous all the time. Besides, I revel in the lesson scene. I can
do just as I please there and it always amuses me when I introduce music that
was written years after Rossini wrote the opera.
—Quote attributed to Adelina Patti

Patti may or may not have uttered these playful sentences,[56] but whether they are historical reality or blatant forgery is immaterial, for they summarize perfectly her approach to the lesson scene. She made her debut as Rosina during the 1859–1860 season in New York City as an energetic sixteen-year-old, and the role quickly became one of her warhorses. She appeared in *Il barbiere di Siviglia* continually until her retirement from the opera stage in 1897, performing it in nearly every important opera house throughout Europe and North America (figure 5.1 provides a caricature of Patti as Rosina). Over the course of these decades, her impersonation of

54. Richard, Earl of Mount Edgcumbe, *Musical Reminiscences, Containing an Account of the Italian Opera in England, from 1773* (1834; reprint, New York: Da Capo Press), 98–99.

55. Abbate, *Unsung Voices,* 10. On the effects of coloratura singing, see also Heather Hadlock, "Return of the Repressed: The Prima Donna from Hoffmann's *Tales* to Offenbach's *Contes,*" *Cambridge Opera Journal* 6 (1994): 240.

56. John Frederick Cone, *Adelina Patti: Queen of Hearts* (Portland, Ore.: Amadeus Press, 1993), caption under picture no. 28, n.p.

FIGURE 5.1.   Adelina Patti as Rosina. *Source:* © V&A Images / Victoria and Albert Museum, London.

Rosina became legendary. Indeed, this coloratura soprano left an indelible mark on Rossini's opera—and on the lesson scene in particular—that affected generations of prima donnas who filled the role in her wake.

The few eyewitness accounts that remain from her earliest appearances suggest that during some productions of *Il barbiere di Siviglia,* Patti followed the lead of her predecessors, substituting only one aria into the lesson scene. That this was not always the case, however, is illustrated in Jack Belsom's detailed account of Patti's three-month engagement at the Théâtre d'Orléans, New Orleans (December 19,

1860–March 22, 1861).[57] During this period, Belsom recounts, she sang the role of Rosina three times, her choices for the lesson scene growing more elaborate with each repetition. For the first, she introduced only "Ah! non giunge," a predictable selection given her familiarity with the music (it was among the first arias she sang in concert as a child prodigy in 1851).[58] In her second appearance she sang "Ah! non giunge" again, but her audience also demanded an encore, to which Patti complied with the traditional Scottish song "Twas within a Mile of Edinboro' Town." In her third and final appearance, the lesson scene grew even more elaborate, for as Belsom reports, "in addition to 'Twas within a Mile' and [Carl] Eckert's 'Swiss Echo Song,' she now added 'Home, Sweet Home' [by Sir Henry Bishop]."[59] In her earliest appearances as Rosina, Patti gleefully and indelibly transformed the lesson scene into what one twentieth-century commentator has negatively characterized as a "show-stopping cabaret."[60]

This transformation from a site of one-to-one substitution into a mini-concert was not without precedent: Pauline Viardot, Malibran's younger sister and a famous prima donna in her own right, introduced a selection of "Spanish songs" and played Chopin mazurkas at the piano during the lesson scene; and when Sontag and Emilia Taccani performed Rode's variations, they were sometimes encored, to which they both responded by introducing the "Tre Nozze Polka" by Giulio Alary.[61] It was through Patti's example, however, that the tradition of substituting more than one aria into the lesson scene shifted from being the exception to the rule.

The process through which her "mini-concerts" evolved into an established component of her appearances as Rosina is significant, moreover, for as was the case in New Orleans, she rarely "planned" on introducing more than one number into the lesson scene.[62] Her avowed intent, rather, was to showcase her voice in one coloratura showpiece only. (As the epigraph that opened this section suggests, the arias from which she most often selected her lesson-scene music were, in fact, all composed years after Rossini had written *Il barbiere di Siviglia:* either "Merci, jeunes amies," the bolero from Verdi's *Les Vêpres siciliennes* [1855]; "Ombre légère qui suis mes pas," from *Dinorah* [1859]; or "Je veux vivre" from Gounod's *Roméo et Juliette* [1867].) When she did add a second or even a third number into the lesson scene, it was typically in response to demands by her adoring fans. A critic describing her

<hr>

57. Jack Belsom, "En Route to Stardom: Adelina Patti at the French Opera House, New Orleans, 1860–1861," *Opera Quarterly* 10 (1994): 113–30.

58. Herman Klein, *The Reign of Patti* (1920; reprint, New York: Da Capo Press, 1978), 24. *La sonnambula* was the work in which she made her full-stage opera debut, just weeks before her first appearance as Rosina. Thus Bellini's music would have been particularly familiar to her at that time. See "Adelina Patti," *Enciclopedia dello spettacolo* 7: 1778–79.

59. Belsom, "En Route to Stardom," 120–22.

60. Richard Osborne, "Il barbiere di Siviglia," in *Grove Music Online,* ed. L. Macy, http://www.grovemusic.com (accessed May 19, 2007).

61. A review of Viardot appears in *Fraser's Magazine* 37 (March 1848): 341. Reviews of Sontag and Taccani performing encores appear in *Illustrated London News* 19, no. 511 (August 23, 1851): 234, and *Gazzetta musicale di Milano* 16, no. 6 (February 8, 1857): 47, respectively.

62. The exception was benefit performances when it was announced in advance that she planned to introduce more than one aria. See, for example, Klein, *Reign of Patti,* 109–10, for a description of her benefit that occurred on August 15, 1862 at Covent Garden.

appearance at London's Royal Italian Opera in 1867, for instance, writes that "the song introduced by Mme. Patti in the lesson-scene was the well known *bolero* from Verdi's grand opera 'Les Vêpres Siciliennes' [. . .] *This being unanimously encored,* Mlle. Patti substituted 'Home, Sweet Home,' and to the evident satisfaction of the audience, gave it in the original language" (emphasis mine).[63] And a review published over fifteen years later mirrors this report: "We have heard the bolero from 'Les Vêpres Siciliennes' interpreted with greater showiness and theatrical effect, but never with like facility and elegance; and her delivery of 'Home, Sweet Home,' *which was given in deference to the encore which followed the bolero*—this being introduced into the 'lesson scene'—was a thing to be remembered" (emphasis again mine).[64] Just as she typically selected her initial arias from a stable repertory, so, too, did she recycle her encores, all of which offered contrasting, lighter fare: "Home, Sweet Home" from Bishop's *Clari;* "The Last Rose of Summer," from Friedrich Flotow's *Martha;* "Il bacio" by Luigi Arditi; "Swiss Echo Song" by Eckert; and traditional songs including "Twas within a Mile of Edinboro' Town," "Comin' Thro' the Rye," and "Lo, Here the Gentle Lark."

The encores Patti received during the lesson scene may have originated as unplanned gestures of appreciation on the part of her spectators, and initially, they may have come as a surprise to the singer. But the regularity with which this happened over the decades, combined with the consistency of her responses, suggests that at a certain point the "encores" were no longer spontaneous; rather, they had become fixed and predictable components of her appearances in the lesson scene. Multiple arias were now expected, but they were not guaranteed. A certain amount of interplay on the parts of singer and spectator was required, Patti agreeing to tack on an extra aria or two, but *only* if she were asked. What was already an opera-within-an-opera accrued an extra layer of performativity in which audience members participated as actively as the singer herself. A colorful and lengthy review of her appearance as Rosina at Chicago's Auditorium Theater in January 1890 depicts the intensity with which her spectators took up this role and the liveliness with which she played along:

> It was in the singing lesson scene of "The Barber" that she came forward with the music sheet in her hand and warbled the shadow song from "Dinorah." Now was the time for an encore. A mighty storm of applause swept down from the galleries and crashed over the stage [. . .] For a moment Patti seemed to hesitate. She was coy even in the face of such a tumultuous recall. But at last she stepped forward with her hand on her heart and courtesied her assent. The applause ceased for a moment and then broke forth again in another storm, when the bows began to creep across the strings in the melody of "Home, Sweet Home." The prelude ceased and with it the applause. Patti's first nightingale notes rippled over the footlights in an unbroken, breathless silence. The great house was hushed. Not the slightest rustle of a skirt broke the fairness of the melody. When the last cooing note of the first chorus had melted there was a wild roar from the pits and the balconies. The madam sang the second verse as well as she had sung the first, and never when her voice was youngest and freshest did she sing the first

<hr>

63. *New York Times* (May 19, 1867): 1.

64. This performance occurred in November 1884, at the Academy of Music in New York City (*New York Times* [November 11, 1884]: 5).

verse better. Men and women rose from their seats and cheered as she drew back, bowing and smiling. The balconies rained programs and handkerchiefs on the pit. Six thousand men and women can make much noise, and these six thousand were taxing their powers to the limits. The madam tried a smile. It failed to allay the tumult. She tried three or four bows. They only made the waves mount higher. Either Patti must sing or "The Barber of Seville" must suffer and dinner must wait [. . .]

So Patti sang. She whispered to the conductor of the orchestra, and the band struck up Arditi's "kiss waltz," "Il bacio." The audience recognized it and cheered [. . .]

The applause was almost as stormy after the kiss song as it had been after "Home, Sweet Home," but Mme. Patti had sung all she was going to and she answered no more calls.[65]

Patti's audience had no intention of leaving without hearing her "in concert," as it were, and Patti had no intention of disappointing them. This shared understanding was kept under wraps, however, allowing the carefully planned mini-concert of the lesson scene to unfold in a seemingly spontaneous manner. As was the case with earlier productions in which prima donnas substituted only one aria, concerns for plot and narrative were set firmly aside. With Patti, however, the audience became complicit in the changes made to Rossini's score, actively and enthusiastically enticing her away from the fabric of the opera. Although the result may have been to deprive Rosina of her true character, no one noticed or cared, for the rewards far outweighed the consequences. Patti provided "several thousand dollars' worth of song for nothing," as her Chicago critic concluded, though more than money was at stake; more significant was that she permitted her fans a spectacular moment of direct communication, and in so doing, altered the "realistic" landscape of Rossini's lesson scene for decades to come.

Most of Patti's contemporaries followed her lead, transforming the lesson scene into their own mini-concerts and approaching their additions as their model did—through the guise of the "encore." A critic observing the Russian contralto Mlle. Belocca in the role of Rosina at the Théâtre Italien (October 1873), for instance, comments that "in the lesson scene she chose one of her own national songs, 'The Nightingale,' and, being encored, sang the *brindisi* from 'Lucrezia Borgia' with so much spirit and fire, as well as with such full volume of voice, as to be obliged to repeat the second verse";[66] and a review of the Hungarian soprano Etelka Gerster in New York City (March 1881) notes that she "introduced the 'Carnival of Venice' [a variation set by Jules Benedict] into the singing lesson scene, and put such life into it as to win an encore, in response to which she sang a polka by Arditi, 'Fior di Margherita.'"[67]

The repertory of coloratura showpieces introduced into the lesson scene shifted noticeably with Patti. The arias that she introduced by Bellini, Verdi, Meyerbeer, and Gounod were taken up by subsequent Rosinas, as were a few of the century's other most ornate numbers: the mad scene from Donizetti's *Lucia di Lammermoor* (1835); "Charmant oiseau" from Félicien David's *Le perle du Brésil* (1851); "Je suis

65. *Chicago Daily Tribune* (January 5, 1890): 1.
66. *New York Times* (October 26, 1873): 4.
67. *Critic* 1, no. 6 (March 26, 1881): 85.

Titiana" from Ambroise Thomas's *Mignon;* "Où va la jeune Hindoue," the Bell Song from Leo Delibes' *Lakmé* (1883); Benedict's "Carnival of Venice"; Proch's variations; and a few others became the favorite lesson scene music of the most famous prima donnas.[68] This change of repertory not only reflects an increased demand for vocal pyrotechnics and extravagant displays of technique that began filtering through opera houses during the third quarter of the nineteenth century, but it is also the result of the fact that the part of Rosina was taken over almost entirely by coloratura sopranos from the last quarter of the nineteenth century into the first quarter of the twentieth. Transposing this role upward had long been a component of the opera's performance history, of course, but these years witnessed a new dominance of coloratura divas singing the role in the leading opera houses, and with them came a new set of lesson-scene arias.[69] It is worthwhile recalling here, however, that "Contro un cor" was always included in the Ricordi orchestral parts for *Il barbiere di Siviglia,* which were used in nearly every opera house throughout the twentieth century. This aria was never entirely lost, in other words, and as a result, some prima donnas did still opt to perform Rossini's original aria, although it was rare.

As was the case with Patti and her contemporaries, most of her successors performed interpolated arias, introducing "encores" following a coloratura showpiece. By the 1890s, the conceit of the encore was no longer compulsory, for the assumption that multiple numbers belonged in the lesson scene was by then taken for granted. Nellie Melba, the Australian soprano who appeared regularly as Rosina at the turn of the century, went on record in an interview during her 1898 tour of the United States, revealing that, "[f]or the singing lesson I have two numbers, 'Sévillane' by [Jules] Massenet, and a song by [Francesco Paolo] Tosti, which he taught me, 'Mattinata.' "[70] Significantly, she does not describe Massenet's coloratura *tour de force* as the "main attraction" or Tosti's sentimental song as the "encore," but rather introduces both as bearing equal weight. Indeed, after Patti, it was understood that prima donnas should prepare at least two arias that contrasted stylistically not only with each other, but with the surrounding opera as well. To flout this expectation was to risk the sort of mild criticism Melba faced when she broke her promise to perform Massenet's aria, substituting a far less virtuosic number in its place: "The

68. The first evidence of a prima donna introducing Lucia's mad scene into Rosina's music lesson comes in the form of a poster for Covent Garden in which it is announced that for a performance of *Il barbiere di Siviglia* scheduled for July 23, 1900, "Mme. [Nellie] Melba will sing, in the Lesson Scene, THE MAD SCENE from 'LUCIA DI LAMMERMOOR' " (Covent Garden Theatre Archive, file 1900). A review for this performance, which comments negatively on Melba's performance of the mad scene appears in *The Saturday Review* (July 28, 1900): 113–14. That this aria was not used as the lesson-scene music until this late date is significant, for, as Romana Pugliese has shown, it was Nellie Melba who first performed the famous cadenza with flute obbligato (see "The Origins of *Lucia di Lammermoor*'s Cadenza," *Cambridge Opera Journal* 16 [2004]: 23–42). It became useful only as a lesson-scene aria, in other words, once the cadenza had become a fixed component.

69. Indeed, when mezzo-soprano Luella Melius took on the role of Rosina at the Chicago Auditorium during the winter season 1925, veteran critic Edward Moore found the sound so unusual that his review of the performance was titled "Melius Sings a Rosina That Is Different" (*Chicago Daily Tribune* [December 17, 1925]: 21).

70. *Chicago Daily Tribune* (March 14, 1898): 5. "Sevilianne" is "Sevilanna" from Massenet's *opéra comique Don César de Bazan* (Paris, Opéra-Comique, 1872).

comedy element was well sustained, and the singing lesson, if not all that might have been wished in the matter of selection, for Mme. Melba gave 'Old Folks at Home' instead of the Massenet number promised, it proved exactly what a large mass of her auditors desired. And Mme. Melba sang it charmingly. Preceding this she gave a Tosti song, 'Mattinata,' to which, as in the case of the old-time one, she played her own accompaniment."[71] Why Melba made this last-minute change is unclear, but even though her critic was disappointed, her audience was pleased, having been treated to the spectacle of one of their favorite prima donnas accompanying herself at the piano in addition to singing two arias. It was a veritable one-woman show.

Indeed, the decades roughly between 1880 and 1920 might be characterized as the golden age of the mini-concert tradition when prima donnas took fullest advantage of the lesson scene, accompanying themselves at the piano if they were able.[72] Foremost among these was the Polish soprano Marcella Sembrich (1858–1935), who critics described as Patti's rightful successor to all things *bel canto,* one remarking that, "Sembrich is now the only representative of the school of fine-voiced vocal virtuose of which Patti was the most brilliant member."[73] (See figure 5.2 for a photograph of Sembrich as Rosina.) Sembrich first took on the role of Rosina in 1884 and performed almost annually in productions of *Il barbiere di Siviglia* throughout Europe and the United States until 1909. The liberties she took went further than most of her predecessors, including Melba and Patti, in transforming this moment into a full-blown showcase. American critics—especially those writing for the *New York Times* and *Chicago Daily Tribune*—were particularly careful to record which arias she sang and how her spectators reacted, often devoting lengthy paragraphs to the lesson scene. Sembrich always introduced at least three and sometimes as many as four arias, the last performed in response to an "encore," the others sung as if the scene were a traditional concert program. Like Patti and Melba before her, she selected music that offered significant variety in both style and language. During an appearance at the Chicago Auditorium in November 1898, for example, she introduced "Voci di primavera" (also known as "Frühlingsstimmen"), a concert aria by Johann Strauss Jr., followed by the song "Życzenie" ("Maiden's Wish") by Chopin, which she sang to her own piano accompaniment, and then concluded with "Ah! non giunge." Three years later she varied this program, retaining the Strauss and Chopin pieces, but replacing "Ah! non giunge" with an unidentified German lullaby *and* Lucia's Mad Scene.[74]

Amid the flashiness of her lesson scenes, which were so fundamentally distinct from anything Rossini could have had in mind, it is possible that Sembrich attempted to pay at least cursory attention to the original plot. A hint appears in a

71. *Chicago Daily Tribune* (March 17, 1898): 8.

72. There is precedent for prima donnas accompanying themselves in the lesson scene. We have already noted above that Viardot was fond of sitting down at the keyboard and performing Chopin mazurkas. Several reviews of De Lagrange, moreover, indicate that when she sang Rode's variations, she accompanied herself (for instance, *Teatri arti e letteratura* 1154 [March 21, 1846]: 20, and *Teatri arti e letteratura* 1255 [February 24, 1848]: 203).

73. *Chicago Daily Tribune* (February 26, 1901): 7.

74. *Chicago Daily Tribune* (November 11, 1898): 5, and *Chicago Daily Tribune* (February 24, 1901): 40.

FIGURE 5.2.   Marcella Sembrich as Rosina. *Source:* psnypl_mus_824 Karoli & Pusch, Marcella Sembrich. Marcella Sembrich Papers, 1790–1988. 1880. Series 9, Box 3, Folder 221. Photograph; New York Public Library, New York, N.Y.

review of one of her earliest appearances in the role at Haverly's Theatre, Chicago (June 1884). On this occasion the music lesson began with a rousing rendition of Proch's variations, followed by "an English love-song," a mixture of virtuosity and lyricism that had become a rather predictable combination by that time. Sembrich concluded with "Ah! non giunge," but before doing so, she took a break from singing full-scale arias to sit at the keyboard. The critic describes what happened next: "Rosina's vocal exercises at the piano, which she indulges in to conceal the love passages between her and Almaviva, were also not only superbly executed, but were given in the most charming and insinuating manner."[75] What were these vocal exercises, and what is meant by "love passages"? Though it is impossible to pinpoint precisely, this account implies that Rosina and Almaviva carried on an "operatic" conversation similar to the one that occurs in the *tempo di mezzo* of "Contro un cor." Sembrich, an exceptional pianist as well as singer, may have improvised scales and arpeggios at the keyboard, alternating vocal exercises with frantic verbal exchanges. In the middle of her one-woman show, in other words, she stepped back into character, thus retaining a semblance of the narrative structure built into the original aria. There is no evidence that Sembrich ever performed these "love passages" again, or that any other prima donna followed her lead. Nevertheless, this episode is significant, for it suggests that at the moment when Rosina's music lesson had drifted furthest from Rossini's work, it also began edging its way back.

In the immediate aftermath of Sembrich's appearances as Rosina, however, prima donnas who took on the role were confronted by the legacies left behind by multiple "authors," Rossini and Sterbini ranking least among them. Prima donnas faced the challenge of attempting to respect the traditions initiated by Patti, Sembrich, and others, while simultaneously endeavoring to leave their own individual mark. By the time Amelita Galli-Curci became the world's premiere Rosina (between 1913 and 1923), these expectations dictated the success or failure of a prima donna. The following review, describing one of her many performances at the Chicago Auditorium in 1917, bears witness to the web of references that had accrued around the scene:

> That her success in "The Barber" surpassed her earlier triumphs was due, in large measure, to her expected employment of expert if obvious showmanship in the lesson-scene: here she piled not only Pelion on Ossa, but also Patti on Sembrich, and Tetrazzini on top of both by, first, giving the bell-song from "Lakmè" as it had not been sung since the youthful and voiceful [*sic*] prime of Emma Nevada, whose especial implement it was; then "The Last Rose" and "Home! Sweet Home" in English, to her own accompaniment on a spinet as tenuous and tinny in tune as that on which Rossini composed "The Barber," and ending the "scene" by exhuming, for good-measure, a clever laughing-song from Auber's forgotten opera on the subject of Manon Lescaut.
>
> When Patti sang "The Last Rose" or "Home! Sweet Home!"—and they were her hokum until the last farewell—the reporters of musical occasions always wrote that, "as the last strains died away, there was not a dry eye in the house." There was not a wet eye last night: Galli-Curci's singing was nothing to cry about; and it was something to make everybody who heard it glad to be there, and eager to go again.[76]

75. *Chicago Daily Tribune* (June 26, 1884): 5.
76. Frederick Donaghey, "Galli-Curci Top-Notch as a Soubrette in Bully Revival of 'The Barber,'"

Galli-Curci's arias, which included two that were intimately associated with Patti, one with Sembrich, Tetrazzini, and Nevada, and one that was perceived as her own contribution to the lesson scene, were no doubt selected with an eye toward both past and present, and for this she was rewarded with lavish applause.[77] Her real accomplishment, however, lay in the relationship to Patti that she communicated, paying honor to her most illustrious predecessor (the "author" in many ways of this lesson scene), while simultaneously resisting the long shadow that she cast over the opera. Galli-Curci inverted Patti's reception, turning tears into laughter, and delivered a performance that was completely new to audiences already intimately familiar with the opera. As such, she achieved a goal as vital as it was noteworthy, enticing her spectators to return for yet another performance of *Il barbiere di Siviglia,* filling the theater to hear this opera again and again.

THE DECLINE OF A TRADITION

Despite Galli-Curci's positive reception in 1917, the mini-concert tradition began a gradual decline toward the conclusion of her career, her three or four arias dwindling to two at most by the time she retired.[78] Almost all of her successors from the 1920s through the 1950s—including Nina Morgana, Elvira De Hidalgo, Toti Dal Monte, Mabel Garrison, Margherita Salvi, Patrice Munsel, and Bidu Sayao among others—returned to the pre-Patti tradition of inserting only one piece into the lesson scene.[79] The exception was the American soprano Lily Pons, who initiated her twenty-five-year-long relationship with *Il barbiere di Siviglia* in 1931 at the Metro-

---

Chicago Daily Tribune (January 2, 1917): 13. Ring Lardner (American novelist, sports writer, and satirist) published a fascinating review of this production a few weeks later in which he parodies Galli-Curci's lesson scene in his own idiosyncratic style, remarking, "And another place where Rossini was lazy was sticking in a scene where Miss Galli-Curci is supposed to be taking a singing lesson and to save himself the trouble of writing new stuff Rossini rung in some outside numbers for her to sing namely The Bell song by Edgar Allen Poe and the Last Rose of summer by Irving Berlin and Home sweet Home by Carrie Jacobs Bond. And the orchestra union rules is that they can't play nothing that ain't in the score so Miss Curci had to play her own cords [*sic*] on a piano that had the mandolin attachment pedle [*sic*] stuck down." "In the Wake of the News," *Chicago Daily Tribune* (January 16, 1917): 16.

77. As the inventory by Radiciotti cited above suggests, Patti may have interpolated the laughing song from Auber's *Manon Lescaut* into the lesson scene. I have yet to locate confirmation that she did so, however.

78. As early as 1918, she began scaling back, performing only Lakmé's Bell Song and "Home, Sweet Home" during a production of *Il barbiere di Siviglia* at the Chicago Auditorium (*Chicago Daily Tribune* [December 4, 1918]: 18). Later appearances feature her singing "Ombre légère" or the Polonaise from "Mignone," both followed by "Home, Sweet Home" (*New York Times* [February 6, 1921]: 5, and *Chicago Daily Tribune* [January 4, 1923]: 17).

79. These prima donnas preferred to introduce into the lesson scene the coloratura arias that had become popular during the "golden age" of the mini-concert tradition. Elvira De Hidalgo, for instance, sang Proch's variations in her appearance at the Chicago Auditorium in 1910 (*Chicago Daily Tribune* [April 23, 1910]: 6), and "Ombre légère" when she appeared, fourteen years later, with the Chicago Civic Opera (*Chicago Daily Tribune* [November 26, 1924]: 13). Toti dal Monte preferred Benedict's "Carnival of Venice" (*Chicago Daily Tribune* [November 28, 1925]: 11). When prima donnas sang an aria that was unusual for the lesson scene, critics would take note. When Bidu Sayao introduced "Deh vieni" from Mozart's *Le nozze di Figaro* into a production at the Metropolitan Opera (December 1845), for example,

politan Opera by substituting two numbers: Proch's variations and "Lo Here the Gentle Lark."[80] Throughout the remainder of the 1930s, Pons consistently sang two arias during the lesson scene, but even she abandoned this practice in the 1940s, introducing either the Proch variations or variations on "Ah! vous dirai-je maman," but not both, throughout the final fifteen years of her career.[81] By the mid- to late 1950s, many prima donnas ceased substituting their own choice of aria altogether, returning Rossini's "Contro un cor" to its original spot.[82]

The factors triggering this decline were no doubt diverse, differing with each country, theater, and singer. Nevertheless, a few general shifts in the cultural and musical landscape during the first half of the twentieth century had widespread influence throughout the world's primary and secondary opera houses. As early as the 1910s and 1920s, for example, clear signs of dissatisfaction toward the practice of altering the lesson scene started to emerge in newspaper reviews, suggesting that some factions—powerful or otherwise—were agitating for performances of Rossini's aria and none other. The critic of Galli-Curci's 1917 Chicago performance concludes, for instance, "I suspect that there will be sad, sapient things said about the unities, whatever they are, and the destruction of illusion by her singing in English, thus leaving the libretto [. . .] prone on its back."[83] Though he himself disagrees, this comment marks one of the earliest signs that change was afoot, that some listeners wanted to hear "unified" performances shorn of "encores" and the spectacle that often accompanied them.[84]

These calls for unity were, at bottom, the product of an increasing belief among twentieth-century conductors—the new leaders of the operatic world—that the "intentions" of composers had to be respected. The true pioneer behind this effort was Arturo Toscanini, whose concept of faithful adherence to the composer's score (regardless of what that concept was with regard to modern-day ideas of "adherence") not only affected how he interpreted the music of Rossini and others, but also emboldened generations of conductors after him to do the same. Toscanini never conducted *Il barbiere di Siviglia,* but his wide-reaching legacy is discernable in the work of two later conductors who were influenced by him. The first was Vittorio Gui, who scoured original source material in order to reconstruct Rossini's "intentions" for the 1942 production of the opera at the Teatro Comunale, Flor-

---

Olin Downes had this to say: "In the lesson scene Miss Sayao elected to sing Suzanna's 'Deh vieni,' and this demonstrated two things: the inherent superiority of Mozart's air to any of the coruscating music of Rossini's, and also the fact that in such a setting Mozart was out of place. A bravura aria is expected and advisable as interpolation in this scene" (*New York Times* [December 8, 1945]: 17).

80. *New York Times* (February 5, 1931): 29.

81. See Fitzgerald, *Annals of the Metropolitan Opera,* 423–640.

82. At the Metropolitan Opera, for instance, the production of *Il barbiere di Siviglia* featuring Roberta Peters as Rosina, in February 1954, restored "Contro un cor." According to the Metopera database, http://archives.metoperafamily.org/archives/frame.htm, prima donnas chose this aria rather than substituting one of their own from this date onward until January 23, 1971.

83. Donaghey, "Galli-Curci Top-Notch as a Soubrette in Bully Revival of 'The Barber,'" 13.

84. It is also significant that at least one critic active during these years, Edward Moore, began calling for an end to all encores in *Il barbiere di Siviglia,* stating that they "distort operatic art all out of recognition" (*Chicago Daily Tribune* [January 4, 1923]: 17).

ence, and who also conducted this version numerous times thereafter at Glynde-bourne. The second was Alberto Zedda, whose critical edition of *Il barbiere di Si-viglia,* published in 1969, weeded out the bulk of "corruptions" that had affected the score throughout its first century and a half of performances.[85] For decades thereafter, this score, with "Contro un cor" firmly intact, represented the authoritative version of the opera. It goes without saying that performances led by these conductors, and those sympathetic to their views, did not include substitution arias for Rosina in the lesson scene.

It is not insignificant, moreover, that the mini-concert tradition and its subsequent decline overlapped with important watersheds in the history of technology, the first of which was the widespread availability of acoustic recordings from 1900 to 1925. The primitive resources available during this era limited reproducible music primarily to arias and duets, and thus the majority of commercial recordings issued during the first quarter of the twentieth century contained only excerpts, "greatest hits" sung by the world's most famous prima donnas and leading men. Patti, Melba, Sembrich, and Galli-Curci all produced recordings during these years, and the music they selected invariably included some or all of the arias that constituted their lesson-scene mini-concerts.[86] Given the widespread popularity of these records, the case might be made that consumers became accustomed to hearing their favorite Rosinas "in concert," a desire for which spilled over into opera houses, fueling enthusiasm for the recital format of the lesson scene. These recordings, in other words, may have generated what Mark Katz has termed a "phonograph effect," in which recordings have a direct and tangible influence on musical production and perception.[87]

If such a phonograph effect was generated by acoustic recordings, then a related outcome might be discerned with the arrival of electric technology in 1925, and then in 1950 with the invention of the LP. These developments brought affordable recordings of complete operas, and consequently, a heightened appreciation of the "work" in its entirety (or, at least the "work" as it was represented on the recording). As consumers became familiar with *Il barbiere di Siviglia* through these records—none of which contain "mini-concerts" and most of which include "Contro un cor"—the demand for change in live presentations of the lesson scene was replaced by the desire for admirable performances of the opera "as written." Of course, vocal recitals

85. See Vittorio Gui, "Storia avventurosa di alcuni capolavori del passato," *Bollettino del centro rossiniano di studi 25* (1985): 56–60; and Gioachino Rossini, *Il barbiere di Siviglia,* ed. Alberto Zedda (Milan: Ricordi, 1969). For a discussion of the problems concerning the Ricordi edition that circulated through opera houses prior to the publication of Zedda's edition, see Gossett, *Divas and Scholars: Performing Italian Opera* (Chicago: University of Chicago Press, 2006), 113–16.

86. Recordings of these singers are now widely available on compact disc. Patti's recordings include the following of her favorites for the lesson scene: "Il bacio," "The Last Rose of Summer," "Home, Sweet Home," "Comin' thro' the Rye," and "Twas within a Mile of Edinboro' Town" (see "The Complete Adelina Patti & Victor Maurel" [Marston, 52011]). Melba recorded Lucia's mad scene and Tosti's "Mattinata," as well as a few others that she introduced into the lesson scene (see "Nellie Melba: The Complete Victor Recordings" [Romophone, 81011]). A similarly diverse selection can be found for Sembrich and Galli-Curci (see "Marcella Sembrich: The Victor Recordings" [Romophone, 80126], and "Amelita Galli-Curci: The Victor Recordings" [Romophone, 81021]).

87. Mark Katz, *Capturing Sound: How Technology Has Changed Music* (Berkeley: University of California Press, 2004), 3.

remained popular during the LP era and beyond, but now these events were distinct, separate entities from an operatic work. Thus although Toscanini's ideals, Gui's seminal performance of *Il barbiere di Siviglia,* and Zedda's critical edition all represent important influences in bringing the opera as a whole—and the lesson scene in particular—back toward its original shape, I would posit a fourth, equally prominent participant: Maria Callas. Her 1957 recording—which today serves as the standardbearer for many singers and listeners—is not an entirely faithful representation of the score (what recording or performance is?). As John Ardoin remarks, however, Callas sings the majority of Rosina's music in the mezzo range, and more important to this study, she performs "Contro un cor."[88] Like Ronzi de Begnis and Sontag, Patti and Sembrich, Callas "authored" the lesson scene. That her vision was one and the same as Rossini's is no less significant, for it was she (more than he) who convinced mid-twentieth century audiences to demand fidelity, and it was she who convinced future Rosinas to deliver.

The lesson scene is one of the few moments in the repertory in which prima donnas might still introduce arias of their own choice without fear of reprimand. The most straightforward approach to altering this scene, conforming closest to traditions initiated during Rossini's lifetime, would be to trade in "Contro un cor" with one aria—"Di tanti palpiti" perhaps, or "Nacqui all'affanno e al pianto." Even as I make this eminently sensible suggestion, however, something nags: what, I wonder, would be the harm in staging a post-1860 mini-concert in the context of the lesson scene? I would not advocate for a return to the tradition of transposing the role of Rosina for soprano, for Rossini's music suffers unnecessarily with this change, especially in ensemble numbers. I wonder, though, would it be possible for a mezzo-soprano to recapture the excitement that was generated by the mini-concerts around the turn of the century? And if so, might it not be worth a try? What I am suggesting, of course, is as selfish as it is unrealistic. Selfish because to ask a prima donna to do such a thing is simply asking too much: performing the role of Rosina is exhausting "as written"; tacking two or three extra arias onto what is already there is surely going too far, even if nineteenth-century singers were willing (a willingness aided, at least on occasion, no doubt, by the unsavory practice of singing other parts of the score at less than full voice, or cutting out bits altogether in order to reserve energy for the showcase moment). Unrealistic because in today's world of tight schedules and union fees, a mini-concert would prove extravagant, if not outright prohibitive.

Setting the realities of the opera house aside and reflecting on the long and colorful history of the lesson scene, however, prima donnas might nevertheless embrace the flexibility that this moment once offered, selecting an aria and perhaps even an encore number that best suit their voices. They might even embrace potential accusations from modern critics of engaging in "absurdity," knowing that such censure would place them in excellent company. Above all, when Almaviva poses his timeworn question, "Che vuol cantare?" today's prima donnas should feel free, even entitled, to look him straight in the face, smile wickedly, and respond as Adelina Patti once did: "Exactly what I please!"

88. The recording was made in London on February 7 and 14, 1957 (EMI 556210.2). John Ardoin, *L'eredità Callas: La cantante, la diva, le incisioni,* 4th ed. (Milan: Il Saggiatore, 1997), 133.

CHAPTER 6

AN INSERTION ARIA SPEAKS

The lesson scene of *Il barbiere di Siviglia* presents a vivid reminder that even as aria insertion began to fade from the day-to-day procedures of opera production, singers, audiences, and critics remained engaged in the practice. After 1850, prima donnas and leading men continued to introduce arias of their own choice into operatic performances, just as they had decades before, and as Rossini's comic opera demonstrates, there was no identifiable "cutoff" point when aria insertion suddenly became universally extinct. Indeed, *bel canto* operas that were affected by these sorts of alterations during the 1820s, 1830s, and 1840s continued to be reshaped by aria insertions well into the second half of the nineteenth century and later. As long as works by Rossini, Donizetti, Bellini, their predecessors, and contemporaries remained integral components of the repertory, so, too, did many of the performance traditions that had accrued around them. As Verdi's star rose during the 1840s and 1850s, however, older operas and composers that had once dominated theatrical rosters started to be crowded out, and with them the contexts in which aria insertions flourished. As explored in the first chapter of this volume, Verdi's operas were by no means impermeable, but he was able to command a relatively higher degree of stability for his works than were his predecessors, and by the 1850s evidence that singers were actively and independently removing arias or ensembles in favor of others grows scarce. In the 1860s and 1870s, moreover, as theaters throughout Italy and beyond began to cultivate repertories that were more "international" in character—including operas by Gounod, Meyerbeer, and Wagner—aria insertion became even more anomalous.

In chapter 1 I sought to identify some of the aesthetic and cultural forces that began to regulate this practice during the first half of the nineteenth century, a discourse against which singers negotiated their aria insertions, and that slowly helped tip the balance of authority away from performers toward composers. In this concluding chapter, I would like to step out of the opera house once again and turn back to discourses that accrued around this practice. Whereas I began by examining traces of aria insertions left behind in a variety of documents, here my attention falls on only one rather idiosyncratic text: a short story titled "Memoir of a Song." First published in the London-based periodical *Fraser's Magazine* in 1849, this fictional autobiography emerged toward the conclusion of the time period under consideration in this study (with the exception, of course, of the investigation of *Il barbiere di Siviglia*).[1] This relatively late date of publication highlights an important distinction between the discussion that will follow and the one that initiated this book: whereas the contracts, theatrical treatises, letters, and critical reviews that occupied chapter 1 may have had a direct impact on the manner in which singers, composers, audiences, and critics began to perceive the "integrity" of operatic works, no such claim can be made for "Memoir of a Song." Though this story was probably read by thousands, it appeared on the periphery of the *bel canto* tradition, a reflection of, rather than an active participant in, aesthetic change.[2] Like the lesson scene of *Il barbiere di Siviglia,* however, it provides a glimpse at the "afterlife" of aria insertion, this time from a perspective that shifts past one individual opera toward broader aesthetic issues concerning the relationship between singer and song, image and actuality, opera and audience.

Overflowing with gripping plot twists and charming details, the significance of "Memoir of a Song" for this study stems from one of its strangest features: the identity of its narrator. (The appendix contains the short story in its entirety.) This diva-like protagonist reveals something of itself in the opening lines of the story: "I am an old song now, and have been often sung. Mine has been a long and brilliant career; and though now put on the shelf amid the dust of departed forefathers, let me, ere I sink into annihilation, retrace the early years of my glorious being, when I flew triumphant from throat to throat, roused the heart, and filled the eyes of man with gladness, sympathy, and love." As these flowery remarks suggest, this narrative is not reported by any of the usual suspects of the opera world. Though prima donnas, composers, and amateurs play prominent roles, theirs are not the personal histories disclosed. Instead, "Memoir of a Song" is just that: an autobiography told through the voice of a song. This, however, is no ordinary song: "a private history is written in my pages. I wish to keep my incog., so shall say no more; *but I have been introduced into many operas,* and have made my appearance at the Philharmonic, and the Hanover Square rooms have rung with my fame. Ah, it is a fine thing, I assure you, to be a popular song!" (emphasis mine). Unwilling to reveal its precise identity, this description makes one thing clear: the narrator of this memoir is an insertion aria. Its disclosure that it has been introduced into "many operas" is amplified later in the story when it announces, "I have appeared in the dress of fifty different editions," and then further on, "I am here! I am there! I am everywhere! My being extends from Calcutta to Paris. At the same instant of time I live fifty times. Swifter than the *Tempest's* Ariel I fly round the earth more nimbly than

---

1. Anonymous, "Memoir of a Song," *Fraser's Magazine* 39 (January 1849): 17–28.

2. *Fraser's Magazine* has been described by Miriam M. H. Thrall as "one of the most important organs of progressive thought [. . .] in the Victorian age." See *Rebellious Fraser's: Nol Yorke's Magazine in the Days of Maginn, Thackeray, and Carlyle* (New York: Columbia University Press, 1934), 6. Though sales figures for the January 1849 issue of "Memoir of a Song" are not available, we know that by the end of the periodical's first year of publication (1830), it had a readership of 8,700, and that this number rose steadily through the 1830s and 1840s (see Thrall, 14). In addition, this story was reprinted in three American magazines: *The Albion* 8, no. 6 (February 10, 1849): 61–63; *The Eclectic Magazine of Foreign Literature* 16, no. 4 (March 1849): 420–29; and *Littell's Living Age* 20, no. 250 (3 March 1849): 397–404.

thought." This aria's ubiquitous presence on the world's stages (as a concert as well as an insertion aria), and its translation into various "editions" (perhaps for private as well as public consumption) is similar to many of the real-life "favorite insertions" encountered in chapter 3, arias that made their way "through the world." That this strange protagonist presents itself as having attained one of the most privileged positions in the musical realm is only one of many surprises and questions tucked into the pages of this hitherto unnoticed story.

In adopting an object rather than a human being as its narrator, "Memoir of a Song" is not without precedent. Beginning with the publication of Charles Gildon's *The Golden Spy* (1709), the genre of fiction known interchangeably as *object narratives, object tales,* and *it-narratives* circulated widely.[3] These stories—some short, some full length, most published in English—use a variety of inanimate items as their narrators: sofas, bedsteads, pulpits, reading desks, mirrors, old shoes, smocks, waistcoats, wigs, watches, rings, coins, and so on.[4] Readers follow these personified objects as they embark on adventuresome quests resembling those that might be undertaken by "real" heroes and heroines. "Memoir of a Song" differs from other object narratives in a few significant ways, however. Intangibles were rarely employed as narrators, and this story is unique in featuring a musical work as its protagonist. More important, by 1849 object narratives had drifted out of vogue; they were an eighteenth- and early-nineteenth-century fad that held little currency by the mid-1800s.[5] This story, in other words, takes up an outmoded form of discourse in an attempt to explore the "life" of an object—and by extension a performing tradition—that was itself falling out of fashion. It is perhaps no coincidence, then, that the narrative of "Memoir of a Song" is a retrospective one; the song "speaks" from the position of having become a popular insertion aria, but the events it discloses regarding its rise to fame belong to the past. Indeed, "Memoir of a Song" rarely deals explicitly with the reception of aria insertions, engaging only occasionally with the day-to-day realities of the practice; there are no accounts, for instance, of this aria being introduced into a particular opera performance; no imagined critical reviews. Rather, the ontology of the main protagonist is presented as a given, a symbol of one of many traditions and habits of the operatic world that function together as a whole.

At the same time that "Memoir of a Song" employs a narrative frame that had fallen out of fashion, it also contributes to a body of literature that was flourishing throughout the nineteenth century: fictional representations of music and musicians in general, and of women singers in particular. In her study of E. T. A. Hoffmann's tales and their adaptation for the operatic stage, Heather Hadlock remarks, "[t]he operatic diva, a singer of strange songs, and too often a turbulent, unkind girl, haunted

3. For detailed discussions of this genre, see Christopher Flint, "Speaking Objects: The Circulation of Stories in Eighteenth-Century Prose Fiction," *Proceedings of the Modern Language Association* 113, no. 2 (1998): 212–26; and Jacob Lamb, "Modern Metamorphoses and Disgraceful Tales," *Critical Inquiry* 28 (2001): 133–66.

4. This list is only a partial sample from the one Flint provides in his article. See "Speaking Objects," 215.

5. According to Flint, "the narrating object appears in a surprising number of satires published between 1709 and 1824," though "most were published between 1770 and 1800." Ibid., 214–15.

the nineteenth-century imagination."[6] This haunted imagination is placed on display in "Memoir of a Song," a story in which "strange songs" and three opera singers (not all unkind) occupy the attention of the main protagonist, the aria, as it embarks on its adventures. Indeed, folded into every episode of this tale and into each description of its characters are familiar sentiments that resonate through the fiction of popular romantic and Victorian authors including Hoffman and Balzac, Meredith and Moore, Eliot and Sand.[7] Like their short stories and novels, "Memoir of a Song" engages with tropes concerning the "nature" of the prima donna and the transcendent musical work. Hadlock investigates these tropes in Hoffmann's tales, paying particular attention to the ambivalent attitude taken toward women performers. "How," she asks, "do these stories about female singers contrive to contain and manage the singing woman's authority? And how does the prima donna's voice repeatedly make itself heard, eluding and overcoming narrative attempts to shape or contain its turbulent noise?"[8] Similar questions focus this discussion, but the identity of the narrator in "Memoir of a Song" invites a modified approach: How does this story about an insertion aria contrive to contain and manage its authority, and by extension, the authority of performance? And how does the aria's "voice" repeatedly make itself heard?

This chapter approaches these questions first through an analysis of the aria, and then of the three singers who bring this music to life. Because "Memoir of a Song" has lain buried in the pages of *Fraser's Magazine* for over 150 years, it is worthwhile initiating this discussion with a synopsis.

ADVENTURES OF AN ARIA

Part revenge narrative, part cautionary tale, "Memoir of a Song" is a literary performance of the inevitabilities of theatrical life described by an experienced professional. The "autobiography" opens at a critical moment in the narrator's prehistory: Stefano, the aria's twenty-five-year-old Italian composer, whose personality and actions bear what is perhaps an intentional resemblance to Goethe's Werther, has met and fallen passionately in love with a rising star, the soprano Giulia. ("This Giulia was the very girl to drive Stefano crazy. He imagined he saw her enacting the part

6. "Return of the Repressed: The Prima Donna from Hoffmann's *Tales* to Offenbach's *Contes*," *Cambridge Opera Journal* 6 (1994): 221.

7. The manner in which musicians, particularly women, figure into this fiction has been the subject of much recent scholarly attention. See Sophie Fuller and Nicky Losseff, eds., *The Idea of Music in Victorian Fiction* (Aldershot, England: Ashgate Press, 2004); Susan J. Leonardi and Rebecca A. Pope, eds., *The Diva's Mouth: Body, Voice, Prima Donna Politics* (New Brunswick, N.J.: Rutgers University Press, 1996); Margaret Miner, "Phantoms of Genius: Women and the Fantastic in the Opera-House Mystery," *19th-Century Music* 18 (1994): 121–35; Susan Rutherford, "The Voice of Freedom: Images of the Prima Donna," in *The New Woman and Her Sisters: Feminism and Theatre, 1850–1914*, ed. Vivian Gardner and Susan Rutherford (Ann Arbor: University of Michigan Press, 1992), 95–113; Ulrich Schönherr, "Social Differentiation and Romantic Art: E. T. A. Hoffmann's 'The Sanctus' and the Problem of Aesthetic Positioning in Modernity," *New German Critique* 66 (1995): 3–16; Ruth Solie, *Music in Other Words* (Berkeley: University of California Press, 2004); and Phylis Weliver, *Women Musicians in Victorian Fiction, 1860–1900: Representations of Music, Science and Gender in the Leisured Home* (Aldershot, England: Ashgate, 2000).

8. Hadlock, "Return of the Repressed," 221.

of Zara in his *Montezuma*. He followed her everywhere. He besieged her with bouquets, letters, and songs. One night he set forth, and stood in a severe shower beneath her window.") Stefano attends her performances, captures her attention, and then gets himself hired as a chorister with her opera troupe in order to spend more time with her: "He thought he was in high favour, and the next idea was to sing with her on the stage. This was a hope, however, too brilliant to be fulfilled. 'Oh, how blessed an existence,' he thought, 'to sing, to act, to feel that idealised brief life of the stage, true to one's own heart!' He went to the *impresario*. Pisani was a courteous and kind Italian. He would do his *possible* to get him a place in the chorus; the opera in preparation was the *Barbiere*. Well, he might stand beneath Rosina's window, and sing among the tenors." As the romance between Stefano and Giulia blossoms, the aria takes form in fits and starts in his mind. Significantly, he finishes its slow movement after hearing her perform an insertion aria in the lesson scene of *Il barbiere di Siviglia:*

> To some minds the slovenliness of a great performer becomes a superb mystery, when from that cloud of physical drawbacks emerge in power the grandeur, the unique talents, the charms of genius and beauty. Thus felt Stefano, when, after contemplating in silence the baggy outline of the great signora's head, the orchestra struck up the air she was to introduce as the famous music lesson. It was ill-played: the fury started up. She threw off her head-dress and dashed it to the ground; tore open her shawl to give her arms fair play; then, with a roll of music as a wand of witchery and command, she came forward, and there stood revealed *la dea di tutti cor.* Subtle as quicksilver, her voice twisted through the intricate *fioriture* of her song. The air seemed illuminated in Stefano's eyes by the delight that he felt. How he envied the tenor! Even the Barber's part would have been something. Well, he would be patient, and sing his best. That very Thursday he finished my adagio.

For the most part, however, Stefano is able to work on the aria only in moments of anguish, the last of which is brought on by harsh betrayal: though Giulia has accepted a pearl ring from Stefano and has pledged to "live for him," she calls their relationship off abruptly when an Englishman, Lord Vane, sees her perform at the Teatro la Fenice, Venice, and displays an interest. Stefano reacts violently, shaking Giulia and nearly strangling her landlady. After receiving a "good beating" from Lord Vane, Stefano returns to his rooms and finishes the aria in one last agonized burst. His final gesture before killing himself is to send the completed piece off to Giulia. ("The last time I saw poor Stefano's face, he was sealing me up in a blank cover. Next morning there was a crimson pool at the door, when a servant passed early in the morning, and it was found that the maestro had cut his throat!")

At a gathering of friends a few nights later, Giulia attempts to perform the aria, but she lacks the ability to execute it well ("she sang a most indecent caricature of my finale, bearing false witness to every cadence and every measure"). Once finished, she tosses the score in the air, allowing it to land at the feet of a thoughtful young violinist, Spiridion Balbi ("Spiro"), who takes it to his rooming house and gives the aria its first satisfying performance. ("He took out his violin, and swept over some chords in a masterly manner. Ah! what a flood of rich and exquisite sounds! He opened me up, and, for the first time, I felt my every fibre vibrate and live in his hands"). This eroticized performance attracts a "feminine" knock at the door. Xanthi enters: "The girl seated herself and listened. She hid her face in her hands, and my voice rose up. Tears forced themselves into the great eyes of Xanthi, so touching was the tale that I told of injured love and dying reproach. That room for me was transformed into an enchanted palace. I glorified the air with my breath, and sighed out my soul in a wordless song of rapturous perfection." Despite this favorable reception, Spiro does not bring out the piece again for many months, involved instead in an "Italian conspiracy" that takes him to Austria and lands him in prison. ("He, and two dozen other poor boys, after exciting their patriotic feelings to madness by noisy singing and rabid speeches, committed some excess at the Opera House, and they were lodged in gaol that night. The only things that Spiro contrived to take with him were a flute and myself!") While incarcerated, Spiro passes time by playing the aria on his flute. Day after day, Löttchen ("Lisa")—the fifteen-year-old daughter of an Austrian officer "with no great looks, and a tough voice"—listens and cries, "as if her heart would break." She brings him a violin ("nothing for this [aria] but the violin or the voice," he begs), but even with this sustenance, Spiro is no match for prison life; he weakens and dies, leaving the aria with Lisa.

Aspiring to the life of a famous prima donna, Lisa moves to Vienna for training, and then to London to make her mark ("I was to go to England—to London—the promised land of needy genius, where princely pay is offered for what most of them, honest people, don't understand"). She practices laboriously, but unfortunately never improves. Nevertheless, armed with a letter of introduction, she enters London's elite musical world, performing at a dinner of Lord Gorehampton, an amateur composer and general music "fanatico." Her host requests that she sing one of his compositions, after which a familiar character, Lord Vane, arrives. Now an established connoisseur of London's musical scene—in part owing to his romantic association with Giulia—Vane distracts himself from the ignorant guests by flipping through Lisa's portfolio. Coming across the aria and perceiving its uniqueness, he asks Lisa to sing it:

> She sat down, and, with a voice veiled with fear of failure, she breathed me forth. I only half existed on paper, it was while floating through space that I truly lived and felt the joy and glory of life. I passed through those mirrored and gilded chambers, and felt that splendour added no ray to my own brightness. Better to rise up beneath the humble roof of a cabin encircled by loving hearts and longing ears, than under the cold gilding of a palace with a fool on the music-stool. Lisa could not give me my full honours, but she was true and good as far as she went.

Overall, the evening is a failure, and Lisa leaves without having secured any future engagements.

Lacking any prospects, she spends her days at her boarding house ("dreary lodgings, such as foreign song-birds must have for their cage in London"), where a new tenant, a young woman unable to speak English, arrives and is settled into the room next door. This seemingly unremarkable event is followed the next day by an astonishing one: Lisa receives an invitation to sing "the piece performed at Lord Gorehampton's" at "the Ancients."[9] Thrilled and frightened, she sets out to practice the

9. The "Ancients" refers to the Ancient (Antient) Concert Series, one of the mainstays of London's musical life from 1776 to 1848. For a historical survey and exploration of its cultural significance, see

aria. As she begins, however, her door is thrown open: standing in it, visibly shaken, is none other than Xanthi, the house's new lodger. In a tearful reunion, Xanthi and the aria meet "like long-parted lovers," and the aria trembles, "beneath the joy of a full interpretation by a voice and a genius of matchless power." Understanding that she is hearing a performance far superior to anything she herself could accomplish, Lisa makes the ultimate sacrifice and offers Xanthi the opportunity to appear in her place at the Ancients.

As the story closes, both Xanthi and the aria have had unparalleled success at their mutual debuts: "That grave audience of dowagers and directors was delighted out of its propriety. But who shall recount the surpassing glories of the Wednesday night, when I was encored by the queen, and lauded by the bishops present, and when a venerable countess was removed in fits to the tea-room, and Field-marshal the Duke of Wellington said 'Good!' twice, and when the *Morning Post* screamed it-self hoarse with admiration next day?" Giulia, meanwhile, falls ill and is cast off by Lord Vane. In her final demand as prima donna, before Xanthi usurps her place at the opera house, Giulia sends for a copy of the aria. Her reaction once she glimpses its title can only be guessed, as these parting words bring the story to a close: "again I met the prima donna's eyes, and she read on my brow, *Addio Giulia!*"

THE ARIA

"Memoir of a Song" is a treasure trove of opera trivia. Shot through with references to famous singers (Pasta, Sontag, Mario, Piček), composers (Bellini, Donizetti, Meyerbeer), operas (*Tancredi, Il barbiere di Siviglia, Il crociato in Egitto, La sonnambula*), and their arias, this story continually reaffirms its setting in the first half of the nineteenth century. Against this realistic backdrop, however, the main characters including the aria exist in a timeless dimension, their identities by no means clear-cut. Xanthi, Stefano, Spiro, and most of the others bear slight resemblances to historical figures, but none corresponds to a single person or place.[10] This skillful imbrication of fictional and real magnifies a set of convictions concerning the nature and performance of aria insertions that can be navigated effectively through questions of identity.

"I am an old song now" — "I am by birth Italian" — "I am of no age, country

William Weber, *The Rise of Musical Classics in Eighteenth-Century England: A Study in Canon, Ritual, and Ideology* (Oxford: Clarendon Press, 1992).

10. Two secondary characters have identities that almost certainly correspond directly to historical figures: Costa and Lord Gorehampton. Costa, the man Giulia orders to find her a copy of "Addio Giulia" at the conclusion of the story, must be Michael Costa (1808–1884), London's premiere opera and symphonic conductor who led the orchestras of the King's (and later Her Majesty's) Theatre, the Royal Italian Opera, and the Philharmonic Society for nearly forty years. Lord Gorehampton bears a resemblance to Lord Burghersh (1784–1859), the founder of the Royal Academy of Music. The connections are tenuous, yet suggestive: Burghersh, like Gorehampton, was a prolific composer of operas, though none became known beyond the productions he produced in his own home; they both insisted on the performance of their works (turning themselves into the butt of many jokes); and they both hosted regular gatherings of musicians. For a contemporary review of one of Burghersh's operas, see "Lord Burghersh's Opera," *Quarterly Musical Magazine* 10, no. 38 (1828): 200–203. For a full-length study of Burghersh, see Aubrey S. Garlington, *Society, Culture and Opera in Florence* (Aldershot, England: Ashgate, 2006).

or school" — "I am the proud offspring of an inspired father" — "I am like the air, a 'chartered libertine'" — "I am here! I am there! I am everywhere!" — "I am all earthly fire." So many declarative sentences beginning with "I am." What is their function? These statements highlight the narrator's obsession with its own identity, which is grounded, necessarily, in sound. Throughout this story, which shifts focus rapidly from character to character and country to country, practically the only factor to remain constant is this aria's compulsive tendency to describe itself. So frequent are references to its structure, form, musical content, and affect that a question emerges: what does this character think (or hope) its listeners will hear?

The narrator addresses certain components of this question directly. In the second paragraph of the story, for instance, it reveals that it consists of two movements, an *adagio* and an *allegro*. A few pages later on, moreover, a detailed, yet far more ambiguous description appears: "I felt myself growing rapidly as my creator wrote; an electrifying chord stunned me. I was almost shivered by a sudden plunge into the key of D five flats. I melted into the minor; I wailed, I lamented awhile there; then sharp throes shot through me in chromatic runs. I quavered beneath a shake on G, again I relapsed into a regretful minor, then I gasped in broken snatches of recitative, and then I hurried on to my termination." This account reveals the subjective nature of what it means to hear this aria. What, after all, does a "regretful minor" sound like? And how might "wailing" and "lamenting" be manifest in a musical work? The responses are many, as are those to all of the aria's descriptive turns: it consists, it tells us, of "superb organization"; it is the "*loveliest* harmony ever created!" (original emphasis)—lofty characteristics indeed, but perceptible only to the individual imagination.[11] In steering clear of objective associations to any real aria, the narrator allows itself freedom to depict itself as an artwork that ultimately reflects the Romantic-modernist belief in the ideology of the aesthetic.[12]

In an essay focusing on this ideology and its implications for music consumption and criticism, James Webster writes, "This ideal demands that the artwork be complete and intelligible on its own terms, that it exclude everything superfluous or contingent, that it be incapable of alteration without violating its essence and that it stake a claim to the realms of spirituality as opposed to materiality."[13] Intentionally or not, the narrator of "Memoir of a Song" personifies many of these qualities. When the aria states boldly, for instance, "I belong to no opera, mark, O reader! I stand alone," it is asserting one of the most critical characteristics of the ideology of the aesthetic—its unique synthesis of content and form allows it to stand completely independent, a coherent thing unto itself. Though it might travel from work to

---

11. The subject of "unsounded" music is far reaching and has been explored in detail by Carolyn Abbate, *In Search of Opera* (Princeton, N.J.: Princeton University Press, 2001). Christopher Hatch also touches briefly on this idea in reference to Keats's "Ode on a Grecian Urn," concluding with the provocative notion that the piper depicted on the urn in the poem transforms "he who is looking at it" into a composer for an instant. See "The 'Cockney' Writers and Mozart's Operas," *Opera Quarterly* 3 (1985): 55.

12. See Terry Eagleton, *The Ideology of the Aesthetic* (Cambridge, Mass.: Basil Blackwell, 1990), and James Webster, "Haydn's Symphonies between *Sturm und Drang* and 'Classical Style': Art and Entertainment," in *Haydn Studies,* ed. Dean Sutcliffe (Cambridge: Cambridge University Press, 1998): 222–23.

13. Webster, "Haydn's Symphonies between *Sturm und Drang* and 'Classical Style,'" 223.

work (perhaps elevating those new contexts), there is no single opera that might claim dominion over it, nor are those surroundings essential. Indeed, it can stand alone in concert performances, as was the case with many "favorite insertions" such as "Il soave e bel contento." Moreover, the aria voices deep displeasure, even dread, at the prospect that its notes and text might be rearranged for instrumental, vocal, or other combination: "Popularity puts one into the vile interior of a hurdy-gurdy," it grumbles; and one cannot miss a sense of *schadenfreude* in a snide revelation about the aria's nemesis, "Ciascun lo dice" from Donizetti's *La figlia del reggimento:* "let him tremble. I heard him on the Pan's pipe last Thursday morning; and our butcher's boy thinks nothing of whistling him on the area steps!" An ideal performance, this aria asserts, is achieved only when music is interpreted "as written," though it also makes exceptions when it is performed extremely well, as when Spiro plays it on his violin. The insistence on "ideal" performance emerges as much from the process of its composition as from the internal attributes of a work. It is significant, therefore, that this aria also describes its own genesis in painstaking detail.

"It was fully two years from the time that the first bars of my being were laid down in the brain to that when, in an hour of despair, agony, and insanity, I was put down onto paper and brought out into the world." Fundamental in this account of the aria's creation is the notion of time: this music is the product of a long, arduous period of gestation—*fully two years*. To all familiar with the myriad accusations of haste flung at Rossini, Donizetti, and other composers of *bel canto* opera, the reference is clear: the years spent writing this piece set it apart from most of its Italian predecessors and contemporaries. More important, however, is the composer's mindset while writing the aria: Stefano is raw with misery. There are fleeting moments when he manages to escape his melancholy, as when the opportunity to perform the role of Don Basilio to Giulia's Rosina renders him "half-crazed with delight." Unfortunately, good moods are bad for good art, and while happy, Stefano manages to write only ornamental (i.e. inconsequential) fragments ("he wrote down the brilliant passage in my third page; he polished my new cadenza, and added a chromatic flourish to my recitative"). When he believes Giulia is in love with him, he forgets about the aria entirely ("I lay sulking in a drawer"). True artistic creation occurs only in times of Stefano's darkest despair, the substance of the aria spilling out of him in the hours just prior to his suicide. This aria is ideal, however, not because it is the product of passionate suffering, but because it *is* this suffering, a characteristic the aria refers to repeatedly: "a stern and awful despair reigned throughout me"; "there lay imprinted [in me] the terrible earnestness of [Stefano's] sufferings—a Song! No! I was a death-cry, a dirge, written in blood and gall"; "[Stefano] laid his faint hand on my breast and tears and sobs passed through me, and filled my spirit with a stormy sorrow." This aria, in other words, represents "an autonomous expression of its maker's personality," the all-embracing union of creator and creation achieved, conveniently, at the moment of Stefano's death.[14]

14. The trope of the composer completing (giving birth to) a masterpiece just prior to dying is, of course, common in romantic literature. In Wilhelm Wackenroder's "The Remarkable Musical Life of the Musician Joseph Berlinger," for instance, the description of Berlinger's final compositional gesture is highly reminiscent of Stefano's: "as often as [Berlinger] sat down to work, he burst into a flood of tears;

If, however, this aria reflects many characteristics of the ideology of the aesthetic, it is unclear how to make sense of its status as an insertion aria. It seems counterintuitive, after all, to narrate these lofty positions from the perspective of a musical work that, by its nature, disturbs the "integrity" of a larger aesthetic object. One explanation emerges by taking the timing of the story's publication into account. It is possible that in 1849, readers still imagined that an insertion aria, particularly a "favorite insertion," could exemplify the same lofty ideals as a tried-and-true classic by, say, Beethoven or Mozart. It is not insignificant that when this aria is performed well, it claims to join the "good society" of Beethoven's "Adelaide" (ca. 1794–1795) and Mozart's "Non più di fiori" (1791), the former a self-standing *lied* that, by then, had circulated in the repertory for over fifty years, the later an integral component of a "classic" opera, *La clemenza di Tito*.[15] The thought that an insertion aria might attain a similar longevity because it is both product and reflection of the ideology of the aesthetic, therefore, may not have seemed farfetched.

This explanation could suffice, were it not for one complicating factor: the aria plainly recognizes that it is destined for obscurity—it is not, after all, a true representation of the ideology of the aesthetic. In the opening lines, it reveals that it will soon reach its "annihilation," and throughout the remainder of "Memoir of a Song," it voices a deep fear of death: "Forgetfulness is my only dread. I tremble lest I should go out of print,—then, I imagine, the sufferings of a song must be indeed dreadful. A silent shade longing in vain to unburden its sorrows, and hovering round the spot of its past pleasures, is the only thing to which I can compare the state of a musical phantom." Most revealing is its admission that it lacks a pure, spiritual core: "I have not a tinge of sacredness in my being. I am all earthly fire, and must perish with the things of the earth [. . .] I may not hope to unite myself to the eternal melodies of heaven." The consequences of this deficiency are dire, for as close as this narrator draws to symbolizing the ideology of the aesthetic, it fails in one crucial respect. It cannot, to return to Webster's definition, "stake a claim to the realms of spirituality"; much to its dismay, it remains grounded in the mundane, a disappointing emblem of musical materiality. Just as the most popular favorite insertions fell out of style once their function as aria insertions became obsolete, so, too, was this aria fated to disappear. Its ambitions toward an "ideal" state are, thus, futile, and its rather gloomy outlook extends beyond the "life" of this one aria toward a broader message concerning the performance of aria insertions in general. An obvious point eludes the narrator, but it need not escape the reader: an artistic

---

his tortured heart would not let him recover himself. He lay deeply depressed, buried among the leavings of this world. At length, by an effort, he tore himself free, stretching out his arms to heaven in an impassioned prayer; he filled his soul with the most sublime poetry, with a full and exultant hymn, and, in a marvelous inspiration, but still violently shaken emotionally, he set down a Passion music which, with its deeply affecting melodies, embodying all the pains of suffering, will forever remain a masterpiece" (in *Strunk's Source Readings in Music History,* ed. Ruth Solie [New York: Norton, 1998], 29). This image of the composer dying while creating his masterpiece continues to be influential up to the present day, as witnessed in the dramatic manner in which Mozart's *Requiem* is depicted as "killing" the composer in Peter Shaffer's 1984 film *Amadeus.*

15. See Emanuele Senici, "'Adapted to the Modern Stage': *La clemenza di Tito* in London," *Cambridge Opera Journal* 7 (1995): 1–22.

climate dominated by the ideology of the aesthetic renders aria insertions anachronistic at best, obsolete at worst. Performances dedicated to conveying what is perceived to be the composer's "vision" alone must, by necessity, reject interpolations and substitutions. The aria's fear of drifting into obscurity, in other words, is well founded, and ironically, it is brought on and hastened by the very same aesthetic stance that it admires and advocates. Its situation is not entirely hopeless, however, for "Memoir of a Song" makes clear that longevity (if not permanence) is attainable for those musical works that forge a "spiritual" connection with a performer or group of performers. In this story, this viewpoint is articulated through the aria's diverse experiences with Giulia, Lisa, and Xanthi, and more important, through the rhetoric it employs to frame each of these singers.

THE SINGERS

To describe "Memoir of a Song" as a revenge tale, as I did in the synopsis, may initially seem unproblematic. It is clear, after all, that at the conclusion Giulia receives her just rewards, but what precisely was her transgression? What is the wrong that gets put right by her defeat? One might argue that the story culminates in avenging Stefano, whom she so cruelly jilted. The composer, however, warrants little sympathy, stalking the object of his affection, insinuating himself into her place of employment, and then resorting to violence when she rejects him. Retaliation on his behalf does not seem entirely justified. In fact, the question of who or what is avenged in "Memoir of a Song" extends beyond individuals. Satisfying answers emerge when taking into account the stereotypes that this story employs for its three singers, interpretations of the nineteenth-century female voice that were already familiar from the fiction of E. T. A. Hoffmann.

As do many of Hoffmann's divas, Giulia, Lisa, and Xanthi each symbolize personas that together represent the "nature" of the prima donna, and the messages conveyed through these stereotypes ultimately serve to justify Giulia's downfall. "Memoir of a Song" does not blandly replicate all of Hoffmann's tropes, however, but rather plays with and inverts some of the aesthetic issues embedded in his tales. One such inversion is central. According to David Charlton, "In Hoffmann's philosophy, an almost mystical triangle connects composer, singer and auditor, one that suggests music's acoustic immediacy of impact."[16] A similar triangle is constructed in "Memoir of a Song" in which composer and singer are present; but, significantly, the independent auditor is absent for most of the narrative (the only people who seem to listen are the singers themselves); the third corner of the triangle is replaced by the thing meant to be heard, the aria. As such, the images of the prima donnas depicted in this story—Giulia's capriciousness, Lisa's domesticity, and Xanthi's idealism—convey specific sentiments concerning the intimate relationship between singers and the music they are compelled to perform. The discussion of who and what each of these characters represents can begin, once again, with issues of identity.

Of the three singers featured in "Memoir of a Song," Giulia is unique in display-

---

16. David Charlton, ed., *E. T. A. Hoffmann's Musical Writings* (Cambridge: Cambridge University Press, 1989), 37. Cited in Hadlock, "Return of the Repressed," 223.

ing a resemblance to not just one, but several real-life prima donnas. The most obvious analogy is to Giulia Grisi (1811–1869), only in part for the correspondence between their names. Stage life for Grisi began in Italy, where she made her operatic debut in 1829, but like the fictional Giulia, she abandoned that country early in her career (in October 1832, to be precise), and settled in Paris and London. For the next thirty years, she alternated between those two cities, appearing almost annually in each until her retirement in 1861. During the decades she spent there—as well as on tours through major centers in Russia and the United States—Grisi specialized in the lead roles of many of the operas referred to in "Memoir of a Song" including *Il barbiere di Siviglia, La gazza ladra, Semiramide,* and *Norma.*[17] She was at the height of her popularity during the 1840s, and thus for readers of this short story the connection between her and Giulia would have been a quick one to make.[18]

Some readers, moreover, also might have noted in Giulia references to Angelica Catalani, the soprano who played an indirect role in shaping performances of the lesson scene in *Il barbiere di Siviglia,* as explored in chapter 5. Midway through the narrative, for example, Xanthi, having heard Spiro perform the aria, asks, "how does the Signora Giulia sing it, pray?" His response, "Very like the cat," is reminiscent of the nickname applied to Catalani in moments of derision, the implication that her singing was like a cat's "squall" striking at the heart of her most valuable asset.[19] At the conclusion of "Memoir of a Song," moreover, Catalani is alluded to via one of her signature tunes, "Rule Britannia," the aria-narrator stating sardonically that "the tide of fashion left Giulia stranded on the shore where she had ruled the waves, like Britannia, for some sixteen years."[20] Finally, her actions after trying,

17. Thomas G. Kaufman, "A Chronology of Grisi's Operatic Performances," *Donizetti Society Journal* 4 (1980): 197–223. For a detailed description of Grisi's voice, her career, and her relationship with her husband (the famous tenor Mario), see the comprehensive entry on her in the *Enciclopedia dello spettacolo,* 9 vols. (Rome: Casa editrice Le Maschere, 1954–1962), 9: 1787–90.

18. When "Memoir of a Song" was published in *The Albion* (see footnote 2), it was prefaced by an editorial note that made a direct connection between Grisi and Giulia: "There may be a reader here and there who will not immediately recognize Madame Grisi as the heroine; but she is undoubtedly the Giulia here portrayed. For fifteen years *the* Prima Donna of Europe, she is verging now upon 'fat, fair and forty,' and must be content at last to have rivals near her throne."

19. The most visible use of this nickname was during the so-called old-price riots, which occurred at Covent Garden in 1809. At issue was the raising of ticket prices, a policy for which spectators partially blamed Catalani. The nickname was incorporated in a poem of protest published in the *Chronicle,* the offending line being, "This is the Cat engaged to squall to the poor in the pigeon-holes." See Henry Saxe Wyndham, *The Annals of Covent Garden Theatre from 1732 to 1897,* 2 vols. (London: Chatto and Windus, 1906), 1: 341; Tracy Davis, *The Economics of the British Stage, 1800–1914* (Cambridge: Cambridge University Press, 2000), 26; and Mark Baer, *Theatre and Disorder in Late Georgian London* (Oxford: Clarendon Press, 1992), 210–14. A similar reference to Catalani appears in a review published in *Fraser's Magazine* a few years prior to the publication of "Memoir of a Song." In it, the anonymous author refers to the nickname in order to disparage another singer, Jeanne Anaïs Castellan, arguing that she knows "no better than the cat" (see "Some Words about Music at the Modern Opera," 36 [October 1847]: 440).

20. Catalani performed this song frequently in concert performances, particularly after she retired from the opera stage. Ellen Creathorne Clayton relates a colorful (though highly dubious) incident in which Catalani spontaneously sings "Rule Britannia" while on a pleasure trip aboard a ship manned by twenty sailors: "The sailors, taken by surprise, rested on their oars to listen, and tears sprang to the eyes of more than one weather-beaten old tar." *Queens of Song* (New York: Harper and Brothers, 1865), 206.

and failing, to sing the aria are revealing, for she turns to a second familiar Catalani warhorse: "At last she tossed me aside and caroled away at Rode's air—a trumpery twaddle, in my opinion. A foolish fellow he is, too. He is so vain of having been Sontag's pet; but he is as noisy and as empty as a drum, and I wonder how he has made his way so well in the world." Of course, none of these references establishes that Giulia is literally Catalani: Giulia sings *like* "the cat"; Catalani resided in London eight, not sixteen years; and Rode's variations are identified here (not incorrectly, as we saw in the last chapter) as "Sontag's pet." Beyond these specifics, however, there are nods toward modes of behavior and a manner of singing that make Giulia, if not a precise stand-in for Catalani, then at least an heir to her legend. This legend, which might be described generally as that of the capricious and rebellious diva, surfaces in much of Hoffmann's fiction as well.

"Hoffmann rigorously segregates the two female-performer archetypes in his tales, denying common ground or connection between the human prima donna and the transcendent artiste."[21] Of the two types identified here by Hadlock, there can be no doubt as to which one the fictional Giulia resembles: she is a close sister to Angela, the willful, demanding, and sometimes violent prima donna of "Councillor Krespel"; and to Olympia, the unfeeling automaton of "The Sandman" who has "a voice like the sound of a glass bell, clear and almost piercing," but whose singing is ultimately "spiritless." Both characters possess extraordinary voices capable of mesmerizing their spectators, but both are very much linked to the "human" realm, unable or unwilling to overcome their reliance on empty virtuosity in favor of true expressive singing. They lack, to put it simply, "heart," a charge that was flung at many real-life prima donnas, including Grisi and Catalani. Of a production of Marliani's *Ildegonda* starring Grisi in 1837, for example, a critic for *The Musical World* commented that "what she wants is tenderness of expression."[22] More than most, moreover, Catalani was accused of performing like an automaton, her singing reportedly void of transcendent qualities. In his *Life of Rossini,* for example, Stendhal regrets, "God somehow forgot to place a heart within reasonable proximity of this divine larynx," and having heard her perform in Naples in 1817, the composer Louis Spohr expressed similar displeasure: "what I most missed in her singing, was *soul*" (emphasis his).[23] Similarly disappointing was Catalani's alleged refusal to perform alongside any prima donnas who were as accomplished, or even nearly as talented, as she was. Instead, she insisted on appearing only with third- or fourth-rate singers whose weaknesses highlighted her strengths, an insistence summarized by her husband's infamous remark, "Ma femme, et quatre ou cinq poupées, voilà tout ce qu'il faut!" (My wife and four or five puppets, that's all that's necessary!)[24] To

21. Hadlock, "Return of the Repressed," 225.

22. *The Musical World* (July 28, 1837), 110. Cited in Rutherford, "The Voice of Freedom," 96.

23. Stendhal, *Life of Rossini,* trans. and ed. Richard N. Coe, 2nd ed. (London and New York: John Calder and Riverrun Press, 1985), 337; and *Louis Spohr's Autobiography* (1865; reprint, New York: Da Capo Press, 1969), 27. Stendhal contradicts this sentiment later on in his book, however, describing Catalani as someone "whose prodigiously beautiful voice fills the soul with a kind of astonished wonder, as though it beheld a miracle" (367).

24. See Edgcumbe, *Musical Reminiscences* (1834; reprint, New York: Da Capo Press, 1973), 107; and T. J. Walsh, *Opera in Dublin, 1798–1820* (Oxford: Oxford University Press, 1993), 49.

compensate for the lack of an adequate ensemble of singers, operatic events with Catalani consisted of moments of soloistic abandon for her, many of which would have featured one or more of her favorite insertion arias.[25]

Giulia is a direct descendent of these fictional and real-life prima donnas. There is no doubt, for instance, that she is an excellent singer. The aria-narrator of "Memoir of a Song" describes her voice as possessing a supernatural range ("three octaves and two notes"), with which she is able to execute the most difficult *bel canto* roles and bravura showpieces in the repertory. She lacks "heart," however, not only in her cruel behavior toward Stefano, but in another important respect: she is inexplicably unable to sing the aria that he wrote with her voice in mind. It is possible, of course, that Stefano overestimated her abilities, but the narrator hints at a deeper explanation: "She had not the pure ore of genius, which combines science and poetry [. . .] she had not one spark of devotional feeling in her whole being." The notes themselves, the "scientific" aspects, in other words, were not problematic; rather, it was the spirit, the "poetry" behind them, that eluded her, a clear sign that she is unable to achieve transcendence. What is more, Giulia exhibits tendencies similar to Catalani, treating her choristers poorly and refusing to cooperate with her costar "attendants": " 'Ah, yes, it is a fine thing to be a prima donna! Fancy Giulia getting her two and three hundred a-night, while we have to starve and dance for twenty.' So sighed Mademoiselle Carlotta, in a pink gingham, and white satin shoes with orange bindings. 'And she is such a vain wretch, and so shabby to the chorus! Fancy her poor women, who attend her in all her deaths and faints, not to speak of other things, never get a farthing from her.' " If Giulia was in fact modeled after fictional representations of prima donnas like Angela and Olympia, and after real-life prima donnas like Grisi and Catalani, then her defeat at the conclusion of "Memoir of a Song" can be read as more than the downfall of one person. It might also represent a hopeful farewell to a mode of behavior, and more important, an approach to opera performance that was perceived more and more as aesthetically bereft. Furthermore, it signals the defeat of a singer, and singers like her, who might have resorted to performing insertion arias whenever they felt remotely challenged by the music they were meant to be singing (Giulia's willingness to replace the aria-narrator with a standard aria insertion, Rode's variations, when she finds the former too difficult is noteworthy). Once again, "Memoir of a Song" signals an awareness that aria insertion was becoming a thing of the past. There are indications that this prediction might not apply uniformly across the entire practice, however, for the relationship between musical work and individual performer explored in the story's descriptions of Lisa and (especially) Xanthi suggest that when sung in particular circumstances, some aria insertions were not necessarily in immediate danger of extinction. It is significant, after all, that Giulia's downfall does not correspond with

25. During the 1806–1807 season, when Catalani was starring at London's King's Theatre, for instance, she inserted arias into nearly every production in which she appeared. During performances of Portogallo's *Il ritorno di Serse,* for example, she sang two arias by Mayr, "Oh quanto l'anima" and "Contento il cor nel sen" (libretto, GB: Lbl: 11779.aa.74); and during performances of Mayr's *Il fanatico per la musica,* she sang Paisiello's "Nel cor più non mi sento" (*The Times* [July 16, 1807], and William C. Smith, *The Italian Opera and Contemporary Ballet in London, 1789–1820* [London: The Society for Theatre Research, 1955], 86).

the aria-narrator's. Indeed, this music "takes flight" only after she has disappeared and after her position has been usurped in the narrative by Lisa, and then ultimately by Xanthi. With these two singers, "Memoir of a Song" completes the picture of the female voice that began with Giulia.

Lisa, the next prima donna to take possession of the aria, is everything that Giulia is not: she is "a girl of fifteen, with no great looks, and a tough voice; as unruly as a wild horse on the prairie: but the heart! there lay her matchless power!" Unlike Giulia, Lisa comprehends the spiritual qualities embedded in the narrator, but much to her dismay, she is incapable of communicating this knowledge to others. In part, this inability might be explained by reference to what Susan Rutherford identifies as a third prototype of female representation in early Romantic fiction, particularly in Hoffmann's narratives: the drawing-room singer.[26] According to Rutherford, these singers are domestic women who receive music educations that serve to contain the seductive "supernatural vocalising" that is characteristic of the public virtuosa (like Giulia). The drawing-room singer "must cleanse her voice of its troublesome egotistical desires, and subject its purified tone to the demands of others."[27] This description conforms to what we know of Lisa: she undergoes rigorous training in Vienna and London to improve her skills, and even though she tries, she never appears in a public setting, remaining confined to the private sphere. Unlike the prototypical drawing-room singer, however, Lisa's voice is incapable of pleasing her auditors, for it is hard and inflexible; the aria itself complains that it feels "banged about," "maimed, murdered," and "suffocated" in her throat. In their opposing talents, in other words, Lisa and Giulia might seem to represent polar opposites, each possessing only half of what is required of an "ideal" performer (flawless technique and inward sensitivity). They are, however, quite similar, each representing the reality of performance, the sweating, spitting bodies that are the primary medium of operatic production; both conform neatly to the Hoffmannnesque prototype of the "human prima donna."

An early review published in *Fraser's Magazine* (a review with which readers of "Memoir of a Song" might have been familiar) laments the necessity of relying on these mundane creatures: "The composer, however high his aspirations, is perpetually dragged down to earth; he is the slave of circumstances; he is compelled to give utterance to every inspiration of his mind, to every feeling of his heart, through organs by whose capabilities he is impassably circumscribed, and organs of which he has not the choice. These organs are the *artistes* for whom he is obliged to write—they are the channels through which he must pour forth his soul, and if the flood be unsuited to the receptacle, failure is inevitable."[28] That this language is echoed in the story's descriptions of Giulia and Lisa is, perhaps, understandable—these sentiments, after all, were quite widespread. The most visible moment of "Memoir of a Song" takes place right before Giulia's "debut" of the aria in front of friends: "I trembled lest I should be misrepresented on my entrance into life, and I feared, above all things, being first interpreted by Giulia. *I knew that she would bring*

---

26. Rutherford, "The Voice of Freedom," 97.
27. Ibid.
28. L. C. H., "On the Italian Opera: Desdemona," *Fraser's Magazine* 4 (1831): 227.

me down to her own level" (emphasis mine). That "Memoir of a Song" constructs an alternative to this reality in the character of Xanthi, however, is compelling, for not only does this character fulfill a fantasy in her ability to convey both virtuosity and sensitivity, "science and poetry"; she is noteworthy also for her mystery, the only one of the three singers about whom the reader learns almost nothing.

Unlike Giulia and Lisa, for instance, it is not immediately evident that Xanthi can sing. When first introduced to the aria by Spiro's violin playing, in fact, her reaction provides only the subtlest hint that she harbors any potential talent or that she might pursue a life on stage:

> "Oh!" cried Xanthi, "to sing that and die, signor!"
> "Live to sing it, rather," said Spiro.
> "I shall never sing it," said the girl sadly.
> "If you could! When you can, you will be the greatest singer in Europe," said Spiro.

This exchange inverts an earlier conversation between Stefano and Giulia described by the aria: "he told Giulia that he would die for her. She thought the compliment well chosen, and returned it with stating that she meant to live for him." Xanthi comprehends the cues that elude Giulia; death, not life, is the proper response to this aria; like Lisa, Xanthi possesses the sensibility necessary for genuine understanding.

Coincidentally or not, moreover, this scene between Spiro, his violin, and Xanthi also invokes an emotional incident in Hoffmann's "Councillor Krespel" that occurs between Antonia and her father, Councillor Krespel. Recall from chapter 4 that Antonia (the daughter of Angela) is gifted with a voice more beautiful than her mother's, but is cursed with a physical ailment that will weaken and kill her if she tries to use it. Following one particularly harrowing episode when, despite her better judgment, she sings and becomes ill, Antonia takes a vow not to transgress again, and distracts herself from her true calling by assisting her father: "she helped him to dismember old violins and construct new ones. *'I don't want to sing any more, I want to live for you,'* she would say, smiling gently at her father, whenever she was invited to sing and had declined" (emphasis mine).[29] Again, singing is placed at the juncture between life and death, and even though Antonia selects life at this moment, she and Hoffmann's readers understand that death for her is the only option. This spiritual link to music, one so strong that she is willing to make the ultimate sacrifice, places her in the realm of Hoffmann's second female-performer archetype: the transcendent artiste. It is this type of singer that serves as the model for Xanthi. She is not Antonia's identical twin, however, for a few features distinguish the two fictional singers and suggest, once again, that "Memoir of a Song" presents a variation on Hoffmann's philosophical leanings, this one concerning the agency and authority of the "ideal" prima donna.

The first indication that Xanthi is not modeled precisely on Antonia appears directly following Antonia's vow to quit singing forever. Understanding the depth of her sacrifice, Krespel attempts to assuage his daughter's sorrow and comes upon a

29. E. T. A. Hoffmann, *Tales of Hoffmann*, ed. and trans. R. J. Hollingdale (New York: Penguin Books, 1982), 181–82.

solution unwittingly when, rather than dismantling the Cremona violin for his "experiments," he plays it for her instead:

> Hardly had he sounded the first notes than Antonia cried aloud: "Ah, that is I—I am singing again!" And the silver-bright bell-like tones that came from the instrument did indeed possess a wonderful and unique quality which seemed to have been engendered in the human breast itself. Krespel was moved to the very depths; he played better than ever before; and as he rose and fell, rose and fell again, with grand expressiveness and with full power of tone, Antonia clapped her hands together and cried in delight: "Ah, how well I did! How well I did!"[30]

As in "Memoir of a Song" a woman's vocal revelation is had at the hands of a male violinist, but the stories differ in one important respect. Whereas the instrumental "voice" in "Councillor Krespel" signifies the end of singing for Antonia, Spiro's violin playing marks the beginning for Xanthi, suggesting that she is not as reliant on her male counterparts as are Hoffmann's prima donnas. She need not surrender everything for them. A second, closely related distinction between the two singers emerges toward the conclusion of "Memoir of a Song" when Xanthi reappears following a long absence, when her identity is once again shrouded in mystery. Just as "Hoffmann urged self-negation to be practiced by any 'true artist,' "[31] so, too, does "Memoir of a Song" by placing Xanthi under a veil, and compelling her, as we shall see, to forgo her identity. Unlike Antonia and Hoffmann's other true artistes who "exist only to be sacrificed for the production of their sublime music," however, Xanthi pays no such price, living and thriving long after the aria's narrative comes to a close.[32]

When she first arrives at the boarding house, the aria refers to her obliquely as "a lady" and "a stranger." This initial obscurity suggests that without sublime music, Xanthi is somehow incomplete, a character lacking living energy. As the strains of the aria resound through the house the following day, however, she is shaken back to life, and for the first time since her reappearance, she becomes recognizable: "it was she! Xanthi, the long-remembered, the adored of Spiro, the Ionian girl I had seen years before at Florence, and *I* had dwelt in her heart ever since." Significantly, this recognition scene includes the only clue to her origins provided in the whole story—she is Greek, a fact hinted at in her name but not stated explicitly prior to this moment.[33]

Until now, nationality has played a straightforward role in differentiating the personalities of its prima donnas. As an Italian, Giulia can be read as representative of the unruliness and excessiveness of the south; and as an Austro–German, Lisa embodies the disciplined and domesticated north.[34] What, then, might Xanthi's Greek

---

30. Ibid., 182.

31. Charlton, *E. T. A. Hoffmann's Musical Writings,* 37.

32. Heather Hadlock, *Mad Loves: Women and Music in Offenbach's "Les Contes d'Hoffmann"* (Princeton, N.J.: Princeton University Press, 2000), 223.

33. The name Xanthi may refer to the city in Greece of the same name, a popular tourist destination during the nineteenth century.

34. As David Charlton points out, Hoffmann also used nationality to delineate the personalities of his individual characters: "In his fiction, Hoffmann would further have his singers symbolize, *inter alia,*

origins "stand for"? If Xanthi is a modern Greek, the answer to this question is unclear, but if she can be identified as an ancient Greek, a possibility emerges: as a member of an extinct society of idealized musicians, Xanthi comes to signify a figment of the historical imagination, a fantasy. Perhaps to emphasize this status, she is compelled to renounce her identity almost as soon as she is recognized. Lisa's offer is pivotal: "you, Signora, are the most fit to take my place. See, take my music; *my name too;* and, *as Lisa,* sing this divine song better than poor Lisa herself ever will" (emphasis mine). When Xanthi first appears in public, and possibly in all future engagements, she does not do so as herself. She sheds her identity, and as such, becomes the ideal "receptacle" for this ideal piece of music: just as composer mapped onto aria, aria maps onto performer—the three entities merge, indistinguishable from one another.

This interpretation of Xanthi foregrounds a long-standing philosophical impasse: simply put, that which Xanthi symbolizes—the perfect vehicle for the composer's intentions—does not exist. As such, she might be read as an end as dead as Giulia, an unwelcome reminder that "ensemble" between aria and singer is unattainable. To leave it at this, however, is to assume a confidence on the part of "Memoir of a Song" in a hierarchy of performance that privileges the composer's intentions and insists that ideal music making occurs only when singers cast off their own creative visions. This, of course, summarizes Hoffmann's hierarchy, which this story partially mimics. "Memoir of a Song," however, does not promote an equally unambiguous confidence in this composer-centered aesthetic, for alongside its insistence that singers "engage with the very spirit of the composer, and actually become its Romantic essence," it also conveys an anxiety over the precise status of this authorial figure.[35] This anxiety is uncovered by reflecting once more on the story's structure as an object narrative.

In his survey of these narratives, Christopher Flint illustrates that the appearance of speaking objects in eighteenth- and early-nineteenth-century fiction was "linked to authorial concerns about the circulation of books in the public sphere."[36] Although publication yielded the benefit of public recognition, it also imposed the surrender of control over one's own work. Object narratives literalize this loss by rendering the "author" (the speaking object) of the story inanimate, unable to exert any agency over its own transmission. These narratives, in other words, draw attention to "the disjunction between writer and written matter," to the dangers inherent in forfeiting power over one's works to the public realm.[37] "Memoir of a Song" introduces a variation on this theme of authorial alienation, for the speaker is an artwork whose creation and subsequent alienation from that process are made explicit within the narrative itself. Though this aria bears the direct imprint of its composer, it is incapable of controlling its means of transmission. That it is an insertion aria makes its unfastened nature even plainer, drifting as it does in and out of a multiplicity of contexts.

---

the spirit of national styles of music: Antonia and Angela in *Rat Krespel,* Lauretta and Teresina in *Die Fermate,*" *E. T. A. Hoffmann's Musical Writings,* 37.

35. Ibid.

36. Flint, "Speaking Objects," 213.

37. Ibid., 214.

This story, in other words, presents an allegory of musical performance in which the composer is not in complete control, nor should he be. Rather, it implies that an "ideal" performance is one in which authority is shared between singer, composer, and musical work. Without the aria-narrator, Xanthi has no reason to exist, and when she sings, she is impelled to self-negate. Conversely, without Xanthi, the aria itself has no reason to exist. It is she who gives voice to this music, and as they both achieve fame, this narrator becomes associated not with Stefano the composer, but with her—it is *Xanthi's*. Her interpretation of this work, in other words, is more influential than the original compositional gesture, and as such Xanthi is no fantasy, but rather a stand-in for dozens of very real figures of the nineteenth-century operatic world, many of whom have participated as protagonists throughout this book.

CONCLUSION

In the end, "Memoir of a Song" presents a probing analysis of the relationship between musical works and the individuals who brought those works to life. The fictional Xanthi mirrors an enthusiasm for performance in general, and for aria insertion in particular that remained integral to the nonfictional world of Italian opera throughout the first half of the nineteenth century. Though no real-life singer could scale the heights of perfection that Xanthi achieved, some came close, and they did so not by obediently following directions, but by making their own decisions regarding how they sang and, more important, what they sang and when they sang it. Like Xanthi, these performers forged a spiritual union between their voices and a set of arias that they introduced into various operatic productions—a relationship that proved doubly beneficial: not only were they able to attain and perpetuate their fame through spectacular performances of these pieces, they also focused attention on, and provided exposure to, a group of arias that might otherwise have drifted quickly and irretrievably into obscurity.

Opportunities for performers to participate in the practice of aria insertion in modern productions are rare. There are, of course, a handful of operas (Italian and otherwise) still circulating in the repertory in which traditions of insertion have become fixed (both "tolerated" and "accepted" to return one final time to the words of Nicola Tacchinardi). In addition to *Il barbiere di Siviglia,* Donizetti's *La figlia del reggimento* and Johann Strauss's *Die Fledermaus* come immediately to mind.[38] These works represent the exception, however, and the aria-narrator's fear of obscurity explored above has proven quite prescient. Although performers might attempt to alter any number of scores with aria interpolations or substitutions, they run the risk of criticism, if not outright condemnation, by doing so. To take one notorious instance, when Cecilia Bartoli performed a pair of insertion arias in a production of *Le nozze di Figaro*—numbers that Mozart himself had composed for that very opera—the reaction among spectators and critics was fierce. Bartoli was lambasted, accused of typical diva-like "egocentricity," one critic summarizing the event by re-

---

38. See Andrew Lamb, " 'Die Fledermaus' and Tradition," *Opera* 42 (1991): 1405–9; and Judith Tick, "Clara Kellogg and the Memoirs of an American Prima Donna," in *Music in the USA: A Documentary Companion* (New York: Oxford University Press, 2008).

calling (almost gleefully) that an angry audience member "cared enough to boo. It is shocking to say it, but Bartoli deserved it."[39] Bartoli did not deserve it—she was perfectly justified in making this alteration, as a handful of critics and scholars have also argued.[40] The negative reactions against Bartoli's alterations were magnified because she was "tampering" with Mozart, a composer whose "vision" still possesses more clout than most. The taboos that she ran up against, however, are universal, serving to limit, and largely prohibit, aria insertions in most operatic productions today.

Such inhibitions are by no means wholly negative. Only by reasserting the composer's authority have modern audiences had the opportunity to experience operas by Rossini, Bellini, Donizetti, and Verdi in forms that attempt to replicate what those artists may have had in mind when they wrote their works. This aesthetic has yielded countless superb productions and recordings, and although performers today are rarely able to engage with the practice of aria insertion, their freedom to engage creatively with the operas in which they appear has by no means been eradicated. What I have attempted to suggest in each of my case studies of individual operas and arias, and in the analysis of "Memoir of a Song," however, is that a composer's authority is not the only authority worth reasserting. As this book has tried to show, singers, too, played a vital role in shaping individual operas, and it was with their aria insertions that they raised their voices most powerfully. Ultimately then, just as Xanthi and her aria companion strike a note of hope for the practice of aria insertion, my hope is that this book has been able to do the same.

39. The production occurred at the Metropolitan Opera House in the fall of 1998. Bartoli sang the role of Susanna, and the substitute arias she performed were "Un moto di gioia" (in place of "Venite inginocchiatevi") and "Al desio, di chi t'adora" (in place of "Deh vieni, non tardar"). The quote cited is by Martin Kettle, "How to Make a Farce out of Figaro," *The Guardian* (November 14, 1998).

40. Critics who took Bartoli's side included William Weaver, "The Met Takes a Fresh Look at 'Figaro,'" *The Financial Times* (November 12, 1998), and Hugh Canning, "Wedded Bliss," *Sunday Times* (November 15, 1998). For a detailed discussion of this event, see Roger Parker, "Ersatz Ditties: Adrianna Ferrarese's Suzanna," in *Remaking the Song: Operatic Visions and Revisions from Handel to Berio* (Berkeley: University of California Press, 2006), 42–66.

MEMOIR OF A SONG

Oh, that I were the viewless spirit of a lovely sound,
A breathing harmony!

I am an old song now, and have been often sung. Mine has been a long and brilliant career; and though now put on the shelf amid the dust of departed forefathers, let me, ere I sink into annihilation, retrace the early years of my glorious being, when I flew triumphant from throat to throat, roused the heart, and filled the eyes of men with tears of gladness, sympathy, and love.

I am by birth Italian. I was created by the maestro in his twenty-fifth year. It was while rocking lazily on the moonlit lagunes of Venice that I first became conscious of existence: in the magic hall of the brain I first bestirred my wings, but found the quarters too confined for my ambitious and expanding energies. I was, however, allowed to move, as the Scotch say, "butt and ben," between the head and the heart, for from both I sprang. Ay, thy life-blood, poor Stefano, ran in my veins, with the wild fire of its burning passion, and the pathos of its sombre melancholy, indelibly impressed on the wild earnestness of my adagio and the marvellous rapture of my allegro! The author of my being had been a poet and a musician from his earliest years. In the poverty-stricken home of his father there were few opportunities for the improvement of any but such a one as Stefano. His was the heart to which all Nature speaks in her fondest and deepest tones; the airy tongue that addressed the spirit of Stefano whispered ceaselessly in the ear willing to hear, of all that was beautiful, poetic, and ennobling.

Now to return to myself. Shall I tell the secrets of the brain? Shall I reveal to Mr. Faraday[1] the electric flashes which accompanied my gradual formation in the thoughts and will of my creator? Shall I trace my being back to its first dawn, through its gradual perfecting, to the full splendour of its perfect organisation,

---

1. Michael Faraday (1791–1867): known for his pioneering experiments in electricity and magnetism, and considered by many to be the greatest experimentalist who ever lived. See A. J. Meadows, *The Great Scientists* (New York: Oxford University Press, 1987).

when, consigned to the throat of a great prima donna, I first spread my wings and sailed forth triumphant, conquering and to conquer?

It was fully two years from the time that the first bars of my being were laid down in the brain to that when, in an hour of despair, agony, and insanity, I was put down upon paper and brought out into the world. Talk of Minerva, all ready armed, leaping, bucklered and helmeted, from the brain of Jove! what was *her* start into life compared to mine? In me were centred a thousand perfections, for I came adorned and crowned with Love's idolatry,—an offering, a dying offering, to the only woman Stefano ever loved in his life. Of course, *I* was in all his secrets. Giulia was a young actress—you do not need a description of her, she is in all the London print-shops; but yet she is not now as she was *then*. Ah! *era stella del mattin.* Originally a flower-girl at Florence, she had a voice of three octaves and two notes, a head of glorious form, and a face of enchanting loveliness. At sixteen, she had the grace of a nymph and the ease of a child. She was taken in hand by old Giorgio, and taught to sing, some time before she learnt to write or read. She was the strangest girl,—a mixture of vanity, vice, fascination, and good-nature, with some superstitions, that made her very diverting when she took a fit of fright about a new character. I know that she vowed fifteen pounds to St. Mark if she got through *Casta Diva*,[2] with an *encore* to the quick part. By the way, I have a spite at *Casta Diva* ever since she was preferred to me at the San Carlo. But to return. This Giulia was the very girl to drive Stefano crazy. He imagined he saw her enacting the part of Zara in his *Montezuma.* He followed her everywhere. He besieged her with bouquets, letters, and songs. One night he set forth, and stood in a severe shower beneath her window.

Giovinetto cavalier![3] sung out Giulia from an attic window.

This was enough for Stefano. He thought he was in high favour, and the next idea was to sing with her on the stage. This was a hope, however, too brilliant to be fulfilled. "Oh, how blessed an existence," he thought, "to sing, to act, to feel that idealised brief life of the stage, true to one's own heart!" He went to the *impresario.* Pisani was a courteous and kind Italian. He would do his *possible* to get him a place in the chorus; the opera in preparation was the *Barbiere.* Well, he might stand beneath Rosina's window, and sing among the tenors.

Oh, obbligato, mille grazie![4] cried Stefano. And he went off as happy as if he had just found fifty pounds in his empty pockets.

For those who like it, it is a charming thing singing in a chorus: to the real lover of the stage, to the real denizen of the green room, this will be easily explained. To feel that one forms one billow of that tide of music,—to feel that one is joining in the ruling passion of a multitude, and making one's own noise besides,—all this combines to create an elevated feeling of enjoyment and delicious excitement. The eventful rehearsal came. Into the dim, dark, nasty theatre, walked Stefano, very triumphant. There stood the pale, ill-washed chorus; the dirty scenes; the disenchanted gardens of the Spaniard's home; and lolling on a chair, sipping *eau sucrée,* in a filthy white shawl, with an old handkerchief over her head, sat the Giulia, very

---

2. "Casta diva": aria, act I, Bellini, *Norma.*

3. "Giovinetto cavalier": *canzonetta* contained in the trio of Act I, Meyerbeer, *Il crociato in Egitto.*

4. "Oh, obbligato, mille grazie!": text derived from opening chorus of Rossini's *Il barbiere di Siviglia.*

tarnished and shabby, certainly. People who know nothing about these things are fond of saying and believing, that all the falsehood of the stage, all the vain trickery of the performers, cure the too-ardent admirer in the morning of the passion that he felt at night in an illuminated theatre. This is far from being altogether true. On the contrary, to some minds the slovenliness of a great performer becomes a superb mystery, when from that cloud of physical drawbacks emerge in power the grandeur, the unique talents, the charms of genius and beauty. Thus felt Stefano, when, after contemplating in silence the baggy outline of the great signora's head, the orchestra struck up the air she was to introduce as the famous music lesson. It was ill-played: the fury started up. She threw off her head-dress and dashed it to the ground; tore open her shawl to give her arms fair play; then, with a roll of music as a wand of witchery and command, she came forward, and there stood revealed *la dea di tutti cor.* Subtle as quicksilver, her voice twisted through the intricate *fioriture* of her song. The air seemed illuminated in Stefano's eyes by the delight that he felt. How he envied the tenor! Even the Barber's part would have been something. Well, he would be patient, and sing his best. That very Thursday he finished my adagio. He wrote me down on paper, but I was voiceless as yet almost. He could only sob me out, poor Stefano! at intervals. He was unfortunately situated. Ah, Stefano, you and I should have existed in the golden days of the song-loving Past, life, love, and livelihood! Stefano was poor to misery, very much in love, and only in the chorus at a very low engagement. These were depressing circumstances.

A fortnight after, Stefano received an intimation from the *impresario* that Don Basilio was sick, and that he might take his part for that night. Stefano was half-crazed with delight: he was getting on in the world. That evening he wrote down the brilliant passage in my third page; he polished my new cadenza, and added a chromatic flourish to my recitative. I was daily improving now.

That evening Stefano was in good voice. He had risen to the dignity of an actor, and Giulia spoke to him; and he stood at the side of the stage, listening enraptured to the mellow tones of love-making on the stage. He was not jealous of the tenor, for *he* had a squint and a large family. And then it was so charming the way that Giulia came forth, to curtsey with enchanting coquetry, and sing, in round, crisp tones, her *Buona sera, buona sera,* as he retreated, bowing truly in spirit to her. Then he was asked to supper, and he went. It was an extremely lively and amusing meal; light wines, and light laughing, and light talking: very pleasant for Stefano, who had never before felt so great a man. When he came home, I lay sulking in a drawer. I was pitched too high for him that night.

The next day Stefano twanged away at the guitar songs of successful love: foolish things, how I hated them! silly addresses to Nice, *mio ben,* and *idol mio.* In my silent, tragic greatness, I lay, and could have gnashed my notes for fury. Well, well, my time was coming. Stefano scraped together all his money to purchase a pearl ring, and he sent it to Giulia. She put it on her lovely little finger, and she acted Ninetta that night. Stefano sang the part of Pippo *faute de mieux,* in the way of a contralto.[5] It was at a small, Italian theatre, and Giulia was only rising into fame.

---

5. Pippo and Ninetta are characters in Rossini's *La gazza ladra.* Pippo is a role composed for contralto *en travesti* and thus having Stefano sing the part adds a revealing, "feminizing" touch.

He got through it wonderfully well, and acted the part in the most impassioned manner.

That evening he told Giulia that he would die for her. She thought the compliment well chosen, and returned it with stating that she meant to live for him. Oh, those light stage vows and green-room promises! Well, this was the state of affairs for one fortnight; they acted together, and never better than one evening, the last but two of their engagement. The walls of the town were chalked all over with homage to Giulia: *Eterno onore all'immortale sirene! Divina Giulia!* and a few other such truisms.

Two idle young Englishmen came to Ferrara. What was to be seen? "Oh, horrid place!—ducal palace—Parisina—wicked woman—poem by Byron, and all that sort of thing."[6]

"There's an opera," said Lord Vane; "let's go."

"Ah! what is it?"

"Semiramide—Giulia."

"Well, let us go."

So they went to the little, dark theatre, filled with the gentry and *beau monde* of Ferrara.

"'Pon my honour, not so bad," said one.

"Very good," said Lord Vane.

He leant over the box—he was interested; and a chorus of women struck up the magic music of the *Serena e Vaghi rai.*[7] How grandly lovely was Giulia in her despotic tenderness! There was a contralto, with an ill-conditioned turban on her head for Arsace; but regal was the love-making of Giulia. And how grandly did she summon the Assyrian courtiers to do their homage to her! *Giuri, a sommi dei.*[8] There was a superb tyranny in her cadences and imperial embellishments. Stefano gloried in her every note; there was not a brighter face than his in the theatre. It was a sight of rapture and triumph to him,—that rapture in the triumph of another that has not even the restlessness of vanity to irritate and mar its enjoyment.

Giulia yet stood in her crimson robes and diadem when Lord Vane addressed her. He spoke French and Italian beautifully. The Italian, subtle from the time she had cut her first tooth, soon saw and enjoyed the admiration of one man and the frantic jealousy of another. Next evening a diamond ring effaced the pale pearl one on her hand; the engagement at the theatre was prolonged for an additional week. The English milor and his admiration of the prima donna was no secret subject of conversation; cruel vanity and heartlessness shone in the fiery glances of Giulia. It was one evening, the last of the stay of the opera *troupe,* that Stefano made his way alone into the presence of Giulia. It was after the performance. She had gone home to her lodgings, and it was late when Stefano rushed up the stairs that led to her apartment. He knocked hurriedly.

Chi c'è? said the sweet treble voice.

6. Byron, "Parisina" (1816).

7. "Serena i vaghi rai": chorus, Act I, Rossini, *Semiramide.*

8. "Giuri, a sommi dei": a reference to "Giuri ognun a' sommi Dei," the ensemble within the finale of *Semiramide.*

Son io! shrieked Stefano, as he burst in. He laid hold of her, and shook her till her teeth chattered, then fell down on his knees, and rolling himself on the ground, made abject protestations of despair and devotion.

Prendi l'anel ti dono,[9] said Giulia, retreating with a scornful grin, and tossing his ring in his poor face. He seized it, and bit the slight gold circlet in two.

Mangi pure, said the malicious woman.

With a scream he seized hold of her, and clasped her in his arms,—

Eh m'ami ancora, dimmi che m'ami.

Sicuro, mia vita! said Giulia.

So Stefano was pacified, like a silly young man as he was, and they sat down. Giulia opened the window, and hung her head out. She wrapped a mantilla round her, and hummed *Di tanti Palpiti.* Then she stopped, and there was a silence for a little while. At last there followed the sound of shuffling feet, and the soft, mellow twang of guitars—that sound full of warmth and starlight to me; and then there rose up a serenade. *Addio, Delizia,* came over and over again from a band of men's voices. Stefano was silent, till the old landlady entered.

Una serenata, signorina mia, dalla parte di milor; sicuro dalla parte di milor.

Stefano asked no more, the Italian blood was lit up with the fury of long-suppressed revenge; he flew on the old woman and nearly strangled her.

Ahi! Soccorso! aiuta! aiuta! And the yells of the two women brought up the whole street to the door in two minutes. Stefano met Lord Vane, who gave him a good beating; and then, dashing through the crowd, he made his way home. He never saw Giulia again. Early next morning he received an intimation that his services were no longer required; that his cadences were as incorrect as his conduct; that Signor Baretti, from Milan, had kindly consented to take all his parts; and that the *corps* wished him health and much prosperity in the book-binding line, to which he had been apprenticed when they first had had the honour of his acquaintance. He got the letter, and lay staring at it for some time; and then he heard the sound of carriages, and looked out in the street. The *corps opératique* were departing for Bologna, and with it light, love, life, and hope, and all the ambitious aspirations of a genius. There is no such thing as genius without ambition; there is no such object in creation as genius without a pole-star for its thoughts, hopes, and aims. That aim may be fame, or love, or power; generally it is all three at once. In the case of Stefano it was so. Those strolling players, with their bales of trumpery and tinsel, were all the world to him: most contemptible, or most tremendous engine, the drama—the stage—the play; that subtle theatrical influence, that throws its baleful rose-pink hue over the very face of heaven, and the fresh green glories of Nature,— who can trace its many-shaped disguises, its pernicious and transfiguring might? Seducing beyond all other enchantments, it colours the face of reality only to corrupt and destroy all Nature and Truth. Miserable delusion! Let the lives and sins of the denizens of the green-room declare loudly the downward tendency of that idolatry of representation which fills the theatres of my native land.

I belong to no opera, mark, O reader! I stand alone; a private history is written in my pages. I wish to keep my incog., so shall say no more; but I have been intro-

9. "Prendi l'anel ti dono": duet, Act I, Bellini, *La sonnambula.*

duced into many operas, and have made my appearance at the Philharmonic, and the Hanover Square Rooms have rung with my fame. Ah, it is a fine thing, I assure you, to be a popular song! The worst of it is, that popularity puts one into the vile interior of a hurdy-gurdy; and we all know how unrevenged have been the most cold-blooded murders of our ill-used class. *Di Piacer*[10] once said to me at a concert, that he had overheard Lady ____ call him "a tiresome old thing," and wonder how any one could like him. Poor, dear old bravura, I was sorry for him. Ah, I was in the heydey [*sic*] of my youth then!

Well, Stefano—master, father, creator—let me return to thy parting hour with me. I was thy favourite child, for I was with thee in thy agonies. Tell me, dost thou, from beyond the stars, still listen to the melody thy heart sent forth like the dying swan? Dost thou remember *me,* the Ariel and familiar of thy spirit? Didst thou hope that night we parted that I should float upwards to thy soul's home, on the tones of that harmonious voice to whom thou didst dedicate my existence?

It was, I suppose, about half-past ten at night, when I felt myself rudely laid hold of, and crushed in a trembling and burning hand. A pen and wild blotches of ink soon made me what I am now: a stern and awful despair reigned throughout me. I felt myself growing rapidly as my creator wrote; an electrifying chord stunned me. I was almost shivered by a sudden plunge into the key of D five flats. I melted into the minor; I wailed, I lamented awhile there; then sharp throes shot through me in chromatic runs. I quavered beneath a shake on G, again I relapsed into a regretful minor, then I gasped in broken snatches of recitative, and then I hurried on to my termination. It warms my old tones to think of myself as I *have* been sung. Mine was a glorious ending in a full storm of musical passion: runs that swept through the whole range of the voice; shakes that tore the air; notes up! up! like a daring rocket to the skies; and tones sinking low, as if overwhelmed with the weight of sorrow and despair. It has been well remarked of me, that I am of no age, country, or school. I might have been the wrathful farewell of an ancient Greek; Medea might have sent me to the false Jason; Sappho might have united me to her own words. I have always thought my style was more antique than modern; and every wretch that sings imagines that he can interpret me! *I* should take a lifetime to study! One woman only has ever entered completely into my meaning, and she was not the person for whom I was written.

I did not hear myself speak the first night of my creation. I only knew that I existed. The tears of my creator fell over my face—such tears as only the children of music and poetry can shed. I lay before him like his own heart, torn asunder, and exposed to view; there lay imprinted the terrible earnestness of his sufferings—a Song! No! I was a death-cry, a dirge, written in blood and gall. Since that night I have appeared in the dress of fifty different editions, none of which to my heart can never be so dear as that first garment which I wore in my master's presence—a dirty, begrimed, blotted, and blurred sheet of flimsy paper, dearer far than the gilded books in which I have since revelled [*sic*] as an honoured guest. Stefano finished: the pen was still in his hand. He wrote on my brow, *Addio, Giulia!* and pressed the name to his white lips; then he laid me down and looked on me as one to whom he would

10. "Di piacer mi balza il cor": cavatina, Act I, *La gazza ladra.*

consign his dying wishes. He laid his faint head on my breast, and tears and sobs passed through me, and filled my spirit with a stormy sorrow. I earnestly trusted that I might stick in the throat of the wretched woman who had caused all this misery.

Oh! ye men and women who have written on the sufferings of the ill-conditioned children of genius, with the kind intention of proving that it is all their own fault, had you been in the way of my experience you would be more merciful in your judgment. I know, allow me to say, better than any one, the secrets of passionate suffering; and had you ever lived as I have done, for several months, in the fitful cells of an excited brain, you would bless your good fortune for your own stupidity. Extreme nervous susceptibility is the price paid for being a poet; and if you are a musician into the bargain, I assure you the thoughts, and airs, and rhymes in your head, have very indifferent treatment, inflammatory food, and frequently an unexpected and lamentable conclusion.

The last time I saw poor Stefano's face, he was sealing me up in a blank cover. Next morning there was a crimson pool at the door, when a servant passed early in the morning, and it was found that the maestro had cut his throat!

This added a tragical interest to my *début*. I was sent to Giulia. When she took me out of the cover, I looked up into her face; she was looking very handsome; her hands were cold as they clasped me; she laid me on the music-desk and turned me over; she hummed a bar or two, invoked the aid of the Virgin, and attempted my allegro. How I gloried in my own difficulties!—she could hardly read me properly, for Giulia was only gifted with a glorious organ and a subtle ear. She had not the pure ore of genius, which combines science and poetry; her physical splendour was unequalled in Europe, but she had not one spark of devotional feeling in her whole being. She turned me over and over, but into my heart she could not make her way. At last she tossed me aside and caroled away at Rode's air—a trumpery twaddle, in my opinion. A foolish fellow he is, too. He is so vain of having been Sontag's pet; but he is as noisy and as empty as a drum, and I wonder how he has made his way so well in the world.

The evening after my arrival Giulia invited some friends to supper. It was after the opera, and I still lay unnoticed on the spot where she had thrown me down in despair in the morning. I listened with some anxiety to the conversation of those around me. My ambitious hopes urged me to wish for a successful *début*. I trembled lest I should be misrepresented on my entrance into life, and I feared, above all things, being first interpreted by Giulia. I knew that she would drag me down to her own level; and thus, defenseless, passive, and hopeless I lay, my leaves trembling in the soft wind that floated through the open window overlooking the Lung' Arno of Florence.

They were very merry, those actors and actresses. The glitter of their professional life follows them every where. Once on the high road to fame—a way strewn with gold and flowers—how light and intoxicating becomes the atmosphere that surrounds the successful singer! They have all the love—the composer all the labour. Poor Stefano, how have thy blood and thy tears rested heavy on my spirit, when I have sailed forth triumphant on the air that beat and fluttered with the raving applauses of hundreds and hundreds! At such times I feel that I am the proud offspring of an inspired father; and I glory in the tears that I have wrung from radiant eyes, believing such to be the best peace-offering to an unavenged and com-plaining shade.

In the meantime Giulia sang, and laughed, and coquetted; and at last she spoke of my arrival and previous melancholy history. She put on a pretty air of sentiment, and even wiped her eyes when she mentioned Stefano's name. She laid me in the hands of the buffo singer; and he, putting on his most admired Leporello grimace, chanted forth my first bar in a style that almost made me laugh at myself.

Brutta assai! questa romanza mi pare, said the tenor, still engaged with the eatables.

Senti un po! said Giulia; and she sang a most indecent caricature of my finale, bearing false witness to every cadence and every measure.

How I was banged about that night! No song of my rank ever suffered so much from the calumny of human beings; yet I felt proudly conscious that I was misun-derstood—that I was a stranger of an illustrious birth, thrown by an evil charm amid a class incapable of comprehending my elevation and dignity; and, like an un-recognized price, I resolved to bide my time, and trust to the all-pervading power of truth to place me in my right position in the world. The gay Giulia finished me with an exaggerated flourish, then rolled me up and tossed me up to the ceiling, from whence I fell at the foot of a silent and thoughtful-looking young man. He picked me up, looked me through, and put me in his pocket. Soon after he took me home. I found myself in a small lodging in a street of Florence. The mean room contained only a bed, a chair, and a table; a violin case lay on the latter, some rosin and music-paper beside it. This young fellow, Spiridion Balbi, I found was of Greek and Venetian combination, by means of an Ionian mother and an Italian father. He had left the island where he was born at an early age, and had become a violinist of some note in Italy. He was playing in the orchestra of the Pergola at the time that I first saw him. He took out his violin, and swept over some chords in a masterly manner. Ah! what a flood of rich and exquisite sounds! He opened me up, and, for the first time, I felt my every fibre vibrate and live in his hands. I felt my latent pow-ers distend and swell into majesty, and my might extend through the airy empire of sound. Joy! glory! and honour to thee, Spiro mio! for that first interpretation of me to myself. I felt then that I stood alone, the *loveliest* harmony every created! I only wanted my words; but who could have missed them, really, amid the passionate weeping and wailing of that marvellous catgut? The violin had all the ecstasy of the human voice in Spiro's hands. He sang, he spoke, he cried, he shrieked, he laughed by turns, on the strings of that magical instrument. He played me through three times that night. I admired myself more and more. I became insatiable, as a young beauty for many mirrors to reflect her charms. At last the violin was laid down, and a female step was heard at the door.

Posso entrare, said the voice of a girl. And Spiro replied by opening the door: and I saw a young, slight figure enter. I had never, I thought, seen beauty before. Giu-lia appeared coarse beside the heavenly outline of Xanthi. Her hair was bound round her head like a golden glory; her eyes were blue; her face and brow white, as if her life had been passed in seclusion even from the warm glances of the sun; and there was a languid and careless grace about every movement, that might have suited a sultana in the prime of her days.

Signor, she said, respectfully, *la cena è preparata.*

Bellissima verrò! ma pria, ascolti un po!

The girl seated herself and listened. She hid her face in her hands, and my voice rose up. Tears forced themselves into the great eyes of Xanthi, so touching was the tale that I told of injured love and dying reproach. That room for me was transformed into an enchanted palace. I glorified the air with my breath, and sighed out my soul in a wordless song of rapturous perfection.

"Oh!" cried Xanthi, "to sing that and die, signor!"

"Live to sing it, rather," said Spiro.

"I shall never sing it," said the girl, sadly.

"If you could! When you can, you will be the greatest singer in Europe," said Spiro.

"Ah!" sighed Xanthi, "how does the Signora Giulia sing it, pray?"

"Very like the cat," replied Spiro.

Ah, me ne godo! cried Xanthi, suddenly. And she took me up to muse over me for a few moments, while Spiro played a strain of enchanting beauty; and I began to feel myself in the good society of such airs as *Adelaide,* [11] *Non più di fior,*[12] *Perfida Clori.*[13] It was with the first of these that I have always maintained the strictest friendship. Long may that dear and esteemed harmony hold her place and rank in Pischek's[14] throat; and may no upstart standard-bearers supersede her claims to notice and respect. We old songs have a great deal to put up with from the rising generation of songlets, ariettas, and above all, that impertinent sutler's girl, the *Figlia,* as she is familiarly called. On this subject I cannot contain my indignation. That snob, *Ciascun lo dice,*[15] holds his head very high; but let him tremble. I heard him on the Pan's pipe last Thursday morning; and our butcher's boy thinks nothing of whistling him on the area steps!

I have not always dwelt "in marble halls." I have followed on the steps of adversity and ruin. I would not wish only to tickle the ears of rich fools and the outer skin of gay hearts. My desire for public life remained for many months ungratified. My first professor revealed me to no one. He was a strange, vain, idle, fantastic wretch, that Spiro Balbi. I am sure the ancient secret of the Greek fire lay in his veins. He lived in a world of wonderful fancies; his plans were to regenerate the world by means of music—to organise a Greek republic with a senate of fine tenors, and a choir of good basses for church matters. In the meantime he entered into an Italian conspiracy, *pour passer le temps.* It was in the Austrian States that he made his *début* as an agitator. He, and two dozen other poor boys, after exciting their patriotic feelings to madness by noisy singing and rabid speeches, committed some excess at the Opera House, and they were lodged in gaol that night. The only things that Spiro contrived to take with him were a flute and myself!

11. "Adelaide": Ludwig van Beethoven, op. 46.

12. "Non più di fiori": rondo, Act II, Mozart, *La clemenza di Tito.*

13. "Perfida Clori": Luigi Cherubini (1782).

14. "Pischek": Jan Křtitel Pišek (1814–1873).

15. "Ciascun lo dice": Act I, Donizetti, *La figlia del reggimento.*

And he played in his dungeon. I floated through the dark, dank air, and I was happy in my own existence—as happy that night, and happier, than the brilliant evening that I reveled beneath the gilded ceilings of the Tuileries, and Belgiojozo[16] pronounced me worthy of my fame. Spiro was sent to a fortress! Bah! the emperor could not put *me* under lock and key. I am like the air, a "chartered libertine;" and a glorious life of ubiquity has mine been since then. I am here! I am there! I am everywhere! My being extends from Calcutta to Paris. At the same instant of time I live fifty times. Swifter than the *Tempest's* Ariel I fly round the earth more nimbly than thought. Once created, my existence is of indefinite length. Forgetfulness is my only dread. I tremble lest I should go out of print,—then, I imagine, the sufferings of a song must be indeed dreadful. A silent shade longing in vain to unburden its sorrows, and hovering round the spot of its past pleasures, is the only thing to which I can compare the state of a musical phantom. I shall never forget what I felt at hearing an interesting little old Scotch ballad tell the story of it restoration from a long trance—a crotchety little old thing it was, too, but an air full of character and feeling. He had been born before the battle of Bannockburn,[17] and had felt himself dying by degrees, until he only lay asleep in the mind and half effaced from the memory of an old nurse. Mercifully she hummed him to a sick child one day; the lady of the house overheard her, rescued my poor friend from oblivion, and, with the cordial of a good accompaniment, he is now going about the world as active as ever he was. I remember, too, I was at the Ancient Concerts the night that Prince Albert caused the unlooked-for resurrection of that glorious old warrior, *Chanson de Roland*. He had been almost in a dying state for several hundred years. He who had been borne on the breath of Taille-fer, he who had been chanted by the Normans of the Conqueror, lay silent and neglected in some dark hole for centuries of suffering! Imagine, I beseech you, what his feelings must have been to find himself in Mario's throat,[18] flung out into the nineteenth century, in the very teeth of such fops as "*Voi che sapete,*[19] *Quel bricconcel Amore,*"[20] and so on. It was a night of triumph such as seldom falls to the lot of any song!

I remained in perfect seclusion with my master. It was only at night that I came forth, to wander awhile about his dungeon and hover round the bars of his prison window, yet there I felt the mission of music was indeed gloriously fulfilled. I was the spirit of love and hope, that fluttered above a worn and weary head, to anoint it with the dews of fresh enjoyment, and strengthen it to bear the wrongs and cruelty of man.

But Spiro sickened—the hand grew faint, and the voice low; the days grew short and dim, and in the long nights, who crept to the prison window still to listen and cry, as if her heart would break?—Löttchen was an officer's daughter, a girl of

---

16. Belgiojozo: A mispelling of Cristina Trivulzio, Princess Belgioioso (1808–1871). Italian princess, expatriate, and patron of the arts who lived in Paris. She hosted the famous duel between Liszt and Thalberg in 1837. See chapter 3, "Making Their Way through the World: Italian One-Hit Wonders."

17. Battle of Bannockburn: a decisive battle in 1314 in the Scottish Wars of Independence.

18. Giovanni Matteo Mario (1810–1883). Tenor and husband of Giulia Grisi.

19. "Voi che sapete": aria, Act II, Mozart *Le nozze di Figaro*.

20. "Quel bricconcel d'amore": aria attributed to the composer Giuseppe Farinelli (1769–1836).

fifteen, with no great looks, and a tough voice; as unruly as a wild horse on the prairie: but the heart! there lay her matchless power!

One evening she came with her father into the prisoner's cell, and, with a red face and stammering tongue, begged to know the name of *the* air.

Cos'è? Cos'è? muttered poor Spiro. The girl, with difficulty, replied in my first bar. *Ah, ma brava!* said the dying musician. He took me out and once more he played me through, but cried out, "Nothing for this but the violin or the voice;" and a violin reached him next day, and Lisa came once more and sat down to listen to such a lesson as she never received before or since. It was a revelation, more than a lesson. I remember that night I felt much solemnised; I was the last gasp of the dying Spiro; all the glory of his race and his lost land seemed to lighten up his brow before we parted. It may be harsh for flesh and blood to part, but the spirits of the living and the dead shall meet again. But for me, what remains hereafter? To wander hither and thither, and find no place in the choirs of heaven, for I have not a tinge of sacredness in my being. I am all earthly fire, and must perish with the things of earth; unlike the holy songs, the spiritual strains which have breathes above the fires of martyrdom, I may not hope to unite myself to the eternal melodies of heaven. Oh, that I were Mozart's *Agnus Dei!* oh, that I breathed the words of ineffable sweetness and the harmony that is a foretaste of the peace beyond all understanding!

I remained at my master's pillow till he died. It was a sad and fearful separation— the thoughts of the mind and the departing soul. My image became overclouded, my voice rung faint in his ears, and at last I lay again alone and cold of my crumpled sheet of paper.

Lisa took me to herself. I was put into a drawer, and time passed on. I became impatient of my long seclusion, and was truly glad to find myself packed up to go to Vienna. Lisa was to study as a music-teacher, not for the stage, she said; but there is no believing the sincerity of a woman's intentions when under orchestral influence.

It was strange that Lisa never took me to her class; she kept me under lock and key, and I only had exercise at night, when other things were done: then Lisa took me from my cell to sing me and cry over me, and despair over my difficulties.

No one knows what a life I led then,—banged about, transposed into a key below my taste, maimed, murdered, suffocated, brought to life again: no one can tell what racking tortures I suffered. Oh, Stefano! Spiro! did you hear my cries in the invisible world where ye dwelt?—I, your child, your beloved, thus ill-used and deprived of the glory that was my due from birth.

Lisa was a very persevering girl; she had a heart, but it was a German heart, and that did not quite suit me as an Italian born and bred. She ploughed me up fearfully, and there was none of the vindictive grace of an ancient Fury in the turn she gave to my final measures. I remained only a half-disclosed mystery to her. What was to become of me? I should, perhaps, be brought out at the Mannheim Opera House, and find myself degraded and lost for ever to all hope of success. In the meantime, Lisa laboured ten hours a-day, with a voice as tough as shoe-leather, and hoarse and uncertain; but on she went, as dogged in her obstinate industry as if she were doing something wrong: in which case people always are obstinate, I have observed, especially the women. Well, time and practice do wonders, and Lisa determined to go to England and try her fortune; and I was to go to England—to London—the promised land of needy genius, where princely pay is offered for what most of them, honest people, don't understand. But, no, let me be fair; I am now indulging in the clap-trap of Italians and such "Children of the Sun," and the stage! I will tell the truth. Of all poetry, give me the poetry of an English heart. Poetry, not selfish passion usurping the name. Give me the refined intellectual love of idealised nature, which has dictated the chaste gaiety of Milton's *Allegro,* and the healthy, wholesome loveliness, that shines on the face of the poethood of Britain. Honour to thee, little, chill, north-western isle! Set in the grey waters of a disagreeable channel, thou art the home of holy and homely affections. I have felt humbled to the dust before an English ballad, ridiculous enough too; but it was so good a creature, breathing of simple, pure affections, and all that language of the heart which touches in prose or poetry. The poetry of common life; there the British bards and singers reign, indeed, alone!

We came to England; it was the beginning of the season: May was shewing her dear, smiling face, over the very chimney-pots of the great city. And that great city! the annual fever was beginning to throb in her veins, and the Opera House was open, and concerts were ringing through the Hanover Square Rooms[21] morning, noon, and night, and my poor Lisa wanted to sing at "the Ancients." Alas! I feared that Madame Vestris[22] would have been as likely to perform some Olympic *espièglerie* on that platform, as my poor Lisa to bring me before an admiring public. She had a letter of introduction to the *élite* of the musical world of London; and to the tender mercies of Lord Gorehampton she was expressly commended by her *ci-devant* master at Vienna. The nobleman asked a few select friends to dinner, and Lisa was to be trotted out in the evening, and her merits to be decided on. Poor girl! she took me from my portfolio, and sang me through six times before breakfast. It was a fearful ordeal that she had to go through. She went at ten, as she was ordered to do, and found Lady Gorehampton, who was slightly deaf, asleep on a sofa. A page wakened her, and she begged Lisa to take a seat, and then looked through her portfolio. I was looked at, and passed over, and at last the gentlemen entered. The party consisted of Lord Gorehampton, a nobleman of well-known musical enthusiasm. He had written sixteen MS. operas, and several things which he called airs of his own. It was giving himself very great airs to call them so. He had kindly patronised Pasta, and had done a great deal for Catalani; the Philharmonic would have been at zero without him, and the Ancients looked to him as a tower of strength. He sat in an arm-chair, with his eyes on the ceiling, looking fiddles and kettle-drums at every body, beating time on his snuff-box to a march played by his lady from his own opera of *Edmondo Ironsides,* an Anglo-Saxon *spectacle* with British music.

The next distinguished personage was the Hon. Harry ———, an *aging* tenor, full of airs (not of music though), with a much finer manner than he had a voice, and looks more saucy than supercilious. He had been the "tame man" of fashionable singers for many a long year, and he had been the Rubini of his own set until he far surpassed the great tenor in consequential capers. There was, besides, a spite-

---

21. Hanover Square Rooms: London concert room, opened in 1775; the site of the series of subscription concerts organized by J. C. Bach and C. F. Abel up to 1782, and of the Salomon Concerts.
22. Lucia Elizabeth Vestris (1797–1856).

ful middle-aged bass, a Mr. Melville, and an old gentleman whom every one declared to be a person of exquisite taste—for nothing, however, but his dinners, that I could see or discover. This was the party, with the addition of one more gentleman, who arrived late.

I was looked through.

Stefano! Ah, non lo conosco! murmured Lord Gorehampton. He spoke Italian on high days and holy-days. He begged to be spared the infliction of any obscure music, and invited Lisa to try her mettle on an aria for William the Conqueror in the grand opera of *The Norman Conquest,* written by himself. He kindly sat down to accompany, and I listened to a performance of loathsome length. Such an indecent clattering of ivory I never before gave ear to. It was a mixture of Balfe[23] and Bunn,[24] and a delicious dash of Donizetti's dregs. Shade of Orpheus! had you only heard the imbecile pomp of the conclusion, you would have dashed your golden lyre from the seventh heavens down on the nodding head of his lordship of Gorehampton, and have silenced him thus for ever!

He was just finishing his air on the unusual word in an Italian song, *Felicità, felicità!* when the door opened and a gentleman entered, and approached the piano.

"Ah, there you are! Good night Vane. I'm busy you see, as usual. Just listen to this idea of a Norman-Gothic cadence," and my lord plunged both his hands into a flat ninth, and then danced up and down like a cat's fugue for few minutes, then he stopped and looked up.

"It's more Danish, do you know, *I* think," said Lord Vane, quite gravely.

"Oh, my dear fellow, excuse me there!" cried the performer. "*This* is Gubba the Dane's flourish, you know, in *The Herdsman's Cake.*"

"Ah, yes!" said Vane, with an assumption of interest, the rogue. "By the bye, when is your *King Alfred* to appear? Can't you get *some* of the airs sung at 'the Ancients?'"

"Why no," said Lord Gorehampton. "You see they won't sing things there till one is dead. It is a great bore that one must die first one's self. Isn't it, now?"

"A shameful regulation!" said Vane; and, to conceal a smile, he began to examine me. I saw his noble and intelligent face, and longed to be introduced to his notice and love. He soon became absorbed in me. He put me on the music-desk. "You will sing this for me," he said, to the trembling Lisa.

She sat down, and, with a voice veiled with fear of failure, she breathed me forth. I only half existed on paper, it was while floating through space that I truly lived and felt the joy and glory of life. I passed through those mirrored and gilded chambers, and felt that splendour added no ray to my own brightness. Better to rise up beneath the humble roof of a cabin encircled by loving hearts and longing ears, than under the cold gilding of a palace with a fool on the music-stool. Lisa could not give me my full honours, but she was true and good as far as she went. She had the artistic heart of a faithful disciple, and she interpreted clearly the outline of my intentions. Vane listened attentively, and soon after went away. The evening concluded with another selection of airs from Gubba's *répertoire,* and then we went

23. Michael William Balfe (1808–1870).
24. Alfred Bunn (ca. 1797–1860).

home;—home to dreary lodgings, such as foreign song-birds must have for their cage in London. And their prospects of Lisa darkened daily; she put me away from her sight, and it was only by a chance opening of my portfolio that I overheard the following dialogue between Lisa and an old friend, a dancer, whom she had known at Vienna:—

"Ah, yes, it is a fine thing to be a prima donna! Fancy Giulia getting her two and three hundred a-night, while we have to starve and dance for twenty." So sighed Mademoiselle Carlotta, in a pink gingham, and white satin shoes with orange bindings. "And she is such a vain wretch, and so shabby to the chorus! Fancy her poor women, who attend her in all her deaths and faints, not to speak of other things, never get a farthing from her. And she never pays her Medea and Norma brats; not a bit, poor things! Besides, she is a pest to the prompter, and a disgrace to the profession. Ah well, it's a fine thing to be a prima donna! But I don't want to have diamond shoeties at the expense of my peace of mind. I could not do the pirouette with any weight on my conscience."

"Lord Vane admires her, does he not?"

"Oh, that is an old story! Oh, yes, I dare say. Who does not *admire* her? But I am sure he cannot *esteem* her; and what is love without respect?" said Carlotta, with much dignity. "However, she expects to be a viscountess some fine day. *Vedremo noi altri.*"

That evening Lisa sat alone, musing over the past and the gloomy present. She heard voices on the stair, and her landlady entered. She said that there was a lady below asking, she supposed, for lodgings, but that she could not comprehend her; and she begged Lisa to come and help her, for Lisa spoke a little English. A stranger stood on the stair; she wished for lodgings; she had just come from abroad, and was anxious, if possible, to procure them that night. She was established accordingly in a room next Lisa's. She went to bed early, and Lisa saw no more of her that night.

It was about noon the next day that a note reached Lisa. It was an offer to her to sing, at the Ancient Concert of the following Wednesday, the piece performed at Lord Gorehampton's. Lisa almost fell on her knees with gratitude, and accepted the engagement without delay. Then, poor girl, she hurried out to buy gloves, a wreath, and a pair of new shoes, and I was left alone.

"Ho, ho!" I thought, "now my time is come. I feel frightened rather. Ahem! I wonder how I shall sound." Lisa came home heated, feverish, and penniless, for she had been more extravagant than seconda donnas should be; and it was with a very uncertain voice that she sang me through, or rather, she had only begun to sing, when the door was suddenly opened and the stranger stood there. She sprang forward and listened.

Canta pure! she cried; and then she leant over the piano, and tears fell over her face. Lisa finished and rose, and the stranger approached the piano, seized me, and kissed me with tears of joy.

Ti ritrovo ancor! and then she paused. She laid her hand on the chords: like a prophetess preparing to declare her awful mission she stood. Lo! what sound of unearthly sweetness invested itself in my form! a meaning, new and unexpected, dawned on Lisa's mind. I rose with an unapproachable glory on the ear and heart of the sole listener. She could have fallen down on her face before the form of the

Greek, for it was she! Xanthi, the long-remembered, the adored of Spiro, the Ionian girl I had seen years before at Florence, and *I* had dwelt in her heart ever since. We met like long-parted lovers, and I trembled beneath the joy of a full interpretation by a voice and genius of matchless power. I had at last met with my equal; I was fitly mated at last. Ah! were we now to part?

It was the morning of the rehearsal at length, and I trembled for my fate. Poor Lisa, I did thee injustice! At eleven o'clock she came and took me up, looked at me once with tears, and then walked to the door of the next room.

"I am ill!" she said: "you, signora, are the most fit to take my place. See, take my music; my name too; and, as Lisa, sing this divine song better than poor Lisa herself ever will!"

Joy! joy! I entered the concert-room in Xanthi's hand. That grave audience of dowagers and directors was delighted out of its propriety. But who shall recount the surpassing glories of the Wednesday night, when I was encored by the queen, and lauded by the bishops present, and when a venerable countess was removed in fits to the tea-room, and Field-marshal the Duke of Wellington said "Good!" twice, and when the *Morning Post* screamed itself hoarse with admiration next day? But I am becoming quite too confidential.

One paragraph more. Xanthi made her appearance at the Opera House, Giulia took the jaundice, and Lord Vane took his leave of a termagant whom he had never loved. The tide of fashion left Giulia stranded on the shore where she had ruled the waves, like Britannia, for some sixteen years.

"I could poison, kill, burn, mangle the wretched woman!" said Giulia to her favourite tire-woman, as she sat glaring over the last tirade of praise. "And what *is* this monstrous song that she sings fifteen times every night? It makes me sick and faint to hear of such sinfulness. I'm sure it's ugly. Tell Costa[25] he must get it for me without delay."

Costa obeyed; the original sheet was procured; again I met the prima donna's eyes, and she read on my brow, *Addio Giulia!*

25. Sir Michael Costa (1808–1884).

BIBLIOGRAPHY

Abbate, Carolyn. "Opera; or, the Envoicing of Women." In *Musicology and Difference: Gender and Sexuality in Music Scholarship,* ed. Ruth Solie, 225–58. Berkeley: University of California Press, 1993.

———. *In Search of Opera.* Princeton, N.J.: Princeton University Press, 2001.

———. *Unsung Voices: Opera and Musical Narrative in the Nineteenth Century.* Princeton, N.J.: Princeton University Press, 1991.

Adamo, Maria Rosario, and Friedrich Lippmann. *Vincenzo Bellini.* Turin: ERI, 1981.

Angelis, Marcello de. *Le carte dell'impresario: melodramma e costume teatrale nell'Ottocento.* Florence: Sansoni, 1982.

———. *Le cifre del melodramma: l'archivio inedito dell'impresario teatrale Alessandro Lanari nella Biblioteca nazionale centrale di Firenze.* 2 vols. Florence: La nuova Italia, 1982.

Anonymous. *I giudizj dell'Europa intorno alla Signora Catalani, ossia articoli concernenti il merito musicale di lei, tratti dalle più riputate opere periodiche di Londra, Parigi, Berlino, Amsterdam, Lipsia, Annover, Milano, ecc., preceduti da un breve compendio della sua vita.* Milan: Antonio Fortunato Stella, 1816.

Anonymous. *Life of Henriette Sontag, Countess de Rossi.* New York: Stringer and Townsend, 1852.

Ardoin, John. *L'eredità Callas: La cantante, la diva, le incisioni.* 4th ed. Milan: Il Saggiatore, 1997.

Armstrong, Alan. "Gilbert-Louis Duprez and Gustave Roger in the Composition of Meyerbeer's *Le Prophète.*" *Cambridge Opera Journal* 8 (1996): 147–65.

Ashbrook, William. *Donizetti and His Operas.* Cambridge: Cambridge University Press, 1982.

———. "Popular Success, the Critics and Fame: The Early Careers of *Lucia di Lammermoor* and *Belisario.*" *Cambridge Opera Journal* 2 (1990): 65–81.

Aspden, Suzanne. " 'An Infinity of Factions': Opera in Eighteenth-Century Britain and the Undoing of Society." *Cambridge Opera Journal* 9 (1997): 1–19.

———. "The 'Rival Queens' and the Play of Identity in Handel's *Admeto.*" *Cambridge Opera Journal* 18 (2006): 301–31.

Azevedo, Alexis. *G. Rossini: sa vie et ses oeuvres.* Paris: Heugel, 1864.

Azzaroni, Giovanni. *Del teatro e dintorni: una storia della legislazione e delle strutture teatrali in italia nell'ottocento.* Rome: Bulzoni Editore, 1981.

Bacchelli, Riccardo. *Rossini.* Turin: Tipografia Torinese, 1945.

Baer, Mark. *Theatre and Disorder in Late Georgian London.* Oxford: Clarendon Press, 1992.

Balthazar, Scott. "Ritorni's *Ammaestramenti* and the Conventions of Rossinian Melodramma." *Journal of Musicological Research* 8 (1988–1989): 281–311.

————. "Rossini and the Development of Mid-Century Lyric Form." *Journal of the American Musicological Association* 41 (1988): 102–25.

Barblan, Guglielmo. "Lettura di un'opera dimenticata: *Pia de' Tolomei* di Donizetti (1836)." *Chigiana* 24 (1967): 221–43.

Bellini, Vincenzo. *I Capuleti e i Montecchi.* Introduction by Philip Gossett. New York: Garland, 1989.

————. *I Capuleti e i Montecchi.* Piano-vocal score. 188–; reprint, Milan: Ricordi, 2006.

————. *I Capuleti e i Montecchi.* Edited by Claudio Toscani. In *Edizione critica delle opera di Vincenzo Bellini.* Volume 6. Milan: Ricordi, 2003.

Belsom, Jack. "En Route to Stardom: Adelina Patti at the French Opera House, New Orleans, 1860–1861." *Opera Quarterly* 10 (1994): 113–30.

Bini, Annalisa, and Jeremy Commons, eds. *Le prime rappresentazioni delle opera di Donizetti nella stampa coeva.* Milan: Skira, 1997.

Brewer, Bruce. "Il cigno di Romano—Giovan Battista Rubini: A Performance Study." *Donizetti Society Journal* 4 (1980).

Brown, Jennifer Williams. "'*Con nuove arie aggiunte*': Aria Borrowing in the Venetian Opera Repertory, 1672–1685." Ph.D. diss., Cornell University, 1992.

————. "On the Road with the 'Suitcase Aria': The Transmission of Borrowed Arias in Late Seventeenth-Century Italian Opera." *Journal of Musicological Research* 15 (1995): 3–23.

Budden, Julian. *The Operas of Verdi.* 3 vols. 1973–1981. Reprint, Oxford: Clarendon Press, 1992.

Bushnell, Howard. *Maria Malibran: A Biography of a Singer.* University Park: Pennsylvania State University Press, 1979.

Cambi, Luisa, ed. *Bellini: Epistolario.* Milan: A. Mondadori, 1943.

Cametti, Alberto. *Il Teatro di Tordinona poi di Apollo.* 2 vols. Rome: A. Chicca, 1938.

Cavalcaselle, Giovanni Battista. *Tipi di scritture teatrali attraverso luoghi e tempi diversi.* Rome: Athenaeum, 1919.

Charlton, David, ed. *E. T. A. Hoffmann's Musical Writings.* Cambridge: Cambridge University Press, 1989.

Chilesotti, Oscar. "Giovanni Pacini." *I nostri maestri del passato.* Milan: Ricordi, 1882.

Chorley, Henry F. *Thirty Years' Musical Recollections.* Edited with introduction by Ernest Newman. 1862. Revised edition, New York and London: Alfred A. Knopf, 1926.

Christensen, Thomas. "Four-Hand Piano Transcription and Geographies of Nineteenth-Century Musical Reception." *Journal of the American Musicological Society* 52 (1999): 255–98.

————. "Public Music in Private Spaces: Piano-Vocal Scores and the Domestication of Opera." In *Music and the Cultures of Print,* ed. Kate van Orden, 67–93. New York: Garland, 2000.

Christiansen, Rupert. *Prima Donna: A History.* New York: Viking, 1985.

Ciarlantini, Paola. "Fanny Tacchinardi Persiani: Biographical and Artistic Portrait of the First Lucia." In *Il teatro di Donizetti: Atti dei convegni delle celebrazioni,* ed. Francesco Bellotto and Paolo Fabbri, 125–52. Bergamo: Fondazione Donizetti, 2001.

————. *Giuseppe Persiani e Fanny Tacchinardi: due protagonisti del melodramma romantico.* Bologna: Lavoro Editoriale, 1988.

Clayton, Ellen Creathorne. *Queens of Song: Being Memoirs of Some of the Most Celebrated Female Vocalists Who Have Performed on the Lyric Stage from the Earliest Days of Opera to the Present Time.* New York: Harper and Brothers, 1865.

Colas, Damien. "Melody and Ornamentation." In *The Cambridge Companion to Rossini,* ed. Emanuele Senici, 104–23. Cambridge: Cambridge University Press, 2004.

Collins, Michael. "Bellini and the *Pasticcio alla Malibran:* A Performance History of *I Capuleti e i Montecchi.*" *Note su note* 9–10 (2002): 109–52.

———. "The Literary Background of Bellini's *I Capuleti e i Montecchi.*" *Journal of the American Musicological Society* 35 (1982): 532–38.

Commons, Jeremy. "Una corrispondenza tra Alessandro Lanari e Donizetti." *Studi Donizetti* 3 (1978): 9–74.

Conati, Marcello. "Presenze delle opere di Donizetti nei teatri italiani nella prima metà dell'Ottocento." In *L'opera teatrale di Gaetano Donizetti. Atti del Convegno Internazionale di Studio, Bergamo, 17–20 settembre 1992,* ed. Francesco Bellotto, 433–36. Bergamo: Comune di Bergamo, 1993.

Cone, Edward. *The Composer's Voice.* Berkeley: University of California Press, 1974.

———. "The World of Opera and Its Inhabitants." In *Music: A View from Delft,* ed. Robert P. Morgan, 13–28. Chicago: Chicago University Press, 1990.

Cone, John Frederick. *Adelina Patti: Queen of Hearts.* Portland, Ore.: Amadeus Press, 1993.

I copialettere di Giuseppe Verdi. Edited by Gaetano Cesari and Alessandro Luzio. 1913. Reprint, Bologna: Forni, 1968.

Corte, Andrea della. *L'interpretazione musicale e gli interpreti.* Turin: Vincenzo Bona, 1951.

Cowgill, Rachel. "Mozart Productions and the Concept of *Werktreue* at London's Italian Opera." In *Operatic Migrations: Transforming Works and Crossing Boundaries,* ed. Roberta Montemorra Marvin and Downing Thomas, 145–86. Aldershot, England: Ashgate, 2006.

———. "Re-gendering the Libertine, or, The Taming of the Rake." *Cambridge Opera Journal* 10 (1998): 45–66.

———. "'Wise Men from the East': Mozart's Operas and their Advocates in Early Nineteenth-Century London." In *Music and British Culture, 1785–1914,* ed. Christina Bashford and Leanne Langley, 39–64. Oxford: Oxford University Press, 2000.

Cox, H. Bertram, and G. L. E. Cox, eds. *Leaves from the Journals of Sir George Smart.* London: Longmans, Green, 1907.

Crutchfield, Will. "What Is Tradition?" In *The Fashion and Legacy of Nineteenth-Century Italian Opera,* ed. Roberta Montemorra Marvin and Hilary Poriss. Cambridge: Cambridge University Press, forthcoming.

Cusick, Suzanne. "Gender and the Cultural Work of a Classical Music Performance." *Repercussions* 3 (1994): 77–110.

Davies, James Q. "'Velluti in Speculum': The Twilight of the Castrato." *Cambridge Opera Journal* 17 (2005): 271–301.

Davis, Tracy. *The Economics of the British Stage, 1800–1904.* Cambridge: Cambridge University Press, 2000.

Dawes, Frank. Review of *Eleven Piano Duets by the Masters.* In *Musical Times* 106, no. 1467 (1965): 370.

Dean, Winton. "Shakespeare and Opera." In *Shakespeare in Music,* ed. Phyllis Hartnoll. London: Macmillan, 1964.

De Simone, Roberto, ed. *La cantante e l'impresario e altri metamelodrammi.* Genoa: Edizione Costa and Nolan, 1988.

Donizetti, Gaetano. *Le convenienze ed inconvenienze teatrali.* Edited by Roger Parker and Anders Wiklund. In *Edizione nazionale delle opere di Gaetano Donizetti.* Milan: Ricordi/Bergamo: Fondazione Donizetti, 2002.

Dotto, Gabriele. "Opera, Four Hands: Collaborative Alterations in Puccini's *Fanciulla.*" *Journal of the American Musicological Society* 42 (1989): 604–24.

Eagleton, Terry. *The Ideology of the Aesthetic.* Cambridge, Mass.: Basil Blackwell, 1990.

Ebers, John. *Seven Years of the King's Theatre.* London: Carey, Lea and Carey, 1828.

Edwards, H. Sutherland. *The History of the Opera.* 2 vols. London: W.H. Allen, 1862.

———. *The Life of Rossini.* London: Hurst and Blackett, 1869.

———. *The Prima Donna.* 2 vols. 1888. Reprint, London: Remington, 1978.

Escudier, Marie et Léon. *Vie et Aventures des cantatrices célèbres.* Paris: E. Dentu, 1856.

Everist, Mark. "Enshrining Mozart: *Don Giovanni* and the Viardot Circle." *19th-Century Music* 25 (2001–2002): 165–89.

———. "Lindoro in Lyon: Rossini's *Le Barbiere di Séville.*" *Acta Musicologica* 64 (1992): 50–85.

Fabbri, Paolo. "Fosca notte, notte orrenda." Program notes for *Marino Faliero* at the Teatro la Fenice (Venice, 2003).

———. "Per un'edizione critica del *Pirata.*" *Chigiana* 45 (2004): 187–217.

Feldman, Martha, and Bonnie Gordon, eds. *The Courtesan's Arts: Cross-Cultural Perspectives.* Oxford: Oxford University Press, 2006.

Fenner, Theodore. *Opera in London, Views of the Press, 1785–1830.* Carbondale: Southern Illinois Press, 1994.

Ferranti, Maria Giuliani. *Giuditta Pasta e i suoi tempi: memorie e lettere.* Milan: Cromotipia E. Sormani, 1935.

Ferris, George T. *The Great Singers: Faustina Bordini to Henrietta Sontag.* New York: D. Appleton, 1888.

Fitzgerald, Gerald. *Annals of the Metropolitan Opera: Chronology 1883–1985.* Boston: G.K. Hall, 1989.

FitzLyon, April. *Maria Malibran: Diva of the Romantic Age.* London: Souvenir Press, 1987.

———. *The Price of Genius: A Life of Pauline Viardot.* New York: Appleton-Century, 1964.

Flint, Christopher. "Speaking Objects: The Circulation of Stories in Eighteenth-Century Prose Fiction." *Proceedings of the Modern Language Association* 113 (1998): 212–26.

Florimo, Francesco. *La scuola musicale di Napoli e i suoi conservatorii (1880–83).* 2nd ed. 4 vols. Naples: Stabilmento tip. V. Morano, 1880–1883.

Freeman, Daniel E. "An 18th-Century Singer's Commission of 'Baggage' Arias." *Early Music* 20 (1992): 427–33.

Freeman, Robert. "Farinello and His Repertory." In *Studies in Renaissance and Baroque Music in Honor of Arthur Mendel,* ed. Robert Marshall, 301–30. Kassel: Bärenreiter, 1974.

Fuller, Sophie, and Nicky Losseff, eds. *The Idea of Music in Victorian Fiction.* Aldershot, England: Ashgate, 2004.

Gara, Eugenio. *Giovan Battista Rubini nel centenario della morte.* Bergamo: Industrie Grafiche Cattaneo, 1954.

Garlington, Aubrey S. *Society, Culture and Opera in Florence.* Aldershot, England: Ashgate, 2006.

Gattey, Charles Nielson. *Queens of Song.* London: Barrie and Jenkins, 1979.

Giazotto, Remo. *Maria Malibran (1808–36): Una vita nei nomi di Rossini e Bellini.* Turin: ERI, 1986.

Giger, Andreas. "Social Control and the Censorship of Giuseppe Verdi's Operas in Rome (1844–1859)." *Cambridge Opera Journal* 11 (1999): 233–65.

Glixon, Beth. "Scenes from the Life of Silvia Galiarti Manni, a Seventeenth-Century Virtuosa." *Early Music History* 15 (1996): 97–146.

Goehr, Lydia. *The Imaginary Museum of Musical Works: An Essay in the Philosophy of Music.* Oxford: Clarendon Press, 1994.

Gordon, Bonnie. *Monteverdi's Unruly Women: The Power of Song in Early Modern Italy.* Cambridge: Cambridge University Press, 2004.

Gossett, Philip. *"Anna Bolena" and the Artistic Maturity of Gaetano Donizetti*. Oxford: Clarendon Press, 1985.

———. *Divas and Scholars: Performing Italian Opera*. Chicago: University of Chicago Press, 2006.

———. "Music at the Théâtre-Italien." In *Music in Paris in the 1830s,* ed. Peter Bloom, 327–64. Stuyvesant, N.Y.: Pendragon Press, 1987.

———. "A New Romanza for *Attila*." *Studi Verdiani* 9 (1993): 13–35.

———. "The Operas of Rossini: Problems of Textual Criticism in Nineteenth-Century Opera." Ph.D. diss., Princeton University, 1970.

———. Review of Gioachino Rossini, *L'assedio di Corinto,* recording on Angel Records SCLX–3819. *Musical Quarterly* 61 (1975): 626–38.

———. "The Ricordi Numerical Catalogue: A Background." *Notes* 42 (1985): 22–28.

Greenspan, Charlotte. *The Operas of Vincenzo Bellini*. Ph.D. diss., University of California, Berkeley, 1977.

Greenwald, Helen. Review of Giacomo Meyerbeer, *Opern-Arien: Sopran.,* ed. Peter Kaiser. *Notes* 58 (2002): 944–46.

Grisley, Roberto, ed. *Niccolò Paganini: Epistolario*. Volume I: 1810–1831. Milan: Academia Santa Cecilia, 2006.

Gui, Vittorio. "Storio avventurosa di alcuni capolavori del passato." *Bollettino del centro rossiniano di studi* 25 (1985): 56–60.

Hadlock, Heather. *Mad Loves: Women and Music in Offenbach's "Les Contes d'Hoffmann."* Princeton, N.J.: Princeton University Press, 2000.

———. "On the Cusp between Past and Future: The Mezzo-Soprano Romeo of Bellini's *I Capuleti*." *Opera Quarterly* 17 (2001): 399–422.

———. "Return of the Repressed: The Prima Donna from Hoffmann's *Tales* to Offenbach's *Contes*." *Cambridge Opera Journal* 6 (1994): 221–43.

———. "Women Playing Men in Italian Opera, 1810–1835." In *Women's Voices across Musical Worlds,* ed. Jane Bernstein, 285–307. Boston: Northeastern University Press, 2004.

Hatch, Christopher. "The 'Cockney' Writers and Mozart's Operas." *Opera Quarterly* 3, (1985): 45–58.

Head, Matthew. "Rethinking Authorship through Women Composers." *Women and Music* 6 (2002): 36–50.

Heartz, Daniel. *Haydn, Mozart, and the Viennese School*. New York: Norton, 1995.

Heron-Allen, Edward. *A Contribution toward an Accurate Biography of Charles Auguste de Bériot and Maria Felicita Malibran-Garcia: Extracted from the Correspondence of the Former*. London: W. Wakebam, 1894.

Hoffmann, E. T. A. *Tales of Hoffmann*. Edited and translated by R. J. Hollingdale. New York: Penguin Books, 1992.

Hogarth, George. *Memoirs of the Musical Drama*. 2 vols. London: Richard Bentley, 1838.

Holmes, William C. *Opera Observed: Views of a Florentine Impresario in the Early Eighteenth Century*. Chicago: University of Chicago Press, 1993.

Huebner, Steven. "Operatic Texts: Ours, Yours, and Mine," *Current Musicology* 84 (2007): 117–26.

Hunter, Mary. *The Culture of Opera Buffa in Vienna: A Poetics of Entertainment*. Princeton, N.J.: Princeton University Press, 1999.

———. "'Se vuol ballare' Quoted: An Early Moment in the Reception History of *Figaro*." *Musical Times* 130, no. 1758 (1989): 464–67.

———. "'To Play as if from the Soul of the Composer': The Idea of the Performer in Early Romantic Aesthetics." *Journal of the American Musicological Society* 58 (2005): 357–98.

Jacobson, Robert. "Viewpoint." *Opera News* 46 (1982): 7.

Johnson, Janet. "Donizetti's First 'Affare di Parigi': An Unknown Rondò-finale for *Gianni da Calais.*" *Cambridge Opera Journal* 10 (1998): 157–77.

———. "*Il barbiere di Siviglia.*" In *The Cambridge Companion to Rossini,* ed. Emanuele Senici, 159–74. Cambridge: Cambridge University Press, 2004.

Katz, Mark. *Capturing Sound: How Technology Has Changed Music.* Berkeley: University of California Press, 2004.

Kaufman, Thomas G. "A Chronology of Grisi's Operatic Performances." *Donizetti Society Journal* 4 (1980): 197–223.

———. "*Il cigno di Romano,* the King of Tenors: Giovan Battista Rubini, A Performance Study." *Donizetti Society Journal* 4 (1980): 116–24.

———. "Giulia Grisi: A Re-evaluation." *Donizetti Society Journal* 4 (1980): 180–96.

Kerman, Joseph. "A Few Canonic Variations." *Critical Inquiry* 10 (1983): 107–26.

———. "Lyric Form and Flexibility in *Simon Boccanegra.*" *Studi Verdiani* 1 (1982): 47–62.

Kimbell, David. *Italian Opera.* Cambridge: Cambridge University Press, 1991.

Klein, Herman. *The Reign of Patti.* 1920. Reprint, New York: Da Capo Press, 1978.

Kreuzer, Gundula. "Voices from Beyond: Verdi's *Don Carlos* and the Modern Stage." *Cambridge Opera Journal* 18 (2006): 151–79.

Lahee, Henry C. *Famous Singers of To-day and Yesterday.* Boston: L. C. Page, 1898.

Lamacchia, Saverio. *Il vero Figaro o sia il falso factotum.* Turin: EDT, 2008.

Lamb, Andrew. "'Die Fledermaus' and Tradition." *Opera* 42 (1991): 1405–9.

Lamb, Jacob. "Modern Metamorphoses and Disgraceful Tales." *Critical Inquiry* 28 (2001): 133–66.

Lawton, David, and David Rosen. "Verdi's Non-Definitive Revisions: The Early Operas." *Atti del IIIo Congresso internazionale di studi verdiani,* 189–237. Parma: Istituto di studi verdiani, 1974.

Lazarevich, Gordana. "Mozart, Haydn, Cimarosa: Insertion Arias as Reflections of Operatic Customs." In *Internationaler Musikwissenschaftlicher Kongress zum Mozartjahr,* ed. Ingrid Fuchs, 725–50. Baden-Wien Tutzing, Germany: Schneider 1993.

———. "Mozart's Insertion Aria 'Alma grande e nobil core,' K. 578: Criticism of Cimarosa or a Compliment to the Composer?" *Mozart-jahrbuch* (1991): 262–67.

Legouvé, Ernest. *Maria Malibran.* Paris: J. Hetzel, 1880.

———. *Soixante ans de souvenirs.* 4 vols. Paris: J. Hetzel, 1888.

Leonardi, Susan J., and Rebecca A. Pope, eds. *The Diva's Mouth: Body, Voice, Prima Donna Politics.* New Brunswick, N.J.: Rutgers University Press, 1996.

Levin, David J. *Unsettling Opera: Staging Mozart, Verdi, Wagner, and Zemlinsky.* Chicago: University of Chicago Press, 2007.

Lippmann, Friedrich. "Pagine sconosciute de 'I Capuleti e i Montecchi' e 'Beatrice di Tenda' di Vincenzo Bellini." *Rivista italiana di musicologica* 2 (1967): 140–51.

Liszt, Franz. *An Artist's Journey: Lettres d'un bachelier ès musique, 1835–1841.* Translated and annotated by Charles Suttoni. Chicago: University of Chicago Press, 1989.

Locatelli, Tommaso. *L'appendice della Gazzetta di Venezia. Prose scelte di T. L.* 16 vols. Venice: Tip. del Gondoliere, 1837–1880.

Long, Richard M. "'Nel cor più non mi sento': Notes on Paisiello's Aria and a Few of Its Interpreters." In *The Consortium on Revolutionary Europe Proceedings,* ed. Donald D. Horward, Harold T. Parker, and Louise Salley Parker, 417–423. Athens, Ga.: Consortium on Revolutionary Europe, 1986.

Lumley, Benjamin. *Reminiscences of the Opera.* London: Hurst and Blackett, 1864.

Malherbe, Henry. *La passion de la Malibran.* Paris: A. Michel, 1937.

Marcello, Benedetto. *Il teatro alla moda.* Venice: Aldiviva, 1733. Translated by Reinhard Pauly. *Musical Quarterly* 34 (1948): 371–403 and 35 (1949): 85–105.

Martello, Pier Jacopo. *Della tragedia antica e moderna.* Rome: F. Gonzaga, 1715. Translated in Piero Weiss, "Pier Jacopo Martello on Opera (1715): Annotated Translation." *Musical Quarterly* 66 (1980): 358–401.

Mauceri, John. "Working with a Living Composer: Multiple Versions of *Candide* and *A Quiet Place.*" Paper read at the Annual Meeting of the American Musicological Society, Houston, Texas, November 2003.

Maus, Fred Everett. "Concepts of Musical Unity." In *Rethinking Music,* ed. Nicholas Cook and Mark Everist, 171–92. Oxford: Oxford University Press, 1999.

Merlin, Countess de. *Memoirs of Madame Malibran.* 2 vols. London: Henry Colburn, 1840.

Miner, Margaret. "Phantoms of Genius: Women and the Fantastic in the Opera-House Mystery." *19th-Century Music* 18 (1994): 121–35.

Moreen, Robert. "Integration of Text Forms and Musical Forms in Early Verdi." Ph.D. diss., Princeton University, 1975.

Mount Edgcumbe, Richard, Earl of. *Musical Reminiscences, Containing an Account of the Italian Opera in England, from 1773.* 1834. Reprint, New York: Da Capo Press, 1973.

Müller, Reto, and Bernd-Rüdiger Kern. *Rossinis 'Eduardo e Cristina': Beiträg zur Jahrhundert-Erstaufführung.* Leipzig: Leipziger Universitätsverlag, 1997.

Osborne, Charles. *The Bel Canto Operas.* Portland, Ore.: Amadeus Press, 1994.

Pacini, Giovanni. *Le mie memorie artistiche.* Introduction by Rafaelo Colucci. Florence: Tipi dei Successori le Monnier, 1875.

———. *L'ultimo giorno di Pompei and Exerpts.* Introduction by Philip Gossett. New York and London: Garland, 1986.

Padovano, Bettino. *Angelica Catalani.* Senigallia: Tipografia Giunchedi, 1949.

Pagannone, Giorgio. "Aspetti drammaturgici e formali nel *Marino Faliero* e nell'*Assedio di Calais.*" In *Donizetti—Napoli—L'Europa,* ed. Franco Carmelo Greco and Renato Di Benedetto, 299–321. Naples: Edizioni Scientifiche Italiane, 2000.

———. *La Pia de' Tolomei di Salvadore Cammarano.* Florence: Olschki, 2006.

Parakilas, James, and Charlotte N. Eyerman. "1820s to 1870s: The Piano Calls the Tune." In *Piano Roles,* ed. James Parakilas, 150–83. New Haven: Yale University Press, 1999.

Parke, William T. *Musical Memoirs: An Account of the General State of Music in England from the First Commemoration of Handel in 1784, to the Year 1830.* 1830. Reprint, New York: Da Capo Press, 1970.

Parker, Roger. *Remaking the Song: Operatic Visions and Revisions from Handel to Berio.* Berkeley: University of California Press, 2006.

———. *Studies in Early Verdi.* New York and London: Garland, 1989.

Pauly, Reinhard. "Benedetto Marcello's Satire on Early 18th-Century Opera." *Musical Quarterly* 34 (1948): 222–33.

Pastura, Francesco. *Bellini secondo la storia.* Parma: Gaunda, 1959.

Pleasants, Henry. *The Great Singers: From the Dawn of Opera to Our Own Time.* New York: Simon and Schuster, 1966.

Poriss, Hilary. "Angelica Catalani, Ensemble, and the King's Theatre, 1806–1813." Paper read at the annual meeting of the American Musicological Society, Washington, D.C., November, 2005.

———. "Artistic License: Aria Interpolation and the Italian Operatic World." Ph.D. diss., University of Chicago, 2000.

———. "A Madwoman's Choice: Aria Substitution in *Lucia di Lammermoor.*" *Cambridge Opera Journal* 13 (2001): 1–28.

————. "Making Their Way through the World: Italian One-Hit Wonders." *19th-Century Music* 24 (2001): 197–224.

————. "To the Ear of the Amateur: Performing *Ottocento* Operas Piecemeal." In *Fashions and Legacies of Nineteenth-Century Italian Opera,* ed. Roberta Montemorra Marvin and Hilary Poriss. Cambridge: Cambridge University Press, forthcoming.

Pougin, Arthur. *Une cantatrice "amie" de Napoléon: Giuseppina Grassini 1773–1850.* Paris: Fischbacher, 1920.

————. *Maria Malibran: The Story of a Great Singer.* London: E. Nash, 1911.

Price, Curtis. "Unity, Originality, and the London Pasticcio." *Harvard Library Bulletin* 2 (1991): 17–30.

Pugliese, Romana Margherita. "The Origins of *Lucia di Lammermoor*'s Cadenza." *Cambridge Opera Journal* 16 (2004): 23–42.

Radiciotti, Giuseppe. *Gioacchino Rossini: Vita documentata, opera ed influenze su l'arte.* 3 vols. Tivoli: Arti Grafiche Majella, 1927–1929.

————. *Teatro, musica e musicisti in Sinigaglia.* 1893. Reprint, Bologna: A. Forni, 1997.

Reggioli, Aldo. *Carolina Ungher: virtuosa di camera e cappella di S. A. R. il granduca di Toscana.* Florence: Polistampa, 1995.

Righetti-Giorgi, Geltrude. *Cenni di una donna già cantante.* Bologna: Sassi, 1823.

Ritorni, Carlo. *Ammaestramenti alla composizione d'ogni poema e d'ogni opera appartenente alla musica.* Milan: Tipi di Luigi di Giacomo Pirola, 1841.

Roccatagliati, Alessandro. "The Italian Theatre of Verdi's Day." In *The Cambridge Companion to Verdi,* ed. Scott Balthazar, 15–28. Cambridge: Cambridge University Press, 2004.

Rogers, Francis. "Henriette Sontag in New York." *Musical Quarterly* 28 (1942): 100–104.

Rose, Michael. "A Note on Giovanni Pacini." *Musical Times* 124 (1983): 163–64.

Rosen, David, and Andrew Porter, eds. *Verdi's "Macbeth": A Sourcebook.* New York: W. W. Norton, 1984.

Rosmini, Enrico. *Legislazione e giurisprudenza dei teatri.* Milan: Ulrico Hoepli, 1893.

Rosselli, John. "From Princely Service to the Open Market: Singers of Italian Opera and Their Patrons, 1600–1850." *Cambridge Opera Journal* 1 (1989): 1–32.

————. *The Life of Bellini.* Cambridge: Cambridge University Press, 1996.

————. *The Opera Industry in Italy from Cimarosa to Verdi: The Role of the Impresario.* Cambridge: Cambridge University Press, 1984.

————. *Singers of Italian Opera: The History of a Profession.* Cambridge: Cambridge University Press, 1992.

Rossini, Gioachino. *Lettere e documenti.* Edited by Bruno Cagli and Sergio Ragni. Pesaro: Fondazione Rossini, 1992.

————. *Il barbiere di Siviglia.* Facsimile of the autograph manuscript. Edited by Philip Gossett. Rome: Libreria Musicale Italiano, 1993.

————. *Il barbiere di Siviglia.* Edited by Patricia B. Brauner. In *Works of Gioachino Rossini,* Kassel: Bärenreiter-Verlag, 2008.

————. *Il barbiere di Siviglia.* Edited by Alberto Zedda. Milan: Ricordi, 1969.

————. *Otello.* Edited by Michael Collins. In *Edizione critica delle opere di Gioachino Rossini,* series 1, vol. 19. Pesaro: Fondazione Rossini, 1994.

————. *Tancredi.* Edited by Philip Gossett. In *Edizione critica delle opere di Gioachino Rossini,* series 1, vol. 10. Pesaro: Fondazione Rossini, 1984.

————. *Il Turco in Italia.* Edited by Margaret Bent. In *Edizione critica delle opere di Gioachino Rossini,* series 1, vol. 13. Pesaro: Fondazione Rossini, 1988.

Rutherford, Susan. " 'La cantante delle passioni': Giuditta Pasta and the Idea of Operatic Performance," *Cambridge Opera Journal* 19 (2007): 107–38.

————. *The Prima Donna and Opera, 1815–1930.* Cambridge: Cambridge University Press, 2006.

————. "The Voice of Freedom: Images of the Prima Donna." In *New Woman and Her Sisters: Feminism and Theatre, 1850–1914,* ed. Viv Gardner and Susan Rutherford, 95–113. Ann Arbor: University of Michigan Press, 1992.

Saffle, Michael. *Liszt in Germany, 1840–1845: A Study in Sources, Documents, and the History of Reception.* Stuyvesant, N.Y.: Pendragon Press, 1994.

Savoia, Francesca. *La cantante e l'impresario e altri metamelodrammi.* Genoa: Edizioni Costa and Nolan, 1988.

Scarton, Cesare, and Mauro Tosti-Croce. "*Aureliano in Palmira:* Un percorso storico-drammaturgico da François Hédelin d'Aubignac a Felice Romani." *Bolletino del centro rossiniano di studi* 41 (2001): 83–165.

Scherillo, Michele. *Belliniana: Nuove note.* Milan: Ricordi, 1885.

Schönherr, Ulrich. "Social Differentiation and Romantic Art: E. T. A. Hoffmann's 'The Sanctus' and the Problem of Aesthetic Positioning in Modernity." *New German Critique* 66 (1995): 3–16.

Scudo, Paul. *Critique et littérature musicales: Première et deuxième séries.* 1856. Reprint, Geneva: Éditions Minkoff, 1986.

Seller, Francesca. "Il *Marin Faliero* da Napoli a Parigi: raffronti testuali." *Donizetti Society Journal* 7 (2002): 31–46.

Senici, Emanuele. "'Adapted to the Modern Stage': *La clemenza di Tito* in London." *Cambridge Opera Journal* 7 (1995): 1–22.

————. "Per Guasco, Ivanoff e Moriani: le tre versioni della romanza di Foresto nel 'Attila.'" In *Pensieri per un maestro: studi in onore di Pierluigi Petrobelli,* ed. Stefano La Via and Roger Parker, 273–88. Turin: EDT, 2002.

Sharp, Elizabeth A., ed. and trans. *Heine in Art and Letters.* London: U. Scott, 1895.

Silvestri, Lodovico Settimo. *Della vita e delle opere di Gioachino Rossini. Notizie biografico—artistico—aneddotico—critiche.* Milan: Fratelli Biatti G. e Minacca, 1874.

Smart, Mary Ann. "In Praise of Convention: Formula and Experiment in Bellini's Self-Borrowings." *Journal of the American Musicological Society* 53 (2000): 25–68.

————. "The Lost Voice of Rosine Stoltz." *Cambridge Opera Journal* 6 (1994): 31–50.

————. "The Silencing of Lucia." *Cambridge Opera Journal* 4 (1992): 119–41.

————. "Verdi Sings Erminia Frezzolini." *Women and Music* 1 (1997): 33–45.

Smith, William C. *The Italian Opera and Contemporary Ballet in London, 1789–1820.* London: Society for London Theatre Research, 1955.

Solie, Ruth. *Music in Other Words: Victorian Conversations.* Berkeley: University of California Press, 2004.

Somerset-Ward, Richard. *Angels and Monsters: Male and Female Sopranos in the Story of Opera, 1600–1900.* New Haven: Yale University Press, 2004.

Spohr, Louis. *Louis Spohr's Autobiography.* 1865. Reprint, New York: Da Capo Press, 1969.

Stendhal, [Henri Beyle]. *The Life of Rossini.* Translated by Richard N. Coe. 2nd ed. London: John Calder, 1985.

Stern, Kenneth. "A Documentary Study of Giuditta Pasta on the Opera Stage." Ph.D. dissertation, City University of New York, 1983.

Strohm, Reinhard. *Essays on Handel and Italian Opera.* Cambridge: Cambridge University Press, 1985.

Suttoni, Charles. *An Artist's Journey: Lettres d'un bachelier ès musique, 1835–1841.* Chicago and London: University of Chicago Press, 1989.

Tacchinardi, Nicola. *Dell'opera in musica sul teatro italiano e de'suoi difetti.* 1833. Reprint, Modena: Mucchi Editore, 1995.

Thrall, Miriam M. H. *Rebellious Fraser's: Nol Yorke's Magazine in the Days of Maginn, Thackeray, and Carlyle.* New York: Columbia University Press, 1934.

Tick, Judith. *Music in the USA: A Documentary Companion*. New York: Oxford University Press, 2008.

Tintori, Giampiero. *Bellini*. Milan: Rusconi, 1983.

Toscani, Caludio. "Bellini e Vaccaj: peripezie di un finale." In *Vincenzo Bellini nel secondo centenario della nascita*, ed. Graziella Seminara and Anna Tedesco, 535–67. Florence: Leo S. Olschki, 2004.

Vaccai, Giulio. *Giulietta e Romeo*. Introduction by Philip Gossett. New York: Garland, 1989.

———. *Vita di Nicola Vaccaj*. Bologna: Nicola Zanchelli, 1882.

Valle, Giovanni. *Cenni teorico-pratici sulle aziende teatrali*. Milan: Società Tipog. de' classici Italiani, 1823.

Viardot, Pauline. *Cendrillon, opera comique en 3 tableaux*. Paris: G. Miran, 1904.

Wackenroder, Wilhelm. "The Remarkable Musical Life of the Musician Joseph Berlinger." In *Strunk's Source Readings in Music History*, ed. Ruth Solie, 19–30. New York: W.W. Norton, 1998.

Wakeling, Dennis W. Review of *Marino Faliero*, Melodram 27030, 2 CDs. *Opera Quarterly* 6, (1988): 121–24.

Walsh, T. J. *Opera in Dublin, 1798–1820*. Oxford: Oxford University Press, 1993.

Weatherson, Alexander. "Donizetti in Paris." *Donizetti Society Journal* 7 (2002): 3–9.

Weber, William. *The Rise of Musical Classics in Eighteenth-Century England: A Study in Canon, Ritual, and Ideology*. Oxford: Clarendon Press, 1992.

Webster, James. "Haydn's Symphonies between *Sturm und Drang* and 'Classical Style': Art and Entertainment." In *Haydn Studies*, ed. Dean Sutcliffe, 218–45. Cambridge: Cambridge University Press, 1998.

Weinstock, Herbert. *Donizetti and the World of Opera in Italy, Paris and Vienna in the First Half of the Nineteenth Century*. New York: Pantheon Books, 1963.

———. *Rossini: A Biography*. New York: Alfred A. Knopf, 1975.

———. *Vincenzo Bellini: His Life and His Operas*. New York: Knopf, 1971.

Weliver, Phylis. *Women Musicians in Victorian Fiction, 1860–1900: Representations of Music, Science and Gender in the Leisured Home*. Aldershot: Ashgate, 2000.

Williams, Adrian. *Portrait of Liszt: By Himself and His Contemporaries*. Oxford: Clarendon Press, 1990.

Wyndham, Henry Saxe. *The Annals of Convent Garden Theatre from 1732 to 1897*. 2 vols. London: Chatto and Windus, 1906.

Zavadini, Guido. *Donizetti: vita, musiche, epistolario*. Bergamo: Istituto Italiano d'Arti Grafiche, 1948.

Zoppelli, Luca. "Intorno a Rossini: sondaggi sulla precezione della centralità del compositore." In *Gioachino Rossini 1792–1992: Il testo e la scena*, ed. Paolo Fabbri, 13–24. Pesaro: Fondazione Rossini, 1994.

———. "'Stage Music' in Early Nineteenth-Century Italian Opera." *Cambridge Opera Journal* 2 (1990): 29–39.

Newspapers and Periodicals Consulted

Il barbiere di Siviglia
Bentley's Miscellany
Il censore universale dei teatri
The Eclectic Magazine of Foreign Literature
L'eco
Fraser's Magazine
Gazzetta musicale di Milano

Gazzetta privilegiata di Milano
Gazzetta privilegiata di Venezia
The Harmonicon
Hellenic Times
Illustrated London News
Knight's Quarterly Magazine
Littell's Living Age
Le notizie del giorno
Il pirata
Quarterly Musical Magazine
The Standard
I teatri
Teatri, arti e letteratura
The Times (London)

INDEX

Page numbers in bold indicate examples or illustrations.